THE CORPUS DELICTI

Illuminations: Studies in Cultural Formations of the Americas

John Beverly and Sara Castro-Klarén, Editors

THE CORPUS DELICTI

·

a manual of argentine fictions

·

Josefina Ludmer

Translated by Glen S. Close

·

University of Pittsburgh Press

Published by the University of Pittsburgh Press, Pittsburgh, Pa., 15260

Translation copyright © 2004, University of Pittsburgh Press

Originally published as *El cuerpo del delito: Un manual,*

copyright © 1999, Josefina Ludmer; Libros Perfil S.A.

Manufactured in the United States of America

Printed on acid-free paper

10 9 8 7 6 5 4 3 2 1

Library of Congress Cataloging-in-Publication Data

Ludmer, Josefina.

  [Cuerpo del delito. English]

  The corpus delicti : a manual of Argentine fictions / Josefina Ludmer ; translated by Glen S. Close.

    p. cm. — (Illuminations)

  Includes bibliographical references and index.

  ISBN 0-8229-4228-3 (cloth : alk. paper)

  1. Argentine fiction—History and criticism. 2. Crime in literature. I. Close, Glen S. (Glen Steven) II. Title. III. Illuminations (Pittsburgh, Pa.)

  PQ7707.C74L8313 2004

  863.009'355—dc22

                              2003027563

Contents

Acknowledgments

This book was written in two worlds, and it owes a great deal to many people. They generously shared their writings, books, facts, witticisms, references, ideas, company, help, and affection, whether in the United States or in Argentina.

Rolena Adorno, Martha J. Barbato (Biblioteca del Instituto de Literatura Argentina, "Ricardo Rojas" of the Universidad de Buenos Aires), Amelia Barona, Marta Cisneros, Nora Domínguez, Gigi Dopico-Black, Marily Fassi, Jean Franco, Roberto González Echevarría, Sandra Guardo, Susana Haydu, Martín Kohan, Luis Martínez (Biblioteca del Congreso de la Nación), Susana Martínez (my research assistant), María Rosa Menocal, Sylvia Molloy, Graciela Montaldo, Cristina Moreiras, Marta Palchevich (Biblioteca del Congreso de la Nación and reader of various parts of the manuscript), César Rodríguez (Latin American bibliographer of Yale's Sterling Memorial Library: he found me the unfindable), Lidia Santos, Horacio Tarcus (Biblioteca del CeDinCI), Margherita Tortora, Alejandra Uslenghi and Mariano Siskind (who oversaw the original edition), and David Viñas. The Yale Center for International and Area Studies and the Whitney Fund awarded me a fellowship for the year 1997–1998, which I spent in Argentina.

This English language edition of the manual is the product of another collaboration between worlds. Glen Close's intelligent, exact, and ironic translation was funded by a grant from the Fundación Antorchas, and publication assistance was provided by the Frederick W. Hilles Publications Fund of Yale University.

I am grateful to my son, Fernando Alcade, for his company, help, and affection in both worlds.

Many thanks to all.

·

introduction

·

Crime as a Critical Instrument

My subject is "crime," and this book is a manual of its body. A manual of "crime" in quotation marks (a manual of crime and quotation marks), because I use the word not in its legal sense, but rather in all senses of the term. And because my field is fiction: sexual, racial, social, and economic "crime tales," tales of professions, trades, and states. Those that form *The Corpus Delicti: A Manual of Argentine Fictions.*

This is a manual of the utility of crime and of crime as a tool. Today, crime is a branch of capitalist production and the criminal a producer, as Karl Marx said in 1863 when he sought to show the consubstantiality of crime and capitalism and, unintentionally, like an astrologer, foresaw this manual:

> A philosopher produces ideas, a poet poems, a clergyman sermons, *a professor compendia,* and so on. A criminal produces crimes. If we look a little closer at the connection between this latter branch of production and society as a whole, we shall rid ourselves of many prejudices. The criminal produces not only crimes but also criminal law, and with this *the professor who gives lectures* on criminal law and in addition to this *the inevitable compendium* in which this same professor throws his lectures onto the general market as "commodities." This brings with it the augmentation of national wealth, quite apart from *the personal enjoyment which . . . the manuscript of the compendium* brings to its originator himself.
>
> The criminal moreover produces the whole of the police and criminal justice, constables, judges, hangmen, juries, etc.; and all these different *lines of business,* which form equally many categories of the social division of labour, develop different capacities of the human spirit, create new needs and new ways of satisfying them. Torture alone has given rise to the most ingenious mechanical inventions, and employed many honourable craftsmen in the production of its many instruments.
>
> The criminal produces an impression, partly moral and partly tragic, as the case may be, and in this way renders a "service" by arousing the moral and aesthetic feelings of the public. *He produces not only compendia* on Criminal Law, not only penal codes and along with them legislators in this field, *but also art, belles-lettres,* novels and even tragedies, as not only Müllner's *Schuld* and Schiller's *Dië Räuber* show, but also *Oedipus* and *Richard the Third.* The criminal breaks the monotony and everyday security of bourgeois life. In his way he keeps it from stag-

nation, and gives rise to *that uneasy tension and agility without which even the spur of competition* would get blunted. Thus he gives a stimulus to the productive forces. While crime takes a part of the superfluous population of the labour market and thus reduces competition among the labourers—up to a certain point preventing wages from falling below the minimum—the struggle against crime absorbs another part of this population. Thus the criminal comes in as one of those natural "counterweights" which bring about a correct balance and open up a whole perspective of "useful" occupations.[1]

In this manual we will use crime like Marx, as a critical instrument that will allow us to carry out various types of operations. "Crime" is a particular conceptual instrument; it is not abstract but rather visible, representable, quantifiable, personalizable, subjectivizable; it does not submit to binary regimes; it has historicity and opens onto a constellation of relations and series.[2]

From the very beginning of literature, crime appears as one of the instruments most utilized to define and found a culture: to separate it from nonculture and to mark what culture excludes. For example, the female crime in Genesis or, later, "the murder of the father" by the primitive horde of children in Freud. To found a culture beginning with the crime of the minor, of the second generation, or to found it on the crime of the second sex, would imply not only the exclusion of anticulture, but also the postulation of a second culpable subjectivity. And also a pact. So, at very first glance, would *fictions of cultural identity with crimes* appear to function.

Let us consider what Sigmund Freud calls the "fantastic" construction in *Totem and Taboo* (1912–1913).[3] Freud links his psychoanalytic conception of the totem (his fiction of the totemic animal as a substitute for the father: love-hate ambivalence) to Darwin's theory-fiction of the primitive horde. Darwin supposes the existence (and he says that this primitive state has not been observed) of "a violent and jealous father, who keeps all the females for himself and drives away his sons as they grow up" (Freud 175); thereafter, each founds his own horde.

Freud relies, then, on Darwin's positivist fiction of the father in order to continue it with his own psychoanalytic fiction of the father. He adds crime and founds it on *a cultural event,* the "celebration of the totem meal." Freud imagines: "One day the brothers who had been driven out came together, killed and devoured their father" in the festival, *putting an end to domination* (176). United, says Freud, they managed to do what would have been impossible individually. Perhaps they had at their disposal a new weapon, he adds (*linking technology with crime or linking the founding crime with a certain "modernity"*). They devoured the father's cadaver, they identified themselves with him, and they appropriated his strength.

For Freud the awareness of guilt is born in the criminal act because the sons, while they eat the father in the festival of liberation, prohibit themselves what he prohibited them, and they renounce sexual contact with the women of the tribe. For Freud the guilt of the sons (*of the "minors"*) would engender the two fundamental taboos ("crimes") which initiate human morality: murder and incest. The totem meal, "perhaps mankind's *earliest festival,*" says Freud, would be "*a repetition and commemoration of this memorable and criminal deed,* which was the beginning of so many things—of social organization, of moral restrictions and of religion" (176; italics added).

"Crime" is, then, one of the tools or *critical instruments of this manual* because it functions, as in Freud, as *a cultural frontier* that separates culture from nonculture, which founds cultures, and which also separates lines in the interior of a culture. It serves to draw limits, to differentiate and to exclude. With crime, guilty consciences and fables of foundation and of cultural identity are constructed.

But in this manual the "tool" of crime serves not only as a divisor, as a fiction of the foundation of cultures (and also as an instrument of definition by exclusion), but also as an articulator of different zones. "Crime," which is a mobile, historical, and shifting frontier (crimes change over time), not only serves to differentiate, separate, and exclude, but also to link the state, politics, society, subjects, culture, and literature. As Marx and Freud well knew, it is an ideal critical instrument because it is at once historical, cultural, political, economic, legal, social, and literary: it is one of those *articulating notions* which is in or between all fields.[4]

Let us attempt to see how the instrument of crime may be used in literature, since this is what *The Corpus Delicti: A Manual of Argentine Fictions* is about. In literary fictions, "crime" can be read as *a constellation* articulating criminal and victim, which is to say, articulating subjects: certain voices, words, cultures, beliefs, and bodies. And also linking law, justice, truth, and the state to these subjects.[5]

Thus, according to the literary representation of the constellation of the criminal, the victim, justice, and truth (elements that seem to meet in literary fictions with crimes), crime as a frontier or line of demarcation can function in the interior of a culture or national literature (and the manual is about this). It can serve to divide certain times of this culture, and it can also divide and define various lines or levels. In each time and in each line the constellation is different because, depending on the literary representation of crime (and its verbal complex of subjectivities, justices, powers, and truths), the frontiers are more or less clear. We will have various lines and times according to who speaks the "I" in the configuration of criminal, victim, investigator, witness (which is to say, according to where crime is subjectivized in the fictions). And we will also have different lines and times according to the type of "justice" or "punishment" applied to crime (in other words, whether or not there is state justice). And we will have different lines according to the relation established between this justice (state or otherwise) and truth: according to the specific type of justice and truth postulated by the fictions.

The constellation of crime in literature not only allows us to mark lines and times, but also to read in the fictions the tense and contradictory correlation of subjects, beliefs, culture, and the state. And this in a multiplicity of times, for cultural beliefs are not synchronous with the division of states, but rather drag along with them previous and sometimes archaic phases and temporalities.

This manual stages crime as a tool, the dividing and articulating power of crime in literature, and at the same time it stages two Argentine dramas or passions: the cultural drama of beliefs in differences, and the political drama of the state at each historical juncture.

The "Stories" of the *Corpus Delicti*

The manual is made up of a mass of "crime tales" from Argentine literature which form the *corpus delicti* (and "the body of crime" can also be "evidence"). The "stories" have subjects and families, they have crimes, criminals, and victims, and they also have "final solutions." They are the type of stories that are found not only in Argentine literature, in fictions, but also in Argentine culture. They are situated beyond the difference between fiction and reality; they are situated between text and context, between literature and culture. Or, if you like, between "literature" and "life," in one of the spaces connecting them. For "crime tales" are stories we can tell among ourselves: they are the conversations of a culture.

Stories of education and marriage, stories of exams, stories of operations, "Argentine" stories (of tango, newspaper vendors, Juan Moreira), stories of writers' manuscripts, of Jews, women, geniuses, artists, famous men: *all with crimes*. And also "stories" of truth and justice with crimes. This is a "manual of conversations" of a culture beginning with the crime tales of its literature.

A "crime tale" can be a moment, a scene in a story or a novel, a quote, a dialogue, but also a long "history" encompassing many novels. The destructuring of narratives in stories and the alteration of their scale; the oscillation of the stories between text and context (between literature and life), the fact that they are all on the same level, allows for the establishment of the desired links. For this reason, the stories of this manual are organized in different forms and move along various temporal trajectories: in pairs, series, networks, families, chains, genealogies, superimpositions, ramifications. These forms and trajectories proliferate and draw the body of the *corpus* of crime, which is a specific field, made up of "crime tales."

This manual's *corpus delicti,* therefore, is neither a corpus of books nor of authors nor of texts (understood as autonomous entities), but rather a narrative *corpus* of stories organized in various ways; a great mobile space-time of "crime tales" that is between fiction and reality: in the conversations of a culture. In the *corpus delicti* all the "stories" relate to each other; they trace trajectories and frontiers and tell "histories."

The Corpus Delicti: A Manual of Argentine Fictions is a floating zone with neither depth nor permanence, a zone in which I can move as I like, in which I can jump from one "story" to the next and also cross (traverse) times and realities. This is the diversion of this manual tool, which uses the very fictions of literature to tell all sorts of tales. A temporary diversion, subject to reformulation.

I

.

from transgression to crime

.

The Subjects of the Liberal State:
Stories of Education and Marriage

The Coalition

In Argentina, the year 1880 represents not only a historical break[1] with the definitive establishment of the state,[2] political and legal unification, and entry into the world market. It also represents a literary break because it introduces a group of young writers (average age thirty-five; President Julio A. Roca is thirty-eight)[3] who form something like the cultural coalition of the new Argentine state. They are not professional men of letters, but rather the first university writers in Argentine culture and at the same time state civil servants. The literary and cultural coalition of 1880 is thus a state coalition, perhaps the first.

This rich culture of 1880 (when Argentina promised to be one of the richest countries in the world with its entry into the world market), one of travelers and diplomats, made the gesture of appropriating all Western and, above all, European literature (and thus not only changed the relationship of the national language to foreign ones, but also founded translation as a literary genre, for example, Miguel Cané's Spanish translation of Shakespeare's *Henry IV*), and it produced a writing that was fragmentary and conversational, novelesque and elegant, substantially cultured and refined: "aristocratic" (in a Latin American country). The coalition that founded and constituted Argentine high culture was homogeneous in its commonplaces of liberalism, positivism, the Club del Progreso, the Teatro Colón, the Recoleta cemetery, and certain carnivals.

But "the coalition" was not only the group of young writers of the "generation of '80," but rather the fabric of positions and subjects of the fictions they wrote. The real writers and the fictional or literary subjects they produced constituted "the subjects of the liberal state": a conjunction of different grades of fictionality (or reality). And this point is essential in the manual because it is not in the actual writers but in the positions written in their literature (the autobiographical first persons and their others) that the relations between the state and culture in 1880 are to be read, along with the invention of "aristocratic" Argentine culture.

Let us imagine, then, that a coalition of writers (which is to say, a group of diverse sectors united by certain objectives) writes fictions for the state and with them produces the "subjects" of the liberal state. The state needs these fictions, not only to organize power relations (and in order to have a complete map of the new society as it is drawn by the coalition in 1880), but also to postulate its own definitions and alternatives. The cultural coalition of the liberal state then appears as a critical construction: a phantasmagoria, a reading device, between "reality" and "fiction."

Its Laws and Its "Stories"

One of the crucial moments of the definitive constitution of the state in 1880 occurred with the discussion of the laws of education and civil registry in 1883 and 1884 (and when President Roca confronted the church and expelled the papal nuncio). The group of writers was directly represented in the elaboration of the laws of secular education and civil registry because Eduardo Wilde, its most fragmentary and humorous member (his autobiography *Aguas abajo* [Downstream] remained unfinished), was the minister of public instruction at that time. Later on, when the law of civil marriage was approved, he would become President Miguel Juárez Celman's minister of the interior.

Around these laws, by means of which the liberal state defined itself, taking possession of the birth, education, marriage, and death of all its subjects, the writers of 1880 wrote a network of autobiographical "stories" of education and marriage. As literature, these stories would become the fiction or the reverse of these state laws, because they singularized the legal universalities (they gave them "I's" and persons), and because it was in the very moment when the laws of education and marriage were violated that the autobiographical subjects constituted their own identity and that of their others. *The transgression of the liberal laws constituted their liberal identities.* The laws of education and marriage not only provided the very material of the tales; rather, their transgression defined the subjects of the state coalition. The literature of the coalition thus shows *the intimate relationship between hegemonic practices and legal discourses.*

The stories of education and marriage of the literature of 1880 revolve around certain school scenes, told as autobiographies. And elsewhere, separated by a distance of space, time, person, or change of world, are the stories that revolve around the marital problems of a character close to the autobiographical narrator, a relative or friend.

The Patricians and Their Autobiographical Stories of Education

The school scene can be biographical or autobiographical, fragmentary or not, postulated as "reality" or fiction (these are some of the variants of the narrative prose of 1880). As for proper names, true autobiographical myths, texts are defined according to their usage: real names, pseudonyms, and anonymity constitute the degree of fictionality of the autobiographical position. They are autobiographies of the realist era. Names also serve to mark the degree of the transgressions: the greater the anonymity, the greater the transgression.

In the autobiographical writing of 1880 one can read two fables of identity at once: that of the nation and that of the person.[4] National history, up to the frontier of the state, coincides totally with personal history. The two times have arrived at a point of arrest and fusion that allows them to be written. In *Juvenilia* (1882, but published in 1884), the real autobiography in the form of "Memories," and in *La gran aldea* (The great village) (1884), the fictional autobiography (in the form of a novel or "Buenos Aires Chronicles"), one reads the first conversations or "stories" about schools and education. They speak about and from secondary schools at the very moment when the state takes charge of free, obligatory, and secular primary education. The two writers, Miguel Cané and Lucio V. López, and also the "Englishman" Eduardo Wilde, the minister who left an unfinished autobiography, were born outside the nation during the political exile of their parents. Cané was born in 1851; he was thirty-three years old when he wrote *Juvenilia*.

Juvenilia and *La gran aldea* open with the death of the father and are told from the present. They speak of school from the memory of youth, of the years of formation. And *the places from which they narrate* these juvenile scenes (in both senses: also where they put the representation of the school) *define the exact positions of the autobiographical subjects,* from which they formulate the fable of national identity coinciding with the autobiography. *Juvenilia* and *La gran aldea* tell the story of the narrator and at the same time the history of the political events that led to the 1880 break in the formation of the state. But the school is situated in the provinces in López, and in Buenos Aires in Cané.

The Amusing Adventures of Juvenilia

Miguel Cané is thus the writer of the cultural coalition of 1880 who writes the real autobiography of his life at school (he uses real names), and who tells the fable of national *porteño* identity (*porteño* refers to the residents of the city of Buenos Aires).

In *Juvenilia,* national history is narrated in a tone somewhere between farcical and picaresque, and the theme is "high school pranks" in the capital, at the Colegio Nacional de Buenos Aires. This tone constitutes the charm and freshness of the text. Memories are organized around a double temporal and spatial inscription because there is a repetition of dates and positions of the author-narrator. On the one hand the date of the father's death, 1863, is touched upon twice; the first time in order to mark the son's entry into high school in chapter 1, and the second to mark his personal participation in the nation's political history and his entrance into the legislature, as the culmination of his pranks or transgressions of the rules of the school, in chapter 29. In 1863 Cané first recounts the death of his father and his entry into high school and finally enunciates his political and family identity: he was pro-*porteño, crudo* (literally, "raw"), and he was a relative of the Varelas.

On the other hand, there is a double inscription of the narration and its relationship to writing because the narrator remembers the school, its space, and its characters twice, or from two places: at the beginning, in the introduction prior to the first chapter, as the minister-ambassador who meets up with his failed former companions ("I had been named minister, I don't know where!, and him . . . !"), and at the end, in the last two chapters (35 and 36), as an examiner: "One day many years later, I returned to the School: in my turn, I was to sit at the fearful table of the examiners" (*Juvenilia y otras páginas argentinas* [Buenos Aires: Espasa Calpe, 1993], 124). "The exams are about to begin, Doctor. We're just waiting for you" (125).

When he returns to the Colegio Nacional to give an exam, and when he recalls it in the last chapter, in 1880, he is a doctor, a state civil servant, and a journalist. He is a typical man of the cultural coalition who turns inward: "I lived overwhelmed by work; beside my university chair, I oversaw the Mail, I spent a couple of hours a day in the Educational Council, and, above all, I edited *El Nacional,* a thankless and exhausting task if ever there was one" (128).

And, finally, the trangressions account is written in 1882 from abroad, in Venezuela, as a diplomat or representative of the national state, in order to "kill long hours of sadness and solitude." In chapter 1 he felt this sadness and solitude when he entered school in 1863 after his father's funeral: "Silent and sad, I hid in corners to cry by myself, remembering my home" (53). In his exile at school, he read long serial novels (in chapter 3, "I went through all of Dumas," 59). And in Venezuela, his other exile, he wrote *Juvenilia.* One writes from where one has read.[5]

To put it another way: in 1880 Cané was appointed general director of Mail and Telegraphs, editor of *El Nacional,* and member of the Council of Education. This is the moment at which he appears as the tired examiner, and during which his memories of school are reinscribed. In 1881 he traveled to Colombia and Venezuela as an Argentine diplomatic representative, and there, far away, alone, and as sad as when he went to school, he wrote *Juvenilia*. In those places or positions, from the internal and external representations of the state of 1880 which serve as the frame of the text (occupying the introduction and the final chapters), Cané recounts and enjoys his juvenile pranks at school and his escapades outside of school between 1863 and 1869.

The Hero of the Nacional Revolution

At the Colegio Nacional de Buenos Aires, the narrator recounts how he led a revolution against the tyranny of the Spanish vice rector Torres and against the lack of food, how he was exiled (they expelled him from school), and how he then returned: "I remember having given a speech about the ignominy of being governed, us, the republicans, by a monarchist Spaniard, and having made reference to the Independence movement, San Martín, Belgrano and I think even the English invasion" (71). There are various amusing and definitive aspects to this story: the beloved French teacher Amédée Jacques,[6] a political exile and the incarnation of science and progress, expels him from school for an anti-Spanish and antimonarchist revolutionary speech (and I would like to think that this is one of the inside jokes of the coalition). He goes off with his trunk to the Plaza de la Victoria, alone and at night. There he is found by the president of the nation himself, Mitre's vice-president serving in his stead, who takes him to sleep at his house because he is a friend of the family. He leaves the previous "nation" (in the form of the revolution against the tyranny of the school), goes into "exile" (and the state itself houses him), and afterward returns to the school. This sequence not only recounts national history but also the history of his own father: his revolution against the tyranny of Rosas, his exile in Montevideo (where Cané was born), and his return. For Cané, and from now on for Argentine "high" culture, the history of the father is the history of the nation.[7]

These sons of the nation and of exile such as Cané, López, and Wilde constitute at this moment, for us, a specific sector of high culture in the Latin American liberal coalition of 1880: patricians who write autobiographies.

The Aesthetic of the Patrician Autobiographies

Cané, López, and Wilde each occupy a double and ambivalent position with regard to the change of 1880: on one hand, they do not fail to represent it and to participate in political modernity, but on the other, they reject a certain cultural modernity.

Their opposition to the new order is not political but cultural, and *it is they themselves who elaborate the separation of the two spheres.* They define themselves as simple, cultured, more or less poor: they are the nation and the nation is simplicity, the past, patriotism (those storekeepers and López's "Flower of a single day"). Therefore, they postulate an "aristocratic" aesthetic of simplicity, and they criticize the French baroqueness of "modern culture," an overloaded and motley new style (Wilde's "Vida moderna" ["Modern Life"]).

In *Juvenilia's* introduction, Cané refers to this aesthetic: "I have never written anything with as much pleasure as I have these memoirs. While attempting to achieve the style I had proposed to myself, I smiled at times when confronted with the enormous difficulties that arise when one wants to write with simplicity. This is because simplicity is life and truth, and there is nothing more difficult than to penetrate this sanctuary" (44).

The War of Transition

In order to continue with the history of the nation, the hero of *Juvenilia* recounts his participation in school as an *abajeño* (one from below) in the war of the *porteños* against the provincials as represented by a foreign priest named vice rector:

> Don F. M. would organize dances for us in the dormitory that previously had served as a chapel. An altar still stood where moral instruction had been given once a week in the time of Doctor Agüero.
>
> It was by no means religious sentimentalism which stirred us to rise up against that desecration; but since in those dances dinner was served and no small amount of dry wine drunk, wine which by virtue of its color served as a visual substitute for sherry, it so happened that many boys got drunk, which was not only a repugnant spectacle, but also authorized certain infamous rumors regarding the conduct of Don F. M. which today I prefer to consider slanderous, but about whose accuracy we then hadn't the slightest doubt. In any case, the simple fact of the dance revealed in that man a criminal condescendence, given that this was a boarding school for young men, whose regimen is abominable in and of itself and can only persist by virtue of vigilance at every moment and military discipline. (86–87)

This indignant paragraph (which says all that will come later, in relation to the discourse of liberalism of 1880) is organized around substitutions and series. In Cané (who thinks like an atheist), the substitution, in the dormitory with the altar, of the drunken dances of F. M. for the moral instruction of Agüero (and also of sherry by the apparent wine), leads directly to repugnance and criminality. And from there, directly to military discipline.

At issue is the fact that Don F. M. sides with the provincials (who are the majority of the boarding students: two-thirds of the total boarding population) and always punishes the *porteños* ("we were the 'State' of Buenos Aires!"). The priest governs with a single party, and this is the motive of the *porteños'* indignation and thus of Cané's heroism.

The *porteño* minority organizes itself. "Vague conspiracy was followed by an organization of Carbonari. I didn't have the honor of being initiated: I was still very young and I belonged to the *abajeños,* those who lived on the ground floor of the Colegio" (87). (Which is to say that this could also have occurred in 1863.) His older friend Eyzaguirre does participate and gives him instructions to attack the nearest provincial when the disorder caused by two small, anonymous bombs breaks out. And it's curious that Cané, when he writes *Juvenilia,* continues to keep the secret of the Carbonari: the name of the student who set off the bombs.

There are expulsions and groundings with no Sunday outings until discipline is in fact affirmed with the entry of the authoritarian Don José M. Torres, whose memory is linked, in Cané, with prison (and also with the "revolution" against his Spanish tyranny).

This episode at the Colegio Nacional recounts at least two struggles for hegemony. The first instance is the internal struggle for hegemony among students of the school, where the number of provincials was far greater than the number of *porteños* because they were boarding in Buenos Aires. The second struggle is for ideological and pedagogical hegemony among the rectors and vice rectors. The episode describes the crucial change represented by the transition from the old rector and priest Agüero, the representative of colonial paternalism in the era of the revolution (moral instruction), to Jacques, the positivist French hero. In the war of transition, the anonymous and sexually "criminal" foreign priest (an interesting association of characteristics), linked to the provincials, is defeated and substituted, or mediated for an instant, by a good priest, the "venerable Dr. Santillán," who is then replaced by the authoritarian Spaniard Torres (who is implicated as the endpoint of the series in Cané's indignant speech against F. M.). And from there to the Frenchman Jacques brought by Mitre. As these amusing episodes indicate, the narrator does not abandon the position of hero of Nacional history. He delivers the speech inciting revolution against Torres and struggles against the perverse priest and his provincials.

The first act of heroism occurs in the first chapter when the narrator invents a "Creole method" in order to continue sleeping in the morning at school; this is the first prank he recounts, *and the first escape from school.* In the market he sees a boy sleeping inside a piece of leather hung under an ox cart, and *a brilliant idea* occurs to him: to apply this method to his own bed. Let us see how the hero experiences his moment of Creole association: "For me it was a bolt of lightning, Newton's apple, Galileo's lamp, Papin's cooking pot, Volta's frog, Champollion's Rosetta stone, Calimacus's curled leaf" (54).

The association is totally Borgesian and Latin American: after a Creole element there follows, inevitably, an encyclopedia (in this case, one of invention or discovery). This association is one of the inheritances left to us by the high liberal culture of 1880 and which Borges brought to its culmination.

The Real Revolution of 1863

The high point of schoolboy transgressions transpires outside, in reality, in one of the escapes from the capital's Colegio Nacional, when Cané recounts his personal participation in the revolution of the *crudos* (the raw ones) and the *cocidos* (the cooked ones). Let us recall that this occurs in the same year as his father's death, 1863, when Cané enters school. But it is narrated almost at the end, in chapter 29, closing the account of rule-breaking at the Colegio as a political history of the nation. And in the very place where he draws the plan of the text, repeating the (strangely inverted) 1880–1863 scheme, he says that he has no plan: "Since I write without a plan and as the memories come, I pause on one which has remained present in my memory with clear persistence. I refer to that famous 22nd of April, 1863, when the *crudos* and the *cocidos* were on the verge of bloodying the city, the *cocidos* for the cause which they championed again in 1880, and likewise the *crudos.* I was a *crudo,* and an *enragé* one at that" (113).

Among the patricians, personal identity is at once political and familial. On that day in 1863 the autobiographical subject defines his family and political identity because he recounts how he personally participated, like his family, in the revolution. *He twice escaped from the Colegio:* during his first escape he saw a Borgesian scene in the Calle Moreno: a knife duel to the death, and men with scarves around their necks. During his second escape, this time across the rooftops, he arrived at the legislature. And the first person he saw there was his relative Horacio Varela, who was "like my older brother," and who sent him home with a message: "that he wouldn't be back until late." And thus he authorized the rooftop escape from the Colegio, *the maximum transgression,* which closes the Nacional history.

The Loves of a Porteño

There ends the political history of personal and national identity; the following chapter, number 30, begins with the end: "It is now time to conclude this chat which has allowed me to pass a few hours sweetly in this sad and monotonous life I lead" (116). And thus begins the economic and cultural history, at once collective and personal.

The collective: "We were atheists in philosophy and many of us upheld in good faith the ideas of Hobbes" (116). "The majority of us were poor and our mothers made all sorts of sacrifices to give us an education. . . . We were disbelieving and somewhat cynical philosophers. . . . We wore our hair long and unkempt. . . . We were, all in all, happy and carefree" (120).

The personal: In chapter 33 Cané returns to his father (who is the personal marker of the narration) in order to construct for himself a cultural identity and something more, outside of the politics of the Colegio: "As for me, I remembered well that from age eight to age twelve I had almost never missed a night at the Opera; my father always took me with him" (120–21). He then recounts how, in *the last escape from the Colegio*, at age eighteen, he found love in the same place where he discovered music with his father. He escapes alone and goes to his family's box at the Colón and falls in love during the opera. "Would that I could love again as I loved then and as one loves only then, pure of heart and lofty of thought!" (122). And to reenter the school, he imitates the voice of the vice rector and knocks over the watchman.

The *porteño* national hero of the revolution is poor and orphaned, but his family, and therefore he himself, is found not only in the legislature, in journalism, and in the company of the president. He is also found, with his children and wives, at the opera. This is the place where the coalition of 1880 finds love and represents it, at the Teatro Colón.

The Loves of a Provincial

While the hero falls in love at the Colón, the provincials fall in love on their ranches, and this is one of the most enjoyable and definitive episodes of *Juvenilia*. At the Colegio's summer location in Chacarita, the hero recounts his equestrian adventures. And he represents, in a totally carnivalesque mode, the other part of national history, that of escapades on horseback and of their leaders. In Chacarita, the students transgress fords, passes, wire fences, limits, and jurisdictions.

The best of these escapes is a sort of excursion on horseback among the Ranquel

Indians, organized by a Riojan enamored of a country girl, in order to attend a dance at a ranch. There an Italian plays the accordion, and an old gaucho asks for light, "like the moribund Goethe" (110). (There is no gaucho without his Goethe in Cané, as in Borges.) The escapees were responsible for bringing yerba mate, sugar, beer, and gin.

Another heroic adventure ensues when the students must return to school, their escape having been discovered and the alarm sounded. The protagonist crosses the fields with five companions on a horse led by the Riojan, with his "pretty." The horse, lent by the old gaucho, trips on a wire fence and falls and dies in a muddy ditch. The fugitives sink into the mud and extract themselves, then undertake a "legendary march" on foot (113). Let us look at the pair of lovers because they also tell another story. The enamored Riojan, organizer of the transgression, was called "crazy Larrea," or "Larrea the parrot," at school ("Let it be understood that I have altered his real surname," 106), and Cané describes him in the following manner: "Larrea's face was a masterpiece. In the first place, that face was only maintained at the expense of a constant struggle against a bushy, riotous, and eminently invasive head of hair. I cannot recall Larrea's physiognomy without the greenish arch that crowned his narrow forehead precisely at the dividing line of his hair and his free skin. It was a thick hair remover of unbearable odor which Larrea applied every night with Benedictine diligence, in order to avoid the capillary advances which I have mentioned" (106–7). His little country girl was delightful, "her only defect being that narrow and scrawny neck that seems to be a distinctive trait of our indigenous race" (108).

The first love of the provincial and the escape among the Ranquel Indians represent one of the amorous universes of the coalition, which plays amusingly against the universe of the first love of the *porteño* and his escape to the Colón. (The two universes will also play in *Sin rumbo* [Adrift] by Eugenio Cambaceres.) This adventure, which ends in chapter 28, immediately precedes the revolution of the *crudos* and the *cocidos*.

A Series of Hairy Brutes

"Crazy Larrea" is one more in a truly insistent series in *Juvenilia*, that of the hairy provincials or foreigners.

One of the culminating moments in the Nacional history, where the subject ceases to be the hero and becomes a contemplator, in chapter 12, is the solitary combat between the incomparable Jacques (who was named by Mitre to teach and direct the school, and whose tomb the narrator [Cané] visits along with those of his relatives) and a fellow student, the *montonero* Corrales, who has no notion of right angles and who has "straight, hard and abundant hair which freely obeyed the impulse of twenty whirlwinds" (74–75). In the heat of the struggle he chants belligerent provocations, short of breath. Then Cané unleashes what is now for us *the classical universal Argentine encyclopedia,* in this case, that of war: "Corrales was a simple *montonero,* a Páez, a Güemes, an Artigas; he had not read Caesar, nor Frederick the Great, nor the memoirs of Vauban, nor Napoleon's notes, nor the works of Jomini. His art was instinctive and Jacques had the strategic science and genius" (76). For this reason the Frenchman of the Encyclopedia triumphs. In 1863–1869, at school and in Chacarita, the political differences between *porteños* and provincials were also cultural, corporal, and racial.[8]

The final brute is the Italian nurse-doorman who had fought in the foreign legion in Montevideo (in other words, who collaborated with the enemies during the anti-Rosas war) and who had been charged with administering injections in the rear end, among other unpopular services in the Colegio. "His person began with a formidable bush of hair which suggests to us the confused and intermingled vegetation of Paraguay, of which Azara speaks. . . . He must have served in the Italian legion during the siege of Montevideo or lived with one of Garibaldi's soldiers in those times, because in the era when he was a doorman. . . . He would enter our rooms singing at the top of his lungs in Italian, with the air of a military reveille. . . . 'Levántasi, muchachi, / que la cuatro sun / e lo federali / sun vení o Cordún'" (94–95). Moreover, the Italian has an indefinite body: no one is sure whether he is thin or fat, like Colonel Buendía. Here the national difference is constructed as at once linguistic, corporal (and capillary), cultural, political, and, perhaps, sexual (as in the case of Don F. M.), because it characterizes a servant of the Colegio.

Seventeen years after writing *Juvenilia,* Cané intervened in this national difference with a book and authorship of a bill crucial to Argentine political history. In the second cycle of the coalition (and of the liberal state: the relations of the cultural coalitions follow a process) in 1899, and as a national senator from the capital, Cané presented his bill proposing a law of residence to the Chamber of Senators, and he published his brief book, *Expulsión de extranjeros* (Expulsion of foreigners), in which he synthesizes the legislation of the principal European nations regarding the right to expel foreigners. Therefore, the author of *Juvenilia* is also one of the authors of law 4144 (1902), called the Law of Residence. It provided for the expulsion from the country of foreigners "of bad conduct" (which is to say, "bad political conduct": anarchists and socialists).[9]

The Depoliticization of 1880 and the Moral of the Story

Let us return to the school in *Juvenilia*.

In the Colegio Nacional, between 1863 and 1869, political and national differences were also cultural differences and something more: differences of hair in one case, of "fine golden sand" in another.

But in 1880, in the frame of the narration, the state employee who has the "I" *depoliticizes the representation* of the differences between companions. And he classifies them by other means, with other names. At the very outset, before he begins to narrate the adventures, Cané, speaking as a doctor and minister and for the cultural coalition of the liberal state, reviews the school's failed students, whom he protects and helps. They failed because they did not know French (as in the case of the famous Binomio, who was a genius in math and who became a poor office worker), or through vice, as in the case of the drinkers or bohemians who suffered from an excess of imagination and were unable to write. And there are no political differences because the year is 1881 and Cané is called "minister." At the end, as the examining doctor of 1880, he blesses the school and recommends, with a final implicit joke directed to the coalition, Boys, go to high school (which isn't obligatory), admire your wise professors, speak French, don't drink, indulge in neither vice nor fantasies, and you will be able to become future state employees, within and outside the nation.

The "education story" of transgressions and national history opens and closes in 1880 with neither politics nor hairy brutes, and with warnings and morals for high school students, who in Argentina continue reading *Juvenilia* and laughing with Cané at his pranks up to the present day.

Juvenilia, *by Minister Cané, Is Promptly and Anonymously Applauded by Minister Wilde*

The letter from Eduardo Wilde to Miguel Cané on the occasion of the publication of *Juvenilia* in 1884 appeared unsigned in *Sud-América*, the official organ of the cultural coalition, on 20 May 1884.

Wilde totally depoliticizes and dehistoricizes the reading, because he compares the memories of *Juvenilia* with his own memories of the Colegio de Concepción del Uruguay (in the province of Entre Ríos), and he says that they are exactly the same. Binomio was a certain Chicharra. The two schools, their food and their sadness, were also the same. What Wilde likes about *Juvenilia* are the common parts he was able to find there: the desolation of the first days as a boarder, the poverty of his family. And, moving on to 1880, he compares the new arrivals at the school with some old, withdrawn member of the Club del Progreso, who goes infrequently and who is received like an intruder. The prediction that the minister of public instruction offers at the end is fulfilled: "It's the best thing you've written. . . . Your book will be read in secondary schools with affection and delight, and outside of them, with that sweet melancholy of memories. . . . And upon concluding the last page and not seeing my name but rather yours at the bottom, a legitimate sentiment has invaded me and I have rightly thought that envy is a grand and noble human quality."[10] A great and noble envy links the members of the coalition.

Juvenilia with La gran aldea

The novel of 1880 is *La gran aldea,* from 1884, because it represents the historical-cultural break that produces the state, and it recounts it after high school, which is situated in the provinces and not in the capital as in Cané. In his fictional autobiography, López speaks of nothing other than the political and cultural change, of the before and after of 1880, and as in Cané, school divides the two epochs. But he speaks not as a real civil servant of the state but rather as a social chronicler (as witness and fictional historian, with a change of names). Thus, *the changes are the substance of the narration:* the change of domicile due to the death of his father (to the house of Aunt Medea and her *mitristas,* at age ten; his mother died when he was born); the change in his situation in the house of his aunt and uncle due to the Battle of Pavón (in 1861, where the narrator represents his family and political identity at age twelve, as in Cané); the change of city to attend school in the provinces, at age fifteen; and the change of situation in the uncle's house after the death of Aunt Medea, when he returns from school after five years. This death makes the uncle her heir and makes possible his second marriage, in 1880, the announcement of which opens the novel and frames it. From then on the narration moves toward the political past, from the final death of the father to school, and toward the final catastrophe (or moral), which leads the narrator back to the space of the school where he fell in love and read at age sixteen. And from there it is written.

La gran aldea and *Juvenilia* not only coincide in their opening with the death of the father in 1860, but also in the frame of 1880; between the two times two subjects are defined. In *La gran aldea,* the space of the school (the autobiographical conversations about schools) divides the theme of the uneven marriages of the uncle, the first to Aunt Medea and the second to Blanca Montifiori. And its second inscription, the return to school, as in Cané, closes the narration. Each of the uncle's marriages represents a part of the novel and a period of history. The first chronicles the previous political nation of Alejandro and Aunt Medea in 1860, and the second chronicles Blanca Montifiori's new culture of 1880. The contrast between one culture and the other (or between one feminine politics and another) is constant, but the true change between the uncle's first marriage and his second (between the two parts of the novel) is the absolute depoliticization of family, social, and cultural life.

The two parts of *La gran aldea,* the fictional autobiography of 1880, divided by secondary school, illustrate *the change in literary representation brought by 1880* and already seen in *Juvenilia:* the account is depoliticized in the second part, making it only social and "cultural." In 1880, the patriotic dates are those of social celebrations: Julio's uncle marries Blanca on 20 June 1883 (Flag Day, commemorating the death of Manuel Belgrano).

As in Cané, the autobiographical subject constructs its political and familial identity on the same day in 1861 as a historical event fundamental to the nation prior to the state. The narrator recounts in the first person how he personally participated, thanks to his aunt by marriage, Medea, first in the news and later in the celebrations of the defeat or the victory of Pavón (where Mitre's city militia overcame the caudillo Justo José de Urquiza's gaucho cavalry in 1861). In the very place of the official news of the victory, in Bringas's patriotic store, the aunt names him (and the chronicler names himself for the first time), and also declares the political identity of his father. Aunt Medea says: this child is named Julio Rolaz, and he is the son of a poor dead *urquista* employee, my husband's brother. The day of the Pavón victory defines his double and split identity: son of an *urquista,* of a loser, who lives in a triumphal *mitrista* household. He is, like the black servant Alejandro, a political enemy of the house of his aunt. In *La gran aldea* the narrator is a witness torn between two periods and two loyalties, a chronicler internally divided *like the nation itself:* his name is Julio. He occupies the place of the previous and internal nation: alone, orphaned, poor, torn between two loyalties and also between two eras. The autobiographical subject of *Juvenilia,* the tired or sad and lonely representative of the state, occupied in his remembered pranks the place of the national *porteño* hero.

The patricians of the cultural coalition define their national identity as at once political and familial. We see in them *the weight of the family and of kinship in the political body* (in Latin America the traditional models penetrate parliamentary and bureaucratic systems, which appear as extended families) *and in definitions of identity* (a feature of "aristocratic" Latin American culture which persists in Borges, Mujica Lainez, and Victoria Ocampo).

In *Juvenilia* and *La gran aldea,* the culture of the previous nation is "national culture." The modernization of 1880 obliges the state to adopt a national culture (*the nationalization of a literature and the literaturization of a nation*) because nationality is a requisite in order to function as a "subject" in the new modern world order. In their "education stories," the patricians of the coalition invent a *national culture that is an agent of cohesion for the state.*

Two Subjects and Two Fables

Lucio Vicente López dedicates *La gran aldea* to Cané when it is published as a book in 1884: "To Miguel Cané, my friend and comrade, L.V. L." *La gran aldea* had appeared in serial form in *Sud-América,* the newspaper which López himself founded in 1884 along with, among others, Pellegrini and Gallo, in order to sponsor the presidential candidacy of Miguel Juárez Celman.

Between them, *Juvenilia* and *La gran aldea* construct two writing positions or two key subjects of the Latin American state from its very emergence: the memorialist official and the chronicler. They are the traditional positions but are occupied by the cultural coalition of 1880 in order to narrate the history of the previous nation. And they are also the *traditional literary positions* in the liberal state of a nation that attained the highest point of Latin American capitalism at that moment, entry into the world market. The memoirs of the official and of the chronicler are the writing of the patricians of the coalition who, nevertheless, construct alternative versions of the previous nation.

Cané's national history has the tone of transgressions or pranks at the Colegio Nacional de Buenos Aires during Mitre's presidency. López's national history, which is the first part of *La gran aldea,* has the grotesque tone of the *mitrismo* of Aunt Medea and her *porteño* friends. Thus, Cané and López differ politically, radically, in the cultural definition of *mitrismo.*[11] (And in the texts we can clearly hear the different tones of the conversations and thus one of the first internal differences of the coalition.) It was thanks to Mitre, Cané says, that we had Amadeo Jacques, the wise European who changed teaching and brought positivism. And López, through "Julio": it was Aunt Medea's ignorant and authoritarian *mitristas* who advised him not to read books nor go to school. And he sees them now, in 1880, moribund and ridiculous with their priest at the burial of Aunt Medea, who dies of rage over a fight among women, her cerebral hemorrhage signifying the end of the previous nation.[12]

I would say that the "education story" of the two canonical books by the patricians of 1880 narrate a fable of identity of the nation prior to the state, one divided (culturally and politically) into two positions and into two opposite versions, one *mitrista* and *porteño,* the other *urquieista* and provincial. For this reason, López's secondary school is in the provinces (and divides the two eras) and Cané's is the Colegio Nacional de Buenos Aires (and unites the two eras).

The Patricians of the State Coalition

The liberal and "aristocratic" coalition of 1880 created a new space in the representation of life. With them there arose a social life as purely cultural life and no longer as political life, as in the literature of the previous moment. The new state and the cultural change recounted in *La gran aldea* are one and the same. The production of this change in the representation of social life was the task of the writers of the cultural coalition. In their literature they constructed a series of subject-positions of the liberal state with their families, places, and solitudes, and also their morals. For now we have only two: Cané's state civil servant (who enjoys remembering himself as a national hero) and López's chronicler (who laments having to represent the nation; López is the first in the coalition who writes his *Viajes* [Travels], and later a *Historia*). On the bases of these, we can advance some provisional hypotheses about the relations between the liberal state of 1880 and this sector of the cultural coalition where Cané and López are found, and which we will call the "aristocratic" patrician wing.

The more or less poor patricians (who represent poverty in their texts: Cané, López, Wilde, the sons of anti-Rosas exiles, and the grandsons of the heroes of independence), who are almost all important officials of the new state, speak of the break and of change, in the form of "real" or fictional autobiographies. Theirs are memoirs of childhood and adolescence written as stories, novels, recollections, chronicles, travel notes, or talks. They recount memories of their education and at the same time, beginning with change and memory, the history of the previous nation in its two opposed political versions, the *porteño* and the provincial. López and Cané represent their political enemies (who are opposite in the two texts: *porteños* in one case and provincials in the other) as uncultured, as the outside of culture. (And if Lucio V. Mansilla's *Memorias* are included, other opposed political and cultural versions are evident.) Within the coalition, the patricians converse heatedly about the political and cultural heritage of the nation.

Their diverse versions coexist, and this is one of the fundamental literary gestures of *the coalition, which affirms itself on the basis of having overcome earlier political differences.* All of them are *culturally, literarily,* valid and true, because 1880 changes literary representation: the writers depoliticize writing when they cross this threshold. In their stories, post–1880 political and social differences are *purely cultural.*

For the liberal state which defines itself as such, the opposed political versions of the patricians are equally valid because it absorbs them, or, better yet, *because it postulates its novelty precisely in the absorption of the political differences of the nation prior to its constitution.* Thus the liberal Argentine state transforms the alternative versions into its cultural complements: into a coalition.[13] And the education stories of *Juvenilia* and *La gran aldea* are transformed into "classics" of Argentine culture.

The Dandies and Their Marriage Stories

A review in order to proceed. Our theme is the cultural coalition of the liberal state because in this first moment we are interested in relations between state and culture in 1880. The coalition is a group of young university writers who produce stories, literature, fables of identity: fictions for the state. The state needs these fictions (the state needs fictions) not only to organize power relations (and in order to have a complete map of the new society such as the coalition draws in 1880), but also to postulate its own definitions and alternatives. With its autobiographical literature, the coalition produces fictions for the state and a series of positions of the "I"—gazes, languages, spaces, perspectives—which we are calling the "subjects of the liberal state." They are the first persons of their stories of education and marriage which "coincide" with the promulgation of the fundamental laws of the liberal state of 1880: those of secular education and civil matrimony. In the stories of education and marriage, the coalition writes these "legal fictions" and "legal subjectivities" for the new liberal state.

In order to be able to imagine the coalition and its different sectors, we need to postulate a certain relationship between the "real" persons of the writers (something of their "biographies") and the "fictional" subjects they invent. We need to operate with at least two degrees of fictionality: the real and the fictional. Up to this point the patricians Cané and López, born in exile, define their familial and political identities on the very day of the occurrence of a fundamental political confrontation prior to 1880. And who place their school stories in Buenos Aires or in the provinces (and put them behind, in the wayward and political childhood prior to 1880) and in doing so install a special type of subject, a third grade of fictionality: the Nacional/national hero of *Juvenilia* (the hero of what we have called the *porteño* fable of national identity), and the autobiographical subject of *La gran aldea,* torn between two loyalties and spaces and between the before and the now ("Julio" the "hero" of the fable of national identity: Lucio Vicente López was the son of the author of *Historia Argentina,* Vicente Fidel López, and the grandson of Vicente López y Planes, author of the Argentine national anthem). In 1880, the patricians constituted the political wing of the coalition and occupied political posts in the liberal state.

But in the literature itself, in literary genre (and here we see the proliferation of grades of fictionality: the plurality of positions which coexist in "the subjects of the liberal state") these patricians of the coalition assume the role of autobiographical memoirist—Cané—and of chronicler—López. Memorialist and chronicler: they are the two most traditional writers' positions of the Latin American state, which appear with its very institution as Spanish colony.[14] These traditional positions, linked to the definition of "the national" and the construction of the previous nation (and it is the patricians themselves who will lead us, with their speeches and bills, from the construction of the nation to nationalism) were not sufficient for the young coalition or for the new state.

Argentina was at the apogee of capitalism for a Latin American country, with entry into the world market (and fables of national identity on the periphery were therefore necessary), but the state was also in full modernization, and new systems for the classification of subjects had to be invented. The present had to be narrated, and more modern positions were required, some sort of "vanguard" in the coalition: the liberal state defined itself precisely by its "modernizing leap." New, more depoliticized, more specifically cultural, and more independent allies, who told other, more "private" stories of education and marriage: for example, the dandy and the man of science. These were the new subjects of the cultural coalition.

The Box at the Colón and the Carnival at the Club del Progreso

The coalition was a fabric converging in certain spaces. Let us listen to what Miguel Cané (who a while back seemed to converse with López, perhaps at the Club, about the cultural legacy of *mitrismo*), had to say about Eugenio Cambaceres (1843–1889), who invented the modern novel in Argentina with a "marriage story" told in the "aristocratic" slang of the Club, and who also invented the new subjects of the liberal state. "That *avant-scène!* Eugenio Cambaceres, with the appeal of his talent, his artistic taste, his exquisite refinement, his fortune, his physical appearance, had it all, as if he had been born under the protection of some beneficent fairy, and he was *the uncontested boss.*"[15]

Cané declares Cambaceres "the boss" of the Teatro Colón, where the men of the coalition go with their wives or to search for a wife; he is the boss of the purely cultural and artistic institution of the representation which accompanies the liberal state as its other face, its fiction, its other self. In 1880, at a moment when politics could no longer be thought of (or performed) as war, there appeared with the Colón this space of illusion and play, where the coalition staged itself, among women, in order to reproduce "in fiction" the scene of the liberal state.

Theater and representation (as performance: spectacularization, fictionalization, simulation, and disguise) allow us to think about the liberal state and its politics of representation.[16] They also allow us to think about its fictions, because what Cambaceres writes when he founds the modern novel is precisely *the theater of the liberal state*. He theatrically represents the private world and writes the first stories of education and marriage of 1880, before *Juvenilia* and *La gran aldea*. In his novel *Pot pourri (Silbidos de un vago) (Pot Pourri: Whistlings of an Idler)*, which appeared anonymously in 1882, Cambaceres chooses the Argentine dandy (or gentleman or *señorito*) as the subject of his autobiographical fiction, and he designates him as an "actor" and "small-time musician" (or the other way around: he chooses as his fictional subject an actor or idler who plays a dandy). And with this purely cultural subject, and "in representation," he will tell the marriage story of the liberal state.

The coalition is a fabric of conversations (the conversations of '80), references, unanimities, ironies, and discrepancies, with different grades of fictionality and in diverse places and spaces. Cané, in *Prosa ligera* (Light prose), places Cambaceres in the Colón, in reality, with his name and as he-who-has-it-all: refinement, fortune, and physique. In the fiction of *Pot pourri*, Cambaceres's "actor" "I" places Cané and the coalition at the carnival dance of the Club del Progreso in the regime of real names, while he represents himself anonymously (and his characters have "generic" names: Juan, María, Pepe). Cambaceres "really" represents the coalition in the Club del Progreso, the 1880 masculine social institution par excellence, in which he was also a boss (vice president in 1873). *But he represents them in the Club del Progreso carnival dance where the masked women choose their partners:*

> In the immediate vicinity of the orchestra (and take note, as this is the most strategic point, the part of this human pond in which the most fishing is done), they spend the sleepless night like wallflowers on the prowl, without so much as a slap from the hand of God to say: "Take that, you miserable wretches!" and in exchange for dislocating their jaws, Miguel Cané, Lucio V. López, Manuel Láinez, Roque Sáenz Peña and others of their lot—rascals and imbeciles one and all—mill about the salons, find themselves chased, assaulted and fought over by the blessed maskers like flies on a pot of jam.
>
> Tell me with whom thou goest . . . No comment. (85–86)[17]

If we compare the "real" tone employed by Cané in speaking of Cambaceres at the Colón to the "real" tone employed by Cambaceres in speaking of Cané and the coalition at the Club (the two purely cultural spaces), we can imagine their places in the coalition. Those tones: the solemn and reverent patrician at the Colón and the (how shall we say?) "amusing" dandy who laughs at the coalition among women, *with the oral and extremely modern language of the Club.* This difference in tone could separate the patricians of the coalition from the avant-garde dandies and show the tensions between them.

I would like to think that the patrician coalition did not forgive him for the joke about the prowling wallflowers and the dislocated jaws, and they did not welcome him into their bosom until 1885, after the publication of *Sin rumbo* (where Cambaceres abandons the satiric tone and the "aristocratic" *porteño* slang) and the fierce attack of the Catholics. At that moment he would be recognized as "the founder of the national novel" in the official organ, the newspaper *Sud-América* where the coalition's official critic, Martín García Mérou, writes in 1885: "The author of *Silbidos de un vago* has founded the contemporary national novel among us."[18]

The "Real Cambaceres"

As we can see, characters in the novels are not the only "characters" in the *corpus delicti.* Let us look at the real character in order to specify his difference in tone within the cultural coalition of the state and to show its tensions.

Eugenio Cambaceres, a first-generation Argentine and a member of the aristocracy of economic power (who represents in his novels the ownership of land and its dramas), is a unique figure in the coalition because he constitutes *its ideological and literary vanguard.* In *Pot pourri,* his first novel, he invents a new subject for the fictions of the liberal state: an anonymous actor who plays a dandy who in the end plays the head of state. And with this multiple subject he invents a new literary language (an aristocratic *porteño* jargon for the jokes of the coalition's Club) and a new fable of identity for "high" *porteño* culture.

Cambaceres is not a state civil servant like Cané (nor a deputy like López), nor the son of exiles, but rather the son and heir of a rancher (the place of entry into the world market) who became a millionaire in the era of Juan Manuel de Rosas. His father was a young French chemist who met the Argentine consul Larrea in Paris and arrived in Argentina in 1829 with an inheritance he subsequently invested in fields and salteries. (And we would like to place this father in the cultural mythology of the nineteenth century: a chemist adventurer or a pioneer of French imperial expansion—adventure as the myth of empire—in the peripheries or colonies where he would become a millionaire. Thus the Argentine dandy is the son of the explorer: two myths of modernity, two cultural fictions genealogically linked in the space of centers and peripheries.)

In contrast to the patricians who were born in exile, Cambaceres, like Lucio V. Mansilla, experienced *rosismo* and its popular culture, and lived in Paris. Their lives synthesize this specific combination of the Creole and the European that is one of the marks of high culture. Cambaceres and Mansilla, the two beautiful dandies of the coalition (whose fathers made money with Rosas while the patricians lost everything in exile): the "true" Creole aristocrats? And their literature: the true aristocratic Latin American literature of the nineteenth century? And their ironic and "familiar" languages, their tones: are they "higher" than the languages and tones of the patricians? We call them dandies (they could be gentleman, *caballeros, gentilhombres, señoritos*), although Sylvia Molloy disputes the designation in Mansilla's case (and she is right because, apparently, the term "dandy" was derogatory *in the patrician sector* of the coalition; this is evident in *La gran aldea* with Montefiori "the dandy").[19] We call them dandies in order to differentiate them precisely from the patricians: because of their "amusing" tones.

In 1880 Cambaceres (who was a lawyer but who did not practice law: he graduated as a doctor of jurisprudence in 1869 with a pragmatic and capitalist thesis titled *Utilidad, valor y precio* [Utility, value, and price]), joined López, Cané, José María, and Ezequiel Ramos Mejía in signing a manifesto in support of Domingo Faustino Sarmiento's presidential candidacy (there were fifty-four signatories and the coalition was set). They proposed Sarmiento as a candidate of peace and compromise against Roca, Carlos Tejedor, and Bernardo de Irigoyen. But Cambaceres was absent from politics in 1880 (and this again separates him from the patricians, who after the pro-Sarmiento manifesto supported Roca) as a result of having been *excessively* liberal or modern to conceive the laws of this Latin American country in the years before 1880. In his youth he was a sort of pure republican, a Jacobin (and according to Paul Groussac, "he was erroneously credited" with a French grandfather: Jean Jacques Régis de Cambacérès, a celebrated legal adviser and delegate named arch-chancellor and duke of Parma by Napoleon I).[20]

The "Frenchman" Cambaceres, like so many others, was a political avant-gardist so radical that he had to abandon politics. As a deputy to the convention of the province of Buenos Aires in 1871 (at age twenty-eight), he had presented a bill for the separation of church and state, and it failed. The bill was founded on a *purely economic liberalism:* Why should the state support the Catholic Church with taxes paid by citizens of all religions?[21] And in 1874, as a national deputy and with a *purely political liberalism,* he denounced the electoral frauds of his own party and no one listened. Within these liberal extremes he found *the limits of the Argentine or Latin American state;* he resigned his seat as a national deputy and withdrew from politics in 1876. He lived from then on in his mansion in Buenos Aires,[22] his El Quemado estate, and his residence in Paris. Between 1881 and 1887 he wrote four novels, and he died of tuberculosis in Buenos Aires in 1889.

He did not marry an Argentine woman (and "the actor" says in the *avant-scène* of *Pot pourri:* Why are women here not educated as in the United States? Why do we follow the ancient Spanish tradition?)[23] but rather, always on stage, an Italian lyric singer named Luisa Bacichi, seventeen years his junior, whom he met in Paris and who died in 1924.

History here proves highly instructive, because this "real" Cambaceres character, who has nothing to lose, exemplifies one of the distortions from which modern liberal Enlightenment thought suffers in Latin America. At the very moment when it is embodied in the modern Latin American states, the scheme appears as impossible, and then as unfulfilled.

The Cambaceres character in my fiction represents the ideological avant-garde of the coalition: he is the writer who has personally experienced the difference between the Latin American, the French, and the North American liberal states. He is conscious of the limits of the periphery, and his fictional subject is one that fails in everything: "However loud my self-esteem might scream, there's no other way to look at it; I'm a complete *raté.*" And so in 1880 he clearly separates the political part of his life, which he consigns to the past as a farce and a failure, from the literary and "theatrical" part, which is the present and *Pot pourri,* where the actor of the marital farce is a depoliticized subject who will represent, in the end, as his limit, the farce of political power.

A "Theory" of the Literary Avant-Garde of 1880

In *Pot pourri (Silbidos de un vago),* Cambaceres writes not only the first marriage story and the first modern novel, but also the first theory of literary modernity at the moment of the emergence of the liberal state, 1882. The "actor-dandy" represents the literary avant-garde of the coalition because:

(1) In his stories of education and marriage he separates literature from party politics, and radically autonomizes it from politics. And because while he travels by train to the ranch of his friend Juan, reading the paper, the anonymous dandy represents politics to himself as a republican farce in four acts: first, *the farce* of the election; second, *the low theater* of the legislative chambers; third, *the simulacrum* of military insurrection; and fourth and last, *the voice* of the

people. (Let us recall Cambaceres's proposal of a separation of the church from the state and of political "cleanness," and then we will be able to compare the three "fictionalities.")

(2) *Pot pourri* is the first novel, therefore, that puts into literary action the metaphor of the liberal state as theater and representation. And it is also the first marriage story of the coalition.

(3) *Pot pourri* is a novel made of fragments and of all the prose of 1880: memoirs, autobiographies, letters, travel chronicles, stories, and journalistic articles (all of which are represented as scenes, in theatrical style: in satire and in farce). (With regard to travel, the actor-dandy seems to refer to López's *Recuerdos de viaje* [Recollections of travel] when he "visits" Juan, but in reality he wants to talk to the *pícara* María: "I reminded her of a book that she had promised me, not with the intention of reading it, it was a travel volume written by a young compatriot. God save me!")

Cambaceres is the antifragmentarian of the coalition and the one who writes a novel with the "fragments of '80" in order to pulverize them. In the literary modernity of *Pot pourri* the fragments are joined by a story of adultery, one of the central themes of the contemporary French novel and theater.[24] (The history of the modern Latin American novel can be read as a history of sexuality in Latin America. Foucault: "The history of the novel cannot be understood separate from the history of sexuality." But also as a history of the state.) *Pot pourri*'s fragments are joined by a marriage story conceived of as the rupture of the *contract* that sustains everything—the others depend on it —and that the system upholds. (I am referring both to the text, to the literary system, and to the political-state system.) The story of marriage and adultery is put in the present and in the insolent gaze and language of the actor who plays the Argentine dandy: a rich, cultured, idle, and unmarried "aristocrat" who has it all, who criticizes everything, and who has seen it all.

(4) But *Pot pourri* is the first avant-garde novel (and the first "theory") of the coalition because, like Luigi Pirandello later, it separates author, actor, and character. And also because it is the first best-seller and the first literary scandal of the coalition, which opens another of our accounts: that of the best-seller stories (or the avant-garde stories?).

(5) Cambaceres represents the literary avant-garde of 1880 because he directly *argentinizes* contemporary European literature: French fin de siècle boulevard theater, realism, naturalism, and modernism-decadence. In order to argentinize them, he superimposes them, he accumulates them, and he exaggerates them. He does likewise in *Pot pourri* with foreign languages—Italian, French, Latin, English—in order to invent an arrogant, uninhibited, and aristocratic Argentine orality: the *"porteño* slang" to which Martín García Mérou alludes,

or "the Creole-aristocratic dialect" disparaged by Paul Groussac. Cambaceres nationalizes not only foreign languages but also everything else he touches: he argentinizes the dandy (*Pot pourri,* 1882), he argentinizes fin de siècle sexuality and illness, again by means of the dandy (*Música sentimental,* 1884, with the same narrator); with decadent naturalism he argentinizes *spleen,* tedium, the loss of beliefs, depression, and he also argentinizes suicide on the ranch, while a farm worker sets fire to it (*Sin rumbo,* 1885). He argentinizes the son of the immigrant with laws of inheritance and Zola's medium in recounting his education and marriage (*En la sangre* [In the blood], 1887), and this is the Cambaceres novel that is read in secondary schools.

(The coalition founds Argentine high culture and translation as a literary genre; Cambaceres's gesture is different and yet the same because he plagiarizes and imports European ideas, sayings, opinions, narrative modes, positions, and genres, but puts them in a space, a tone, and a language that are absolutely Creole or Argentine: he translates them literarily.)

(6) In the series of operations of *Pot pourri*'s marriage story of private life in the society of '80, the position of Argentine dandy oscillates between transgression and scandal *after the first carnival dance* (the actor places himself on the divide and shows sexual inequality and "injustice"), and convention and conformism *after the second:* in the way in which he "arranges" the final solution to adultery he acts as "the law" embodied in the head of state. The place of this new coalition subject, *the place of the cultural avant-garde* or of the dandy, would be this specific movement between transgression and the law and its embodiment, between the two limits which are the serialized carnival dances.

(7) With *Pot pourri* in 1882 the modern avant-garde novel is invented and takes a forward jump so long (that it almost remains unread; it is not reprinted, nor is it read in secondary schools; Jorge Salessi's thesis on Cambaceres sleeps unpublished in the stacks at Yale) that it can be read from the writing of Manuel Puig in the 1960s and 1970s. To read from "Puig and his precursors," in that specific literary position of representation: for Cambaceres, theater (the Colón and the Comédie-Française and the boulevard theater), for Puig, Argentine radio, and North American cinema.

Both writers work with a minimalist theory of representation, with fragments and with a proliferation of dialogized and quoted discourses: "scenic" dialogues, newspaper reports, gossip columns, ads, letters, internal discourses and monologues, footnotes. This links them to a "familiar" orality and to simple, melodramatic story lines, taken from contemporary theater or cinema. With his marriage story, Cambaceres invents a theory of representation for 1880 high life, and he also invents a private aristocratic language and an impersonal tone for an anonymous subject, which is present in Puig for the middle class: a heard language made up of clichés, sayings, proverbs, the common part of "common language." In order to recount the rupture of the contract that sustains everything, Cambaceres invents (like Puig in the sixties) the *"on dit"* of 1880: a discourse about the "speech" of the Latin American aristocracy for his stories of education and marriage.

The Best-Seller of 1880: Author, Actor, and Character

Let us proceed once and for all to the marriage story of the coalition's avant-garde, with its fictional identities, in order to see their proliferation and their coexistence in the new subject of the liberal state. Cambaceres was thirty-five years old when he published his anonymous work as a "slap in the face of good taste." *Pot pourri* appeared in Buenos Aires (published by Biedma) in 1882 without the author's name and with the subtitle "Silbidos de un vago" (which is the same subtitle given the following novel, *Música sentimental,* which appeared in Paris in 1884, again without the author's name and with the same dandy as narrator). Its success was sensational: the first anonymous text of the coalition is *the first best-seller of 1880* and its first scandal or literary "crime": it was attacked, reprinted, and parodied.[25] The edition sold out the same year, and it was followed by a second edition; in 1883 the third appeared (Paris, Denné), still anonymous, with "A Few Words from the Author." The anonymous "author" is a wealthy man of leisure who refers to the *scandal* raised by the first edition and to *"criminal" accusations against him;* he says that he is not the *"flâneur"* or the "idler" of the whistles (and we won't pause to consider the *"flâneur"*); he articulates his avant-garde project of demolishing institutions; and finally he presents himself as well as a "failure": this time as a "failed author" of a farce in which "truth sings out clearly." Let us listen to his quick, conversational language, *at once so Creole and so French,* and let us see the amusing "Argentine aristocrat" of 1880 who has seen it all and who is *the new subject of the liberal state*:

> One morning I awoke feeling adventurous and, fed up to the gills with the tedious routine of my life (rise at noon, luncheon at one, wander aimlessly along Calle Florida, eat wherever I chanced to be at the appointed time, play a hand of bezique at the Club, set off for the theatre, etc.), I thought I might well fancy a change in direction, inventing something new—the first thing that popped into my head—so long as it took my mind off this beastly prospect, whereupon I was struck by an idea as absurd as any: to contribute to the enrichment of the nation's literature.
>
> To contribute to the enrichment of the nation's literature, I told myself, one need only be in possession of pen, ink and paper, and not know how to write

Spanish; I discretely meet all of these prerequisites, and so there is no reason why I should not contribute to the enrichment of the nation's literature.

And in my spare moments—in between yawning as wide as an ocean and smoking a packet of Caporal—I managed to fabricate the concatenation of non-sense with which you are already familiar and which has raised such a storm, such an outcry, such a furor against a certain third-rate specimen of humanity: the author.

Frankly, it wasn't worth it: *le jeu n'en valait la chandelle.* (1–2)

But you see, one does not dig trenches or take up a pick-axe to mine the foun-dations of an edifice with impunity, even if it threatens to collapse and one works with the Christian intention of preventing—should it suddenly come crashing down—broken arms and legs, of avoiding the owner's becoming churlish, com-plaining that his chattels are being assaulted and his home violated. . . .

But, really, I never imagined that they would take it so seriously and would shout themselves hoarse, crying: *à la garde, au voleur à l'assassin!* before a defense-less fellow, an unhappy player who steps out into the open with his hat in his hand, who does not flee from justice as he is neither thief nor assassin and whose only crime is to have written a farce, to have composed a *pot pourri* in which the truth sings out clearly.

I conclude.

I tried to induce laughter and instead induced rage.

Total fiasco; that was not the aim.

Like all mocked maestros, I want to smash my instrument against the floor . . . and yet . . . the love of the art . . .

Will I offend again?

Who can say? (6; italics in the original)

And he did offend again. This is the failed "author" who with the farce of truth touches *the literary limits of the periphery,* between "transgression" and the "verbal crime." The public did not understand the literary contract to "mine the founda-tions of an edifice with impunity, even if it threatens to collapse": it did not under-stand the truth of the "contract" which sustains everything, but it transformed it into the coalition's best-seller.

"A Few Words from the Author" was added to the third edition in 1883. In 1882, *Pot pourri* had opened with the first manifesto-autobiography of the liberal state (we are in the "literary avant-garde"). The speaker is a multiple and anonymous subject (or anonymous because it is multiple) who seems to be always the same (Cambaceres himself): an aristocrat who is the heir to a great fortune, again one who lives off his capital like Flaubert (and Cambaceres is pleased to *épater le bour-*

geois and then, in exasperation, take up the indirect free style in order to introduce himself into other "I's" without ceding the "I" to them), *a man of leisure* who "vegetates" (let us recall the exhausted Cané of *Juvenilia*, who went from the mail to the newspaper to school) because he has a drama: personal fulfillment. *He is a frustrated subject because of the family of which he is heir and* rentier.

He says: "Yes, sir; I was born to act," and he claims to have not only the vocation but also the perfect talent to be an actor: a "plagiaristic intelligence," an *"avenant physique,"* and an ability to interpret "any manner of outpourings of the soul." But: "Unfortunately, the high social standing of my family coupled with the scorn the world heaps on a thespian—an absurd remnant of the times in which the mask of the buffoon degraded the practice of this noble art—assaulted my natural impulses, whereupon I was forced to renounce my most cherished predilection" (8).

The family identity of this "anonymous" subject, who also tells his story of education, is not political, as in the education stories of the patricians Cané (that of the "real" name) and López (that of the pseudonym or fictional name), but rather economic and social. The two fictionalities, that of the failed author and that of the frustrated actor, are joined in the fable of identity of this new subject of the cultural coalition of the liberal state: torn between the economic and the social in these backward peripheries, he becomes, finally, a writer. This is the position of Victoria Ocampo in her autobiography, in another avatar of the relations between cultural coalitions and liberal states in Latin America. And for her as well, adultery, "passion love," for an unnamed man is the center that articulates the fragments of the system.

The Dandy's Gaze: Hatreds and Loves

Like Machiavelli's prince, the actor who plays the dandy in order to tell the marriage story is in perpetual representation and sees the world as representation. And he will use various masks, and this is precisely his transgression of the family prohibition of theater. But the scheme of his position is simple and consists of putting himself outside of and above the conflict (I won't marry),[26] and of oscillating between two limits (or between the limits of the periphery).

In the "magnificent dance" (not a carnival dance) of chapter 3, the dandy, who has seen it all and wears gloves, contemplates from a distance the theater of Argentine elite society with the gaze of "gossip's evil spirit" (18). And there he exhibits another of the characteristic gestures of the historical dandy (one of the themes of the "theory of the dandy"): Baudelaire's "aristocratic pleasure of displeasing":

> I was then experiencing just such an ill-fated moment, and *gossip's evil spirit was goading me on.*
>
> I felt an *evil disposition,* caustic and biting, awaken within me; I would have sunk my teeth into the virgin's white tunic to tear it asunder, and through the *frenzied desire to wreak harm* that assailed me, I saw everything round me painted in the most odious of manners. (18, italics added)

The hateful gaze and the position of the actor-dandy are the argentinization-translation (parody?) of the historical dandy: somewhere between cynical and sadistic, ascetic and evil, misogynistic and androgynous, frivolous and impertinent, intelligent and provocative.[27] This dandy launched against the high life of the theater of the liberal state is our new coalition subject. He represents the economic and cultural aristocracy and exhibits one of the fundamental traits of Argentine high culture: the criticism of his own culture, cultural self-criticism. In order to achieve this, the dandy's hateful gaze (that position and that voice) is situated in his alliances between two limits or languages, the feminine and the masculine: on the divide. The female verbal alliance is that of a "woman friend" who is "what is commonly known as a viper-tongue" and "has made up vile deeds, told disgraceful tales, concocted atrocities" (22). He hears her "stories" and in *verbal-rhetorical alliance with crime* (another of the traits of the historical dandy), he contemplates the parade of characters of the high-life dance. The cultural criticism of the "viper-tongue"—with the theatrical metaphor of the actor and of representation: *with the metaphor of the double identities of theater and of liberalism*—speaks of hypocrisy, farce, and crime in the private life of the aristocratic circle. And it shows the horrible peripheral bourgeois behind the beautiful appearances: utilitarian spirit, vulgarity, conformism, and spiritual lowness.

The male verbal alliance, the other limit, appears at the end, when he leaves nauseated by the venom of his "old female friend," and meets up with a "young journalist" in order to depart with him and happily close the chapter of the "magnificent dance" of "elite society": "Overflowing with talent from head to toe, he is as brilliant, dangerous, and sharp as a straight-edge razor," his "eyes sparkled with pernicious mischief," and his "expression, quite peculiar to himself, was one of permanent sarcasm." He takes him by the hand and the pair go for a "breath of the fresh night air" (31).

Between the evils and the hatreds of the two genders, he who plays the dandy character (or the dandy who plays the actor in order to tell the marriage story) is a "spiritual aristocrat" who exaggerates his singularity and who places himself above all conflict ("I won't marry") in order to "sing the truth" of the private life of (depoliticized) "modernity." His cultural modernity would be defined by that aristocratic rejection of the bourgeois modernity that he attributes to the local high life.

Is it possible to belong to the cultural coalition of the liberal state (to produce fictions for the state) and to attack culturally or "literarily" the social culture that accompanies or produces the liberal state? Perhaps it would be possible given at least the conditions which *Pot pourri* fulfills: putting oneself culturally above and outside, depoliticizing, and oscillating between the left and the right and between the two sexual genders.

With regard to love, the dandy's gaze sees only *negritos* and gauchos.

At the carnival dance, they are marked by diminutives.

> The sweet, darling black kiddies, more than any of the others, bring me true joy.
>
> I cannot even look at their little black faces, their little sky-blue smocks, their little white undies, their little patent-leather boots, their little riding crops, little drums, little bells, and little rattles without my mouth watering at the thought that such grace and salt of the earth is raised up in this land of mine.
>
> Little angels! (83)

The fourth act of the republican political farce in chapter 6 dramatizes the injustice toward the patriotic gaucho soldier:

> There in the most desolate part of the pampas, the noble yet wretched Argentine soldier ekes out his existence, that stoic fellow, the admirable embodiment of a beast of burden's endurance and Christian resignation.
>
> The country demands his all and he gives his all to the country.
>
> His home and family he abandons, his wealth he loses, his life he endlessly exposes to the traps set by savages fighting in an all-out, merciless war.
>
> And what does he receive in exchange? What prize, what recompense for the desperate solitude in which he suffers and dies for others? (54–55)

Reminiscent of José Hernández's *Martín Fierro,* this alliance with the gaucho and denunciation of the injustices of the fatherland is, as we know, one of the discourses of the ranchers.

Finally, the Marriage Story

The dandy tells the story of Juan and María in the following order. First, the "research trip" to the ranch where they spend their honeymoon (María is already bored); second, the first carnival dance, where María suspiciously changes costumes with a friend and disappears; third, the second carnival dance with María's pursuit by the oafish Taniete (the dandy's Galician servant-cum-spy) and his discovery that the intruder is Pepe, Juan's confidant and secretary; and fourth, his own intervention in two times, first with the letter to María and second with the naming of Pepe as consul in Monaco.

The dandy's strategy for resolving his friend Juan's problem with the *pícara* María and the traitor Pepe has various other steps and oscillations depending upon the interlocutors. His strategy moves between limits, "in female" and "in male," between left and right. It moves between transgression and the representation of the law, and this is the movement of the coalition's avant-garde.

First, in transgression. When among equals (in the company of his friends) the narrator/dandy tells "the truth" about sex: he shows natural equality and social inequality (he "transgresses," putting himself "in female"). He dialogues with Juan following the first carnival dance, when he already has suspicions about María, *with footnotes as stage directions:*

> "It's fine that man marries and together with his wife traverses the path of life, but really! Up to a certain point!"
>
> "Man is like a horse: from time to time he needs to take to the fields, twitch his tail, frolic and roll around in the mud, if there's no sand around."
>
> "If man is like a horse, then of course woman must be like a mare, who switches her tail, frolics, and rolls around as well."
>
> "What would you say if your wife used your logic?"
>
> "Stop right there! Man is man and woman is woman; she dons skirts and he wears the trousers."
>
> "Oh, how we men, made in the image and likeness of our Lord, mete out justice in this vale of tears!" (102)

Second, in "the law." After the second carnival dance the narrator writes a letter to María in which he tells her that she is a rascal and that she should forget Pepe, because if she doesn't he will tell Juan. He takes the letter to her (and she answers that an informer is an even bigger rascal), and afterward, *in a monologue "imaginarily" addressed to María,* he tells her "the truth": he reformulates "in male" and from a purely economic liberalism, the place of each sex in the new civil contract of marriage:

> Do you know what you have done by getting married?
>
> You have transferred the use of your person, you have signed a rental agreement; that is exactly what you have done, *as if you were a dwelling;* it is *a contract* in which you cannot be occupied by any objects aside from those your tenant chooses.

Juan has taken you in order to inhabit you and as *Juan possesses his fortune* one can only suppose that he does not want to share you with anyone else, especially when *the intruder is not even paying rent* and is, moreover, actually cheating him out of it like a swine.

In a word, *you are not your own* but another's chattel, and having usufructed yourself clandestinely by a third party you fall—under the precepts of the aforementioned Astete Code—*into mortal sin*, committing *the offence of robbery;* and therefore you are naught but a thieving sinner who deserves no pardon from Our Lord. (135; italics added)

As we have mentioned, the first anonymous text of the coalition is the coalition's first best-seller and its first literary scandal or crime. And one of the central points of the scandal is Cambaceres's *purely economic liberalism* in the discourse of the separation of church and state and also of the "legal" contract of marriage. Female sexuality is now the biological equivalent of capitalism: truth is the body of the woman as property, as a piece of furniture or as a thing, and the crime of robbery is the limit.[28] Still addressing María imaginarily, the narrator states that only Juan represents a *free "nature"* in which *time and money are equivalent*:

But let us admit for a moment that as a son of Adam, it runs in the family, and he will often be of a mind to close the book of matrimonial duties and decree his time off and his holiday periods.

Where is the harm in that? How can it wound you?

Do you fear, perhaps, that your husband might forget you or love you less?

Nonsense, señora! Men's hearts are very large: there is comfortably room for many of you within them, simultaneously.

Our Lord Father and Mother Nature, in their infinite knowledge, have made it so. Why, look no further than cocks and other quadrupeds for proof of what I say.

I once met a man, *verbi gratia*, who used to spend his nights at his mistress's house, and yet, one fine day, to save his father-in-law from a fraudulent bankruptcy, he gave his entire fortune to his wife.

To his lover his time, to his wife his money; and since time is money, it made no difference which; and since *love is measured according to the benefits it brings*, then by giving to both of them *he loved both of them in equal measure*. (135–36; italics added)

The equation of marriage, sexuality, and money is resolved by the dandy into liberal capitalism, thanks to his position "in the representation of the law."

The Head of State and the Final Solution

Pot pourri exhibits the complicity and the double relationship of the state to the actor and to representation: he is its other, its fiction and its transgression, and he is also the same: *he represents it.* Because the actor-dandy, who spoke "in female" to Juan and "in male" to María, finally embodies the head of state who elegantly expels the "intruder" Pepe from the "nation"; Juan won't find out.

He sends Taniete (the "dumb Galician" who played spy) to find Pepe, and when Pepe arrives at his house he tells him his story of education and marriage, and in the last chapter he says,

> "When a man," I continued, "starts off as *a little scamp learning about life on the streets, touting theater tickets* by night and scavenging cigarette butts at the entrance, and fighting other boys over marbles and coppers by day, while his poor, sick mother languishes in bed suffering;
>
> "When another man, feeling sorry for the miserable old woman and pitying the hard luck that has befallen the poor lad, reaches into his pocket for the former and *attends to the education of the latter,* makes somebody of him, calls him to his side and *gives him a position of trust in his own home,* allowing him to come and go as he pleases;
>
> "When this twenty-year-old lad, who is at a time when contact with men and the morbid milieu they mix in has not yet had the chance to pervert his heart, behaves like a barbarian, going so far as to make a common prostitute of his boss's wife;
>
> "When all of this occurs, methinks, I have every reason, and then some, to say that the rascal I am describing has all the makings of a perfect knave." (141; italics added)

He then presents him with a choice between honor and a gentleman's duel: if he admits to the relationship ("if it is serious and the flames of passion burn intensely within your soul"), he will call Juan, he will tell him everything, and he will give them each a revolver so that Pepe will not be able to claim that he was "shot like a defenseless dog." Otherwise, if he "couldn't give a bean about the woman," if he has no honor and is a coward—which is in fact the case—then *l'état c'est moi* and he will be expelled from "home."

> "I have foreseen the event and brought along this case, containing one thousand francs in cash, twenty-franc denominations, this *passport* in your name—*ordering the national authorities and begging the foreign ones* to place no obstacle in the way of your transit—and, finally, this *appointment* for your distinguished self to occupy the demanding post of Argentine Consul in . . . Monaco.

"Go, my young friend, go and join the ranks of those who, with a few honorable exceptions, nobly and worthily *represent the republic* abroad.

"I recommend roulette in Monte Carlo." (142–43; italics added)

The representation of the liberal head of state by the actor-dandy founds and
closes the novel of the coalition. This new subject is perhaps the most powerful
(the one who has it all: the millionaire boss of the Colón), the only one who dares
to "represent" the head of state who names consuls and ambassadors (one of the
fates of the cultural coalition), because the position of the dandy (the physical distance and the gaze which separates him from the world) assures his domination.
He is the boss of the cultural institution of representation that accompanies the
liberal state as its other and as its self. And, in the mode of farce, he names as consuls those whom he would prefer to see far away from his friends' wives.

The liberal state marks the limits of this subjectivity and of this fable of identity. In the Argentine dandy, the transgressive constant of the coalition is verified,
making it a cultural coalition of the liberal state: legal subjectivities have a limit
that is occupied by the state itself (its representative, its actor). And in touching
this limit, the dandy reformulates the male code "of honor": an aristocratic code
that places on one side the gentleman, the *caballero* (Juan's "high" masculinity,
with the "duel of honor," and his own ascetic masculinity), and on the other the
"low" masculinity of Pepe, the "coward" and "traitor" (whose education was paid
for!). At issue is a (Latin American) masculine pyramid of protectors and the definition of the "true gentleman."[29]

Pot pourri with La gran aldea

The "marriage-adultery story" (the contract and the breaking of the contract which
threatens the social order, violates frontiers, and implies contamination and pol-
lution)[30] is the central *narrative institution* of 1880 because it not only constitutes
the correlate of civil law, marks the abandonment of politics, and poses the private
world as a center in the construction of a purely cultural and social universe. It
also provides topics, events, modes of opening and closing narrations. *Pot pourri's*
1882 marriage story opens a series of narrative links which reappear in *La gran
aldea* in 1884: the announcement of marriage opens the narration (in Cambaceres
the autobiographical subject is the friend of the groom; in López, the nephew);
adultery occurs during carnival with a change of costumes (with double identities,
which is a way of representing female transgression and also the liberal theater),
and there is a conclusion or "final solution." Lucio V. López, then, takes up the depoliticized marriage scheme established by Cambaceres in order to narrate the

cultural change of the second part, and he also takes up the new subject of the liberal state, the gentleman or dandy.

Marriage, sexuality, money, honor: these make up the nucleus of the adultery stories of the liberal state and are the unknown factors and the equation which the dandy has to resolve. In *La gran aldea,* the young Blanca Montefiori marries the old uncle exclusively for money: the "new" woman of '80, who "cultivated an interest in letters," separates marriage/money from sexuality. And not only Blanca and not only in Buenos Aires: the autobiographical subject of *La gran aldea* returns at the end to the school in the provinces to search for Valentina, his former girlfriend, and he finds her happily married to a rich old man.

The misogyny of *La gran aldea* culminates in the upper balcony of the Colón,[31] but what interests us is the dandy and the "final solution." The final solution: there is no escape from adultery in *La gran aldea;* the uncle is old and the autobiographical narrator—with neither money nor power—cannot intervene (and besides, he also desires Blanca; he is always torn between two loyalties: he is the "nation"). This precipitates the apocalyptic ending, with a fire at the carnival, a burned girl, a vegetative old man, and the guilty parties who flee, marked by their sexual difference (the adulterous woman flees with her lover and never again sleeps), racial difference (the black servant Alejandro), and national difference (a French maid who was supposed to watch the girl and who instead donned the costume Blanca had worn the previous night in order to attend the carnival dance, disappearing at the end with Alejandro).

Cambaceres and López, with the chronicle of the new culture of 1880, close the relationship among marriage, sexuality, and money in opposite ways and with a notable choice: either it is resolved from within the state, as in *Pot pourri* ("diplomatic" expulsion from the nation) or a catastrophe occurs, as recounted by the autobiographical witness at the end of *La gran aldea*. State or apocalypse (*justice beyond the state*) is the final fictional choice posited by the coalition of 1880 in its marriage stories with violations of its "laws" on the part of women. And we can therefore see the function of the fabric of the coalition, which gives the state the final choice (the nonchoice) when faced with breaking the legal contract that sustains everything.

The autobiographical positions—the subjects of the liberal state—are defined by their allies, and in each one of the parts into which the subject and the narration of *La gran aldea* are divided, a certain male politics is defined, with "fathers" and "protectors." Julio's *political alliance* with Alejandro, his father's faithful black servant, poor and *urquista* like him, dominates the first part but is broken in the second in order to give way to the *social and cultural alliance* with a virtuous and transparent gentleman named Benito Cristal: a happy bachelor who was a friend of his father, who reads Rabelais, who frequented the Club del Progreso since its foundation, and who enjoys "a unique influence" there. In 1880, other family allies are needed, and prior political solidarities are dissolved. So, with depoliticization, the place of the black Alejandro changes totally: he goes back to being a mere servant and, as such, one of those responsible for the final disaster.

La gran aldea provides patrician alternatives to *Pot pourri* not only with its "final solution" but also with the dandy. In contrast to *Pot pourri*'s peripheral reproduction of the historical dandy (in the mode of peripheral farce?), Benito Cristal appears as the dandy's Latin American other, as the good and happy, Don-Juanesque version: the *patrician version of the old bachelor aristocrat* who "suffered the worldly weaknesses of gallantry" and who in the end makes an exemplary marriage to a rich woman "of an age proportionate to his" (181).

The gentleman or *caballero* Cristal is the straight, patrician, Spanish alternative of this "new subject of the liberal state," but he retains certain of the dandy's traits: coldness toward life, mockery and sarcasm of positivism and utilitarianism (of money), and the embodiment of truth and virtue. Cristal: "He loved truth deliriously, and he could proudly say that he had never lied in his life. . . . The *refined honesty of his word* matched the honesty of his actions, and he carried his *worship of virtue* to the delicate point of practicing it in silence, without proclaiming it like the Pharisee" (91; italics added).

As a protector of Julio (in whose house he has one of his adventures), Benito Cristal differentiates himself not only from Cambaceres's dandy, but also from Montefiori, the father of the adultress Blanca, who *is in fact called a dandy,* and we can therefore see, perhaps, what exactly a dandy was for the patrician sector of the coalition, which exhibits the "good taste" of simplicity: "Like all old dandies, after swallowing his health pills, he would submit his appearance to Guerlain's miraculous make-up" (111). The ex-diplomat Montefiori is the "chic" figure of the Buenos Aires aristocracy: he has a boyish air, he is an epicurean, a gourmet, a man of the world, he speaks French and English and bedecks his home with tapestries and bibelots. But the ironies, rejections, exclusions can be seen when he appears as "a reputable Catholic" (138) whose his wife and daughter are adulteresses. For Montefiori the dandy turns out to be not only the father of the adulteress Blanca who marries "the uncle" to spend his money, but also the husband of Fernanda, with whom Benito Cristal has secret relations in Palermo.

The dandy's position of "honor," which appears with the marriage stories, constitutes a new subject of the coalition with its alternatives for the state: in López, rich, ascetic, and misogynistic; in Cambaceres, poor, Don-Juanesque, and proper. This new subject serves the liberal state in representing the "aristocratic male gender" in private, in a purely cultural space, and *in representing its exclusions*.

The new dandies and *señoritos* of *Pot pourri* and *La gran aldea*, who embody the "aristocratic male code" of the coalition, *expel various characters from honor, from truth—and from the nation*. Cambaceres's actor-dandy, as a "president" who names officials for service abroad, expels from the nation the secretary, who entered the house of his friend and protégé Juan in order to cause Juan to lose his honor (and whom Juan protected and paid to educate!). And what the alternative *caballero* of *La gran aldea* will exclude from truth, honor, male distinction, and high aristocratic Latin American culture is the Jew as the representative of money, in whose "cave" (the character's surname is de la Cueva) his friend-protégé Julio can lose his honor (and he therefore clearly separates money and honor). He will also exclude him from the "nation."

La gran aldea is the novel of 1880 because 1884 contains the emblems of the whole decade, including the stock exchange and the Jew (and it also contains the "final apocalypse"). In telling its marriage story, *La gran aldea* recounts the change (depoliticization, modernization and its spaces, new alliances, new subjects, money, the stock exchange, and the Jew) and also all the "dangers" and threats of change; it narrates from the nation. We would like to pause a moment to examine this figure of the Jew Eleazar de la Cueva in *La gran aldea* (which leads directly to Julián Martel's 1891 *La Bolsa* [The stock exchange], the classic anti-Semitic novel of Argentine literature) because this "Jew" opens in the patrician political sector of the coalition of the liberal state a history which extends up to the present. De la Cueva opens the "stories of Jews," which appear in chapter 6.

In chapter 10 of *La gran aldea*, after the great change of 1880 and after returning from school in the provinces, Julio works in the "business office of Don Eleazar de la Cueva, a man whose business dealings were the most vast and complicated in the Argentine republic and who wielded great influence over governments, banks, the stock exchange, everyone. A mild and *Christian* man, above all, very devout and faithful . . . he was a sort of astrologer in his business dealings" (89).

Julio remarks: "Don Eleazar was above all a speculator; in his trading house nothing but stock exchange papers were bought and sold," and he had "the patience and tenacity of an *Israelite*" (92). (And here we can observe a vacillation regarding the speculator: on the one hand he was a Christian; on the other an Israelite: is it possible that the construction of the Jew in the literature of liberalism may include this sign of vacillation in naming?)

De la Cueva declares bankruptcy and tells Julio: "I've lost everything! Starting today I'll be living off the charity of my relatives; yes, sir, from the charity of my family" (99). And here Cristal intervenes against de la Cueva and says to Julio: "His bankruptcy is a bankruptcy which neither ruins him nor brings him to court; for him everything is solved by not paying" (96).

This is confirmed *precisely* at the wedding of Blanca Montefiori and his uncle, because there *Julio says ironically:* "my ex-patron, Don Eleazar de la Cueva, a bankrupt man, in a desperate financial situation, had thrown a cascade of pearls and diamonds over the head and neck of the lovely bride. 'But Don Eleazar is famous,' *Monefiori exclaimed,* admiring the *old Jew's* splendid jewelry . . . 'He's an artist and *un homme de monde!*'" (150; italics added, ellipses in original, and no more vacillation in naming).

Eleazar not only fakes bankruptcy and regales the dandy's daughter with diamonds. With him there appears for the first time in Argentine literature what will appear in almost all the later pamphlets: the "Jewish politics" of the two sides. Julio remarks:

> Don Eleazar, without being a man of the world, without being a political man, had a certain political influence; without being a party man, he intervened and participated in all parties . . . he made his name and his influence felt in a thousand different ways: in *elections* he was always present *on both sides* without giving his name, and he contributed efficaciously to the triumph of both parties with hefty sums of money . . . *he was promiscuous* with everyone, for in the Lord's vineyard, he reasoned, it was as good to be a Jew as a Christian. (89; italics added)

And Cristal remarks to Julio, in order to expel him from the "nation": in the stock exchange, "his agents, divided *into two factions who operated against each other, prepared their coup*"; de la Cueva sows terror "without the least consideration for *patriotism*" (94–95; italics added).

The "final solution": the gentleman who "loved truth deliriously" and defended "all the rules of gentility" advises Julio to leave de la Cueva: "Friend, friend, find yourself another fate, beware the danger in Don Eleazar's house! It's better to run the risk of losing your shirt, *like me,* than to expose yourself to *losing your honor there*" (92).

The new subjects of the marriage stories (their fictional proliferation: the "boss of the Colón," property-owning millionaire, dandy, misogynist, actor, "president of the republic" on the one hand, and the patrician, club-going, Don-Juanesque gentleman of the truth on the other), are those who represent (*those in charge of "representation"*) a private space of marriages and a purely social-cultural public space which serves as a map, fiction, or phantom of the liberal state. They represent the coalition at social events and among women: at the Club del Progreso, at the Colón, at carnival dances, and at wedding celebrations. They criticize the modern culture of their own circle for the inauthenticity of its values, for bourgeois utilitarianism and hypocrisy. And they produce alternatives (or "final solutions") in the face of the scandal of adultery, of sexuality and money, in order to postulate for the coalition and for the state a new fable of identity (a private one of gender). A male aristocratic fable for the liberal Latin American state, which time and again expels from the nation—from their houses—those who "threaten honor" or behave promiscuously: Pepes and Jews. What is needed is a depoliticized male subject with an exemplary ethic in regard to money, honor, and truth (and the "nation") to represent the state culturally and to represent, therefore, its exclusions of honor.

The Map of the Cultural World Is the Map of the Liberal State

In depoliticizing the family identity of the autobiographical subject and representing it as an actor or a social chronicler, or better yet, in depoliticizing representation from 1880 onward (and to depoliticize is, in reality, to produce a reformulation of the political),[32] the coalition's new subjects (the dandies, the gentlemen and their alternatives) inaugurate cultural criticism and *the new cultural politics* which accompany and represent the liberal state. They construct social, cultural, sexual and racial names, classes and genders in relation to marriage, sexuality, money, and honor: a series of categories for those who are present in or who enter their houses or private worlds: women, "confidants," Pepes, immigrant servants, blacks, and Jews. And they represent them as enemies because they can threaten honor, truth, and the "nation." These purely cultural differences draw a phantasmic map of private life which is at the same time a map of the liberal state: the coalition "statizes" private space, for it is in the private theater that "internal difference" is represented as a supplement (and threat) to national states.

Physics Exam Stories: Insanity, Simulation, and Crime at the Colegio Nacional de Buenos Aires

Suddenly in 1887, we come across a physics exam at the Colegio Nacional.

> Sure of the terrain he tread, absolute master of himself, the word sprung forth easily, fluidly, frankly from his lips, in the hushed silence of the room; the timbre of his voice sounded with the purity of crystal and a slight quaver of emotion . . .

It might have seemed *a fiction at times, more like a false imitation* of knowledge and talent, the glitter of *a theatrical apotheosis,* rehearsed, artificial, gaslight simulating the sun.

It was a triumph, however, a splendid moment of triumph. The highest, the most honorable of grades; a special mention by the members of the committee, congratulating Genaro for his superb exam; general applause, the congratulations of his companions, even those whose haughty disdain he had always felt weigh upon him most painfully and who now approached him with a smile on their lips to shake his hand solicitously.

And all of this would *be published,* Genaro thought, full of proud jubilation, he would be seen in print, *his name,* his obscure and unknown name, the name of the "son of the gringo tinker," would appear in the columns of the press, it would circulate from hand to hand, surrounded as if by a brilliant aura of *fame* and prestige. (Eugenio Cambaceres, *En la sangre* [Buenos Aires: Imprenta de Sud-América, 1887], 95–96; italics added)

And shortly thereafter, in 1889, we come across another physics exam, also at the Colegio Nacional.

Shortly after entering the exam area, a name unknown to all is called out, and suddenly, as if moved by a pinprick, while we were all looking around to find the owner of that surname, the individual was on his feet, trembling, transfigured, and he turned the handle of the urn to get his ball. On the second crank one popped out: the fateful number thirteen was inscribed in relief with black ink on the wooden sphere. Bad omen, we thought, and sure enough, the unfortunate fellow began to rustle his program, shift in his seat, fake a slight cough, and, finally, he said with a faint voice: "I don't know." "Eh? Pick another one," said the ill-fated Doctor Bartolazzi, with his easygoing and kindly tone; the urn was cranked and another ball, jumping nervously, falls into the wooden dish: such-and-such a number. Number . . . with a soft sigh and an air of Christian resignation that could have been the envy of martyrs, he uttered another "I don't know." "My boy, pick another, go ahead, pick another," the professor tells him again, inspiring him with a little courage to hide the shame of his rejection. The third ball, more skittery than the first two, leaps out and the unfortunate fellow opens his eyes immeasurably wide, his arms fall like two hanged men, and he again stammers his refrain: "I don't know."

"And what do you know?" the professor asks, at the end of his patience.

"I know magnets."

"Magnets? Well, tell us about magnets."

"Magnets . . . ," the stricken examinee begins, "magnets . . . sir . . . I don't know . . ."

He disappeared like a shadow surprised by a ray of light which erases it unexpectedly; and he slipped away down the stairs with his long, emaciated shinbones clacking and his worn-out shoes puffing like bellows. (Manuel T. Podestá, *Irresponsable: Recuerdos de la Universidad* [Irresponsible: Recollections of university] (1889) [Buenos Aires: Editorial Minerva, 1924], 20–25)

What reader doesn't like to read exam stories? And especially stories about physics exams, which put certain "superiorities" to the test?

Today we may relive the fateful moment of trembling in front of the tribunal because we find "physics exam stories" in the literature of the cultural coalition of the liberal state which we have taken as our point of departure for narrating certain histories. The stories of education and marriage and *Juvenilia*'s stories of the Colegio Nacional culminate in the physics exam stories. They are told by a new sector of the coalition (different from the patricians and the gentlemen), through the voice and gaze of the positivist subject and in the second phase or juncture of the liberal state, which is approaching its first crisis. The coalition's scientific section is its most modern and open, the one which leads us to the future, but what is important at this moment is precisely physics: the knowledge of the laws and the forces which move bodies.

With the positivist subject and its cases we put an end to the fiction of the coalition, because it is this subject that carries us to the frontier of crime, the theme of this manual.

The problem of the scientific and naturalist fictions of this new subject of the liberal state is the problem of the epistemology of the state.

What does the state need to know, given modernization and what José María Ramos Mejía, the author of the first Argentine psychiatric text (*Las neurosis de los hombres célebres* [The neuroses of famous men], published between 1879 and 1882), calls in *Los simuladores de talento* (The simulators of talent) "the leveling tendencies so insolently carried even to the tabernacle of genius"? What need it know about equality and differences, promotions and demotions, winners and losers?

This is the time of social mobility produced by the expansion of literacy; *the time of celebrities* linked to the professionalization of journalism and with the culture industry; it is also the time of the insane and of the criminals and freaks who accompany the famous like two sides of the same coin.

What does the state need to know in a modern culture defined by education and the press? Or better yet, what knowledge does it need, what type of specific knowledge? How is an epistemology of the state defined?

It is necessary to control liberal social mobility and to give it meaning; to draw a map of winners and losers and define their relative positions; to establish scientifically a new hierarchical classification of men according to their merits or capabilities; to know how to differentiate true (unique) geniuses from the fakes, from schemers, from mediocrities (the majority), and also from the "abnormals" who go astray. We are in full capitalist expansion: differential networks must be redefined. And this must be done in a rigorous and "scientific" fashion, on the basis of the physical and material components which govern biological and social processes: forces, masses, movements, transmissions, resistances, speeds, intervals of time. And finally, this knowledge must be organized into laws.[33]

Everything must be submitted to examination, and the physics exam stories of the Colegio Nacional will articulate some of these enigmas because they belong to naturalist literature, which is the literary counterpart of scientific materialism: it recounts processes of generation (Cambaceres's character is named Genaro) and degeneration (that of "the crazy magnet fellow"), and it connects economy and sexuality.[34] The problem of naturalist literature, the problem of the scientific position of the coalition, and the problem of the epistemology of the state is the relationship between two fields of determinations, one biological and genetic, the other social. Where should the duality be articulated? And moreover, how should scientific knowledge and ethical and legal judgment be linked? What is required is a bridge that will permit us to slip from genetics to society and law. And it is there that the physics exam story appears before us as a "rigorous" event that produces the conversion of genetic information into responsible or irresponsible (guilty or innocent) social conduct. The exam on the scientific laws of bodies articulates the two corporalities and articulates science and law. The exam draws the legal network: the laws of physics, the laws of heredity, social and penal laws. For the coalition's scientific subject, knowledge rests on laws and leads to law.

The narrators of the naturalist novels *En la sangre* (1887), by Eugenio Cambaceres, and *Irresponsable* (1889), by the medical doctor and insanity specialist Manuel Podestá,[35] submit certain "abnormal cases" of social mobility within the liberal state to "physical examination" before the authorities of the Colegio Nacional. These "abnormals" ascend or descend the staircases of the school and enter where they should not the day of the exam. And they recount to us the black hole of the exam (everything is performance and the spectacle of modernization) in order to draw the map of a specific type of difference and to base these differences scientifically on genes and on society, which is to say, on the deterministic codes of biology and sociology. When political differences fall, the human genome project commences, represented by the scientific-literary sector of the coalition.

The characteristics of the naturalist esthetic, *determinism and degeneration,* are applied to these "abnormals" of physics. "The son of the gringo tinker" with his square head,[36] a first-generation Argentine (in Cambaceres's novel) and the son of the wealthy alcoholic, who wears a top hat but whose shoes are worn out (in Podestá) are cast respectively as "winner" and "loser" in the physics exams.

These scientific novels present for the first time the biographies of certain subjects: the simulator of talent and the madman, who will occupy the attention of writers, scientists, and jurists, and who are defined in opposite ways in the physics exams, by the success of one and the failure of the other. The simulator's physics exam and the madman's physics exam articulate science with bodies, science with law, heredity with society. From the perspective of the "family" of scientific identity (from the autobiography of the insanity doctor in *Irresponsable* or from the naturalist gaze of *En la sangre:* this is a "fictional" scientific subject, the other a "real" one) insanity and simulation must be defined (along with these new characters) as the very negation of the universal laws of the liberal state.

For this reason, the physics exam stories inaugurate not only the history of those who represent an "abnormal" social-institutional mobility or crossing, but also the history of *a new correlation,* a singular pairing (they were made for each other) of the scientific position of the liberal state with the simulator of talent and the madman. This correlation structures the fable of identity of the coalition's scientific subject, which requires a specific type of other (a Judaized one, as we shall soon see) in order to exist and to define itself. An autobiographical and scientific "I" (and a communitarian "we") in Podestá, or an omniscient naturalist narrator in Cambaceres, penetrates an other (a "he" opposed to "them" and "us"), opens this interiority (in the indirect free style, without granting it the "I"), gives it an identity, and puts as its limit crime and the law: that is the fable of identity of the coalition's scientific or naturalist subject, and its fiction for the state.

The man of science, the simulator and the madman (and the press, fame, winners and losers) are the characters who simultaneously close our history and open it to the future because they constitute the passage between the culture of the liberal state and the new culture (a postmodernity) which arises at the end of the century. (This transition can be clearly seen in the relationship between the works of the scientists José Ingenieros and José María Ramos Mejía on the theme of simulation. With their differences, the two unite simulation with insanity and carry both to the frontier of crime.)[37]

The Fable of the Simulator of Talent

"The only talent he had was one for deceiving others into thinking he had any at all!" says the scientific narrator of *En la sangre,* who recounts the biography of Genaro Piazza from the day of his birth until he declares himself no more responsible for his crimes "than snakes for their venom." The simulator of talent links himself to the double identities of fin de siècle literature through representation, and therefore through the liberal scene and liberal theater.

Let us look at *the moment prior to the exam:* the number thirteen ball, the "I don't know," the open door of the examination room, the urn . . . and the robbery:

> At the end of the year, among the elevated number of his fellow students, Genaro had just *descended the wide staircase* that carried them *from the examination room* to the ground floor.
>
> He went about anxiously . . . completely absorbed, engrossed in a single worry: his exam.
>
> The fact was that everything was riding on this game, which was a matter of life or death, he told himself . . .
>
> Moreover, an idea pursued him, fixed, embedded in his brain; increasing his uneasiness, a sad presentiment plagued him with the implacable tenacity of an obsession.
>
> Overcome by a profound, irresistible aversion to one of the subjects included in the year's program, he had shied away from studying it.
>
> It was physics, *the coefficient of the expansion of gases.* When he first approached the point, it had been impossible for him to understand, he had toiled, he had become agitated, it had made a labyrinth in his brain. [. . .]
>
> But how he deplored it, it weighed on him now, the *thirteenth* of the month and a Friday, he thought, thirteen the number of the question on the exam, thirteen the number of his name on the list! . . .
>
> All he needed was to start believing in witchcraft, him too, in bad luck, and to start wearing horns to protect himself, like his father after buying a watch . . . [. . .] but why, in any case, that strange coincidence of three *thirteens* together?
>
> He would go himself with a tremulous and hesitant hand, like an accused man turning himself in, to take the ball from the urn, the first, the last, whichever . . . the ominous ball, the fateful, cabalistic ball: thirteen . . . it was inevitable! . . .
>
> Genaro sees the open door and enters the examination room:
>
> But the damned urn, resembling a messenger from hell, attracted him, fascinated him, cast upon him a devilish spell of temptation.
>
> In vain he exhorted himself, he struggled, he resisted, it was impossible for him to divert his gaze from it, he followed it, he enveloped it despite himself with a *Jew's avaricious eye.*

And the robbery:

> Then, as if snatched from the floor by the lash of some furious hurricane, with all the initiative of the brave, with all the hesitancy of the coward, incapable of discerning, without the least awareness of his acts, as if he were contemplat-

ing another in his place, *Genaro saw himself standing by the urn*. He had stuck in his hand, he had felt the sensation of the bite of liquid lead in his flesh; bristling with terror, he had taken it out. [. . .] *he had robbed it . . . or perhaps not, it had placed itself between his fingers of its own accord! . . .*

It was time: the Rector, the professors, the other students were coming up the stairs.

Sheltered, curled up in a hollow in the wall, his instinct alone, his marvelous fox's instinct had saved him. (*En la sangre*, 79–93; italics added)

In the moment prior to the "instinctive" robbery, when he debates the crime, Genaro is a dialogized subject with two voices inside him: the atavistic voice of his Neapolitan father and that of his Argentine education. His conscience is in a perpetual debate, and the novel will carry the exploitation of double meaning to an extreme: heredity as genes and money; the ball from the exam, which he steals, and the black ball at the Club del Progreso, which vetoes his name and his entry into the space of the gentlemen; Piazza is his surname and it is in the plaza of the park that he is judged and absolved.

The simulator of talent is a new subject "in representation" and a "criminal" of truth. Clever as a fox, *he crosses all social classes* from the tenement where he was born to the ranch of his wife Máxima, daughter of a patrician millionaire who immigrated in 1840 and served as an officer under General Juan Lavalle. He marries her after *raping her in a box at the Teatro Colón during carnival* and leaving her pregnant, and thus marries her "inheritance." He arrives at the Colegio Nacional de Buenos Aires thanks to the inheritance left him by his greedy Neapolitan father and also because he is intelligent, as his teacher and a lawyer friend told his mother. (The immigrant mother, a good old woman, wants him to become a doctor: "Doctors were everything in America, judges, deputies, ministers"). At the moment of the exam, the son of the immigrant is positioned, with his two "inheritances," in high school and at the starting point of the middle class.

And *after the exam*, during the celebration with his peers, he simulates drunkenness in order not to talk. Ramos Mejía also dwells on the solemn silence of the simulator of talent, but Cambaceres's indirect free style says more: "Nothing . . . not a phrase, not even two sensible, pertinent, appropriate words would he have believed himself capable of emitting from his lips . . . nothing . . . And with all the dexterity, all the cunning of a comedian, he, too, pretended to be drunk; he dulled his vision, he separated his legs one from the other, he tilted his body as if cut loose from his seat, he nodded, drooled, stammered, called for more wine" (105; ellipses in original).

And henceforth, the "actor" extends himself until he reaches the social summit (his only limit is the Club del Progreso, because of the "black ball"), he speculates with Máxima's money, he forges her signature, he robs her, mistreats her (and also mistreats the workers on the ranch), and at the end of the first edition of *En la sangre* (censored in the later editions, for secondary school?) he tells her: "The owner, you say? Of your money, but not of your ass, I'm the owner of that!" This is the son of the Neapolitan tinker, the first generation of intelligent Argentines, who robs a ball to "win" at the physics exam; the series composed of simulation, fraud, forgery, and crime reappears clearly in Roberto Arlt (along with the physics exam).

The Fable of the Insane Man: Rights by Mistake, the "Wandering Jew," and Demotion

> He was a fifth-year student who was going to take the exam; no one knew him, he'd never attended class, and we only learned of his objective in risking such a hazardous mishap when he himself, with a maidenly shyness, asked us without addressing himself to anyone in particular: "Is there a physics exam today?" "Yes, sir," someone answered him, and our man, without saying a word, went *by mistake directly into the examination room,* whose door opened directly onto the stairs
> . . .
> Someone pointed out to him that there a *Law exam* was being given and that he could take his physics exam in the adjoining room . . .
> A figure who was never erased from our memory, a physiognomy which we only needed to see once more, many years later, to remember it intact, a *wandering Jew* of the University, a pariah, who searches still for a career, a fortune, untouched yet by the magical finger of treacherous and biased fate. (20; italics added, ellipses in original)

> Physicians, lawyers, engineers, ministers, deputies, businessmen . . . even the most useless had climbed to the top of the mountain; what talent denied them, fortune conceded them; but in the end, by struggling, by falling and getting up, they had climbed . . . And he, who sunk ever lower down the worm-eaten stairs of chaos. (209, 222; ellipses in original)

In *Irresponsable* (by the physician Manuel Podestá) the narrator is an anonymous doctor who recounts, along with his own scientific autobiography, the life of a man who passes through his educational and scientific institutions with the pseudonym of "the magnet fellow." He saw him at the physics exam in the Colegio Nacional and later in the dissection amphitheater at the medical school, and finally in the asylum; thus he establishes the stages of his own ascent and at the same time the descent and fall of the insane man. At the physics exam, he couldn't answer the questions even about what he said he knew, magnets. In the dissection amphitheater of the medical school, he bursts into tears over a dead prostitute instead of observing the cadaver scientifically. Later came politics, and at a demonstration he spoke heatedly against his own partisans, who turned against him and lynched him, as if he were a member of the opposition. As a result, he suffers an attack of epilepsy, loses his top hat, and is arrested and then taken to the insane asylum, "like a dog."

The insane man is "well-to-do" (he wears a top hat, and when he loses it, he, too, is lost), but his alcoholic heredity and his desire to marry a prostitute to "redeem her" ("I had abandoned my family, my friends, my career, everything for her, I had sacrificed everything . . . I had imposed upon myself a mission, I wanted to redeem this woman at the cost of my own sacrifice") precipitated him toward the abyss of *insanity, which is to say, to the negation of the educational and marital institutions of the liberal state.* She was extremely beautiful, depraved, and irredeemable because she lacked the gene of "moral sense"; she was "crazy, hysterical, corrupt. Her organism was so formed" (196). He leaves her, she commits suicide, and her cadaver appears nude in the dissection amphitheater, where the autobiographical scientist describes her at length. (The realist-naturalist novel seems to require the figure of the prostitute: a way of em-bodying "the fall" and of making the social visible. The visibility of the prostitute and of the realist novel as a seeing machine.)

A friend of the insane man (a double of the narrator, who was promoted through sacrifice and study, while the insane man was rich and abandoned his career) tells him: "you are a wretch, one of many in whom a law of heredity is fulfilled, from which few can escape" (263). He also tells him: "It has been a blessing for you that your situation has not led you to more dangerous extremes. When you were delirious with the impressions which upset your mind . . . you could have been a criminal" (266; ellipses in original).[38]

But there is no crime in the insane man or in his descent; he is "irresponsible" and ends up "like a dog."

The Laws of Physics: Those Who Know What They Don't Know

But why is the physics exam story the one that defines the simulator of talent and the insane man, new "other characters" of the liberal state, narrated by the scientific subject? They find their "truth" in the physics exam because there is always a ball (a law of physics) that these subjects know that they don't know, and there is also the thirteen, the law of luck.[39] The son of the Neapolitan tinker is named Genaro Piazza and knows that he does not know the coefficient of the expansion of gases, which is ball number thirteen (and this occurs in chapter 13 of *En la sangre*);

the son of the alcoholic draws the number thirteen ball first, says he doesr
the answer, and that he only knows about magnets, which he says aftei
doesn't know, and thus he acquires his literary and scientific name: "the magnet
fellow." *Irresponsable* has thirteen chapters.

The laws that they know they don't know at the moment of the exam are laws
of expansion (Ramos Mejía uses this word for the simulator of talent: "individual
expansion") and laws of attraction. *What they know they don't know is what they embody:* a law of physics, in both physical corporality and social corporality, in
schools and marriages. This law is the center of their histories and it determines
them inexorably. I only know that I don't know the expansion of gases, says the
simulator of talent to himself before stealing a ball and later ascending socially to
the very summit through his marriage with the aristocratic Máxima. I only know
that I don't know magnets, says the insane man, magnetized by the beautiful prostitute whom he tried to marry, before descending into jail and the insane asylum.
And yet the narratives recount the attractions and expansions of these characters
as they cross with their heredities through society, institutions, and female bodies.

The scientific gazes of Cambaceres's naturalist narrator, who erases the process
of enunciation, and of Podestá's insanity doctor, who recounts his scientific life in
the form of memories, explain, in the physics exams, the history of those subjects
marked by the thirteen. Both transgress the laws of education and marriage. Both
serialize institutions and social classes in order to pose the limit of crime and the legal
distinction between those who are responsible and those who are not. The insanity
of the magnet fellow, in his process of degradation, is defined as the "irresponsible"
negation, one by one and in series, of the institutions of the liberal state: education, science, marriage, politics (and even friendship). And Genaro's simulation is
defined, in his process of expansion, as a violation "in crime" of the barriers between social classes: Genaro is born in the tenement, crosses the middle class in the
Colegio (where he steals a ball), and arrives at the ranch thanks to his marriage.

There is a network which links the topics of the physics exam of the simulator
and the insane man (and that same network is the one that draws the scientific
subject of the liberal state): they enter where they should not and thus transgress
rights and the law, the insane man by mistake (he is "irresponsible"), the simulator
by decision (he is "guilty); both have the number thirteen as their fate and destiny,
both know that they don't know and bet everything on the exam. *And both are
"like" Jews:* Cambaceres's "like" an "avaricious" Jew is a "modern" and "realist"
consciousness; a false Enlightenment consciousness (as Peter Sloterdijk says in
Critique of Cynical Reason). He represents the cynical diversion, and he proceeds as
if laws existed only for the stupid: one must survive, one must win, and one must

keep up appearances. He is "the winner." Podestá's "like" a wandering Jew is the demented pariah who blunders into the law and the fatal law of heredity: he has the "illusion" of marrying the prostitute and "redeeming" her, and he abandons everything for this "literary dream." He is the "loser."

The network that unites the topics of the physics exam in the coalition's stories of education and marriage constitutes what we could call a cultural configuration, which becomes *a cultural artifact* (an interwoven, mutating complex of positions, accounts, and final solutions), and it opens in a multiplicity of directions. As it reappears and traverses the history of culture, stories are installed at each one of the points of which it is made, and these stories form series, chains, families, and genealogies, carrying us to the future. For example, the history of the exam stories.[40] Or the "stories of simulators," the "stories of the insane," the "stories of winners and losers," and the "stories of Jews."

II

.

the frontier of crime

.

Transmutation Operation Stories

The voyage through the *corpus delicti* includes territories, stations, and frontiers. We are about to arrive at the frontier that closes the trajectory "from transgression to crime"; let us review before arriving. The voyage from transgression to crime crossed a "classic" field of Argentine literature and culture because it was an exam story for my teachers. We moved through the stories of education and marriage of the coalition that founded aristocratic culture in Argentina, through the distinguished, refined, and novelesque language and the ironies and self-criticism of the subjects of the liberal state. Between them, they invented a tone and a mode of speech that attempted to represent "the best of the best" of a Latin American country at the moment of its entry into the world market, and which became "classic" in Argentina. And between, *with that same tone,* they also invented a language suffused with arrogance, xenophobia, sexism, and racism. With those tones they wrote their legal fictions for the liberal state: the stories of the national hero, the nation, the dandy, the scientist, and all their others, and they became secondary school classics in Argentina.

The frontier is not only the limit of a state but also a particular conceptual instrument: an inclusive-exclusive zone, a fissure that sutures. And the frontier we are approaching marks the mutation "in crime" of one of the subjects of the liberal state, the scientist, and it closes a cycle, that of the coalition. For this reason, "transmutation operation stories" are now being told. The frontier of crime is a mobile zone made up of mutations in evolution that create new cultural and literary species (to use the Darwinist tone of the time) by means of magical processes of genetic engineering of literature and culture (to use another tone). Or, in other words, the transmutation operation stories of the frontier are transgressive experiments by scientists in which the functioning of crime as a divisor of cultural lines can be seen. They bring forth a limit (where there is danger, secrecy, illegality), and they affirm the existence of a difference.

The frontier of crime is a place of collision or contact and it opens in all directions. Its resonant space is that of the transmutation operation stories written in Argentine literature between 1890 and 1914.[1] In these stories, the gaze and the voice of the coalition subject who could "scientifically" identify a simulator or a madman and decide whether or not he was criminal (responsible or irresponsible) appear as mad, simulating, or criminal. Crime marks a cultural limit that shows another side, a "beyond," something new ("the new"). And then the logic of differentiation opens in other directions, into other territories and stories. The frontiers "in crime" (mobile frontiers: cultural mutations) function as passages that allow us to travel through time and through culture. They separate (and unite) cultures, they found cultures, and they also separate (and unite) lines within cultures.

The transmutation operation is simple and consists of installing a frontier in the very heart of the "man of science," placing this subject and this position "in crime" and submitting it to another justice and other laws. The mutations undergone by the position of the man of science in the transmutation operation stories could be seen, perhaps, in the mutant biographies of those who wrote them.[2] In the time of the frontier, and in Argentina, there are at least four operation stories.

First Transmutation Operation

The first transmutation operation was that of the man of science into a detective in 1896. The detective tale is born in Argentina with *La bolsa de huesos* (The bag of bones) (1896) by Eduardo Holmberg (1852–1937). The man of science commits a crime with the protection of his own jurisprudence, the corporate (*not state*) jurisprudence of his own "scientific" professional group, which is beyond "social laws."

In *Irresponsable,* the narrator presents himself as a physician, and his family (and his autobiography) was the family of science; from there to the detective there is a step and a mutation. *La bolsa de huesos* is the first detective tale of Argentine literature (a sexual scandal in the Faculty of Medicine: crime and transvestitism), told autobiographically (and with a light and self-mocking tone: "scientist's humor") by a natural scientist who "plays" detective in order to write a novel. He, the man of science, must identify the murderer, and this identification is that of his or her sexual identity, of the female signs of the fin de siècle, and of female crimes. The scientist receives help from a phrenologist friend, commenting that "our medical science, represented by its worthy priests, commits more errors in diagnosis or treatment than a friend of mine whom I have never seen make a single mistake as a phrenologist" (178). (With this detective tale there is born a whole new symbolic field and a new literary genre which mixes the learned with the popular; for us, in the manual, "the story of women who kill" is born.)

The man of science in *La bolsa de huesos* (who is also a physician) transmutes himself into a detective not only to investigate the mystery of the female sex in the name of the law (for the state), but also to write a novel "that will deceive": "Some will say it's a novel, others that it's a story, others a narrative; some will think that it's a police inquiry, many that it's a lie, few that it's the truth. And, thus, no one will know what to believe" (232). He says that "official justice" must not intervene in his investigations (201), and the resolution itself is made outside the law, given that this physician-detective-writer, when he arrives at "the truth," witnesses the transmutation operation of the murderer from "man" into woman (contemplating it ecstatically), and imposes "literary justice." He induces the beautiful criminal to take a double portion of the same Peruvian drug, unknown to science, which she used in her serial murders of medical students, and which produces ecstasy followed by death. And with this he commits a crime that does not incur state justice and remains a "medical secret," beyond "social laws" (the frontier is the place of the secret and of the "beyond"). Holmberg's tale is dedicated to his friend Belisario Otamendi, chief of the police department, and the other two medical characters in the fiction are named Doctor Pineal and Doctor Varolio, "two cerebral names," as the narrator himself says. Let us listen to our man of science in conference with the phrenologist, inside "the circle" and at the classic moment of the detective tale:

"There were two similar skeletons, forgotten in the same way, by the same mysterious person. *The person must be identified.* From the first investigations, I suspect that it's a woman; the idea of a drama of passion occurs to me, I pursue it and I arrive at the ending. *It is a woman.* But I'm the one who carries out the inquiry, as a novelist, as a physician, with a romantic spirit—the woman interests me, and I set out to save her—and I save her, that is to say, I save her from the clutches of the police; but in order to do so, I must see that she takes a double dose of poison."

"*But you are guilty, you are a criminal,* as the instigator of a suicide."

"Very well. Did you know who Clara was? Did you know how much it mattered to me to keep her from her natural judges? You don't know anything about that, nor will you ever know. *Now medical secrecy intervenes.*"

"But wretched man! *You will be the victim of your curiosity.*"

"Agreed. *That will not keep me from thinking that medical secrecy outweighs other social laws.*"

"When will you publish the novel?"

"Very soon. Don't you see? I'm almost done. I'll send it to print with the ink still fresh."

"And the polishing?"

"That will come."

"And success?"

"I don't know."

"But it's about a scandal, about several crimes."

"No, sir. It's about the application of the general principles of *legal medicine,* which is a science, and demonstrating that science can conquer all fields, because it is the master key of intelligence. Science will conquer man, who has not yet conquered religion or politics." (131–33; italics added)[3]

The phrenologist, who operates outside academies, accuses him of being a criminal and asks him about success, and our scientist-detective-writer (a "new" subject) puts himself beyond social laws, "the clutches of the police" and "natural judges," and beyond science (in literature) in order to say that the novel demonstrates that the science of the state (legal medicine) will conquer all fields in order to conquer "man."[4] He is both a "scientific-legal" subject of the liberal state and a "criminal" writer; it is perhaps this ambivalence (this hybridization) between science and literature that defines the first transmutation of the man of science into a detective *and constitutes it as a frontier.* Would he find success with his "scientific and detective" novel about the female sex and its crimes at the end of the century? Is it read in secondary schools?

Holmberg is a "frontier" writer because he belongs to two coalitions, that of 1880 and that of the *modernistas;* and he is also ambivalent as a frontier because he is our first and last "physician-writer" of the series of "physicians in crime" that follows; from here on, the authors of the transmutation operation stories will no longer be university men (like those of the coalition), but rather professional writers who earn their living by writing. And here, on the frontier and in the dispute between literature and science over "truth" (and "justice"), another new subject appears: the journalist-writer, or the subject of *modernismo.*

The frontier is not only the limit of a state but also a zone of aperture and creativity. The "international" culture at the end of the nineteenth century produced Conan Doyle's novels, Freud's texts, the study of signs (semiology), and Charles Sanders Peirce's theory of abduction. Another type of rationality is born out of traces and details: *a new epistemological model, another form of knowledge.* On the "national" side of the frontier as well, there arises a passion for studying and deciphering the "mystery" of the mind, and the operation of disclosure knows no bounds: the minds of artists, scientific researchers, geniuses, famous men, and also the minds of criminals and women become objects of inquiry on both sides, in fiction and in science, in the occult and in the visible sciences. And with the passion for deciphering comes interpretive indeterminacy, the textuality of the enigma, and *ambivalence in literature.*

In Holmberg we see the ambivalence of the frontier of crime (his literary detective is a man of science "in crime"), and also the proliferation it produces (aperture in all directions). Holmberg wrote not only detective tales, founding the genre in Argentina, but also works of fantasy and science fiction.

Second Transmutation Operation

Leopoldo Lugones (1874–1938) published "El Psychon" (Psychon), an "international" *modernista* story (fantasy or science fiction?) in *Las fuerzas extrañas* (Strange forces) (1906). In it, the man of science transmutes into an "occultist" (*at the margin of the academies*) and into an inventor of machines for the transmutation of "forces" or "bodies" which turn against him and lead him to annihilation. The foreign man of science "transmutes" thought and finds madness.

In the state coalition described in this manual's "From Transgression to Crime," continuity and identity were created among the biological, the social, and the legal realms; in the *modernista* variant, which is antiacademic and scientific-occultist in Lugones's stories, identity or continuity would be created between thought and the universe, and between physics and metaphysics. The stories of *Las fuerzas extrañas* are founded on an animist-occultist principle, which is developed at the end in the form of a "Cosmogony in Ten Lessons" by a shaman or theosophist master who preaches the sameness of laws of thought and laws of the universe. The men of science involved with the "strange forces" (outside of academies or institutions, transgressive "foreigners" in the Cosmopolis, like anarchists) prove their animist hypotheses in light, sound, and thought, and they build machines to carry out operations of transmutation.

"El Psychon" is on the frontier not only because it is about the transmutation of thought, but also because it continues with the "physics" of the liberal state (and with gases, which no longer expand but are liquefied), and uses it to define madness. Holmberg's tale was narrated in the first person by the man of science / detective, and the victim was "the belle of the Faculty of Medicine"; in Lugones a former patient of the physician, who is also an initiate, narrates, and the victim is Dr. Paulin, the scientist himself. Paulin, a foreign doctor of physics and medicine, studied mental suggestion and the liquation of gases, but, says the narrator, he had a "grave defect": he was a confessed spiritualist. He maintained that the spirit rules the tissues and the physiological functions, and the academies mistrusted him. The initiate narrator attends his experiments (and reproduces his scientific discourse full of names, numbers, formulas, techniques, and apparatuses) following his arrival in Buenos Aires to study medical applications of botany. But it is precisely in Buenos Aires that Paulin discovers a gas or "a body" that "could be volatilized thought," which he calls Psychon. He attempts to liquefy it by reducing it to a temperature close to absolute zero in an apparatus that consists of "three concentric spirals made of connecting copper tubes."

The narrator wonders, "If this little bit of clear water that I have before my eyes could be translated, I thought, what would it *say*? What *pure* child's prayer, *what criminal intent,* what projects could be contained in this receptacle? Or perhaps some failed *artistic* creation, some discovery lost in the *shadows of illogic?*" (168). But when the thinking liquid begins to escape from the apparatus, other transmutations occur:

> I noticed a sardonic expression on the doctor's face which was entirely strange under the circumstances; and almost at the same time, the stupid and preposterous idea of jumping over the table entered my spirit; I had barely thought it, when the piece of furniture passed under my legs, and I had time to see that the doctor was tossing his cat in the air like a ball . . . What's for sure is that for an hour we were performing the most outrageous stunts. . . . I vaguely remember that amid the laughter I was assaulted by *ideas of crime* interspersed in a vertiginous enunciation *of mathematical problems* . . . the pure thought that we had absorbed was surely the elixir of madness. (169; italics added)[5]

The sameness of the laws of thought and of the universe, the continuity between "matter" and "spirit," the transmutation of liquid thought into the "elixir of madness." Madness, before the transmutation, is linked to art (just as crime is linked to the child). After the "operation," madness is made up of outrageous stunts, laughter, ideas of crime, and mathematical problems. Pure thought leads to crime and madness; Dr. Paulin disappears the following day, and the narrator believes that he repeated his transmutation because "he is in a convalescent home in Germany." Across this dangerous frontier we travel from Cosmopolis to Locopolis.

For in leaving the subjects of the coalition behind and crossing the frontier of crime, what matters is *the antistate gesture* of Lugones's new scientists, who are "outside of the academies" (like Holmberg's "phrenologist"); *the attack on official science* implicit in the incorporation of theosophical theories presented as "scientific": the demolition of the scientific subject of the coalition. In 1897 José Ingenieros and Leopoldo Lugones began to publish *La Montaña: Periódico socialista revolucionario* (The mountain: Revolutionary Socialist newspaper).[6] In issue 11, an article titled "La ciencia oficial y la Facultad de Ciencias Herméticas" (Official science and the Faculty of Hermetic Sciences) appears signed with José Ingenieros's initials (J. I.), and in it he attacks the "monopoly which those sages whom we can call official presume to exercise over science," comparing it to the Inquisition, and he contrasts it with *"a revolutionary science* which provokes discussion, exposes methods and systems, accumulates proofs, attempts demonstrations." He refers to Annie Besant, Madame Blavatsky, Rochas, Aksakoff, and others, and to their "important studies of Occultism and Theosophy [that] have revealed to us indisputably real phenomena which are in contradiction with *the so-called laws of the official sages*" (italics added). Ingenieros applauds the foundation of a Faculty of Higher Studies in Buenos Aires where courses in occultism, the cabala, occult therapeutics, and transcendental magnetism would be given, and he recommends a course in hyperchemistry and a section of experimental work. "Although we do not share in their entirety the principles which inform the creation of this Faculty of Hermetic Sciences, we hope for its progress *despite our official scientific world,* which has greeted it with absolute silence and with smiles which betray its crass ignorance of the subject" (italics added).

Third Transmutation Operation

The man of science is a torturer and murderer in *El hombre artificial* (The artificial man) (1910) by Horacio Quiroga (1878–1937), a text that also fits into another series which we could call "torture stories" or "Toward a Literary History of Torture in Argentina."[7] *El hombre artificial* was published in six installments between 8 January and 12 February 1910 in the series "Folletines de *Caras y Caretas*" under the pseudonym S. Fragoso Lima.[8] There, between advertisements for El Abuelo port wine and Bu-Bu biscuits, articles about the first airplane in Buenos Aires, the "oriental revolution," a radical cure for colitis, and the wind in Mar del Plata, it coincides in issue no. 589 with a chapter of Eduardo Wilde's autobiography *Aguas abajo,* and in issue no. 590 with Amado Nervo's "El angel caído" (The fallen angel).

In *El hombre artificial,* the operation of the literaturization of science (or the operation of the transmutation of scientist into criminal, which is one of the central features of the frontier) is recounted by an external narrator, a modern chronicler who uses flashbacks. The novel presents an international circle of scientists in the characters of the Russian physician Donissoff, the Argentine Ortiz, who studied electrical engineering in Buffalo, and the Italian physician Sivel; all have broken with their families as the result of some tragic story, and *all have renounced their inheritance.* They enclose themselves in a laboratory in Buenos Aires "equipped with the most perfect kinds of machines and instruments *which they ordered expressly from the United States*" (chemical, anatomical, and bacteriological apparatuses, electric lamps), in order to bring a rat to life and then to build an artificial man. They call him Biógeno, but they need to bring him to life with feelings; Donisoff argues "scientifically" that *a production of pain* in the nervous system is necessary to elicit sensitivity in the artificial man. Here begins the transmutation operation story.

Donissoff (he is noble, has the beautiful face of an archangel, and speaks French and English) goes out in search of a victim and returns with *"a poorly dressed, very thin man with a yellowish complexion"* and dark glasses. "And turning to Sivel and Ortiz, he said to them quickly *in English:* We must tie this man down immediately. Let's not lose a moment because he's going to get suspicious." They tie him to a gurney to torture him for "the scientific ideal," and the torturer is Donissoff himself, a revolutionary prince who once handed his noble guardian over to the group of anarchist terrorists to which he belonged in Russia.

> A cry of horror, a heartrending shriek, had come out of the poor devil's throat when he heard *torture.* Already infinitely frightened by the trap they had laid for him, by that laboratory with its hellish aspect, and by the three man-devouring demons, his whole being had broken into a shriek when he saw what awaited him.
>
> He made a terrible effort to break the restraints and rolled around on the floor in a convulsion. They picked him up, sat him down again, and Donissoff, putting a hand on his arm, said to him coldly:
>
> "It's useless to scream; no one can hear anything at all from the street. Now, if the knowledge that we are suffering more than you from your pain can be of any comfort, rest fully assured. . . .
>
> The immobilized man felt Donissoff approach and sensed the contact of Donissoff's fine hand with one of his. For five seconds the poor being's heart beat wildly, dying of suspenseful anguish. And suddenly he let out a terrible cry: one of his fingernails, caught by the edge with pliers, had just been ripped backward.
>
> It was a single cry, but one which carried with it a delirious paroxysm of pain. . . .
>
> The poor tortured being now looked as thin as a cadaver. His abdomen was horribly sunken and his prominent ribs, projected upward in contrast, seemed to break the skin. His face was livid and his eyes were sunken deep in their sockets. From his nostrils ran two streams of blood that cut across his lips and disappeared into his beard. Not a single nail was left on his fingers. (130)

The others (the Italian and the Argentine) can't tolerate "the session" and withdraw, but "the Russian genius" continues "the operation" until Biógeno absorbs the tortures of the other man and appears to come alive, touching his nails, crying out in pain, and speaking with the voice of the tortured man. "We've made a horror, Donissoff," Sivel protests, running his hand across his anguished brow. "This man had no life of his own. He is a mannequin; we have transmitted the other man's soul to him." The tortured man ceases to feel and dies, and his is the second life sacrificed by Donissoff. The Russian then decides that Ortiz and Sivel should hypnotize him so that he can receive Biógeno's excess charge, and at this moment he recalls the scene of the secret revolutionary committee in which he "had sacrificed something more than his own life" by saying that another prince (the guardian who cared for him after he was orphaned, and whom he loved enormously) had to be executed. Donissoff ("sublime creature, archangel of genius, will and beauty," says the narrator-chronicler) lies down next to Biógeno in "the torture room," extends his hand to him, cries out, and falls, "destroyed by that abominable machine of pain that he had created with his genius and which ended up discharging all his accumulating suffering at once: he had exploded, killing Donissoff" (132).

The "modernity" of the frontier, its plural ambivalence, and its tunnels into the future. In *El hombre artificial,* in 1910, the relationship between *ethics and science* is posed at the same time as the relation between *ethics and revolutionary politics* in the figure of Donissoff, who as an *anarchist* in Russia hands over a fellow noble ("for the sake of the revolution") and as a *scientist* in Argentina tortures a poor man ("for the sake of life") using *North American* instruments *and speaking English with his peers so that the skinny, poorly dressed victim will not understand him.*[9]

Fourth Transmutation Operation

Here the man of science is a Frankenstein who performs a transmutation operation on a Moreira! (Another Argentine Frankenstein had already appeared years earlier in *Caras y Caretas*.)[10] Again he commits a crime, with his operation on Moreira, and again he is protected by secrecy and by the *private jurisprudence* of a "scientific" professional group: a jurisprudence that is "beyond social laws." The satirical and utopian novel is born with *La ciudad de los locos (Aventuras de Tartarín Moreira)* (The city of the madmen [Adventures of Tartarín Moreira]) by Juan José de Soiza Reilly (a journalist for *Caras y Caretas*), which was published in Barcelona by Maucci in 1914. *La ciudad de los locos* is the Virgil of this manual because it is inhabited by celebrities, madmen, geniuses, monsters, Moreiras, physicians, journalists of truth, and criminals, and it opens and continues infinite series. With this operation we definitively cross the frontier between Cosmopolis and Locopolis.[11]

In the *corpus delicti,* Moreira undergoes various operations of transmutation in black and white. In "The Moreiras," discussed later in the manual but returning to 1880, we shall see in Eduardo Gutiérrez's *Juan Moreira* the transformation of the gaucho Juan Moreira into a landlord named Juan Blanco (White): a "whitewashing operation." And here, in *La ciudad de los locos* from 1914, we witness the "blackening operation" intended to transform the "little madman" Tartarín Moreira into a superman-genius by injecting him with fluid from a black idiot. (Tartarín Moreira is the "French" Moreira of the upper-class gangs of the end of the nineteenth century: the other face or the same face of the sons of the liberal state.) The two transmutation operations performed on Moreira, a true mutant in black and white, are sustained by *the desire for celebrity, for fame,* and they inscribe crimes on certain bodies and in certain languages. And both are recounted by organic journalists of key media: Gutiérrez, who wrote for the newspaper *La Patria Argentina* in the 1880s, and Soiza Reilly, who wrote for *Caras y Caretas* at the beginning of the twentieth century.

In chapter 5 of *La ciudad de los locos,* titled "Empieza la novela" (The novel begins), we are introduced to the "madness doctor" in charge of the insane asylum:

> The director was a man of short stature. He spoke rapidly, like all beings of nervous spirit. He was fond of changing subject without transition. His face wasn't ugly. Only his eyes were too cloudy and too small. Too malicious. . . . His body was undoubtedly ugly. He possessed special features that made him resemble a camel. He was lame and also hunchbacked. When he walked, his enormous hump swayed with the impulse of his strange lameness. [. . .] His spirit was lame. His heart had humps. His brain ruminated ideas. . . . He treated the sane and the mad alike with aggressive disdain. He was a learned man. But ill mannered. This disparity between brain and action is constantly observed in men who study excessively. (40)

The "experimental" operation performed by the Frankenstein of the insane asylum in order to transmute his stepson, Tartarín Moreira, into a superman-genius and in order to win fame for himself,[12] is not only the pearl of the transmutation operations but also one of my favorite stories in the *corpus delicti*. It is recounted by a satirical and cartoonish journalist called Agapito Candileja and it is found in chapter 14 ("Un experimento salvaje" [A savage experiment]):

> "Well, dear doctor," said the hunchback, "I believe that my experiment will turn out magnificently."
> "And the fluid?" the other inquired.
> "I extracted it from the brain of a hypertrophic patient. *An Abyssinian black.* A most curious case. He was *a perfect idiot.* My theory is this: "supreme wisdom must arise from supreme idiocy."
> "And the inoculation? Where?"
> "In the base of the cranium. The procedure consists of delivering the germ of idiocy to the encephalon. Then the brain is enlightened. Intelligence is enlarged. And, through the collision of mental fluids, the superman will be born. The genius . . ."

"Can we try it?"

"Very soon."

"On whom?"

"On my son, that is to say, on my wife's son. On Tartarín."

"And he agrees?"

"At first he refused. "I don't want to be a guinea pig," he joked. But I gave him plenty of money to bet at the racetrack and to squander in cafes. He accepted. . . . But he thinks it's a simple experiment. A simple test of scientific curiosity, like a vaccination, without any danger."

"He doesn't know that he could die in the test, or that even at the very best, he could go mad?"

"He doesn't know anything about that." [. . .]

The other physician—whose name the reader shall never know because he has not yet died and because it was he who told me this unique story—helped to position Tartarín face down and lengthwise on the table. The hunchback took a hollow steel needle with a small rubber valve at the upper end. He inserted it into a mysterious glass tube so that it would absorb a bluish liquid. Then, with a *pleasant diabolical smile, the humpback climbed up on a bench.* He dug around with his fingers at the back of the victim's neck. He pulled back the hair and while the other physician held the patient's arms down, he quickly sunk the needle into his brain with *Herculean strength.* (98–101; italics added)

The other physician inquires:

"And if the experiment doesn't work? And if when your wife returns from the theater, she finds her son dead?"

"No one will be able to say it was me who . . . operated on him. Unless you . . . !"

"Doctor! . . ."

"No! I know. I trust you. But, in short: did Doctor Jenner not also sacrifice his own son in order to bequeath to the world the prodigious invention of vaccination?" (102)

Tartarín Moreira goes stark raving mad, and the mother moves from the theater to the insane asylum (from Cosmopolis to Locopolis, like us), where she leaves her son, *a victim of science* (and of the mixture of the black Abyssinian idiot with Tartarín Moreira, himself a Creole-French-Cocoliche mixture). The hunchbacked monster (whom we will later learn is called Jacinto Rosa), whom she married for his money (in order to protect her dear son), rebukes her for having brought him to the asylum he runs. "A superior light has reached his brain. Your son is a genius. Your son is now, thanks to my science, a superman. . . . He's not mad! You should not have brought him! Bad mother!" (103).[13] The narration continues:

The only one in possession of the *barbarous secret* besides the director and his physician assistant was Doctor Plomitz. In his studies of the transmission of cerebral fluids, he had arrived at the same conclusions as the director. They discussed the subject often. It was Doctor Plomitz who showed him the best place to insert the needle. When he examined Tartarín the night they brought him to the asylum, it occurred to him to examine his occiput. There he found *the revealing sign.* . . . He knew that the boy was the director's stepson. He understood everything. And he also understood the failure of the experiment. *He didn't say a word. The crimes of science are beyond the domain of law . . . !* (103–4; italics added)

Again the secret, the signs, and the crimes of science on the frontier. *La ciudad de los locos* has a particular humor because it reads with the pace and visual logic of a comic book, narrated backward and forward (ahead is behind), and made of superimpositions that mix traditions and cultures. The names of the characters, their actions, the presence of one of the most durable imaginings of mass culture (that of the scientist as monster and madman representing evil, or the evil and the power of knowledge), define it as a "North American" novel, popular and journalistic, made of the embryos of mass culture and with the particular type of *satire against power* that is born with mass culture. It is a modern novel, a *modernista* novel with Rubén Darío in the prologue, and also an Argentine popular novel, with Moreira and Agapito Candileja. And it appeared serialized in *Caras y Caretas* and later as a book in Barcelona. It has mad scientists, journalists of truth, secrets, confessions, crimes, and also a utopia, because Tartarín Moreira will later set fire to the asylum and found Locopolis, the city where desires are fulfilled.

This is why today, on the frontier, if I were obliged to choose among the four transmutation operations (or among the crimes of science), I would choose this one and carry it into the future. I keep the "unread," discarded part of literary history, and I discover that if history is read from there, if "the very much read" are read from "the unread," something of the *modernista* and utopian satire can enter into the linear succession of "the very much read" and break it. For this reason, *La ciudad de los locos* (the territory of *Locopolis*) is the Virgil of this manual.

The "Other Side," or the Fiction of Crime

The crime of the scientist has carried us from one modernization to another: to the "other side." In the four transmutation operation stories of the frontier,[14] crime stories with criminals, victims, and secrets finally appear. Madness, torture, fame, unofficial science, the globalization of Latin American literature, the United States, English, and mass culture in Argentine literature also appear.

The transmutation operation, which fuses the scientific subject with the monster, the occultist, the detective, or the torturer (with another power, with "crime," other justices and *laws other than that of the state*) produces a break and a jump to another side, and it opens new writings, textualities, spaces, and literary genres. (And it also opens series and stories in the manual.) Here a new subject appears: the journalist-poet, the professional writer, who is precisely the one who puts the man of science "in crime." This cultural war between the poet (or writer or artist) and the man of science over truth and justice, a war of hybridizations and ambivalences between "science" and "literature," is what the transmutation operation stories recount. They are cultural operations, produced with the dividing and articulating instrument of crime. They introduce us into a modern (and *modernista*) journalistic culture motivated by *the desire for fame*, which writes lists and collections of celebrities, which speculates about genius, talent, and madness, and which classifies men in hierarchical scales. And which can *threaten*, like anarchism and revolutionary socialism and like occultism, *the hegemony of the scientific discourse of the law and the state* (what we have called the state epistemology of 1880). Because it brings another truth, another modernization beyond the modernization of the liberal state; a more "international" and global postmodernization: the modernization of the communication media which is already evident at this moment, with large journalistic enterprises such as *La Nación* and *La Prensa* and new magazines such as *Caras y Caretas*. The appearance of the culture industry is accompanied by a break in Spanish American literature and culture, and this break is what the frontier of crime recounts.[15]

Into this weave of relations (journalism, *modernismo*, occultism, anarchism, socialism) the men of science "in crime" are inserted, and they introduce new subjects (new modes of subjectivity) and new human symbols in literature and in culture: the apostle, the theosophical master or shaman, the poet or artist (Rubén Darío arrived in Buenos Aires in 1893), the superman, the genius, the revolutionary (and even the femme fatale): all subjects "beyond" the state who take charge of *the limits of science:* of mystery, of desire, and of the spirit. And with them other circles appear, different from the official coalition: "the sect" and the esoteric groups of initiates, bohemian poets, media writers, scientists outside of the academies, anarchist conspirators, and revolutionary socialists (all in contact with one another). With these circles there arise states within the state with their own powers, forces, laws, and justices. And beyond the frontier of the national state, the United States emerges as an imperialist political force that threatens the spirit or culture of Latin America with its materialism and its pragmatism.[16]

The detective tale, the fantastic tale, science fiction and utopian satire: these new genres cultivated by journalist-writers (the genres of the frontier "in crime," of the scientist and the limits of science) introduce us into modern culture through passages or tunnels, and they pose various crucial problems. In the production of culture, they are defined as marginal and popular (by their place of enunciation and also, sometimes, by their place of publication) and at the same time as central; they are machines of power dominated by ambivalence and by a certain interpretative indeterminacy: are they challenges to state law or its supplements? Are they antistate fictions or simply fictions that have become independent of the state? Are they works of delegitimization?[17]

The Crime of the Artist: Portrait Stories

But the man of science is not left alone with his crime and his ethics to open new genres on the frontier. Suddenly, in the same space of *Caras y Caretas,* beside the scientist as torturer (in *Toward a Literary History of Torture in Argentina*), we find the artist as torturer and "in crime." Alongside Horacio Quiroga's *El hombre artificial* there appears "Historia de un espíritu" (Story of a spirit)[18] by Juan José de Soiza Reilly, the "unread" writer who allows us to read other "very much read" writers. The two texts appeared in the same medium—*Caras y Caretas*—and in the same period, and they represent the scientist and the artist as torturers and criminals. Both characters embody the passion for "the new," and both, the Russian scientist who is a "sublime creature" ("genius," "archangel") and the "ingenious" (and therefore mad) artist who wants to paint the sublime "damned soul" of his generation, invent a "pain machine" in order to give life or create, and both commit murder and annihilate themselves.

In "Historia de un espíritu" the narrator is a journalist who, in order to write an article, goes to contemplate the final gesture of *a painter of famous canvases,* thirty years old, who is about to be shot. "The agony of a man of talent is a beautiful spectacle which only poets, birds, dogs and women can comprehend," says our Virgil of the manual. The famous man is a *"poor modern artist,* whose pictures were always *ingenious* because they had a good deal of *madness"* (32; italics added). He speaks ("is interviewed") and explains why they are going to kill him.

> *"I sought to do something new.* Something worthy of my century. Something aesthetic. Something beautiful . . . I sought to feel and interpret better sensations. New ones . . . I sought to enjoy invisible mysteries. Sins."

"But, your crime?"

"Well. I'm getting to that . . . *Don't call it a crime. Call it the experiment* of an enraged soul which is dying of hunger and thirst . . . They are going to kill me just for that! (33; italics added, ellipses in original)

His *passion for the new* was such that he sought out hungry, *skinny, and black* models because he wanted to paint "a collective soul." ("The vindication of the 'poor' and 'weak,' for they are not, as we believe, humble or unfortunate, but rather fearsome men who have only a collective soul," say Gilles Deleuze and D. H. Lawrence at the end of this manual). "Through my studio passed all the skinniness, all the squalidness, all the dried out flesh *of the tenements, the alleys, the hospitals and the asylums*" (34; italics added). Finally he chooses for his transmutation operation a scrawny old vagabond who is *black and mute* (his tongue lost to cancer).

I tied him with strong ropes to a post of nandubay wood. [. . .] And I sat down in front of the mute. In front of the horrified man. I was waiting . . . And I waited two long days like that. Three days. Four, Five . . . [. . .] Every ten hours I gave him a piece of bread and a drink of water so that he wouldn't die. I wanted to bring his skinniness to an extreme degree without extinguishing his life. I hastened the thinning of that withered body with a whip. The black man wanted to cry out. But how? What about the cancer? Where was his tongue? . . . Believe me; it was a lovely scene. Most lovely . . . After eight days, my model's curly hair turned white. It was a silent tragedy. Gradually his teeth fell out. His eyes escaped an inch from their sockets. His spinal column became twisted. [. . .] By the tenth day, my model was becoming acceptable . . . I prepared my brushes. [. . .] Awaiting the tragic grimace. Yearning for the dreamed of skinniness. The beautiful final gesture . . . [. . .] Out of the blue, like an act of fate, a moonbeam dressed the black man's cadaver in white light . . . Damnation! A cadaver with a silver shroud was no use for my picture . . . I couldn't do it . . . They arrested me . . . Now they're going to kill me with eight shots. What a vulgar death! What a shameful death! . . . I deserve to die the death of the black man . . . Thus, in my own agony, in my own skinniness, in my own pain, I would find sufficient strength to copy the neurasthenic and wretched soul of my generation. (35–36; ellipses in original)

The new on the frontier: "the collective soul of the skinny blacks" and the artist as torturer and criminal, together with the scientist as torturer and criminal.[19] This "criminal artist" announces, from *modernismo* and from *Caras y Caretas,* the grimaces from the alleys, hospitals, and asylums of the aesthetics or "collective soul" of the social literature of the Boedo circle.

The conception of a purely aesthetic sphere separate from ethics and *with its own laws* (beyond social laws) which leads to crime, to madness and annihilation, parallels the conception of a purely scientific sphere, also separate from ethics and with its own laws, leading to crime and annihilation. Science and literature have become independent from the state, they have become autonomous and institutionalized, and they constitute "states within the state" with "their own laws." The *scientist as criminal torturer* and the *artist as criminal torturer* go together and arise in Argentine literature at the same moment, on the same frontier, and also in the same popular medium, and they coincide at the point of "the new" and in their torture victims: the "dogs," the "skinny," and the "black" of society who are picked up in the street, in tenements, hospitals, and asylums. From Cosmopolis to Locopolis across the frontier of crime.

Coda

With the fall into crime of one of the subjects of the liberal state of 1880 in the transmutation operation stories of the 1890–1914 frontier (and with the appearance of the journalist-poet and the artist as new subjects), a cycle of "the subjects of the liberal state" appears to close (the first one, that of emergence). But "aristocratic" Argentine culture also crosses the frontier and beyond, in the future, it incorporates the poet and the artist "in crime" and places them opposite the man of science: there is a crime *between* them. And with this it marks a second cycle of the coalition which turns back on itself and returns, paradoxically and "in *modernista* mode," to the high culture of the liberal state of 1880. In this way it closes (and closes *for us*) the cycle from transgression to crime. The literature of what will be the coalition of the journal *Sur* of 1955 (another liberal and state coalition, but one associated with a military state), will continue the tradition of the aristocratic culture of 1880, incorporating the artist "in crime" from 1940 on as another of its subject-positions *opposite* the man of science. There is a crime between them.

This occurs in *Las ratas* (The rats) (1943) by José Bianco (1909–1986) and *Los ídolos* (The idols) (1953) by Manuel Mujica Lainez (1910–1984).[20] Both recount, in the history of certain families, the history of aristocratic liberal culture, from 1880 and 1890, closing in their respective presents. Both recount a cultural history through family history; they recount what was the "high culture" from its origin at the end of the century; they stage, in these histories, Latin American aristocratic culture. In that history, art and science appear as brothers or close friends, but it is art (and literature) that is put, in both cases, "in crime." The "high" culture has passed through *modernismo* and the frontier, and the crime of the artist and of the poet links the two stories (and links them also with Ernesto Sábato's *El túnel* [The tunnel])[21] to close the familiar cycle of the coalition's man of science.

In the two novels (both bildungsromans like *Juvenilia* or *El juguete rabioso* or *Don Segundo Sombra*), the man of science accompanies the "adolescent artist," and a crime occurs which is not punished by justice and which is secret and ambivalent. In *Las ratas* the young piano "artist" appears to have murdered his half-brother Julio, a Frenchman and a scientist (who worked with rats in his laboratory and in his biochemical research), and he confesses this crime in the work. In *Los ídolos* the young poet Gustavo sinks in the river in Stratford-upon-Avon along with his idol Sansilvestre (who had stolen the poems in *Los ídolos,* the book which made him famous, from an adolescent friend). The drama is narrated by the physician and man of science who was an adolescent friend of the young poet Gustavo and who gave him the portrait of the supposed author of *Los ídolos*.

Let us first enter *Las ratas,* a text of initiation that sustains itself in the utopia of telling all, and which tells it in a secretive, veiled, ambiguous way. It not only narrates the perfect (family) crime (considered a suicide), but also *crime as a change of place,* as a passage from one space to another, from one language to another, and from one art (music) to another (literature), as in Sábato's *El túnel.* The story is *the history of the family* and its relationship to Europe, and also *the history of a portrait* (like that of Dorian Gray). It is told by the youngest, Delfín Heredia, who has the same name as his grandfather and who confesses to the murder of his half-brother to close the circle or cycle.

He takes 1880 as his starting point (the Colegio Nacional of *Juvenilia* and support for Roca and Juárez Celman), and he closes in the present of the 1940s. Everything moves between France and Argentina, between the two languages;[22] among the law (of the father: he is a criminal prosecutor), art (painting-music-literature), and science (Julio); between different "mothers" and their voices. And between the church (the Jesuits and Franciscans) and liberalism (*the two cultures of the Latin American upper class*: the "feminine" religious culture and the "masculine" liberal Masonic culture). And it also moves between high culture, represented by the modern music of Prokofiev which Delfín performs on the piano, and modern mass culture, represented by the cabaret songs that his mother's friend sings and which seduce the scientist. In this vacillation, the tale reveals the family's hypocrisy (it is not truly upper class; a previous generation lived in a pasture belonging to the church of San Francisco), its duplicity, and the ambiguity (ambivalence) of the artist as criminal and the man of science Julio, to whom he gives rat food, a solution of aconitine which cures and kills.

Following Julio's death (considered a suicide), the mother says to the young criminal artist, "I know you didn't resemble one another. Julio had different eyes, a different voice, different interests. Is there anything more different from a man of science than an artist? Is there any relation between biology and music? Nevertheless I relate them, and your piano, for example, that piano at which you practice so savagely, sometimes reminds me for some unknown reason of his rats. The resemblance isn't physical, it isn't intellectual. You have something deeper in common: your character" (24).

Character unites them. *Las ratas* (full of literary quotations and "conversations about literature," one of the marks of the Argentine high literature of the period) alludes to *The Picture of Dorian Gray*[23] (to the duplicity of the portrait, to double subjects, to falseness and hypocrisy) and so to the aesthetic and "criminal" culture of the fin de siècle. The portrait that hangs by Delfín's piano in *Las ratas* is a self-portrait of the father painted thirty years before when the father was Julio's age and wanted to be an artist. (He studied in France, returned with an illegitimate son, Julio, and gave up painting to marry and transmute into a criminal prosecutor.) It resembles Julio: for Delfín, it is both his father and his half-brother. "The duplicity of the portrait is our duplicity," says Delfín, the fourteen-year-old murderer-narrator who "speaks" with "him" every afternoon as he plays Liszt's sonata and passes into "another reality."

And we move on to Mujica Lainez's *Los ídolos*. In the chain of passions and idolatries among adolescent men, everything revolves around a book and portrait that are fetishized, and also around death. At issue is the construction and destruction of "idols," the idolatry of the writer admired as a "genius" and who turns out to be a "criminal," a literary thief. All the references link Europe with Buenos Aires, and also Buenos Aires with the ranch (the marker of the "true" upper class; in *Las ratas* there is no ranch, only a farm), and each element is valued in relation to a European place and to a work of art—literature or painting. The novel is narrated in (or from) the difference between science and art.

At the end of the first part, the narrator, a physician and researcher, imagines: "Sansilvestre, who did not write *Los ídolos,* who kept its precious manuscript, unknown to anyone, following the death of Juan Romano (assuming he was its real author) gave in to the temptation to put it into print under his name, and that is how it appeared. He never guessed that its repercussion would be so enormous, and since then he lived, over the course of a long existence, tortured by *the crime* that reduced him to a terrible slavery" (83). Sansilvestre, the false "author" of *Los ídolos*, secretly keeps *a portrait* of Juan Romero, the dead "real author"; the narrator gave Gustavo, at age sixteen, *a portrait* of Sansilvestre, who was his idol. The history of the family and the history of the portrait are fused and are repeated in the theme of the portrait of Aunt Duma (which reproduces, at the ranch, the story of idolatry in the painter, in his brother, and in the madwoman of the servants' quarters).

The physician-narrator (a researcher and disciple of a famous man of science), who was the poor, passionate friend of the rich, passionate admirer of the poet (who in turn was the passionate friend of the dead young poet from whom he stole in 1908 the texts of *Los ídolos,* his only and ingenious book, which brought him fame), shows the agony of this high culture, its swan song between 1937 and 1952 (Peronism) with the swans of Shakespeare, the swans of *modernismo* in *Los ídolos* (the sonnets to the night, to death, from 1908), and the swans of Palermo, where the monument to Sansilvestre and Gustavo is erected.

In 1950, in the garden of the last family house, the physician "I" of *Los ídolos* contemplates a manifestation of high culture: the full-scale *copy-reproduction* of an eleventh-century tapestry from Bayeux (with knights, incidents of conquest, monsters, horses: *a medieval encyclopedia*) on which Gustavo's aunts have worked their whole lives, and which they finish on the day that Gustavo dies in the Avon River with Sansilvestre, his idol. He contemplates the combination of this European reproduction, which is like the weave of a destiny, with the patio of the old house in the southern barrio, and he marks the apparently contradictory association of the "Creole element" with "the encyclopedia" that is one of the features of the high culture of 1880:

> How disconcerting was the medieval frieze as one advanced among winter plants on their rusty nails, earthenware jars and bird cages! . . . everywhere, throughout the extent of the cloth measuring half a meter in height by seventy meters in length, the most characteristic "themes" of our old houses—the cistern, the eaves, the brick floor, the geraniums—mixed their familiar presence with chivalresque fantasy, with the fabulous bestiary. . . . The juxtaposition of the usual, the quotidian, the known, the all-too-well known—manifested in that cistern, those big cages full of cardinals and canaries and those flowerpots—, and the chimeric, overflowing with remote, legendary allusions—which the Bayeux cloth symbolized—, *the marriage of the two apparently contradictory "traits" which with invariable insistence characterized Gustavo's family,* achieved its fullest expression that noon, in a big, quiet house in the south of the city. (186; italics added)

The novel closes in 1952 with the scientific "I" reading *Los ídolos,* imprisoned in a mesh of passions, destinies, and crimes of adolescent artists: "Any day I can die with *Los ídolos* in my hands and it will be as if I were to go on reading. I won't even notice. It will be as if I were to go on reading, with Gustavo beside me" (235).

In the "aristocratic" culture of the second coalition, these texts about the relation between art and science (which is resolved by the crime of the artist) seem to mark the literary cycle which goes *from autonomy to self-reference:* they read like a closed system that turns back on itself not only because literature is spoken of in the texts, but also because both revolve around doubles, doublings, and duplicities, and *around portraits.* The effect is an evanescent fiction, full of ambivalence and indeterminacy. "High" writing introduces the fiction of the enigma of the portraits and the doubles to recount the crime of the artist and his relation to the man of science. The subjects of the liberal state separated the political from the cultural and the literary in their stories of 1880; paradoxically, they autonomized literature from politics with their fictions for the liberal state. Now, in the 1940s and 1950s (in the future of the frontier), autonomy takes another step and what became independent turns back on itself in order to contemplate itself in a family portrait with men of science. In cultural and social, and not only literary, self-reference, these portrait stories add the frontier of crime to 1880 in order to close the second cycle of the subjects of the liberal state and of aristocratic Argentine literature.

The two bildungsromans openly display the high cultural tradition they represent. They maintain European languages and translation as a literary genre; literary erudition, art, and travel; the joining of a Creole element and a European encyclopedia;[24] high social and family spaces; clean writing and texts which converse among themselves, and thus, the constitution of a circle or coalition. And they also maintain a constant feature of high culture, which is a double critical definition: one for the newcomer and another for their own social sphere, which appears in decadence. Which *is born* in decadence when it is represented for the first time in 1880, with López and Cambaceres. Cultural criticism of the oligarchy is one of the fundamental features of oligarchic high culture in Argentina. It was not Mujica Lainez or Bianco or Victoria Ocampo (of the cultural coalition of the liberal-military state of 1955), then, who invented this critical posture that closes the cycle from transgression to crime. What the *Sur* coalition does, with its artists "in crime," is to fill the cycle with the mysteries and enigmas of *modernismo,* to pass it through the ambivalences and secrets of the frontier. With the fiction of the man of science and the crime of the artist, they invent a way of turning back on themselves, and a way of crossing the frontier of crime in order to court their own demise.

III

.

the moreiras

.

Argentine Stories

1

I am going to introduce you to a character who doesn't get out of Argentina much. His name is Juan Moreira and he is a national hero of violence and popular justice. Though the historical Juan Moreira died in 1874, he moved on to the serial novel in 1879, joined the circus in 1884, and founded the national theater in 1886. And with the theater he founded a genealogy extending up to the present; we call this genealogical history of foundations "The Moreiras."

The first Moreira is one of my favorite heroes of the *corpus delicti,* and not only because he is handsome and bejeweled: "His beautiful head was adorned with a thick mane of black hair whose magnificent curls parted over his shoulders; he wore a full beard, a magnificent and silky beard descending to his chest. On his pinky he wore a diamond of great value, and on his chest, falling toward one of his small pockets of his belt, there shone a thick golden chain which held a *remontoir* watch."[1] He is also a favorite because his violent spatial and corporal practices constitute a multidimensional language that circulates, reappears, and changes with history; organizes social relations and tribes; constitutes subjectivities; marks physical and symbolic trajectories and territories; defines lines; forms conflicting blocks; founds literary genres and sexual genders; and articulates current, mythical, progressive, eschatological, cyclical, and virtual temporalities. Moreira tells "Argentine stories," and his violent body announces a politics of visibility, technology, language, and death.

1879: Two Popular Heroes

Juan Moreira appeared in literature as a criminal in 1879, with the process of modernization and immigration, at the very moment of the end of the civil wars, the annihilation of the Indians, the political and legal unification of the nation by the liberal state, and at the very moment in which Argentina reached the highest point of capitalism for a Latin American country: entry into the world market.

Juan Moreira is the popular hero of this specific cycle, that of the moderniz-

83

ing leap of the end of the nineteenth century: a Latin American modernization through internationalization of the economy. We can read this conjunction in Latin America of modernizing leaps, liberal states, and entry of the regional economies into the world market as a process involving certain changes of position in culture and literature. In Argentina, new literary representations appear, sharply distinguishing the "popular" (defined as Creole) from the "high" or "learned" (defined as European and scientific). At the opening of this cycle, in the same year of 1879, two popular heroes are born: the peaceful gaucho and the violent gaucho. They are the other face and the reverse of the subjects of the liberal state, because they appear simultaneously in literature, showing the two paths of the popular in the era of the modernizing leap and speaking precisely of the use of force or the body either for the economy or for violence. (So we return to the beginning of the manual, to 1880, to "the subjects of the liberal state," to tell another side of the same story, to retell "history.")

Popular Latin American heroes relate to each other and form networks and contrasts: each one embodies a specific position at a given moment in the discourse of a culture. Moreira does not appear alone in 1879, but rather accompanied by the peaceful old gaucho of José Hernández's *La vuelta de Martín Fierro* (The return of Martín Fierro). The peaceful gaucho and the violent one are born at the same time, and we must read them together. Both are continuations of *El gaucho Martín Fierro* (The gaucho Martín Fierro), from 1872, and they thus constitute two possible versions of what comes after the confrontation, violence, and exile that conclude the first *Martín Fierro*.

La vuelta de Martín Fierro closes Hernández's scheme: in 1879 the popular hero is a father who returns from exile, addresses his children, and sings to them in traditional gaucho verse of forgetting the oral justice of confrontation: forgetting popular violence. He uses the book of the old man's proverbs to recommend pacification and integration into the law through work, and in this tone and with this pact he closes the gaucho genre. The gaucho's voice is *almost* the voice of the triumphant liberal state, the official voice.

In contrast, Eduardo Gutiérrez's *Juan Moreira* appeared in 1879 in serial form in the opposition newspaper *La Patria Argentina* to follow through with confrontation and violence and to impose popular justice. The violent hero is *like* an antistate subject; the voice of the national *mitrista* opposition within liberalism.

The pacifist hero and the violent one, the two popular faces of the modernizing leap, arise together in literature from different writings, genres, technologies, and temporalities, and they open processes that are central in Argentine national culture. These processes include intense debates culminating in the theater, which was the place of opera and the "high" (liberal, scientific, and European) modern culture of the end of the nineteenth century, and also, *at the same time,* the place of the circus and Creole drama, of national popular culture. At the end of the century, with the modernizing leap, the cultural divide is formulated *in the space of representation:* in one theater Lugones europeanizes Martín Fierro, and in another Juan Moreira is dramatized and nationalized.

The destinies of the new popular subjects of modernization were foreseeable. With *La vuelta de Martín Fierro,* Hernández's old gaucho is legalized as a worker in Argentina's wealthy agro-export economy. *Martín Fierro* culminated in 1913 with Leopoldo Lugones's lectures at the Odeon Theater in front of the president of the republic. Speaking in the theater and as the official poet, Lugones said that Martín Fierro, Argentina's national *payador* (or gaucho singer), was the Homeric bard of epic poetry, and he thus presided over the final ceremony of nationalization and canonization, which consisted of europeanizing and thus universalizing the gaucho singer. In the theater, in 1913, *Martín Fierro* was reborn as an epic poem and as an exportable symbol of national identity.

Juan Moreira, meanwhile, founded the institution of the national popular theater in 1886. And he has managed to transform himself and to maintain his visibility in different genres, textualities, and media up to the present day. In the theater he founded, the violent Moreira initiated an infinite chain of representations.

Journalism and the Railroad: The Visibility of Violence

The first Moreira lived and died not only in reality, but also in the serial novel that appeared in *La Patria Argentina* in 1879 and 1880. The author was Eduardo Gutiérrez and the newspaper was his family's and belonged to the liberal *mitrista* opposition. The novel is narrated by a modern journalist who investigates the life of the real character in order to write a biography of the last years of his life, 1874 and 1875. (During these years, the first Martín Fierro, the popular hero of 1872, lived in exile among the Indians, enjoying a respite from his confrontations with power.) Juan Moreira was the popular hero of the age of the press and of technological and cultural modernization, *a really existing dead gaucho* whose life and deeds the journalist recounts, quoting witnesses and using real names. The violent gaucho who pursues confrontation to the end seems to be a literary construction of Latin American modernization that coincided with the new journalism and its *technologies of truth:* proof, investigation, witnesses, real names and places, exact dates, scientific statements.[2]

To put it another way: violence appears where power is threatened. Moreira arises at the moment of the emergence of the liberal state and extreme national populist political opposition which threatens the state from within liberalism itself. (Moreira's first violent gesture is killing an immigrant in an economic conflict, and his second is killing a representative of political-military law who used an instrument of torture against him and who allied himself with the Italian immigrant.) Moreira is invented or narrated by a modern subject belonging to this political opposition: the writer of national crime stories in the form of gaucho serial novels published in newspapers.[3]

Before becoming an outlaw, Gutiérrez's hero was "a good gaucho": an honest, independent worker, married and with a young son, and also an authentic henchman—and bodyguard—of the boss Alsina (the *caudillo* of *porteño* populism), whose arms—the horse and the dagger—he bears proudly. Before his fall, Moreira was the owner of "a fleet of carts, which was his most productive capital. Thanks to his spotlessly honest reputation, great stockpiles of the fruits of the country were entrusted to him for delivery to the nearby train station" (11). The hero is situated in the chain of transportation that connects rural culture to urban culture. This is the exact place of the popular hero of violence who arises in 1879 and 1880, narrated by the modern journalist in the first moment of the liberal state. Rural transportation and journalism's technology of truth link the two cultures and the two new subjects to produce *the most extreme visible violence.*[4]

For the gaucho Moreira's modern particularity is that, as the avenging serial novel hero, he represents the passage from old forms of rural transportation to the railroad (and also the passage from the countryside to the city). He embodies the violence of this modernizing trajectory and this clash of speeds, and the perfect illusion of reality created by the new technology of the press allows him to do so with maximum visibility. It is as if the new railroad were crushing the old cart and as if this bloody massacre were embodied in a discourse of such extreme visibility that it constituted a virtual reality displaying the desire for a future cinema, with the train above the spectators. *The result is the maximum illusion of violence, which is what Moreira represents at this moment.* He directs this violence against power, and power turns its violence on him, annihilating him against the wall of a brothel.[5]

Violence, Justice, and Law

Juan Moreira represents the continuation of the gaucho tradition of confrontation and violence: he follows *La vuelta de Martín Fierro* with a fight to the finish, and he carries it toward a radical new position that is at once anarchist and nationalist at a time when anarchism was associated with foreign immigrants.[6]

Violence is unleashed because Moreira's honor is twice offended: first in an economic dispute and then by an abuse of power. One of the problems of the modernizing leap is the problem of what to do with the past (division, war, exile) and how to relate the old rural masses, their culture and language, with the new immigrants and their languages. Moreira eliminates at the outset the representative of the economic pact, a character whose surname identifies him as an Italian and an immigrant. (Sardetti was the owner of a *pulpería,* or local tavern, and he owed Moreira ten thousand pesos. Sardetti denied the debt before the authorities, refused to recognize the oral pact, the word of honor, and did not return the money.) Moreira kills him in his *pulpería,* and this murder is "just," according to oral country law. So affirms the elderly father of Moreira's wife: your honor was offended, you have killed Sardetti fairly, you are innocent.[7]

Next Moreira kills, also "fairly," the representative of the state: the lieutenant mayor Don Francisco who sided with Sardetti and put Moreira in the stocks (the torture instrument used by the police at the time) because he lusted after Moreira's wife. The lieutenant mayor who tortures men and lusts after women represents the authority of the police and the law of the state. The avenging popular hero Moreira kills him in his own home, where he once lived happily with his wife.

With these two "just" deaths, provoked by an economic injustice and by an abuse of state power, the gaucho Moreira embodies popular justice in its pure state, directed straight at oppression: his victims are the enemies of the people. He articulates "crime" with law, economy, and state power, and he makes the crossing required of a popular avenger: *the passage from legality to illegality because of an injustice.* Once beyond the law, he becomes a serial killer and ends up being gunned down by the police in a brothel. Every time it is represented, his death marks the inexorable triumph of state legality.

Thus far, the scheme of the serial novel of the opposition merely repeats the legend of the heroic criminal driven to a life of crime by an injustice or by committing an act that the state, but not the community, considers illegal. In this respect, Moreira could be a Billy the Kid or a Jesse James, who appeared in the United States in the 1870s along with political organizations that defined themselves as populist in moments of rural discontent with the new political economy.[8]

But in Argentina, the criminal hero produces a change in the politics of language and in the politics of death in relation to the peaceful hero, who is his other face. The politics of language: Juan Moreira is not the gaucho singer of proverbs, like Martín Fierro (nor does he recount his life in the first person), because the technology of the press imposes another subject, another language, and another genre, and the only time he is represented singing in the novel, he sings not in gaucho verse but in the Spanish of *Don Quixote*. (The song is titled "Come, death, so concealed" [102]). *The politics of language and the politics of death go together and define the violent popular hero of liberalism as a dead hero.*

The Circle of Violence

Moreira shows that, in Argentina, the paths of legality and illegality are reversible in violence. For outside the law, after fighting valiantly against a party of soldiers, he switches to fighting with the soldiers against outlaws, and he finally saves the life of Sergeant Navarro, the commander in charge of pursuing him. Moreira kills on both sides of legal violence: he alternates between legitimate and illegitimate violence. And he also kills on both sides of political violence, because he has political "patrons" whom he protects from violence. These patrons "legitimize" Moreira's violence. He was the bodyguard of the boss Alsina and then later, outside the law, he saves another boss, Marañón, from dying in a violent assassination attempt. Alsina and Marañón are leaders of political groups that are enemies at this moment within populism. *Martín Fierro's economic alliances are transformed into political alliances in the new universe of modernization.*

The popular hero of the modernizing leap can be seen as a pure confrontational force because he combines violence with opposing positions. The novel makes Moreira oscillate always between two places, and this oscillation, together with his various faces, enables him to represent *all possible positions within violence at this moment, as well as the circular logic of violence.* He represents popular violence massively, in the form of justice by one's own hand and its final outcome, as well as state violence and the politics that directs it. Juan Moreira's Argentine stories can be read as a theory of popular violence, political violence, and state violence during a modernizing leap and with the new technology of the press, which treated crime as entertainment.

White Moreira

Even before showing himself in the theater, the violent hero cannot lack an internal stage, for the modernizing leap defines the cultural divide in the space of representation.

In the chapter "El guapo Juan Blanco" (The handsome Juan Blanco), Moreira arrives in the town of Salto disguised as Blanco, a rich and elegant rancher who buys and sells land (and whose surname means, literally, "White"). Moreira appears as an end-of-the-century simulator transmuted into a "Blanco" with proud and irresistible black eyes. A hermaphrodite: armed and with feminine extremities (head and feet). A "hero of women": he has a "politics" with regard to women and also a "female" politics. A cultural and social hermaphrodite: a mix of city and country, of ancient and modern, of gaucho and boss. The popular hero of violence has a double legal and political identity, and also a double social and sexual identity.

Blanco and his exploits in Salto present us with the components of a contemporary popular hero in his pure state, and *the alliances of liberal populism are also revealed*. The whitewashing of Moreira lays bare this construction because it adds to it another degree of fictionality. Blanco is not a victim but rather a victor of victims: it is he *who represents them* because he appears in the town in order to do justice and to show what honor and freedom are, and what a man is.

As Blanco, Moreira is the other part of the populist alliance: a rural dandy dressed in leather and studs who imposes justice in el Salto. His exploits inspire suspense, fear, laughter, and applause among members of the popular classes, and he is consecrated as their hero. He acts out the stereotypical confrontations with the lieutenant mayor and with economic power. At a dance at a wake he applies satire, humiliation, and several blows to the lieutenant mayor but does not kill him, preferring to steal his lover away in front of the whole town, which laughs at authority. And in the town pool hall he kills the powerful Rico Romero after playing against him and cheating, under the terrified gaze of the other players. Moreira as Blanco kills Rico (literally, "Rich"), is consecrated as the town's hero, and reproduces various games: the game of popular violence, the economic game between the ranchers, the game of the popular alliance, and also the game of double identities of the "high" official literature of the same period, which is one of the characteristic features of the modernizing leaps. He reproduces them within the novel and *according to the logic of spectacle and representation:* as "simulation," mask, trick, and social disguise.

From the Many Faces of Moreira to the Two Masks

Almost immediately, four years after his birth in Gutiérrez's serial novel, Moreira became visible in a process that followed the cinema: in 1884 he appeared in the circus, in the form of a pantomime, *voiceless* (passing through silence and bodily movement in order to exit the novel). Then in 1886, after two years of pantomime, Eduardo Gutiérrez, the author of the novel, and José Podestá, the actor who played Juan Moreira, reinvented the popular hero of confrontation and violence and wrote the first work of Argentine national theater, which was born in the circus as popular theater. The drama opened on 10 April 1886 in Chivilcoy; in time, and with success, new scenes and new music were added (for example, the national dance from the Creole opera *Por María*), along with new characters such as the greedy Neapolitan merchant Antonio Cocoliche. The *milonga* (a folk dance of the province of Buenos Aires, influential in the origin of the tango) was first danced onstage in 1889 in a Juan Moreira drama.[9]

Drama consists of people, voices, and bodies in certain set situations and practices. The representation of the avenging hero in the circus is a popular celebration that contains within it other popular celebrations with Creole songs and dances. The text simplifies the novel and stages its exact movements. Moreira has two acts and two political and legal faces. In the first act he kills Sardetti and the lieutenant mayor out of hatred for the oppressors, and in the second he kills out of love for his bosses: to save Judge Marañón and Sergeant Navarro, who legalize him and declare him good. Finally he is killed by the police in the brothel. Moreira was consecrated as a popular hero of justice in the traveling circus. There he founded national theater and opened the series of his thousand reincarnations.

Moreira's Virility

The category of survival is central to understanding Latin American popular culture. Moreira's violent body is placed in limit situations of life or death; in these situations of survival and salvation certain popular heroes are defined. And they also define their others as loyal or disloyal. For Moreira is placed not only in limit situations, but also in a *Creole male pyramid,* a hierarchical system that links sons, bosses, *compadres,* and friends in a network of loyalties and betrayals. A male pyramid of powers and also of corporalized affections is represented with bodies in moments of violence or lethal danger. The popular hero represents a series of positions of the male gender in a specific culture and in a precise line of the economic and social pyramid. He relates to other men, addresses them directly, and *his voice calls them amigo, don, patrón, tata, compadre.* In these limit situations, in this pyramid and these verbal relations, Moreira defines a specific type of Latin American masculinity.

1. The Loyal

Moreira (violence) is always an articulator, like transportation, because in the chain of masculine hierarchies of fathers and bosses, he speaks *in the presence of* the *patrón* and father, upward from below, and he also speaks *as* a *patrón* and father, downward from above. His body and his discourse have two directions. He needs two directions, two acts, and a double face in order to be the popular hero of violence at the end of the century and to configure a male gender with its limits.

In the drama's second act (and in a chapter of the novel titled "La pendiente del crimen" [The slope of crime]), the outlaw Moreira thwarts a political assassination attempt in a hemlock grove and saves the life of the (future) Justice of the Peace Marañón (a real character who was a leader of the same oppositional political party as Gutiérrez). Moreira says that he saved him "because I love you," and he calls him *"patrón."* Marañón responds by addressing Moreira as "friend" and by offering him protection: "you know that you can count on me whenever you're in a bind." Here Moreira acts out a popular dream of salvation by the *patrón,* by the love of the boss who is "above." We want to emphasize this close relationship between *patrón* and "salvation," with all the religious weight the terms carry in Spanish and in Latin America. Moreira, outside the law as the result of an injustice, saves and protects the *patrón,* and the *patrón* pardons him, saves him, and offers him protection as his "friend." Upward and downward, the exchange is the same: it is an *egalitarian salvation deal.* The difference in equality resides in the word "salvation," in its corporal and physical meaning for the *patrón,* and in its legal and religious meaning for Moreira. The *patrón* (and later Sergeant Navarro) legitimizes popular violence in Moreira when it serves to protect or "save" him.

In "the salvation of the *patrón"* we can clearly read the populist liberal alliance as *a convergence* of two gazes or two political perspectives (one popular and the other that of the liberal opposition) *in a traditional phrase* (which is also a religious mandate). (The policy of legalizing outlaws is evident in the passage from one *patrón* to another, as in the film *Juan Moreira* by Leonardo Favio.) In the same scene in the novel and in the drama, when Moreira kills the enemies in the hemlock grove, the political violence of the modernizing leap becomes very visible, almost a virtual reality.

In order to see Moreira as a *patrón,* we must change genre, leaving drama and returning to the novel. *For in the circus, Moreira is not a patrón:* his beloved friend Julián is a gaucho like him, his equal and his loyal companion. In the novel Julián was also faithful to the end, to the cemetery itself; Moreira's only legacy was the dog he left Julián as a token of loyalty. But Julián is faithful because he appears as the "poorly attired" countryman of the bejeweled Moreira: he is faithful because he is situated below Moreira in the masculine pyramid. Julián says: "Command me *as if* I were your servant, Moreira my friend." And when they meet in one of the novel's life-or-death moments, the narrator says that "they kissed each other on the mouth *like* two lovers, sealing with their kiss the loyal and sincere friendship they had felt for each other since they were little" (113; italics added).

As a *patrón*, Moreira touches the "like" of the other gender. In the social and economic hierarchy of the *patrones*, Moreira's two positions mark the extreme limits of a possible masculine gender. They mark a configuration of its limits. In the presence of the judge-*patrón*, he is brave, all man, *single-handedly* defeating an armed group. (Hannah Arendt says that "the extreme form of power is All against One, the extreme form of violence is One against All.") As a *patrón*, Moreira is also a man who loves his faithful friend (who is like a servant) passionately, like a lover, with their bodies on the border of another gender. The two faces of the hero of violence configure the limits of a masculine gender clearly defined in situations of survival by the hierarchical relations (upward and downward) between men.[10]

The drama suppresses the lower limit because it radicalizes the hero of the circus and erases in him the voice and the body of the *patrón*: it changes Moreira's genre and gender.

In the chain of fathers in the masculine family hierarchy, there occurs something very similar to what happens in the relations between *patrones*. Moreira appears before the old father and as a young father to his son Juancito. The old man is the legislator of popular justice and he declares Moreira innocent when he appears before him: you have justly killed the enemies of the people, he says. While the *patrones* appear to represent the law of the state and politics (and also "the religion of the *patrones*"), the fathers represent oral law, the "good law" of traditional rural justice.

In this second downward relation, as a father, Moreira almost touches the other gender again. The novel's narrator says that his affection for his son Juancito "shone most sweetly in his pupil, imparting to that manly and beautiful physiognomy an expression of entrancing sweetness . . . he contemplated him in the pale candlelight with an *almost maternal* tenderness and covered him again in kisses as if wanting to recoup, with that supreme pleasure, all his misfortunes" (158; italics added).

To conclude: the violent hero in limit situations represents the amorous affections within the ascending and descending masculine pyramid, and he thus marks the limits of the popular masculine gender for the serial novel of that moment. Looking upward, toward the father and *patrón*, he is the valiant hero of justice for the two laws. Looking downward, as father and *patrón*, he is situated on the "like" or the "almost": like a lover to his friend and like a mother to his child. It is as if at this limit he were capable of the other gender, *of the best* of the other gender. This total masculinity, which is again a sort of double gender identity, is clearly seen in the serial novel and erased in the popular drama.

2. The Disloyal

Speaking of loyalties and genders, it is now time to introduce Moreira's wife and the ranks of the disloyal. The lovely Vicenta has something special which arouses the desire of those in power, the representatives of the law: she is a sexualized woman. The lieutenant mayors want her for themselves, and we use the plural here because there are two of them in the novel, as if to underscore this female position or attribute which touches the sexuality of power. When Moreira becomes an outlaw after killing the first lieutenant mayor, the police torture her old father and kill him. Vicenta is left at the mercy of the second lieutenant mayor and has to define herself as the popular hero's wife (or as popular heroine) and not only as a sexualized body. Therefore, she resists the desire of power and the law until she arrives at *the limit situation* with her child, one of hunger and survival (like "Deceased Correa," another Argentine popular heroine). At this precise moment, in this life-or-death situation, Moreira's *compadre* Giménez arrives to save and protect her, as he promised Moreira. (Giménez was the best man at Moreira's wedding and *provided him with weapons*—two revolvers—when Moreira became an outlaw. At the moment of his departure, Moreira asks him to protect his wife.)

The *compadre* enters Vicenta's limit situation to *save and protect her in exchange for her sexualized body,* and he tells her that Moreira is dead. When Moreira comes home after saving Marañón, he discovers his wife with his *compadre* Giménez, who flees like a coward. Moreira spares Vicenta's life when she kneels before him and begs him to kill her like a dog, like Kafka's Joseph K. at the end of *The Trial.*

Vicenta says in the play (act 2, scene 3), "Don't go, *my* Juan, kill me first. (She clings to his chaps.) Kill me like a dog, because I have offended you, but first pardon me; I was not to blame, they have deceived me saying that you had died, and I have taken this step so that our child would not die of hunger. Pardon me and then I will gladly die." And Moreira responds: "May God not allow it (putting away the dagger). You are not to blame and our child needs you because I cannot take him with me: who will care for him if I stain my hand with your blood? Farewell, Vicenta; we will not see each other again because now I am surely going to get myself killed, since the earth holds nothing for me but bitter sorrows."

Vicenta asks Moreira to declare her innocent and kill her like a dog, which is exactly what happens to Moreira himself in the rest of the play: he is declared innocent by the *patrón* and the sergeant, and then killed like a dog by Sergeant Chirino, shot from behind against the wall of a brothel. With Vicenta, Moreira acts as *father and patrón,* as a judge or legislator: he spares her life, he "saves" her, but only as the mother of his child. And at the very moment of her pardon, he abandons her and transforms her into a guilty subjectivity.

Vicenta's position as a sexualized feminine body who is therefore treacherous or unfaithful without knowing it is very marked in the novel because the narrator gives her another name when she takes up with the *compadre:* he calls her Vicenta-Andrea. The position of Moreira's wife is wholly maintained in the circus and the popular drama. It is, at the end of the century, that of the sexualized companion of the violent popular hero.

Women are not divided like friends into the faithful and the unfaithful, but rather into the unknowingly unfaithful and the professionally unfaithful, the prostitutes. Moreira leaves one and moves on to the other. The soldiers finally find him in the brothel with the faithful Julián and his unfaithful female friends; death and sex are fused in a single image.

Today we cannot read a literary genre or sexual gender without at the same time reading its other or others, which are its correlates. In Moreira we clearly see that male gender is defined between men, and that it also defines the female gender. This violent male gender, always at the limit of the other gender when it occupies the positions of father or *patrón,* corresponds to a female gender defined by heroic resistance to the desire of power, and also a potentially treacherous sexuality, as in the case of the protecting *compadre.* The sexualized female gender is represented as unfaithful, as suffering maternity, and as a guilty criminal subjectivity.[11]

In their interrelations, these positions, bodies, and voices of masculinity and femininity in situations of survival draw something like a Latin American configuration situated between urban and rural cultures. It is the configuration of a genre, that of the hero of violence and justice, who is the popular hero of the press, of melodrama, and of the end-of-the-century modernization. In its successive mutations, reincarnations, and representations, this configuration or artifact of voices, bodies, and limit situations that is Moreira permits us to read historical changes in the design of literary genres and sexual genders in Argentine culture. Here are a few examples.

Moreira and Julián, the "lover-friends" of the serial novel who are censored in the play, take a century to reappear and rewrite their kisses, in the epigraph to Néstor Perlongher's 1987 poem "Moreira," included in his book *Alambres.* Moreira appears as *a torture victim whose tongue has been cut out,* and he leaves his mute legacy to Julián. In the 1980s and in the genre of poetry, the popular hero is at once the martyr of state violence and the lover of his friend Julián.[12]

It is Vicenta's position, however, that undergoes the most mutations in generic configuration. When Juan Moreira enters Argentine cinema for the second time, in 1972, she becomes another Vicenta, the "other" Vicenta. The director Leonardo Favio corrected the literary scandal of the treacherous wives of the end of the nineteenth century (who were also found in the high literature of the same period, in its marriage stories) and represented Vicenta, who does not speak like a Creole, as a popular saint, surrounded by candles after the death of her son: Juancito dies of measles while Moreira is away. This sexless Vicenta lives in perpetual mourning, her only role that of the praying and suffering mother. Only the prostitute who accompanies Moreira before his death has a sex and a body. Moreira's death frames the film, and death also appears personified to claim Juancito, announcing that the hero will leave no heirs or legacy. Favio defended and at the same time condemned Moreira precisely at the moment of political violence in 1972 and 1973. (And the video of his film went back into circulation in May 1995 as a video supplement to the magazine *Página 30*.)

The representation of Moreira in Luis Puenzo's film *La historia oficial* (The official story) (1985) takes place in a literature class in a boy's secondary school in 1983, when democracy erupts and the violence of the military state becomes visible. The literature professor who directs the classroom performance is like a member of the Dead Poet's Society in his radical opposition to the history professor who teaches the "official story." The class stages the final moment in which the soldier Chirino kills Moreira, and in the festive climate of the male representation, Vicenta is embodied by the class "gay."

A century after the first play, in 1994, Vicenta comes full circle and returns to the theater. In 1994, when the director and actor Gerardo Pensavalle presented his independent production of Juan Moreira in the El Colonial Theater and in Buenos Aires plazas, he explained his interpretation as follows: "I decided to be as faithful as possible to the spirit, the adventure, and to add a certain currency to the fundamental conflicts. For example, they kill Vicenta and *disappear the son*" ("La vigencia de Juan Moreira," *Primer Plano, Suplemento de cultura de Página 12* [Buenos Aires], 2 October 1994).

Vicenta's death is finally politicized: both she and Juancito attain the same height as Moreira. In the *Juan Moreira* of 1994, men, women, and children are the popular heroes and the victims of the state violence that invented Moreira.

How to Use the Moreiras, and What For

What to do with the Moreiras and their mysterious, multifaceted genealogical language; what to do with the sinuous and mutating series of practices embodied in them?

Juan Moreira is one of my favorite heroes of the Argentine stories of crimes not only because he is a whole theory of violence but also because his periodic representations (the genealogy of the Moreiras) *constitute a literary history of violence* in Argentina, from the end of the nineteenth century up to the present day. At each moment, the Moreiras can be seen as cultural artifacts (complex ones, with many faces: "real," literary, legal, economic, technological, political, and sexual faces oriented in opposite directions) of a violence that delimits physical and symbolic spaces and varies with history, that measures certain junctures and tells national stories.

For if we read Moreira at a certain juncture, we can clearly see the violences of that moment; Moreira makes visible (technologically ever more visible) the various violences of a specific juncture. This applies to the various senses of "violences" and to the various senses of "visible," because each time the Moreiras appear, they allow us to see the violence of the state, political violence, and popular violence. And they also make visible the technological violence of modernization because they show themselves continually in different media, marking the changes in mass technologies.

But Moreira is not only an instrument for the mediation of violence at each moment, but also an instrument for the mediation of violent literary movements, of literary breaks in Argentine culture. For each time a Moreira reappears or becomes visible, he marks a certain movement of foundation in literature: he founds theater; he founds the Latin American novel for export (according to Rubén Darío); he founds Locopolis, he "founds" Borges; he founds the literary avant-garde of the 1970s (César Aira's ¡*Moreira!*, which is Marxist and Freudian);[13] he founds gay political poetry in the 1980s (Néstor Perlongher's "Moreira"). The Moreiras articulate, divide, and connect cultures; they are associated with the aesthetic avant-gardes (with their aesthetics of war), with literary and political anarchisms (in which they are heroes), and also with scientific, socialist, and literary progressivisms (in which they are criminals). Each time, Moreira as a cultural artifact, as a "real" fiction of the criminal hero, defines some sort of territory, frontier, confrontation, or debate, and unleashes wars of meaning or interpretation in which different lines of Argentine culture are drawn.

2

From Cosmopolis to Locopolis by Way of the Moreiras

1890: "Nationalization"

Now we would like to tell you the "unread" story of the *modernista* Moreira who appeared in *Caras y Caretas* in 1907 and who founded the city of the madmen (*La ciudad de los locos*) in 1914. In order to do so, we must review the network and the trajectory drawn by the Moreiras in a specific historical cycle, that which extends from Cosmopolis to Locopolis, and from crisis of 1890 and the first "revolution" by the Radical opposition to the great concession of the electoral law of 1912 and beyond. The Moreiras traverse the violent process of repression and opening that culminates in the Sáenz Peña law establishing secret and obligatory voting, which begins a new era. In this trajectory they tell stories, they differentiate all the lines of culture, they display their violence in various territories, and they delimit certain male subjectivities and certain "national signs." All by means of violence.

This is, then, a trip from Cosmopolis to Locopolis "by way of the Moreiras," a principle for the organization of groups and tribes who define their identity and their territories through violence.[14]

Juan Moreira is crucial to the end of the century, and not only because he founded the national theater in the circus. He is at the center of a renewed debate over civilization and barbarism, the place of the popular, and also the place of the literary and the political. In 1890, in the circus (where the whole barrio or town went for entertainment), there were at least two Moreiras. One was the martyr of popular justice crushed by the violence of the state, and his drama could be national *and* anarchist (and this is how Alberto Gerchunoff read it a bit later, in 1920). The other Moreira was the brave gaucho of the masculine liberal oligarchy which *nationalized him* in a famous ceremony recorded in the official newspaper *Sud-América* on 11 November 1890 under the title "Originalidades sociales: Juan Moreira" (Social originalities: Juan Moreira). José J. Podestá cites the newspaper in his *Memorias:*[15]

> "The life represented by Juan Moreira is admired today by the capital's most distinguished society," says the chronicle in *Sud-América,* and the circus "up until yesterday the meeting place of a certain specific social class, is now invaded nightly by Buenos Aires's most distinguished elements . . . we see people whose social life

is mythical sitting with attention and excitement, in an excellent humor mani-
fested in the form of frank and expansive laughter, for the almost fantastic feats
of the hero of Navarro have the virtue of stirring them from their remote calm
and sweeping them up in *the boisterous merriment of a circus where urbanity, deco-
rum and order are pure metaphysics.*

"An example to the point: Who has ever seen Dr. Ignacio Pirovano, the famous
surgeon, at any circus? Nevertheless, there he was last Saturday night mixed in
with the immense crowd which was applauding, laughing, and enjoying the various scenes of the life of the *noble and brave gaucho* to whom Adolfo Alsina gave the
famous dagger which he would later use in his heroic adventures on the pampa."
(65; italics added)

The chronicle also portrays General Manuel Campos laughing at the humorous
sayings of the Neapolitan in the national dance, and it says that youth

is happily represented each night by the Englishman Balcarce, Juancito Varela,
Saturno Unzué, Ocampo, Frías, Lynch, Acevedo, etc.

We provide below the places and the names of the most enthusiastic propagandists. It is fitting that those mounting the enterprise should know who they are.

Club del Progreso: Edmundo A. Mackinlay and Servando Ferro
Stock Exchange: the Englishman Balcarce and Ramón Arriola
The Criterión: Alberto Alcobendas and Carlos Dose
The Confitería del Águila: Ricardo Thwaites and César Vivot.

With propagandists like these, the life of Juan Moreira is well assured of a sea
of admirers. (66)

In 1890, as Podestá says, "critics raise the white flag," and Moreira is declared a
"noble and brave gaucho" and "the hero of Navarro" in *Sud-América*. His violence
is legitimized in the circus of the state, and he is transformed into *a national popular classic* because he invades the very centers and spaces of power: he is in science,
in the army, and then in the stock exchange, the Club del Progreso, in the
Confitería del Águila, in the official newspaper, and finally everywhere. In 1890, in
Juan Moreira, a founding and legitimizing gesture of the liberal male oligarchy in
Argentina became visible in the trajectory from Cosmopolis to Locopolis, as did
the organization of tribes through violence. The groups of distinguished men and
youths who attended opera performances with their wives here enjoy themselves
noisily in the very place where popular violence is produced and dramatized, and
they appropriate it. While empowered liberalism ceded political power (in the Labor
Code of 1904 and the Sáenz Peña law of 1912) and also launched repressive laws
(the Law of Residence in 1902 and the Law of Social Defense in 1910, providing for

the expulsion of union agitators and foreign anarchists), it founded certain signs of national and popular identity in its downward incursions (it founded "national-popular culture"). In this same trajectory from Cosmopolis to Locopolis, this male oligarchic gesture (consisting of entertainment and violence) was repeated with the tango, when the "bad *señoritos*" went in groups (in gangs, in mobs, in raiding parties) to enjoy themselves in the brothels and then took the dance of the brothels to Paris.[16]

Exportation

But this occurred a bit later, around 1911, but in 1890 there was another Moreira who was also a founder, and he was found neither at the circus nor at the stock exchange but rather in Gutiérrez's novel as read by the founder of *modernismo*: this is the exportable Moreira. In an article titled "La novela americana en España" (The American novel in Spain), Rubén Darío, who represented the aesthetic vanguard and the new Latin American literary culture which arose with modernization and globalization (and also a new modern subject, the journalist-poet), declares Moreira the hero *who founded the American novel*.[17]

Darío wrote for a Spanish audience that Gutiérrez's serial novels were the first novels that belonged to Latin America in their mix of legend and history and in the originality of their barbarism and violence, and that this was precisely what Europe wanted. In Spain, in the throes of the first globalization of Latin American literature, Darío said that Juan Moreira was exportable literature, and he defined Latin American literature for export for the rest of the twentieth century.

In 1890 Moreira was nationalized and americanized for export in a strange interplay between the circus and the novel, between Argentine elite society and the Latin American and global literary avant-garde. Here, with Darío and beyond national frontiers, we will interrupt this initial trajectory (from the circus to Spain) of the nationalization and (Latin) americanization of the Moreira of 1890, and return to Buenos Aires, jumping ahead to

1907

For this is the year in which our unknown "French" Moreira appears to tell the "story" that we're really interested in telling you. As often happens with the Moreiras, he does not appear alone, because in 1907 Evaristo Carriego, the anarchist and *modernista* poet so linked to Borges and his foundations, wrote the poem "El guapo" (The tough guy), which appeared in the section of his book *Misas herejes*

(Heretical masses) titled "El alma del suburbio" (The soul of the suburb).[18] He dedicates it "To the memory of Saint Juan Moreira. With utmost devotion."

"El guapo" is the idol of violence in the barrio of Palermo (he is Borges's famous Juan Muraña), and Carriego presents him this way:

> The barrio admires him. An exponent of courage
> in the long run, he won renown for his daring
> he won a hundred fights among the boys of the barrio
> and he came out of prison consecrated.

Carriego invented the barrio for Argentine literature, Borges said when he invented Carriego in 1930. In 1907 the anarchist and *modernista* poetry of Carriego, a native of Entre Ríos province, established a collection and a world of the urban "popular." He invented the barrio of Palermo and with it the tango, courage, the tough guy, the margin-dweller, the tenement, the barrel organ, the little old lady, the working girl with tuberculosis, the gringo, the little seamstress, the newspaper vendor, and also Saint Moreira. The heretical saint of Carriego's "El alma del suburbio" (The soul of the suburb) became visible in the suburban violence of Palermo.

Let's leave the San Moreira who appears in the dedication of the "tough guy" (95) and turn to the dedication of the section "Envíos" (42) in the same book. There we find a poem dedicated to J. J. Soiza Reilly (and to the writings of Soiza Reilly), in which Carriego writes, for example,

> Your barbaric murderers, apostles of Crime,
> your poor Margaritas, never redeemed,
> your drunken poets, who hunger for apotheosis,
> your prisoner Nietzsches in their cells of neurosis

This Juan José de Soiza Reilly of the heretical masses is none other than the author of our "French" Moreira. At that same time, in 1907 and 1908, he was writing the adventures of Tatarín Moreira under the pseudonym Agapito Candileja in *Caras y Caretas*. These adventures made up the first four chapters of his novel *La ciudad de los locos: Aventuras de Tartarín Moreira* when it appeared in Barcelona in 1914.

Without leaving Buenos Aires in 1907 (and still traveling from Cosmopolis to Locopolis), let's move on from the book of poems where we find Saint Moreira and Soiza Reilly (leaving from Carriego's *literary space,* which contains Soiza Reilly's literary space) *to the popular weekly magazine* where Soiza Reilly's Tartarín is found (the space of *Caras y Caretas,* for which Carriego also used to write).

Or let's go from the many faces of Moreira, passing through the twin masks of theater to *Caras y Caretas*. There we will be able to see how, at the same moment and in writers so linked to each other (sharing the same literary space) but *in different media,* Moreira makes visible two apparently opposing violences: he is the brave saint of the suburban *compadritos* in Carriego's poems *and also,* in *Caras y Caretas,* the leader of the gangs of "bad boys from good families" who go to carnival dances in the barrios to entertain themselves by exercising violence against the little seamstresses and against the barrio thugs. In literature from the same year, and in writers of the same space, Moreira makes visible the violence of the barrio and the violence of the center against the barrio: he makes visible the circular logic of violence.

(How to think about the vicious circle of the Moreiras' violence, which moves upward and downward and installs itself in the aporia of a mimetic and spectacular figure? The victim's language of violence can approximate that of the perpetrators: Hannah Arendt says that the decisive experience which persuaded Georges Sorel and his contemporary Vilfredo Pareto to emphasize the factor of violence in revolutions was the Dreyfus Affair in France, when they saw the supporters of Dreyfus use the very methods they had denounced against their opponents.)

Caras y Caretas began to appear in 1898, and the Moreiras proliferated because the magazine published not only Carriego, Ingenieros, Payró, and Darío, but also Cané and the writers of the liberal state coalition: all the inventors, supporters, and detractors of the various Moreiras and their violences. All the writers of the Moreiras converge in *Caras y Caretas* (which describes itself as a "Festive, Literary, Artistic and News Weekly") because it is the cultural encyclopedia of globalization and the turn of the century, the mass magazine of Cosmopolis, both international and local: the place where all the cultural lines of the period mix nationally.[19]

This is why a Moreira from this magazine, produced by this very medium, is of special interest: we find in Soiza Reilly's Tartarín Moreira *an organic Moreira of the encyclopedia of modernization* (just as Gutierrez's Moreira was an organic product of *La Patria Argentina*) who leads us from Cosmopolis to Locopolis.

The weekly magazine *Caras y Caretas* contains and mixes all the cultural lines of the cycle (and all the Moreiras, and the thousand faces of Tartarín Moreira) *because as a medium* it is on another level, technologically more modern and thus more massive and "popular," at the same time as it represents the avant-garde of cultural journalism. Howard Fraser says that technological advancements such as the transatlantic telegraph cable, the photogravure, and the linotype machine allowed it to differentiate itself from other magazines and cultural media of the period. All spheres of culture appear in *Caras y Caretas* in a state of fragmentation, contamination, and serialization: in the form of various montages and collages, columns, pictures, and series. *Caras y Caretas mixes everything:* the circus and the Teatro Colón, the national and the international, and diverse tones (festive and serious, amusing and didactic, sentimental and satirical). It makes room for everyone, for the state and the counterstate: official ceremonies and worker demonstrations, violent anarchist acts and strikes. It mixes anarchists with liberals and Radicals with socialists. It mixes the science, literature, and politics of the global era with the new icons of mass culture; it mixes, therefore, high culture and the new popular culture. It combines realities and fictions, and also the written with the graphic and photographic, with advertising and the market.

Caras y Caretas is an encyclopedia because it includes all of the culture of the era and because it represents technological globalization, the illusion of Cosmopolis, and cultural democratization. And so it also represents a new progressive and modernizing, anti-imperialist and futurist culture: the culture of photography, the detective novel, cinema, science fiction, and comics. And a new culture begins a new struggle for cultural power. One of its weapons in this struggle is a form of satire, of attack on the law, of delegitimization, a way of interrupting the transmission of culture that is born with modern mass culture: with magazines, photos, cartoons, comic strips, and silent cinema. And this is what the adventures of Tartarín Moreira by the organic journalist of *Caras* are: a satire that could find no other place for itself, and that uses its backward world to attack all the institutions of the liberal state and to found the territory of Locopolis.

For us, today's hero is this "French" Moreira of fiction and satire who appears in 1907 in the turn-of-the-century cultural encyclopedia, but various other Moreiras are also found in *Caras y Caretas* in this cycle. The journalist and writer Fray Mocho (José S. Alvarez), for example, examined the "true" Moreira in the part of the magazine dealing with "reality." Fray Mocho was a founder and director of *Caras y Caretas* and he also wrote for *La Patria Argentina,* the newspaper that gave birth to the first Juan Moreira: he himself connects the two media and territories of Moreira. He was also a chief of police and, according to his acquaintances, a dandy. Under one of his many pseudonyms, Fabio Carrizo, he wrote a chronicle that appeared shortly before his death, on 4 April 1903 (4, no. 235), titled "Episodios policiales: La muerte de Juan Moreira" (Episodes from police history: The death of Juan Moreira).[20]

Let's go back for a moment in *Caras y Caretas* from 1907 to 1903 to see where this *real and organic* Moreira leads us. Fray Mocho establishes a first difference by contrasting the true Juan Moreira, "a rebellious, insignificant and violent gaucho," with the fictional hero (and this is what José Ingenieros also did in 1910 in his lecture "Psicología de Juan Moreira" [Psychology of Juan Moreira], where he said that the real Moreira was a born murderer).[21] Fray Mocho tries to establish a second difference as well, because he also contrasts Moreira with the suburban *compadrito*. He differentiates between their violences and says that he has done research to reconstruct the scene of the "true" Moreira's death against the wall of the brothel and at the hands of the law. The only participant in the tragedy still alive in 1903, he says, is the retired Sergeant Andrés Chirino, who is precisely Moreira's killer. Fray Mocho then interviews Chirino, who recounts how he killed Moreira and how Moreira shot him with a bullet that damaged his eye and how he cut four fingers off his left hand with a hatchet. In *Caras y Caretas,* Chirino says: "Then they awarded me compensation, which I didn't receive until months later, and as for the 40,000 peso reward they offered to whoever apprehended the outlaw, I never saw a penny of it!"

Moreira and the Argentine stories: In Argentina the word *chirinada* is derived precisely from this Chirino who killed Moreira, and it refers to an attempt at a military coup on the part of officers of lower rank. Through Moreira and Fray Mocho, in *Caras y Caretas* in 1903, the former soldier *denounces the state that does not comply with its promise of compensation for the extermination of undesirable outlaws.*

But there is more about "reality" (and about current affairs) in *Caras y Caretas,* because Fray Mocho's chronicle is accompanied by graphic material: an image of the real, visible Moreira. And there is a photo of Moreira's skull, "kept by Mrs. Dominga D. de Perón, widow of Doctor Tomás Perón."[22]

A "real and organic" Moreira in *Caras y Caretas* leads us, in 1903, to certain military pressures and to Perón's ancestors. The two genealogies coexist in the same space in the turn-of-the-century encyclopedia of globalization: in the manual's "From Cosmopolis to Locopolis."

But "reality" drags us forward, and we find ourselves now in 1905, 1906, 1907, and 1908 in room 15 of the El Sarandí tenement house, home to a couple consisting of "El Cívico" and "La Moreira." A *female* Moreira who gets her name from the knife she wears in her garter belt. "El Cívico" was of southern Italian (Albanian) descent, and "La Moreira" was the daughter of Andalusian gypsies. She worked as a prostitute, robbing her clients, and also as a dancer: *she was among those who spread the fame of tango in its association with prostitution.* El Cívico was an irresistible lady's man and a typical *compadrito* of the tenements and brothels, clever and skilled in the art of the dagger (a king of bravery). He called himself "a supporter of Alem and Irigoyen," and he loved and exploited a female Moreira in 1907. The story is told by José Sebastián Tallón,[23] and he adds: "For what was most frightful in this conceited individual, who proclaimed himself an authentic Creole—and in this respect he was no different from his colleagues—was his love for his woman. 'El Cívico' loved this professional prostitute who kissed him good-bye every evening before going off to the brothel. He loved her constantly, with exclusive and thorough devotion."

La Moreira, in contrast, abandons El Cívico, along with the tenement and the brothel, in search of a better fate. And Marta E. Savigliano uses the couple and the scene of abandonment to compose a "tableau vivant": the founding moment of the tango. She makes La Moreira (a mutant, in the end, like all those of her lineage) *the founder* of a genealogical chain of permutations in tango: *"pebeta, papusa, flor de fango, mina, percanta, milonguita"* (54).[24]

As much as I enjoy this Argentine story, we must continue our journey and arrive finally at the fiction of *Caras y Caretas* and our Tartarín Moreira, who appears in these same years in the series of chronicles published under the pseudonym Agapito Candileja.

In issue number 437/16, from 1907: "Una farra carnavalesca de Tartarín Moreira" (Tartarín Moreira's carnivalesque spree).

In number 446/9, from 1907: "El diputado Tartarín Moreira (Psicología popular)" (Deputy Tartarín Moreira [Popular psychology]).

In number 493/17, from 1908: "Tartarín Moreira en París (Psicología popular)" (Tartarín Moreira in Paris [Popular psychology]).

And in number 513/15, from 1908: "Aventuras morales de Tartarín Moreira" (Moral adventures of Tartarín Moreira).

We should recall that the Tartarín Moreira of *Caras y Caretas* from 1907 and 1908 will become the heroic founder of Locopolis in the satirical novel *La ciudad de los locos,* subtitled "Aventuras de Tartarín Moreira" and sub-subtitled (for export or *modernista* globalization) "Novela Sudamericana" (South American novel), since it appeared in Barcelona in 1914, published by Maucci. Between 1907 and 1914, this Moreira traverses the entire cycle of violence and of the opening of the oligarchic liberal state through the enactment of the Sáenz Peña law and beyond.

The author was, of course, Juan José de Soiza Reilly, an "unread" writer in Argentine literature. He dedicated the novel "To my companions at the *Fray Mocho* magazine" (founded in 1912 by a group of journalists from *Caras y Caretas*), and he included a prologue subtitled "Advertencias de mi honradez" (Warnings regarding my honesty), which is a literary manifesto of the individualist and antibourgeois *modernista* avant-garde, paying homage to Darío and Cervantes. Soiza Reilly, the journalist-writer of *Caras y Caretas* and *Fray Mocho,* was (like Carriego) such a devout *modernista* that he named his son Rubén Darío Soiza Reilly.[25]

Soiza Reilly writes the satirical "French" Moreira of the cultural encyclopedia of modernization because he was, like Fray Mocho, an organic writer of *Caras y Caretas,* a star journalist, the "king of reporters"[26] sent to Europe to interview celebrities: these are the interviews that make up his 1909 best-seller *Cien hombres célebres,* and *Caras y Caretas* established him in Paris.

For *Caras y Caretas,* Soiza Reilly invented not only the grandson Tartarín Moreira, a "modern," urban, festive, and violent youth, but also, during these same years and in a typical *modernista* operation, "Juan Moreira's grandfather." His chronicle "El abuelo de Juan Moreira," included in his book *Crónicas de Amor, de Belleza y de Sangre,*[27] brutally demonstrates Moreira's relation to visible violence, genealogy, technology, madness, and the future.

Soiza Reilly says that his character was called "Juan Moreira's grandfather" because the shape of his head was exactly that of the typical Creole type, but the difference was that his hair and beard were white. Soiza's Moreira is a grandfather, but he lives in the present, after his grandson's death. In this *modernista* genealogical tangle, Moreira's grandfather goes mad when his only daughter, who could have continued the lineage, dies. He was rich, used to travel to Europe with her, and on those trips filmed her in all her beauty. Upon returning to Buenos Aires, the young woman falls ill with tuberculosis and dies. The central problem of the Moreiras is that of genealogies of visible violence; when he is left without descendants, the grandfather becomes the "madman" of cinema and mechanical reproduction (we are now in 1908): he spends all day and all night with the movies of his daughter, and his mania consists of believing that every object he touches is transformed into a camera. (It was also in 1908, after ten years of documentary trials carried out by the Frenchman Eugenio Py and the Austrian Max Glucksman, that a young Italian, Mario Gallo, filmed the first Argentine movie containing a plot and violence: *El fusilamiento de Dorrego* [The execution of Dorrego].)

This *modernista* grandfather is another of the organic Moreiras produced by Soiza Reilly and *Caras y Caretas.* But today we are more interested in the "French" grandson, Tartarín Moreira, who appeared in 1907 in the chronicle titled "Una farra carnavalesca de Tartarín Moreira" under the pseudonym Agapito Candileja.

Juan Pérez introduces the character genealogically: "Tartarín Moreira is an illustrious lad. His ancestry is sonorous. On the maternal side, he descends from an old family in Tarascon. A family most famous for its terrible adventures. On the paternal side he descends from the no less famous Moreira family, which included a certain very brave Juan, or so they say" (*La ciudad de los locos [Aventuras de Tartarín Moreira]: Novela Sudamericana* [Barcelona: Maucci, 1914], 11).

Juan Pérez shows the mixture, the serialization, and the mutation typical of the Moreiras and of *Caras y Caretas:* A nephew of Tartarin of Tarascón (Alphonse Daudet's literary character) came from France and "Settled as a layabout in the Argentine Republic. The first thing he did when he arrived on *porteño* soil was to tell a policeman that he was the son of the Shah of Persia." The policeman takes him to the station and from there they transfer him to the insane asylum. "In the hospital he was able to prove that he really was mad, so they released him" (12). He then went to work as a farmhand on a ranch and fell in love with the daughter of Juancito Moreira ("Gutiérrez's literary character"), and together they had a son who married the daughter of an Italian market vendor ("who claimed to be a count") and a long line of offspring.

Juan Pérez: "The mixture of these diverse races—Tartarín, Moreira, and Cocoliche—formed the original temperament of the young lawyer Tartarín Moreira. . . . Would you like to meet him? He is a gentleman of twenty-three years, very elegant and very modern. He holds a university degree. He speaks French. He's rich. He has horses, cattle, and women. He is very much a Tartarín and very much a Moreira . . . What a coincidence! Here he comes now" (12–13; ellipses in original).

On the French side (that of Daudet), Tartarín Moreira had a totally mad ancestor, according to Juan Pérez. Agapito Candileja, who signs the chronicle, presents himself as a journalist for "El eco de las Mercedes" (The Las Mercedes echo), which was the magazine of the insane asylum of that name (founded in 1906): he is a journalist of madmen or the "mad" side of the satirical *modernista* journalism of *Caras y Caretas*.[28]

Moreira is violence and madness in *Caras y Caretas,* but in "comic strip" mode. The Frenchified Tartarín Moreira represents the convergence of Alphonse Daudet's Cervantine hero of the 1860s (*Les Aventures prodigieuses de Tartarin de Tarascon* is a French satire about the invention of the *local hero*)[29] with the modern journalist of madness. Tartarín Moreira is narrated by Agapito Candileja in *Caras y Caretas:* the violence of Moreira Frenchified by Tartarín and recounted by Agapito (in comic strip mode), Candileja (in Enlightenment mode), journalist of "El eco de las Mercedes" (in the mode of madness). The Enlightenment in Charenton (in the effort that we have yet to make in order to become republicans), recounting the violence of Tartarín Moreira in 1907, in the encyclopedia of modernization.

In the four chronicles, Agapito Candileja's literary Moreira (mixed, serialized, and mutant) explores different professions, positions, madnesses, and violences. Wearing a series of "masks," as if he were a typical *comic strip character,*[30] Moreira traverses the possible positions of the Frenchified "sons of the well-to-do," and he also traverses, as a Moreira, *all violences*. And he is narrated by Agapito Candileja, who explores all the possible positions of the poor, enlightened *modernista* journalist: as journalist of madmen, as satirist, and as unpublished poet.

We turn our attention first to the pair formed by Tartarín Moreira and Agapito

Candileja. For in the same tone of satire and of the maximum visibility of violence, "in comic strip mode," "in *Caras y Caretas* mode," in 1907 and 1908, in a series,
in each of the four chronicles, both members of this pair don another mask in a
series of permutations which do not alter the two places: that of the "illustrious
lad" Moreira, and that of the journalist Agapito who is the witness and accomplice to Moreira's violence, his madness, and his politics. What matters in producing
this violence are the two new subjects (the "well-to-do son" and the "modern journalist") and the medium's new techniques of visibility. Agapito Candileja is directly
related to modern realist journalism and its technologies of truth, and also to the
serial novel's visibility of violence, to Gutierrez's narrator from 1879. But now "the
journalist" appears with a fundamental satiric twist and narrates with other more
modern technologies of the visibility of violence: those of the comic strip.[31]

The "French" Moreira is an organic product of the medium because he is a mixture, he is serial, mutant, popular, satirical, "mad," and modern like *Caras y Caretas*.
Moreira's violence is the violence of the medium, in the form itself.

But let's listen, finally, to Moreira and Agapito in *Caras y Caretas* and accompany
them as they travel to the "Morning Star" ball in the barrio and to Maxim's in Paris.
As soon as Juan Pérez introduces them, Moreira invites Agapito to a carnival dance
in the barrio: "we'll shut off the lights and make off with a few seamstresses . . . You
follow me?" (14; ellipses in original). And so Agapito recounts Tartarín Moreira's
"carnivalesque spree":

> We arrived at the premises where the "Morning Star" society was having its
> masked ball. A delightful gang awaited Tartarín at the door. Each one of those
> boys was a tiger. What wonderful fellows! They were all drunk . . . [. . .]
>
> When we went in, Tartarín, acting very mysterious, explained to us how we
> should begin the scandal. I was insanely happy. Finally I was going to get to enjoy
> an aristocratic party. Just imagine! A spree in the company of Tartarín Moreira
> and his gang! All those happily dancing seamstresses and store clerks were going
> to have to flee from our ruckus . . . So when Tartarín gave the agreed upon signal
> sometime before daybreak, I trembled with pleasure. (14–15; ellipses in original)

Tartarín Moreira is a gang member who entertains himself by provoking scan-
dals at carnival dances in the barrio in this first chronicle from 1907. And he has an
uncle who is a government minister and who gets everyone out of jail and allows
them to repeat the whole nocturnal rite.

In the third chronicle, from 1908, we follow Moreira to Paris in the company of
his gang made up of sons who export their violence to Maxim's. One of Moreira's
companions is the son of a noodle manufacturer who "eats up" the noodles, trans-

formed into pesos, in Paris, and another the son of an ex-president of a republic which Agapito does not care to remember.

There Tartarín "came up with a magnificent plan," says the ever-present Agapito (who was working in the Argentine legation in Paris), and he introduces himself as a representative of the Argentine government on a secret mission to "propagate by my mediation in these parts everything worthwhile in our character, our brain, our race . . . I shall begin tonight by showing you one of our favorite entertainments. In order for me to do so, you will need to lend me your hats" (22; ellipses in original). There ensues a "national" ruckus in which Moreira crushes the hats of all the Frenchmen present and then smoothes everything over with money.

Agapito: "Being the happy dreamer that I am, this lovely spectacle reminded me of Della Valle's painting *The Indian Raid* . . . And I laughed! What an omelet he made! And I thought that Tartarín Moreira will become either the president of the republic or an academic writer, because he deserves to" (25; ellipses in original).

The successive phases of Agapito's Moreira, his mutating positions in the first four chronicles in *Caras y Caretas* (and in the first four chapters of *La ciudad de los locos*) culminate in the last chronicle ("Aventuras morales de Tartarín Moreira") with another very specific violence in a Buenos Aires bar.

Agapito Candileja: "While we were talking, a newspaper vendor came into the café. He approached our table. He offered us newspapers . . . Since we didn't want to buy any, he asked us to please give him an olive. Tartarín got mad. He took the boy by the neck of his old shirt and he threw him hard against the door of the café. The boy's head hit the glass. The glass broke. Big crash . . . The boy collapsed, his head split open, gushing blood" (34; ellipses in original).[32]

In this last chronicle in *Caras y Caretas,* Moreira crushes the newspaper vendor, gives false names—his, "Benito Villanueva," Agapito's "José Figueroa Alcorta"— to the illiterate policeman who intervenes, and then smoothes everything over by giving some money to the café owner. At the same time, Moreira is chief of police in some province he's not familiar with, since he only collects the salary and divides the profit with his uncle the minister: his job consists of sending his uncle the signed receipts. This national institution exists in Argentina today, and such employees are called *ñoquis* (showing up only to collect their checks on the last day of the month, when restaurants serve gnocchi to their cash-strapped customers). In *Caras y Caretas* mode (with the literary violence of comic strip satire), Moreira simultaneously embodies the corrupt Creole political system and violence against newspaper hawkers. (In the second chronicle, Agapito narrates the exploits and the speeches that got Tartarín elected as a deputy from Tachuelas, an office he used to demand publicly an increase in the diet.) The French Moreira represents violence against the popular classes, violence abroad, and the violent and barbaric "South American" politics which Payró will describe in his own *Divertidas aventuras del nieto de Juan Moreira* in 1910.[33] But Soiza Reilly's Moreira operates in the modes of madness, satire, mutation, the series, and the comic strip: in the entertainment and violence of *Caras y Caretas*. In *Caras y Caretas* mode.

Moreira as a principle for the organization of tribes that define their identity and their territories through violence. In 1907 and 1908, the fictional Moreira of *Caras y Caretas* is a representative of Creole politics and also a bad boy from a good family who goes to dances in the barrio *to entertain himself and to exercise violence.* And who takes this same violence to Paris, as an "official Argentine," in an "Indian raid" on the foreigners, and who wields it in the bar against the newspaper hawker, all in the trajectory from Cosmopolis to Locopolis. He is perhaps a son of those who nationalized and legitimized Moreira's violence in 1890, in the circus, one of those who danced the tango and its violences in the brothels of Calle San Juan and then carried it to the center and to Paris, nationalized for export. Like Ricardo Güiraldes in 1910.[34]

The story of the French Moreira is told with that of the upper-class gangs (and also that of the previous upper-class gangs who went to the circus in 1890 to see the first Moreira), which is told alongside the story of tango (also told with a Moreira), its nationalization and exportation to Paris by the future author of *Don Segundo Sombra,* the gaucho who in 1926 marked a literary return to our starting point in 1879. With Güiraldes we arrive at Moreira's other: the peaceful old man. In 1910, the cycle from Cosmopolis to Locopolis signals its limit with the next one.

1914: At the Gates of Locopolis

We are now in 1914 in the novel, at the very gates of Locopolis, and in the first paragraph of the antibourgeois *modernista* manifesto which opens *La ciudad de los locos:* "Normal people will not be able to judge this novel. Imbeciles won't comprehend it. Those who only believe in the beauty of the straight line will say it was written by a madman. Those who need detailed descriptions to comprehend a character will be horrified. Those who need chronology, clarity, logic, and symmetry in order to become involved in the lives of the novelistic protagonists should lock this book away. Perhaps their children will manage to attain, through the refinement of money, the honor of understanding it" (7).

After the four chronicles and in the fifth chapter, which is titled precisely "Empieza la novela," the chronicler Agapito Candileja disappears and madness is displaced, for Tartarín Moreira finds himself in a straightjacket in the insane asylum.

So "the novel begins." I have already recounted how Moreira went mad following the experimental operation intended to transform him into a superman-genius (and how he became a victim of the violence and the scientific crime of his stepfather, the Frankenstein in charge of the asylum who injected him with the genes of a black idiot). At a later point, we'll consider how he lived in the asylum for three years as an ordinary madman while his stepfather, also mad after the "savage experiment," resided in the pavilion for "distinguished" patients; how he delivered a speech about madness from a tree before leading a massive escape and the burning of the asylum; how he founded the utopian and egalitarian city of the madmen, the city of desire; and how it was destroyed.

IV

.

the history of a best-seller:

from anarchism to peronism

.

A Literary Genealogy "in Crime" by Way of the Story of the Submission of the First Manuscript to the Master

The initiation "in crime" is a figure of Arlt's literature that leads us to a constellation and to another writer. It is the figure of entry through the other side or the "crime" of something: science, school, literature. It is the world of Arlt's first texts: the first person, poetry, age sixteen, the dream of being a genius, the struggle for life, the city, the library, the used bookstore, the theosophist, transgression, the horror of descent into hell, the engineers, and finally the verbal crime of the informer. And the "unread" writer Juan José de Soiza Reilly is always present in this world, impregnating it.[1]

Soiza Reilly surfaces in Arlt every time a first-person narrator recounts his "initiation in crime," as if to say "that's where I come from." In *Las ciencias ocultas en la ciudad de Buenos Aires,* the narrator recalls *La ciudad de los locos* (he includes the city of the madmen in the occultist city); in *El juguete rabioso* the boys from the barrio allude to Soiza's chronicles of "dark Buenos Aires" and the Apaches of Paris. Another of Arlt's "stories of criminal initiation" (at age sixteen, involving libraries and cities) was written in 1930, and in it Soiza Reilly appears in person as "the idol of young poets and reformers," *and it is he who publishes Arlt's first text* in 1916 in the *Revista Popular.* Finally the "great" Soiza Reilly appears in and with a title to grant the sixteen-year-old's dream of seeing his name in print. Arlt's recollection appears in a journalistic sketch (an *aguafuerte,* or etching) titled "Este es Soiza Reilly" (This is Soiza Reilly) and is included in Arlt's collection *Nuevas aguafuertes porteñas.* The text is dated 1930 in Rio de Janeiro (and Soiza was still alive when this was written; his death was in 1959).[2]

Let's travel, then, to Rio de Janeiro, for this history occurs "in two cities." Arlt says that when he was in Rio, someone asked him "with an ambiguous smile" what he thought of Soiza Reilly, and he answered: *"Hombre,* I'm going to write an article about what I think. Read it."

We would like to quote this chronicle *in extenso* in order to use the image of Arlt at age sixteen in the presence of "the master" Soiza: the scene of submission of the manuscript, of the library, of fascination, of trembling and doubt, of the publication of the first text bearing Arlt's name in print, along with Soiza's title.

We are tracing a literary genealogy "in crime" by way of "the story of submission of the first manuscript to the master." In this same scene Arlt recites from memory Soiza Reilly's best-seller, *El alma de los perros* (The soul of the dogs), whose history leads us from anarchism to Peronism.

The chronicle has two parts. In the first, "Año 1916 o 1917," Arlt recounts that he went to Soiza Reilly's house in the Calle Ramón Falcón, between Membrillar and "the other one," and entered his library. Arlt refers to himself as "a badly dressed boy" and says:

> The badly dressed boy goes in. He carries inside him *a tremendous excitement*. He is going to speak to the author of *El alma de los perros*, of *Figuras y hombres de Italia y Francia*. Soiza Reilly is, *at that time*, famous among *boys who write*. His chronicles of Paris (the nonexistent Paris of sixteen year olds), of Verlaine, have *sent shivers through the souls of poets in short pants and reformers of the world* who have not yet come of age. The author of these lines, which is to say, the badly dressed boy, is excited as he enters *the library and office* where the servant invites him to sit. And with good reason. "He is going to read some of his work to the great Soiza Reilly." Will the man who saw D'Annunzio listen to him? *If you could feel how fast the badly dressed boy's heart is beating* . . .
>
> He looks out the window at the street, and then at *the library, and he thinks*: "this is how to be a writer. With a room like this, books, a servant. *Will he read what I've brought? Maybe he will* . . . because you can tell by his chronicles that he's a good man . . ."
>
> The door opens and the man appears, stiff in his hairy jacket, cleaning the lenses of his black glasses with a cloth. The man *we all know from the photographs*.
>
> The excited boy stands up and says:
>
> "I want to be a writer, sir. I read everything you write. I know some of your stories by heart. For example: "And the Sheherazade of modern tales spoke. It was a skinny, a very skinny, an extremely skinny dog, the skinniest dog . . ."
>
> "*I wrote that when I was young.*"
>
> "I was hoping you'd do me the favor of reading something I've written . . ."
>
> The man made a defensive gesture.
>
> "Don't worry, it's short and typewritten."
>
> "All right . . . Leave it for me . . . *if I like it I'll publish it* in the *Revista Popular.*"
> (221–22; italics added, ellipses in original)

"The badly dressed boy who writes," who later displays such violent emotions, leaves "sure" that Soiza will like what he's written. And "One month later" ("Un mes después" is the title of the second part) he recounts how he became an author thanks to Soiza Reilly's title of honor in *Revista Popular*.

My friends ask, "Hey, didn't you see your story in *Revista Popular*? And look, there's a title above it that says: '*Modern and Ultramodern Prose.*'"

The author runs at full tilt to the newsstand and buys the magazine. Sure enough, there is his piece, a column in small and dense type, and above it *his name, his own name and surname. Is it possible? His own name! In print, and as a title of honor, "Modern and Ultramodern Prose."* But then . . . he knows how to write . . . he has talent . . . talent . . . *he's a genius! . . . His* article has been published, yet the trains run on and the people walk ever so naturally down the street . . . *while his name, his own name, is printed there in capital letters!*

And for several hours the boy is elated as *only a sixteen year old* can be. They are the most beautiful hours of his life, *the most perfect hours, filled with a deep and terrible joy. He feels as if he can touch the sky with his hand. As if he's been given the keys to paradise. Soiza Reilly likes his work!*

I believe that men and women are naturally ungrateful, joyful and ferocious creatures. . . . But I also believe that these creatures never forget those who first mark them with *a first terrible pain or joy of such intensity.* For this reason, *I have never forgotten Soiza Reilly. His was the first, generous hand which provided the most extraordinary joy of my adolescence.* (223–24; italics added, ellipses in original)

Soiza Reilly published the text of the happy, sixteen-year-old genius and added a "title of honor" to it; he included the "Modern and Ultramodern Prose" in the *Revista Popular,* and with this gesture he illustrates a specific combination which is one of the "marks" of the literary genealogy between anarchism and Peronism. But let us return to 1930 and to Rio de Janeiro in "Este es Soiza Reilly": "*The mature writer* had put 'Modern and Ultramodern Prose' as *ironic praise* for *the boy* who believed that the more 'difficult' terms one used in prose, the more artistic it was. . . . That much *I can swear to . . . I don't know if Soiza Reilly understood the article or not,* but what I do remember is that many sensible people said to me: 'But man . . . one needs a dictionary to make out what you've written. Where did you come up with those strange words?'" (224). In this chronicle, to which the library and the master's title are essential, Arlt recounts his criminal entry into literature and into the *Revista Popular,* thanks to Soiza Reilly.[3]

The figure of betrayal (the verbal crime) permits Arlt to recount his origin. "I believed, but he must have intuited that the disciple would be unfaithful to the master," says the chronicler of the initiation in *Las ciencias ocultas.* In "Este es Soiza Reilly," the betrayal of the master consists of placing Soiza Reilly in 1916 or 1917, he doesn't remember which, when Arlt was a "badly dressed boy" who wrote and Soiza was the "famous" writer with the library, and when Arlt quoted Soiza's 1909 book *El alma de los perros* to him ("And the Sheherazade of modern tales spoke. It was a skinny, a very skinny, an extremely skinny dog, the skinniest dog . . ." "*I wrote that when I was young*"). It consists of not saying what he thinks of Soiza's literature in 1930, after Arlt himself wrote *Los siete locos* (which featured an astrologer, pimps, slang, and madmen), when he is confronted in Rio de Janeiro with the "ambiguous smile" of his interlocutor.[4]

In this fluctuation between 1916 and 1930 and between Buenos Aires and Rio de Janeiro, all the figures of Arlt's "initiation in crime" occur, but we will not dwell on it, for the "history" or Arlt's relationship with Soiza Reilly does not end here. In another story of the submission of a manuscript by Arlt to another writer (which recounts another of Arlt's initiations "in verbal crime"), Soiza reappears with *the prologue* to *Diario de un morfinómano* (Diary of a morphine addict), a first "short novel" which Arlt published in Cordoba with the help of another writer "in crime," José María Vargas Vila.[5]

We can close this first story of the history of Arlt's relationship with Soiza Reilly by observing that in the world of Arlt's initiation stories, at age sixteen, in his stories of cities and libraries (in the "crime" of libraries, verbal and literary "crime"), the entire end of one century and beginning of another is present with all its anarchist and *modernista* elements: cultural journalism, the chronicle, poetry and "the reformer poets," celebrities, photographs, difficult modern and ultramodern prose, the popular, occult and theosophical sciences, the perfection of the social order, madness, simulation, fraud, hallucinations. . . . This is a new combination of "the modern" and "the popular," and Soiza Reilly is present with *La ciudad de los locos,* with *Los apaches* from the dark city, and in person with the *Revista Popular* which he edited in 1916 (and which went bankrupt two issues later). He is also present with the "modern and ultramodern prose" of Arlt's first text published in Buenos Aires and with the prologue to *Diario de un morfinómano,* published and lost in Cordoba.

"Soiza Reilly" as a position, as a space, as one of the links between the end of the century and Arlt. He condenses the period between 1907 and 1914: aesthetic anarchism, *modernismo,* the popular journalism of celebrities and the urban underworld, the fiction of criminals and madmen. He is the writer who wrote (like Vargas Vila) *a best-seller founded on hate, El alma de los perros,* which Arlt recites from memory in the 1916–1930 scene, and which is what allows us to trace an Argentine literary tradition "in crime" and *a cultural and imaginary line leading from anarchism to Peronism.*

☠

We began the genealogy with an *aguafuerte* by Arlt in which he recited the best-seller *El alma de los perros* from memory. We'll proceed with a strange editorial prologue titled "Palabras liminares . . ." (Liminal words . . .), which recounts the scene with Soiza Reilly and the manuscript of his future best-seller.

El alma de los perros was published in 1909 in Valencia with a prologue by Manuel Ugarte (which is to say that it was published in Spain by the *modernistas*). It was reissued in Buenos Aires in 1917 by the socialists of *Nosotros,* then reissued again by Peronism in 1950 (twenty-four editions between 1909 and 1950), and it was also translated into various foreign languages. This best-seller[6] traverses a space and a history, and its editions and prologues draw a virtual genealogy, not only of writers and writings (Manuel Ugarte as Soiza's prologuist in Nice; Soiza as Arlt's prologuist and titlist in Argentina), but also of cultural and literary politics in relation to "the modern" and "the popular."

The twenty-fourth and final edition of *El alma de los perros* in 1950 (*Year of General San Martín, the Liberator*) was that of E.D.E.A. in Buenos Aires (an "official" edition), and it opens with a text signed by *The Editors* and titled "Palabras liminares a la 24ª edición," which recounts the editorial history of the book beginning with "the scene of the unpublished manuscript." In this "modern" scene, cities are countries and continents, and excitement is telephonic.

> Forty-three years ago, in 1907, *a young Argentine journalist* arrived in Paris. *He traveled Europe interviewing its most famous men* for the magazine *Caras y Caretas.* He carried in *his bohemian suitcase the unpublished manuscript* of a book. He wanted *the brilliant writer* Manuel Ugarte, *currently the Argentine Ambassador in Cuba,* to contribute *a prologue* to it.
>
> "Leave me the originals," Ugarte answered him. "I'll read them tomorrow . . ."
>
> The young man left. At two o'clock in the morning, the telephone rang, waking him violently.
>
> "Who is it?"
>
> "I've just been with Manuel Ugarte. I happened to read your manuscript. Your dogs are magnificent!"
>
> "But . . ."
>
> "I want to take your book to Spain to publish it in the *Biblioteca Blanca* in Valencia. It was founded by my father-in-law, Mr. Sampere. I'm the director."
>
> "But . . . who are you?"
>
> "Vicente Blasco Ibáñez."
>
> So it was that *El alma de los perros* by Juan José de Soiza Reilly, *with a prologue by Manuel Ugarte and with the editorial support of the great Valencian novelist,* was disseminated *far from the Americas in three consecutive editions of 50,000 copies each.* (7; italics added, ellipses in original)

We should also note in this scene the "brilliant writer Manuel Ugarte" as ambassador, and the change in meaning of the word "library," which now signifies "collection." "The Editors" of the twenty-fourth edition of the best-seller continue their journey around the world:

> Three editions of 50,000 copies each travel the Americas. In 1910 the book won a gold medal in the Universal Exposition in California. In 1917 the magazine *Nosotros* published it with an evaluation by Rodó, and there followed popular editions, translations into French, Italian, Czech, Hebrew-Yiddish, Arabic, and too many pirate editions.
>
> Overcoming *resistance on the part of the author—who is currently the General Director of Public Libraries in the Province of Buenos Aires—*, we have acquired the rights to this new edition which *we faithfully reproduce from the first edition by Sampere* (Valencia, Spain, 1909), *without cuts, additions or corrections* so that "this most original jewel"—as Darío once called it—might preserve, as its author wishes, *"even the errors of youth."* (8; italics added)

From anarchism, with Darío, to Peronism: in 1907 Ugarte, a *modernista*, anti-imperialist, and expelled socialist, favors the *modernista*-anarchist[7] Soiza Reilly by facilitating the publication of his first "jewel" in the *Biblioteca Blanca*. And in 1950, when the last edition of this best-seller appears, Ugarte (ambassador in Cuba until his resignation) and Soiza (director of public libraries in the Province of Buenos Aires) are state civil servants. They meet not only in the Paris of *modernismo* in 1907 but also in the Buenos Aires of Peronism in 1950 (which is when Arlt begins to be read by the *Contorno* group).

Following the "Palabras liminares" of this last "official" edition of the best-seller, we read Ugarte's prologue dated in Nice, 1909. He says that these pages are "irreverent, crude, full of malice, of frankness, of *frondeur* spirit," and that they are different, the product of an "autonomous sensibility." He also says that *El alma de los perros* is a *cruel* volume, *at times brutal and excessive,* but particularly attractive; despite *the perversity* which is insinuated in certain episodes, this 'lean flesh' is full of *anarchic rebellion.*" Ugarte also says in 1909 that "*A vague pessimism* darkens everything" in *El alma de los perros,* which is a parade of "suffering and needy caravans," "souls downtrodden by destiny," "gloomy lives," and "social misery." And he concludes "democratically": "I have already intimated that *I do not wholly applaud the author's point of view.* . . . *But* the disagreements to which a spirit gives rise are a confirmation of its originality" (italics added).

Following Ugarte's 1909 prologue, there is a third "prologue," which is a personal letter sent by José Enrique Rodó to Soiza, dated in Montevideo, 24 March 1914. Rodó says that he liked the book, that Soiza's style is unmistakable and original, but (*everyone adds a "but"*) he states a personal wish that Soiza might complement his great merits as a writer "with a philosophy more benevolent toward things and men."

At the center of the two linked scenes "of initiation" in libraries, Arlt's and Soiza's, we find the best-seller *El alma de los perros,* with its *modernista*-anarchist aesthetic of destruction, excess, and social misery. It traverses a literary path passing through *modernismo,* anarchism, and socialism and ending in an "official" new edition by Peronism.[8]

Let's close this virtual genealogy "in crime," made up of stories of submission of the first manuscript to the master, with a chronicle by Manuel Ugarte, the prologuist of *El alma de los perros,*[9] in which he recounts how *he submitted his first book* to General Mansilla, how he contemplated *his imposing library,* and how "the diabolical monarch" *devoted a chronicle to him.*

Ugarte's *La vida inverosímil* (The implausible life) (Barcelona: Maucci, 1927) is a book of chronicles combining the modern with popular media culture. It includes chronicles about the novel, cinema, and reality, Russian revolutionaries, crime, hatred, truth, tragic mistakes, prohibition, and trips around the world. It also includes "El ombú del General Mansilla" (General Mansilla's ombu tree) (215–20), in which Ugarte says that everyone races their cars on the roads of France, interested only in speed, and that for this reason few visitors to the Côte d'Azur have noticed a majestic tree that stands on the outskirts of Nice, near the Magnan bridge. Those Argentines who approach on foot stop to marvel at it and murmur, "it's an ombu": the only one in Europe. Ugarte, who dated his prologue to Soiza's book in 1909 in Nice, says that "since it stands only a few paces from the little house where I live most of the year, I go almost every day to sit in its circle of shade, and I often wonder who brought it." A French writer (George Lafond, who lived in Argentina and published a dozen books on "our America") told him that it was General Mansilla: he spent winters on the Côte d'Azur, and one morning the mayor of the city and the Argentine consul appeared to plant "a tree from my land."

Ugarte turns to the "childish" and "ingenuous" past of Buenos Aires and to his emotions in order to measure Mansilla's time in Paris:

> *I remembered* the day I went to visit him for the first time at his house on Calle Paraguay, *taking him a childish booklet of poems* that I had ingenuously titled: "Verses," perhaps so that no one should be deceived if they were so imprudent as to cut the pages. I evoked *the cordial welcome* that he afforded me in *the imposing*

library where he reigned like a diabolical monarch, with his red suit and his pointy white beard. *I relived my reading of the benevolent commentary with which he favored me in one of his chronicles a few days later.* And I measured the time elapsed between that initial visit and *the last time I ate with him in Paris,* at his residence on Victor Hugo Avenue, a few years before his death, *when his monocle kept falling out* and he had to renounce his decorative and original look. (217; italics added)

Lafond tells Ugarte that Mansilla was "a splendid fellow," and Ugarte adds that "he was also an agreeable writer, sometimes at odds with grammar, but always endowed with that synthetic and living agility later perfected by Mariano de Vedia." Ugarte laments that Mansilla has only published the first volume of his *Memorias* and wonders what has become of the others.

The history of the ombu, of the king of the library, and of the "synthetic and living agility" can be followed indefinitely backward, with the "literary initiation in crime" recounted by Mansilla, for example, in "De cómo el hambre me hizo escritor" (How hunger made me a writer), which opens with "I got out of jail. . . ." But we'll stop here because in speaking of jail and hunger, Mansilla stated better than anyone else a certain (modern and popular) commonplace of the virtual genealogy between anarchism and Peronism. With Mansilla, then (with Rosas? with the dandy of 1880 and the best-seller "in crime" of the dandy Cambaceres?), we close this literary series of writers between America and Europe. The series opens with the "radical" dandies of the coalition and includes the journalist-poets of *modernismo,* the anarchists, socialists, and anti-imperialists of the first globalization of Latin American literature. It passes through the "madmen," the "Apaches," the "astrologers," and the "prostitutes" and closes in Peronism.

Nothing is more inconsistent with a manual than the idea of an "alternative" or *maudite* history of literature. As should now be evident, we intend only to tell a series of stories forming pairs, families and trees (the superimpositions, series, chains, and ramifications of the *corpus delicti*). They are articulated in certain common or familiar places, which are the concerns of a manual, and they traverse realities.

The characteristic of the genealogical series of the manual is that they always include missing links between two "very much read" or "classic" writers. A "missing link" connects Arlt and Mansilla (high school "classics"), in this case, the best-seller of hatred, *El alma de los perros,* which is what sustains the genealogy. Incredibly enough, the "unread" or "lost" writer unites the extremes, establishes a continuity, and "recounts a history" which is genealogical and which forms a trajectory through times and realities, becoming a network and a ramification in the notes.

The space between Arlt and Mansilla is the proliferating space of the unread, the place where multitudes of roads begin and form networks and where all the points of the stories branch out.

The genealogy we have traversed by way of the story of submission of the first manuscript to the master seems to consist of a collection of fragments of "conversational" prose linking journalism and the novelesque and the modern-ultramodern with the popular (*and including a specific type of politicization, cultural politicization*) in scenes of cities, continents, libraries, publications, and prologues. This collection of fragments illustrates a network of old avant-gardes, old best-sellers, old utopias, and "literary curiosities" which become hidden and lost in history. A virtual genealogy of what history loses: Ugarte, Soiza, Sux, Vargas Vila; second-rate writers, excessive writers, too hard in their verbal crimes: unread writers.

The genealogy of initiations which joins the very much read with the unread "in crime" is simply a specific mode of exhibiting, from within, "the method" of the manual. And also of framing, in a certain sense, *The Corpus Delicti: A Manual of Argentine Fictions.*

V

.

women who kill

.

Our subject is "crime." However, we do not use the word only in the legal sense, but rather in quotation marks, in a metaphorical sense and in all senses of the term, for our field is fiction: sexual, social, national, racial, political, and economic "crime stories," as well as those of professions, trades, and states. Crime in fiction can affect the totality of differences because it functions, in reality, as an instrument (a theoretical instrument, if you like) that serves to draw limits, to differentiate, and to exclude: *a line of demarcation that changes the symbolic status of an object,* a position or a figure. If located on one side of the limit, the figure can be sublime; if it is on the other, it falls and is degraded.[1]

☠

In the vast world of crime stories, from the end of the nineteenth century until now, a specific case appears in the relation between crime and female gender in Argentine literature.[2] It is the story of women who kill men in order to exercise a justice that is above the state, and which appears to condense all justices, and we would like to title it "Toward a Popular History of Some Female Latin American Criminals."

"Women Who Kill": it not only indicates a female action "in crime," but rather refers to a type of woman who produces in men a figurative death because she has something, she bears weapons. The metaphor is inscribed in language: a man-killer, a killer woman. Certain linguistic formations with marks of crime constitute narrations and histories, and they also constitute "reality" itself: law, medicine, daily life, eroticism. A type of female crime inscribed in language, situated in narrative, in a chain, and in a network of correlations: this is what we will attempt to trace by means of "the story."

Women who kill men appear at the end of the nineteenth century in Argentine literature, together with prostitutes and adulteresses.[3] They appear in the first year of *Caras y Caretas* and in the festive tone of the Buenos Aires of that era: in Paris and with a judge.

> *Las mujeres que matan*
> En París cierta joven a un juez

de un balazo dejóle muy mal
y como esto pasó ya una vez
de las armas de fuego al igual,
nos demuestra que existen ¡pardiez!
Señoritas de fuego central.⁴

[A certain young woman in Paris / shot a judge and left him quite ill / showing once and for all / that women, like firearms, by Jove / have a central fire.]

These killers form part of a constellation of new representations of the feminine, but they are sharply differentiated from the rest. They are the inverse or opposite face of the victims. When men kill women in these fictions, they nearly always accuse them of "female crimes" or sex-body "crimes": abortion, prostitution, adultery; they criminalize their sex before killing them. In this "story," the victims are never mothers. Women who kill men, on the other hand, are differentiated from the victims because they are mothers or virgins, and they possess a "central fire."

They occupy a specific position in language, in culture, in literature, and also in cinema, and it is thus possible to see them in person. For example, Pedro Almodóvar's film *¿Qué he hecho yo para merecer esto?* (What have I done to deserve this?) (1984) synthesizes the story rather well. Carmen Maura plays Gloria, a "decent woman" who is differentiated from the prostitute who lives in the apartment directly next door. Gloria is a mother and a married woman. The first scene of the movie, which takes place in a gym, shows her as strongly sexualized, almost as pure sex, mute and coupling with a stranger. She makes her money cleaning gyms and other people's houses. She lives with her two sons, her husband, and her mother-in-law in a small apartment on the outskirts of Madrid, and her husband is a taxi driver enamored of all things German (he has lived in Germany and he first appears in his taxi singing in German). Her husband hits her for not having ironed his shirt before he has to leave to meet his girlfriend, a German singer, at the airport (she is a nostalgic Nazi who proposes that the husband falsify Hitler's memoirs), and Gloria kills him with a ham. She kills him at the very moment in which he shows his Nazi side or his Franquist nostalgia. The police arrive immediately; Gloria confesses her crime to the "Almodóvar" detective, who doesn't believe her, and she therefore does not receive justice. *¿Qué he hecho yo para merecer esto?*: the title is Gloria's, it is what leads her to crime and to liberation from state justice. At the end, she is also freed from her mother-in-law, who returns to her homeland, to the south, but she also says farewell to one of her sons because the grandmother, played by Chus Lampreave, takes him with her.

☠

A series of stories like this occur in Argentine literature between the ends of the two centuries, between two modernizations through globalization. With them we can trace a chain, historical and changing, of women who kill.

The first is Clara, a beautiful transvestite, false medical student, single mother, and serial killer who founds the detective story in Argentina: the text (which we already mentioned in "the frontier") is *La bolsa de huesos* by Eduardo Holmberg, from 1896.[5] But we could title it "Crimes in the Medical School" because Clara attacks medical science at its root, killing medical students with an unknown Peruvian drug that produces ecstasy and death, and after killing them she removes a rib. She signs her crimes as a "woman": the rib, ecstasy, and death synthesize the justice of her sex. She seduces them and kills them with the Peruvian poison because the first victim broke his promise to marry her when she bore his child. The narrator is a man of science, a physician, and naturalist researcher who makes fun of himself as a writer, saying that he previously published "The Heavy Boot and Gaucho Chaps as Factors of Progress," as well as a dissertation on the mentality of the crab, whose final chapter is titled "The Crab in Administration and Politics." This scientist has now become a detective, he says, because he wants to write a novel and also to show the advantages of legal medicine, phrenology, and handwriting analysis in the discovery of the truth. He wants to demonstrate, in literature, that science can conquer all terrains.

He makes use of a portrait or "male" identikit, reproduced by a photographic studio, but, in following the bags of bones that the "student" leaves in his wake, he soon discovers the female signs of the murderer, the traces left by gender: perfume ("a reminiscence of perfume; something subtle, like a ghost of delight, an aristocratic perfume, more tenuous than a moonbeam" [187]); handwriting ("the end of a letter, of which only a few words remained, and among them a mine, a treasure, a revelation, a name!" [211]): again, the signature of the woman, Clara. He discovers her precisely by calling her Clara, following the last crime, in the wake of the victim whose rib she excised. Named and discovered, she surrenders. The doctor accompanies her to her house and he sees her, as if in the dressing room of a theater, when she emerges from an adjoining room or from behind a screen after removing her male clothing and letting her hair down as he ordered her to do. "I felt as if all my muscles were coming loose from their respective joints. . . . What sovereign beauty my astounded eyes beheld!" (223). He surrenders before the murderous beauty and sympathizes with "that character in Hoffman who sold his reflection on the night of Saint Sylvester" (223). And he then applies what he himself calls a "literary justice": he obliges Clara to take a double dose of the Peruvian poison. He applies a justice beyond that of the state; he orders her to kill herself in order to save herself from "the clutches of the police" (231).

The detective narrates the case while conversing with his collaborator, the phrenologist Manuel de Oliveira Cézar, who accuses him of having committed a crime in ordering the suicide, but the detective alleges that "the medical secret takes precedence over all other social laws" and that he will devote himself to recording these events in his novel (231). With this, the case of "literary justice" closes. Afterward, he medicalizes Clara's mind: he says that she was an unfortunate neurotic, a hysteric ("neuroses have no explanation, nor do they have a beginning or an end; they are like eternity and the infinite; and if you wish in any case to limit them, understand that they begin with the permutation of an indefinable complex, develop without knowledge of their origin, and end when they end, just because" [228]). Finally, he redeems her as a mother because she died, in ecstasy, while clutching in her left hand a ruby-encrusted locket that he believed contained the drug, but which later was found to conceal a photograph of her son. (Dead, she once again produced ecstasy in the police and in the multilingual press operating in Buenos Aires in that period.)

Clara, the first murderer of the detective genre in Argentina, is at once a patient of Charcot and a beautiful avenging Circe who knows medicine. She better than anyone else incarnates the modernity of the end of the nineteenth century in the "scientific literature" of the detective story: she kills men of science when she removes her male clothing, and she does not receive the justice of the state, at the very moment when the first women appear in the medical school of the Universidad de Buenos Aires, which is to say, alongside the first women physicians, who were also among the first Argentine feminists.[6] I want to mark this direct correlation between literature and "reality" in the first stories of the "Crimes of the Medical School" and in "Toward a Popular History of Some Female Latin American Criminals" (an exercise in linear history and in simple correlations). But I also want to mark the other "real" correlation of the modernity of the end of the nineteenth century, the mass which surrounds and penetrates the stories and binds their networks: the beautiful woman and science, hysteria, theater, photography, the detective genre, identifications and identities, semiology and abduction.

Two literary examples of the fecundity of hysteria, with respect to the "crimes" of literature, are found in *L'Invention de l'hystérie: Charcot et l'Iconographie photographique de la Salpêtrière*, by Georges Didi-Hubermann.[7] The first crime is in reality the continuation of the story of Clara and the physician, but in a theater in Paris, and it is found on page 272, when Didi-Hubermann considers hysterical theatricality as a practice of cruelty: *the crime of the beholder.* The hysteric, he says, loves with the image: she hopes with the image, she hates, dies, and kills by means of the image. And he refers to a play dedicated to the great psychologist Alfred Binet and performed at the Grand-Guignol in Paris in 1909 by André Lorde's *Thêatre de l'épouvante* (Theater of terror). It ends with the vengeance of the beautiful Clara: "Claire throws the powerful disfiguring vitriol in the face of her experimenter and physician," writes Didi-Hubermann.

The second literary example of the fecundity of hysteria with respect to the "crimes" of literature also occurs in Paris in 1928, and it is found on page 150. Didi-Hubermann relates that the Surrealists commemorated that year the fiftieth anniversary of hysteria, reproducing the photographed ecstasies of Augustine, *her clichés of ecstasy,* he says, and he quotes Aragon and Breton: "We Surrealists celebrate here the fiftieth anniversary of hysteria, the greatest poetic discovery of the end of the nineteenth century."

Buenos Aires in 1996 celebrated the centenary of Clara, the greatest poetic discovery of the end of the nineteenth century in Argentina.

The plural correlations (or networks) among hysteria, science, theater, and female crime, which conclude with the story of Clara in the Theater of Terror in Paris, form links that connect the stories, for they appear clearly in the second woman who kills, in Roberto Arlt's play *Saverio the Cruel,* from 1936.[8] Susana is a rich young woman who dresses up as a mad queen and conspires with a group of friends in order to mock a young butter salesman named Saverio, who visits her house. The farce is to be played out during "a costume party at the estate." And from the beginning Susana says: "This year no one on the estate will say they're bored. The party has all the proportions of a spectacle" (291).

At the party, during the last act, one character says: "I have the pleasure of introducing you to the inventor of the tragedy and of the most enormous put-on ever seen in Buenos Aires. We *porteños* have specialized in what we technically call a *cachada,* a joke. The *cachada* involves a mischievous concept of life. If my memory serves, the dead writer José Ingenieros organized, along with other like-minded creatures, a *cachada* club, but they all pale in comparison with this, whose author is an impeccable young lady upon whom we all look with passionate eyes" (322).

Ingenieros's *cachada* club was called La Syringa and was exclusively male.[9] Susana's madness deceives Saverio, who is described as physically "defeated" and wearing the "expression of a dog seeking sympathy" (294). Susana fancies herself a queen and expresses a desire to take revenge on the colonel who dethroned her by beheading him. When Saverio sees her for the first time, Susana is in the background with her hair down and dressed as a man. One of the friends, pretending to be a doctor, convinces Saverio to play the colonel who dethroned her in order to help them cure her of her delirium. Saverio declares himself an antimilitarist but finally accepts the role of "comedy colonel," thus falling into the beautiful woman's trap.

In Arlt's theater we find not only the correlation among hysteria, science, theater, and female crime, but also "the dead writer José Ingenieros" and the performance within a performance, cinema and psychoanalysis: the children of the estate owners in the 1930s apply to La Syringa (to the "mischievous" and modernist side of the scientific culture of the end of the nineteenth century in Argentina) the theory of repetition of the traumatic event, which is the mode in which Alfred Hitchcock's cinema will represent psychoanalysis and cure in 1945 in *Spellbound*.

Back in his "modest rooming house quarters," Saverio, "dressed in a uniform like a fantastic colonel from some Central American banana republic" (307), assumes the role of colonel and military dictator and imagines dominating the world: he is Mussolini in front of the mirror, he is the Latin American dictator, he is Saverio the Cruel. He buys a guillotine and says that he does not believe in the fiction of parliamentary democracy, that to govern is to chop heads, that he needs antiaircraft guns. He consults an English arms merchant who represents Armstrong Nobel Dynamite and who recommends Violet Cross Gas. In his rooming house, his simulation is perfect, and when Susana's friends witness it in her absence, they tell him that he resembles Maurice Chevalier in *Hollywood on Parade* (1934). Behind his back, they say he's crazy.

One of Arlt's characteristic modes of representation consists of reversing the logic of the representation at each step of the narrative, so that the sequence becomes a series of twists. In the second act Saverio is the mad one, the actor, and the cruel colonel, just as Susana was a madwoman, an actress, and a dethroned queen in the first. In the third act, in the middle of the party and in a deep red room with a throne, Susana acts like a dethroned queen. But Saverio, dressed up as a colonel, reverses the logic again by telling Susana that he already knows it's a joke. The farce ends and the guests, "dressed up in eighteenth-century costume," retire. Saverio rebukes her for ferociously mocking a poor wretch like himself, and then Queen Susana reverses the logic once again: it is he who dresses up or simulates, not she. And she tells Saverio: I love you, it's no use dressing up as a poor butter salesman, you are the colonel who dethroned me. And she kills him with a revolver. Saverio's last words: it was no joke, she really was mad.[10]

Everything depends on how many turns or twists are given to the "performance" or simulation, always present in Arlt as a multifaceted phenomenon or a double-edged weapon. It either decides a certain meaning or it does not, when read as a machine of exclusions. The wealthy, mad, and simulating young woman kills the poor butter salesman on the estate: here La Syringa functions as a mechanism of social exclusions imposed from above and as a typical social crime of the 1930s. But if the butter salesman is what he simulates in his "madness," if he is Saverio the Cruel (and if Susana is the queen), the representation is reversed, for Susan kills the Latin American fascist dictator of the thirties. She executes another type of exclusion, a political one. And the estate, or the upper class, can thus cease to be the monster and join the antifascist front with progressive groups, as will soon occur in the reality of the 1940s, with the first Peronism. In Arlt, the social problem, the political problem, and the gender problem can be subjected to a double reading (and to an anticipatory function), for with the twists of the woman who kills in the theater of the theater, he touches the limits of representation.

Clara is a hysteric and also a physician; Susana is madness and also the great cinematic actress of the 1930s: her identification with the role is so extreme that she questions, at *the very moment of the performance,* the possibility of representation, and, as a queen, she kills the disguised colonel, Saverio the Cruel, the Latin American military officer who buys arms from England. She will be saved from justice because she can incarnate so well "the simulation of madness in criminals," as Ingenieros himself feared.[11]

We will not pause here to elaborate on the correlation between movie actresses and military officers in the 1930s in Latin America. In 1935 a young woman from the town of Junín arrived in Buenos Aires in search of fame and fortune in movies and in radio: Evita. Let us just say that Evita, who played mad queens and famous women on the radio, shares a moment with Arlt.[12]

Following the limits of representation, let us then move from the estate to the factory and to the third story. As is well known, Borges's Emma Zunz seeks to avenge her father, Emanuel Zunz, "erroneously" accused of embezzlement. She must kill the man responsible, the owner of the factory where she works and where her father was employed as a teller. Emma is an eighteen-year-old virgin who, one Saturday during a strike, visits the owner of the textile factory, a Jew, with the pretext of denouncing her fellow workers, and kills him. This takes place during the 1920s, but the story is written in the 1940s, and it also refers to Emma's present. Between the two times, and in Borges's allegory, Emma is the avenging Virgin, sent by God, and also the factory worker who rises up against the owner during the strike, and also the woman who kills a Jew working on Saturday, or who simply kills a Jew. The woman who kills represents all "justices": that of God, that of the father, class justice, racial justice, and sexual justice. And she finally mocks state justice when she calls the police, confesses her crime, and accuses the owner of having raped her, when hours earlier she dressed as a prostitute and went to bed with a sailor who spoke another language. Before justice, she stages a farce of the truth; she uses the law and the stereotype of the ill-treated virgin (she uses the stereotype of the law) in order to evade the justice of the state and to exercise all justices, allegorically. The story is told by a chronicler, but Borges, in the afterword to *El Aleph*, says that another woman, Cecilia Ingenieros, provided him with the plot. Cecilia was a modern dancer and the daughter of the criminologist-writer José Ingenieros, he of Arlt's La Syringa, the exclusionary joke club. Father and daughter link Borges with Arlt in the chain of modern women who kill.[13] Emma is the textile worker who kills the owner during the strike, and the correlation is almost obvious.[14] (The stories are joined by links: a cultural mass of multiple correlations made up of political, technological, and cultural processes, of names and images.) The stories or dramas of Borges and Arlt are linked by the presence of Ingenieros and cinema; those of Borges, Arlt, and Puig by the cinema of Torre Nilsson and by Peronism. The cinematic adaptations of women who kill in the final stages of both Peronisms, the woman worker and the servant from the provinces, are significant: Leopoldo Torre Nilsson filmed "Emma Zunz" in 1953 with the title *Días de odio* (Days of hatred), and *Boquitas pintadas* (Painted mouths) in 1974. With respect to the specific genre that links them, Arlt, Borges, Puig, and Torre Nilsson (and of course Beatriz Guido, who moves between them) show in these stories the way in which, in each instance, they allude to social realism even as they elude it, devising other twists and versions of the women who kill (just as Almodóvar showed in *¿Qué he hecho yo para merecer esto?* the way in which he alluded to Italian neorealism while eluding it).

The women who kill seem polarized, symbolically and socially, into "the most" and "the least": an incomparable beauty who disguises herself as a university student, the daughter of estate owners who disguises herself as a mad queen, and a factory worker who disguises herself as a prostitute and an informer. This type of polarization is also clearly seen in Manuel Puig's *Boquitas pintadas* (1969), retitled *Heartbreak Tango* in Suzanne Jill Levine's English translation.[15]

Raba, a domestic servant from the provinces (who previously worked in a factory in the capital) kills a policeman who is the father of her son and who would not marry her, but who then became involved with her *patrona*, the young Mabel Sáenz. She kills him with a kitchen knife; she applies the justice of the tango and of the radio and cinematic serial. The story is set in the 1930s in a small town, but the story continues into the present. The young *patrona,* who fears that her relationship with the policeman will be discovered, helps Raba to escape justice by fabricating the story that he was drunk and attempted to rape her at gunpoint. Raba not only evades state justice, like the others, but also is rewarded at the end of the novel: she lives with a peasant widower and she is pregnant, surrounded by children, abundance, and nature. Final justice is also applied to the no-longer-young Mabel, who is left poor and with a polio-afflicted grandson. The story is told by chroniclers and by medical and police documents such as, for instance, the following extract from a "Preliminary Record" of the police department of the Province of Buenos Aires:

> Antonio Josefa Ramírez, twenty-four years of age, confessed to having slain Police Officer Francisco Catalino Páez with a kitchen knife. The confession was interrupted several times by crises of tears and from time to time Miss Sáenz had to hold the accused down in her repeated attempts to knock her head against the wall. Miss Sáenz, to whom the accused had already related the events as soon as she woke up, helped her to fill in the gaps constantly evinced by her memory. The deeds had been precipitated in the small hours of the sixteenth day when the accused saw the decedent enter her room, wearing his officer's uniform. The latter threatened her with his revolver and told her to yield to his wishes right there, despite the proximity of her employers. The accused, bearing much resentment for having been abandoned with an illegitimate son after having been seduced on the basis of empty promises, resisted and alleged to be afraid of waking up her employers, and as Miss Sáenz opportunely vouched, it was Mrs. Sáenz's custom to get up in the middle of the night with acid indigestion and go into the kitchen. (161)

In Puig's "serial novel," women represent social classes and men the connections or relations between classes. The alliance between the domestic servant and her *patrona* in order to evade justice (a female alliance insinuated in the epilogue to "Emma Zunz") follows the logic of the social polarization of the women who kill: they belong neither to the middle class nor to a middle ground.

Raba, written in serial novel style at the end of the 1970s, kills a policeman, like so many female urban guerrillas in that period: she kills a representative of the state.[16] César Aira's *La prueba* (The proof), from 1992,[17] a novella that could be called "Women Who Kill in the Supermarket," features two punk girls who give their names as Mao and Lenin and who present themselves as lesbians. They attempt to seduce another girl, a depressed virgin named Marcia, who encounters them on her way home from school. It is the story of the most recent globalization: among their strategies of seduction, the girls speak of certain television programs, rock music, parties in discotheques with celebrities. The conversation takes place in an Argentine version of McDonald's called Pumper Nic, where the punks brutally insult the female employees. Finally, the punks decide to give Marcia definitive proof of their love, and they head for a supermarket. Mao and Lenin introduce themselves as "Commandos of Love": they empty the registers, burn the supermarket, and kill employees and shoppers, men and women alike, with extreme violence: that of the 1990s.

Lenin: "A man in a white apron was coming out from behind the electronic scale, as if he had taken charge of the situation and decided to put an end to it. Lenin didn't waste any saliva on him. She showed him the point of the knife, and as the man was raising his hands as if to snatch it away or to hit her, she slashed his face with lightening speed. The blade went in point first, opening a horizontal cut reaching down to the bone, to the gum, above the upper lip, from the left cheek to the right" (69–70).

"Listen up, everyone," said Mao over the speakers. She was talking slowly, fully in command of the echoes. She had lent her voice a neutral and informative timbre which was pure hysteria. So intense and so pure that the growing hysteria of the male and female shoppers seemed a homey nervousness in comparison. It made them understand that in order to reach hysteria one needed more than an accumulation or increase in nervousness or fear. This was something else. It was something that, by definition, does not increase, a maximum that has been achieved outside of life, in madness or in fiction. Everything fell silent as the last cash registers stopped working. "This supermarket has been taken over by the Commandos of Love. If you cooperate, there won't be many casualties. There will be some, because Love is demanding. The quantity depends on you. We are going to take all the money in the registers and leave. In fifteen minutes the survivors will be home watching television. That's it. Remember that everything that happens here will be *for the sake of love.*"

How literary it all was! There occurred one of those hesitations that happen at the expense of the real quality of reality. A man in one of the lines let out a resounding guffaw. Immediately a shot rang out, but it made a hole not in the forehead of the man who was laughing, but rather in the leg of a short lady two places in front of him in line. Her leg started spouting blood and the lady fainted dramatically. There was a swirl of movement and shouting. Mao swung the recently discharged revolver a bit and returned the microphone to her mouth. The man, white and stunned, stopped laughing. The shot was meant for him. It was as if he was dead, because in the fiction corresponding to his previous incredulity, the hole really was in his forehead. . . . How much time had passed? Five minutes in all, since they burst into the supermarket? And how many things had happened! Everyone was waiting for the police, for the firemen, but they knew they were awaiting an atavism, because there was nothing to wait for. What everyone felt was the opposite of the imminent arrival of help: they were caught in a centrifugal flight, the Big Bang, the birth of the universe. It was as if everything known was escaping them at light speed to found new civilizations based on other premises somewhere out there in the blackness of the universe. (74–75, 86–87)

The story is narrated from outside and from Marcia's perspective (although without conceding her the "I"), and it narrates a transformation in the perception of the world, a "revolution," because it shows Marcia's conversion after contemplating the "real" violence of the supermarket, *which is intended only for her*. Marcia is the sole recipient of the live spectacle: of the "proof." In the closure of the text we read: three shadows exited "and were lost in the streets of Flores."

La prueba is a text about female revolution and about the revolution of the spectacle and the image, and also about the violence of consumption and the modernization of the 1990s in Argentina. Mao and Lenin, previously guerrillas, now punk lesbians, attack (like Clara, the first) a certain Latin American modernization at its root.

Facets of the Chain

From crimes in the medical school to crimes in the supermarket: between two modernizing leaps, the chain of stories of women who kill seems to have different facets and twists (different types of correlations) which put it in contact with a certain exterior, a certain "reality."

The first of these facets is that of fiction. The chain of fictions (women who kill in chains) seems to enter into almost direct correlation (as has been seen in the notes, with some "real" and numerical facts) with situations of the rupture of domestic power, with certain female irruptions in Argentine culture: the first female university students, the first female factory workers, actresses, guerrillas, and other pioneers.

Toward a popular history of certain criminals: the stories of women who kill say something that is not said elsewhere in Argentine literature; they tell the history of a certain female culture in Argentina. One which does not pass through female writers but rather through other networks, and which recounts the violent irruptions that were foundational not only in politics and in culture, but also in the play of literary, theatrical, and cinematic genres. They also founded female subjectivities. The chain tells this history with a twist, telling it always in the mode of female crime fiction.

Or perhaps: it tells that there is, each time, a new class of women *because* it represents them "in crime." Like the picaresque, as if it were a Kafka text, the chain of women who kill tells that each time a different subject-position makes its way in the interstices of the others (in the linguistic, social, national, sexual, and racial interstices), it is represented literarily in the fiction of crime or before the law. This making way through differences is the crime: an instrument that draws a line of demarcation and transforms the symbolic status of the figure (the pioneer becomes a criminal and is degraded), and also an instrument for the founding of cultures.

The first facet of the literary chain turns this new female reality over and tells it "in crime fiction."

☠

But this twisting of fiction is followed immediately by another, a legal and internal one because, in the chain, female crime does not receive state justice. And this second twist of the chain, that of justice, puts it in contact with other "realities." The female killers do not receive justice for medical reasons, or because no one even suspects them since they are mothers or virgins, or because they perform a farce of truth before justice. Or because they rely on the herbs of exaltation and death, or because they are representatives of God and of the father, or because they are the allegory of justice. Of all justices: private, sexual, paternal, and also social, economic, and political.[18]

Crime is an instrument of differentiation which functions in a precise way because one of the meanings of the exemption of the killers from state justice is seen only when the chain is read (or written) from the female part, which is what constitutes it: from the women who kill in the first person. But in the "Argentine stories" the woman who kills speaks through others because they are narrated in the third person (while the male criminal assumes the first person at the beginning of the twentieth century); what is lacking is the female killer's own story. What is needed is a twist of sexual (or pronominal or narrative) gender, which could also be a national twist, in order to be able to read one of the meanings of this exemption from state justice, which is reiterated in all phases of the chain. To put it another way: it is necessary to include a non-national, Latin American link in the Argentine chain in order to be able to hear the whole story told from the perspective of the woman who kills and thus to see the meaning of justice.

I find this first person in Mexico, in Ángeles Mastretta's 1986 novel *Arráncame la vida* (available in English as *Tear This Heart Out*).[19] Catalina tells how in the 1920s she killed one of the local political officials of the Mexican revolution (a former soldier and governor) who was also her husband and the father of her children. He had ordered the killing of her musician lover. Catalina uses Clara's drug, the poison of exaltation and death, and she gives him a euphoria-inducing but ultimately lethal tea. But she does not act alone; the tea is given to her by a peasant woman whose husband was killed by Catalina's. The two allies, from above and below, perform political and sexual justice at the same time: ecstasy and death for the double murderer of peasants and artists. Of course, the poison is an unknown drug, no one suspects anything, and there is no state justice. And so Catalina concludes in the first person: "There were so many things I wouldn't have to do now. I was alone, with no one to give me orders. So many opportunities, I thought, and there beneath the rain I burst out laughing. Sitting on the ground, playing with the wet earth that ringed Andrés's grave. Enjoying my future. Almost happy" (293).

This external incorporation into the Argentine chain is crucial because it defines its meaning from another place. The stories of women who kill, in chains, constitute at every moment a situation "in crime" of an empowered female representation which escapes state justice. But depending on how it is read, or how it is told, from what "I" (from the perspective of the victim, the chronicler, or the murderer) or according to the perspective from which the chain is observed, the meaning of the exemption from state justice varies, for in the stories of women who kill, gender decides the meaning of the representation. From the perspective of the detective-physician, the medical students, and the poor butter salesman, the killer becomes a neurotic and mad woman, and she receives a medical and social condemnation, but not a legal one: this is the case with Holmberg and, perhaps, with Arlt. If told from the female voice, or from another genre/gender, also literary, or from another national literature, the woman who kills eludes state justice because she performs political and sexual justice, killing a "criminal" and receiving a liberating prize: she wins a future (Mastretta, Puig, Almodóvar, and also, perhaps, Borges and Aira).

Crime (and the cultural artifact of crime and punishment) serves to demarcate areas and also serves as an instrument of differentiation: crime exempted from state justice because of "sickness" (mental or social disturbance), or for the sake of representing another "legitimate" justice. The chain of women who kill poses a crucial problem of meaning, which depends precisely on its gender character.[20]

Let us reconsider the correlation of the chain with a certain reality, from the perspective of gender. The women who kill in the stories are made of "female signs":

they all kill out of passion, love, jealousy, or vengeance, and their crimes are domestic; they kill former lovers or husbands who have not kept their word or who
lie. This is one of the stories of the chain: private crimes, of unchained female passion. And this side of the chain connects directly with a certain "reality," because
domestic crime is dominant among women who kill, according to English-language studies and statistics.[21]

Literature and reality connect through the female signs of the women who
kill. But the reality of literature says more than a certain reality which functions
as its direct correlate, because the women who kill in the linked stories not only act
out the unchained female passion of the reality of domestic crime, but also seem
to condense all female crimes in the field of the symbolic (different from the sex-
body "crimes" of the women victims). They are "criminals" of truth and of legitimacy, the values of the state: they have illegitimate children, illegitimate lovers,
and they situate themselves in the semantic field of duplicity, transvestitism, falsification, and simulation: the false medical student, the false queen, the false prostitute, the false rape victim, the false informer, the false revolutionaries Mao and
Lenin. And with these "female crimes," they evade state justice. The women who
kill in the stories act out "female signs" (those of hysteria: domestic passion and
simulation), and at the same time they apply a twist by using the "female signs" of
justice, like that of the "decent woman," in order to evade it and to postulate themselves as agents of a justice that is beyond that of the state, and which therefore
condenses all justices.[22]

The two final twists of the chain, the pronominal twist of gender, and that of
the symbolic crimes of gender, give meaning to the justice of the women who kill.

☠

But the women who kill are not alone but rather with their victims, who occupy the
political side of the chain and define its correlation with a certain reality. They are
a series of men, also linked, who represent a type of force that was crucial, and
not just in the history of women. The victims are:

- in 1896, the future *physicians* who invented hysteria and the modern science of
  the mind with their photos and classifications; in the detective novella, Clara
  eradicates the scientific power which accompanies the liberal state;
- in 1936, the man who, in the theater of his mirror, plays the *Latin American dictator* aspiring to dominate the world;
- in the other "realist and social" story of the 1940s, *the owner of a factory* on strike
  in the 1920s;

- in the "serial novel" of the 1960s, *the policeman* of the 1930s;
- in the new historical novel of the 1980s, the corrupt PRI *politician* of the 1920s;
- in Almodóvar's cinema of the 1980s *movida*, Gloria kills the Nazi-Franquist *taxi driver;*
- in the short and violent novel of the 1990s, Mao and Lenin kill the supermarket *consumers,* men and women.

The side of the victims is the political side of the chain (that of the correlation and of the political twist)[23] because while the women are polarized socially between the "greater" and the "lesser" (and this appears to be one of the logics of the genre), their men may be said to occupy a set place in the correlation with a certain "reality": in one of the crucial forces (scientific, military, political, economic, police) sustaining the state at each moment. Or sustaining its "modernization." But sustaining it from below, from its very foundations, for the poorest representative of these forces is the victim. The women who kill cut the roots of power or they cut off power at its root, at each moment: science and the university, commerce, the factory, the police, local politics, taxis, and supermarkets. They, the modern women, eliminate one of the powers sustaining "modernization" at these specific junctures.

"Women Who Kill" and "Toward a Popular History of Some Female Latin American Criminals." The key and violent elements of this linguistic, cultural, and literary figure (the elimination of power at its root and the marking of an advancement in female independence) make it especially apt for criminalization, for foundations, and at the same time for allegories of justice. The literary chain, through the correlations it draws (through its fictional, its gender, and its political facets), touches reality constantly, and it touches different layers of reality: it *is* a certain reality, represented and read in the mode of "female crime."[24]

Finally, the chain has a *purely literary side,* that of literary genre. This is fundamental because here the female irruptions, their criminalization and exemption from state justice, coincide with certain literary modernizations that are also crucial. The stories that form the chain define themselves each time in relation to a certain type of naturalism and social realism; they define themselves as its opposite side, more modern and with a more twisted and perverse politicization. The new (scientific) detective novel of the late nineteenth century, the new (cinematic) theater of the 1930s, the other "realist and social" story of the 1940s, the other "serial novel" of the 1960s, the "new historical novel" of the 1980s, and the other violent

novella of the 1990s. This more modern and perverse realism of the chain differentiates itself from social realism *because what matters in the stories of women who
kill is not the reproduction of reality but the reproduction of the image*. For this reason,
the chain of women who kill could also tell a literary history of the reproduction
of the image and the spectacle of passion in Argentina. Of the modern genres of
that image: from Clara's photograph, through Susana's theater and the cinema of
Emma and Raba, to the television of Mao, Lenin, and Marcia.

From crime, from the other side of the frontier, the linked stories of women
who kill open a world of correlations that not only end on a certain side of reality.
Sexual genders, literary genres, and genders of the image and spectacle of passion
could serve historically in similar ways, and they could coincide in their twists,
provided that female representation be placed "in crime."

VI

·

stories of truth and

stories of jews

·

Stories of Truth

We are now entering the world of crimes of truth. A sign on the door reads: "In this sector of the corpus, stories relate in pairs or couples: pairs of stories, pairs of crimes, or couples of criminals."

At the door our guides await us, and we recognize them as a pair of criminals from two Argentine classics of the twentieth century: Emma Zunz (from Borges's 1948 story "Emma Zunz"), who disguises herself as a prostitute in order to avenge her father, and Gregorio Barsut (from Arlt's *Los locos* and *Los monstruos*, 1929–1931),[1] who says things like the following to the pharmacist Ergueta in the chapter of *Los monstruos* titled "Un alma al desnudo" (A soul bared): "I consider myself extraordinarily beautiful. [. . .] Photogenic at the very least. [. . .] Moreover, this conviction has modified my life profoundly. I know I can talk to you because they think you're crazy . . . [. . .] It has modified my life profoundly because it has led me to behave like a comedian in front of others. Many times I've pretended to be drunk in front of my friends when I wasn't; I exaggerated the effects of the wine in order to observe the effects of my supposed inebriation on them. Don't you think I could be a movie actor?" (490).

In this world of pairs, Barsut is the ideal companion for Emma, who kept a photo of Milton Sills (a U.S. movie actor of the twenties) in the same box where she hid the deceitful letter that announced the death of her father and that opens the story on 14 January 1922 (a letter from Fein or Fain, in which the only thing clear was the date, the place, and the false name of Emanuel Zunz). In the world of the crimes of truth, the photo of Milton Sills is Gregorio Barsut.[2]

The fatal Borges-Arlt pair ("A cinematic weekend romance between contemporaries") is united by the common crime of truth perpetrated against the state and by a series of strange coincidences, those that open the door of this new world. Our guides—a woman and an "actor"—introduce us into the semantic field of duplicity, transvestitism, and simulation, which is one of the fields of the crimes of truth. And which is, in literature, the place of the seconds, the illegitimate, the resisters, the women, and also of the "actors." Emma: the young woman who acts like a prostitute and keeps the photo of Milton Sills; Gregorio: the "artist" who wants to go to Hollywood in order to return to Buenos Aires: "People will point at me, saying: 'That's Barsut, the artist Barsut; he's just back from Hollywood, he's Greta Garbo's lover!'" (493).

The "Story" of the Truth

In the stories of our guides, language is acting: performance, representation, simulation, and falsification.

Emma and Gregorio tell us that they are united by cinema and by the twenties, the U.S. cinema of the twenties (and that they are later united by the cinema of Torre Nilsson),[3] but in truth the most striking coincidence is one they do not tell: both kill a "Jew" and later evade justice with their "stories."

One apocalyptic Friday in late 1929, Barsut (who lives off an inheritance) kills the Jew Bromberg (a "slave" of the Astrologer who attempted to decipher the Apocalypse) in alliance with the Astrologer himself, who gives him the revolver and returns the money of which they had robbed him; this murder is told by an omniscient narrator without an "I." Barsut is arrested in a cabaret for paying with the Astrologer's money (which turns out to be counterfeit money printed by the anarchists), and he evades justice by accusing the whole gang, committing a crime of truth that convinces everyone.

This last part is told, and *believed*, by "the chronicler of this story," who exercises the "I" in the chapter titled "El homicidio" (The homicide):

> Barsut had been arrested in a cabaret on Calle Corrientes for attempting to pay his check with a false fifty peso note. Simultaneous with Barsut's arrest was the discovery of Bromberg's charred corpse among the ruins of the Temperley estate. Barsut immediately accused the Astrologer, Hipólita, Erdosain and Ergueta. . . . The discovery of La Bizca's corpse at dawn on Saturday transformed the events we narrate into the bloodiest panorama of late 1929. . . . There remained no doubt that the police were dealing with a perfectly organized gang, one with untold ramifications. . . . Barsut's declarations filled wholes series of columns. There was no doubt as to his innocence. (517–18)

And on 16 January 1922, a Saturday or a Sunday (depending on how the days are counted), the factory worker Emma Zunz (eighteen years old, a virgin) calls Aaron Loewenthal, one of the owners of the Tarbuch & Loewenthal textile factory (a "greedy Jew" whose only passion is money), arranging to meet him that night, with the pretext of the strike; she goes down to the port and goes to bed with a sailor who speaks another language; in the factory, she kills the Jew with "obscene lips" (in both languages, Yiddish and Spanish)⁴ in order to avenge her father, his name, and his honor; she picks up the telephone and evades justice by accusing Loewenthal and perpetrating a crime of truth that convinces everyone: *"Something has happened, something unbelievable. . . . Sr. Loewenthal sent for me on the pretext of the strike. . . . He raped me. . . I killed him . . ."* (219; ellipses in original).

The crime of truth committed by Emma and Barsut, and which convinces everyone, consists of a statement identical to a true and legitimate one, but situated in another place and time and with names other than the legitimate ones. Borges's chronicler defines it as follows at the conclusion of the story. "The story was unbelievable, yes—and it convinced everyone, because in substance it was true. Emma Zunz's tone of voice was real, her shame was real, her hatred was real. The outrage that had been done to her was real, as well; all that was false were the circumstances, the time, and one or two proper names" (219).

The presence of a narrator-chronicler with his temporal and spatial perspective is necessary in order to show the crime of truth as a "believed fiction" (and as beyond the true/false division). Because the "stories" of Zunz and Barsut pose a problem of sequence: they found a before and after in time and space (Emma: he raped me, I killed him). The duplicity constitutes them, because they join two fields of representation (two different orders) in one (and they can thus be read as allegories). The chronicler shows how the two times, spaces, names, and circumstances that are fused into one in the story belong to different orders. Zunz and Barsut, with their stories, reveal the strange coincidence between the crimes of truth and the discourses of truth: the discourses that are believed. For their chroniclers, who say what our guides do not tell us, show that the chronicle is the discourse of truth of a culture founded on a belief in the truth of confession.

The Story of "Fiction"

What Emma and Barsut say in order to evade justice after murdering the "Jew" (verbal simulations, verbal duplicities, verbal falsifications that convince everyone), that verbal decomposition of the truth that closes their stories, is "the fiction" of Borges and Arlt. A story and a crime of truth that imply an ambivalent use of language, where the same goes for two (I came/he made me come on the pretext of the strike). Emma and Barsut do not lie; they place what is true and legitimate in another place and time and with names other than the legitimate ones ("all that was false were the circumstances, the time, and one or two proper names"). They place simulation (and they also place crime) in the field of language, and that is the literary "fiction" of the twenties and forties in Argentina. A fiction that places two simulators, a woman and an "actor," in verbal contact with an institution of truth-justice-legitimacy (not only the state but also, in Arlt's case, "the chronicler of this story") that is believed and that also believes the story. Emma and Barsut are believed, moreover, because in both cases they provide visible proof in order to be believed: a female *body* (Emma's "raped" body and La Bizca's corpse) and a charred Jewish *body*. Which is the *corpus delicti*.

The literary fiction of Arlt-Borges, a fiction that was taken as *the* fiction, rests on that decomposition of "legitimate" truth (on that "falsification").

The Politics of the Story

The stories of Emma and Barsut are performative statements, accusations addressed to the state in order to evade justice, in order to deceive and to convince: they stage a politics of beliefs. Emma and Barsut's crimes of truth cannot be separated from their political textuality because they suppose some type of state or institutional representation (a legitimate institution inspiring belief) that they address in order to be believed. Inasmuch as the reason of state is the rationality linked with "truth," Emma and Barsut's statements would not only be crimes of truth but also crimes of justice and crimes against the state. *Which is to say, political acts.*

But their politics is (like their justice) enigmatic, because it is founded on beliefs. Their politics is to show that the reason of state rests wholly on the apparatus of beliefs and archaic remainders (*which are written on bodies, with blood, and in legitimate names*). The stories of Emma and Gregorio following the murder of Jews are critical instruments that place the truth "in crime" and generate enigmas in relation to the truth of justice.

The Enigmas of the Story

Emma Zunz and Gregorio Barsut both kill a "Jew" in the Argentina of the twenties and forties[5] (a character who was constructed as a "Jew" in the narration through his passion for money or passion for writing), and they both evade justice, convincing everyone and remaining free to serve as our guides in this world. They also kill, in both cases, a "criminal Jew." They kill Loewenthal and Bromberg, who are alternately, never coincidentally, represented by different voices as "Jews" (money and writing) or as criminals (thief or murderer). The Jew is narrated by different voices or narrators in order to divide him between "Jew" and "criminal."

Let's look at the construction of the Jew in Borges on the part of the chronicler or narrator of Emma Zunz.

> Aaron Loewenthal was in the eyes of all an upright man; in those of his few closest acquaintances, a miser. He lived above the mill, alone. Living in the run-down slum, he feared thieves; in the courtyard of the mill there was a big dog, and in his desk drawer, as everyone knew, a revolver. The year before, he had decorously grieved the unexpected death of his wife—a Gauss! Who'd brought him an excellent dowry!—but money was his true passion. With secret shame, he knew he was not as good at earning it as at holding on to it. He was quite religious; he believed he had a secret pact with the Lord—in return for prayers and devotions, he was exempted from doing good works. Bald, heavyset, dressed in mourning, with his dark-lensed pince-nez and blond beard, he was standing next to the window, awaiting the confidential report of the operator Zunz. (218)

This description by the narrator contains one of the fundamental statements of anti-Semitism: the avarice of the Jew and his fraudulent secret pact with God, and it occurs as Emma travels toward the factory to kill him, in 1922.

But in another part of the text (in another previous time, in 1916), Emma Zunz's father swears that Loewenthal, rather than he, is the "real" thief; he swears it to his daughter the last night they see each other, before he changes his name to Manuel Maier and goes into exile in Brazil. (She is the only one who knows his secret name and the name of the real criminal. Or the secret name of the criminal.) And if the last oral, personal message of Emanuel Zunz in 1916, when he swore to his daughter (and in what language?) that the true thief was Loewenthal, was also a deceit in order to save his name before her? Was that why he changed his name? Another farce—crime—of truth? Emma believed him, but the suspicion that her crime is totally gratuitous taints the text. Emma's crime of truth is also based on that secret pact of legitimacy (her name is entirely contained in that of her father, Emanuel Zunz), which elicits belief.

Another enigma: was Emma Jewish, or rather, was her dead mother Jewish?[6] Was the murder she committed like that of Rabin in 1995: a "pure" Jew killing the "real criminal" at sunset on Saturday? Or was the textile worker not Jewish, allowing us to read the text, set in the twenties, as the Borgesian metaphor for the Hitlerism and Peronism of the forties? Emma Zunz as another "Fiesta del monstruo" to pair off with *Los monstruos*?

In Arlt the Jew appears in *Los locos* and the criminal in *Los monstruos*. In the chapter titled "Sensación de lo subsconsciente" (Presence of the subconscious), the narrator says for the first time that Bromberg, or "the Man Who Saw the Midwife," is Jewish, when he poses to the Astrologer "the problems of interpretation" of the Scriptures.

> Soaking and disheveled, the Man Who Saw the Midwife was standing beside the steps.
>
> "Oh, it's you!" the Astrologer gasped. "Yes, I wanted to ask how you interpret the verse from the Bible that says: 'the heaven of God.' Surely that means that there are other heavens not of God's making . . ."
>
> "Whose are they then?"
>
> "I mean, it could be that there are heavens where God does not exist. Because the verse goes on: 'And the new Jerusalem will descend.' The new Jerusalem? Does that mean the new church?"
>
> The Astrologer thought for a moment. He wasn't interested in the matter, but he knew that to keep his prestige in the other man's eyes he would have to say something, so he replied:
>
> "We, the enlightened ones, secretly know that the new Jerusalem is the new church. [. . .] But why from just this one reference do you assume that there must be various heavens?"
>
> Bromberg came and sheltered under the porch. He stared out at the wet, panting darkness and said:
>
> "Because the heavens are something you feel, like love."
>
> The Astrologer stared at him in surprise, but *the Jew* went on:
>
> "It's like love. How can you deny love if it's inside you and you feel the angels making it stronger all the time? It's the same with the four heavens. Everything in the Bible is a mystery, of course, otherwise the book would be completely absurd. The other night I was reading the Book of Revelation. I was sad at the thought we had to kill Barsut, and wondered if it was permitted to shed human blood."
>
> "There's no blood shed when you strangle someone," the Astrologer observed wryly. (212–13; italics added)

The "murder" of Gregorio Barsut by the Jew turns out, at the end of *Los locos* (in the chapter titled "El guiño" [The wink]) to have been a farce, a simulation of murder with the complicity of Barsut himself. But in *Los monstruos* (in the chapter ironically titled "Donde se comprueba que el Hombre Que Vio a la Partera no era trigo limpio" [Wherein it is confirmed that the Man Who Saw the Midwife was not altogether trustworthy]), the Astrologer tells Hipólita and Barsut that Bromberg, the Man Who Saw the Midwife (here he does not say that he is Jewish) was condemned to life in prison for murder, but that he simulated madness and escaped from jail: "Bromberg? . . . Bromberg's story is interesting. A kind of criminal simulator, a little crazy, that's all" (467). At the end of the Astrologer's narration of Barsut's story, "Hipólita understood. She said to herself, 'I wasn't mistaken. This devil was trying to kill time'" (470). She doesn't believe him, but Barsut does, and he has his reasons.[7]

Emma and Gregorio kill those Jews divided between "Jews" and "criminals" by two narrative voices *because they believed the father in Borges and the Astrologer in Arlt.*

Did the father and the Astrologer lie (or commit a crime of truth) about the "criminal" Jew? Emma and Gregorio kill them because they believed them, and afterward their own stories were believed: the chain produces a decomposition of the circle of beliefs. Our guides have led us to his enigmatic point, to the heart of the crimes of truth.

You know or you believe. . . . You know or you know you believe. . . . You believe or you want to believe. . . . say our guides. Because "fiction" as decomposition of the truth, as literary representation, as perpetual ambivalence, as language in which the same goes for two, as indecipherable text, "fiction" as the form of the secret in literature and as a machine generating enigmas, modern Argentine fiction of the twenties and forties, which was represented and read as *the* fiction, is written about the murder of the "criminal" Jew, as defined by the father and the Astrologer.

(But there is *a difference between Borges and Arlt:* in Borges the enigmas are left for the reader; in Arlt for the characters and narrators. It is possible that this abyss separates them.)

A Side Road

Zunz y Barsut . . . they are united by the reproductions of the twenties and also by those of the forties. They are united, in reality, by the strange movement of literary temporalities that takes place between Arlt and Borges, two strictly contemporary writers (Borges was born in 1899 and Arlt in 1900). As contemporary as Emma and Gregorio, who live and kill in the same years, during the twenties. But Emma's story appeared in 1948, when Arlt and the 1920s were dead, while in Gregorio's story, the date of the fiction coincides with that of its writing and publication: the three are strictly contemporaneous, as the author himself establishes in the note which concludes *Los monstruos:*

> *Note:* Given the haste with which this novel was completed, with four thousand lines (out of a total of 10,300) written between the end of September and the 22 of October, the author forgot to mention in the prologue that the title of this second

part of *Los siete locos,* initially called *Los monstruos,* was renamed *Los lanzallamas* at the suggestion of the novelist Carlos Alberto Leumann, who in a conversation one night with the author, insinuated the suggestiveness of the latter title, which the author accepted. This work was finished with such haste that the publisher was printing the first sections while the author was composing the final chapters. (523)

The temporal difference of the contemporaries generates a strange movement, which is the movement between Arlt and Borges and between the twenties and forties in Argentina (and the movement of "fiction"). In it, the enigmas of the present are extended forward, as anticipation, or backward, as memory, and they leap into "another reality."

In "Emma Zunz," Borges places the enigmas of the forties in Argentina in the twenties: Peronism and anti-Semitism. He carries them to the "before," as memory (as "those brief hours of chaos that Emma Zunz's memory today repudiates and confuses" [217]). He knowingly carries Peronism and anti-Semitism to the twenties in order to *represent them strangely,* in a "story," in a crime of truth, in another "reality": in another time and place and with other names.

And all of Arlt in 1929 places (without knowing it, like the Astrologer) the enigmas of the present in the "after" of the narration, as vision and anticipation, and for this reason *it can represent, also strangely,* the "reality" of the forties. It can represent the Hitlerism and the Peronism of Borges's present as a "story" or as a crime of truth: in another place and time and with names other than the legitimate ones. He represents Hitlerism in 1929, in Argentina, with the final solution of *Los monstruos:* the murder of the Jew (by Barsut) and of the squint-eyed woman (La Bizca), and extermination by gases and suicide (Erdosain's). And he can represent Peronism strangely, in the "after" of anarchism (*in the continuity of Argentine culture between anarchism and Peronism*), with the final destination of the former prostitute and the Astrologer, who disappeared with everyone's money (Barsut's included) and were not found, as "the chronicler of this story" reports, closing the story a year later, in 1930. Today we know more than he did: we know that Arlt's couple of the Astrologer and the former prostitute fled fiction in 1929 and returned to the "reality" of Peronism in two different cycles: first her as Eva Perón, and then him as López Rega, forming a pair with the same General Perón. They returned with the strange names that their enemies gave them, Arlt's names.

Let's leave here the movement of these two contemporaries, Emma and Gregorio, where the simultaneities of the present oscillate, in fiction (and in "reality"), between the future and the past. It is, for now, a side road, between zones of time and realities, in the world of pairs and crimes of truth.

The Plan of the Story

Emma and Gregorio guide us and tell us their stories. . . . Both open chronologically, we might say (they say), with money "in crime," together with "the anonymous accusation." As if they belonged to a similar story, framed with the same elements: as if they were made for each other. Emma's story begins with the "crime of the teller"; Barsut's with the "crime of the bill collector." The pair shares not only "the anonymous accusation" and that pure money, that sign-money "in crime" at the starting point of each of the stories. Another instance of money in crime accompanies them and unites them at the endpoint, the day of the murder of the Jew and of the crime of truth, because Emma *tore up the money* (an act of "impiety" and "pride," she says) that she made pretending to be a prostitute, and Barsut was arrested in a cabaret paying with the Astrologer's *counterfeit money*.

Their stories share a certain beginning and a certain end; they also share a movement between beginning and end (the very movement of the narration) which obeys a secret *plan*. A plan which connects money and truth with "crime," with regard to the Jew.[8] A capitalist story (or a capitalist critical instrument) of justice and revolution which can be represented wholly with the language of falsification (verbal falsification, falsification of money, of documents, of proof, of a work of art, of the *Quixote*). The crimes of truth, falsification, and literary fiction link different languages that revolve on the same axis: the same story but in another place and time, and with other protagonists. When Barsut is arrested following the murder of the Jew, he holds counterfeit money made by the anarchists in his hand. And literary falsification is in the very title of Borges's matrix text of crimes of truth, which, like "Emma Zunz," has a name as its title: "Pierre Menard, autor del Quijote" (Pierre Menard, author of the *Quixote*) (dated 1939 in Nîmes), whose narrator, allied with the French aristocracy, says that he will make a "brief rectification" of Menard's "bright Memory," refuting a "deceitful catalog" of his works that "a certain newspaper, whose Protestant leanings are surely no secret, has been so inconsiderate as to inflict upon that newspaper's deplorable readers—few and Calvinist (if not Masonic and circumcised) though they be" (*Collected Fictions*, 88).

(With "Pierre Menard, autor del Quijote," Borges writes his own criminal initiation in "fiction." "Pierre Menard" [a text about a masculine name, about the "restoration" of his "memory"], "He dedicated his scruples and his nights 'lit by midnight oil' to repeating in a foreign tongue a book that already existed" [95]; "His admirable ambition was to produce a number of pages which coincided—word for word and line for line—with those of Miguel de Cervantes" [91]. Which coincided in another language, in another place and time, and with other protagonists: that would be his "fiction," his "falsification," his crime of truth. And that would include the "circumcised").[9]

Emma and Barsut explain that the politics of money and of beliefs, those that rule in this world, connect "fiction" with falsification and with racism in the peripheral capitalism of the twenties and forties. This is the enigmatic point, the heart of the crimes of truth, to which our guides have led us.

The Reproduction of the Story

Our guides point out the final coincidence of the stories of truth and the stories of Jews of the Arlt-Borges pair, all of them "in crime" in the Buenos Aires of the twenties and forties. A strange coincidence in the "epilogues" and in the future. For both Zunz and Barsut escaped state justice to reproduce the "story."

In the afterword to *El Aleph*, dated 3 May 1949, Borges says that the "story," *neither fantastic nor real,* was told to him by Cecilia Ingenieros (see note 13 in the previous chapter). And in the afterword to *Los monstruos*, Arlt's final irony (sarcasm, expressionist satire) is that Barsut tells the story to everyone, for he goes off to Hollywood in 1930 to film it. According to "the chronicler of this story," who uses the "I" and who believes Barsut's declarations (as well as Erdosain's confessions): "Barsut, whose name had gained within days a maximum of popularity, was hired by a cinema company that was going to film the Temperley drama. The last time I saw him he was dazzled and surpassingly content with his fortune: 'Now everyone really will see my name on every corner,' he said. 'Hollywood. Hollywood. This movie will make me a star. My path is clear'" (523). The guides (the body-name of a "woman" and the body-name of an "actor") clear our path because they close the story that is believed with the story of its mechanical reproduction in the future.

On One of the Streets of This World

The declarations of Emma and Barsut to the state following the murder of the Jew define the crime of truth and at the same time define the fiction of Borges and Arlt in the twenties and forties. It is a type of literary representation (which was believed and even postulated as "fiction itself") which puts simulation in language, decomposes the "legitimate" truth, represents the secret in literature, and can be compared or metaphorically linked to the falsification of money. A crime of truth closes the story (or the sequence) of money, the plan, the "criminal Jew" (if the father and the Astrologer are to be believed), and his murder.

That fiction, which is a modern capitalist machine generating enigmas (or a capitalist critical instrument) coincides strangely, in reality, with the stories of the apparatus of anti-Semitism that circulated in Argentina in the twenties, the forties, and up to the present: *fakes and forgeries*[10] (like the "Protocols of the Elders of Zion" and the "Andinia Plan"), which follow the story of Emma and her father, of Gregorio and the Astrologer: the story of money, the secret plan, and the "criminal Jew."[11]

A final clarification, say our guides. In this excursion, we did not intend to show you the supposed anti-Semitism (or its opposite) of our authors, Arlt and Borges (or that of Baudelaire). We accompanied you only to leave you here, on one of the streets of this world of crime, at the point where we observe the enigmatic coincidence of these fictions of modernity of the twenties and forties, fictions that were believed: one revolving around "truth" and another around "the Jew."

Like us (say Emma and Gregorio, taking their leave), those stories implicate each other, they go together even as they change places and signs, each referring to the other, each within the other: they are a true pair.[12]

Stories of Jews

Project for an "Anthology" with Introduction, Characters, Notes, and Coda

Introduction

"Jews"[1] as usurers, as simulators or criminals of truth, and as antipatriots who act politically on both sides and provoke chaos: the figure emerges clearly with the coalition, with Eleazar de la Cueva in *La gran aldea,* 1884. And it is defined by the gentleman-dandy Cristal, who rescues the autobiographical subject Julio ("the nation") from the office-cave of the usurer. The "high" Argentine culture of the liberal coalition opens for us one of the roads that traverses this manual.

The "story" of "the Jews" (a place of margin, alterity, and exclusion) is a story of the Latin American modernity which appears at the end of the nineteenth century to link economic, political, and then pseudo-scientific racial elements in a cultural constellation: an artifact made of symbolic materials (recombinant or recycled signs) and interwoven narratives. This constellation, placed serially in "the anthology," serves not only to represent the figure of money with its "real" and state correlates: liberal or neoliberal "modernizations," economic crises, destabilizations, and coups d'état. It would also serve to mark its writers as organic members of the cultural coalition of the liberal state of 1880 and of the Catholic nationalism of 1890 and 1930: it is the artifact that *situates liberal and antiliberal subjects in relation to each other.*

The "stories of Jews" of the anthology are *fictions of exclusion:* they put into evidence a group of symbolic differences relating to truth, and also a group of empirical differences (a voice-language or a different gaze); these differences are placed "in crime" and in relation to the state. And they circulate not only in literature, but also in political and social "reality." The political and economic "story" of "the Jews" (seen clearly when read from the perspective of crime: "in" the world of crime) appears in Argentina in anti-Semitic pamphlets from the end of the nineteenth century through the present.

"The Jews" as a Cultural Artifact of Money

"The Jews" are always the *representatives of money,* and the narrative that includes them is an economic narrative: banks, stock exchanges, and gold. "The Jews" are the sign of the money sign: a sort of representation squared. Or better yet, "the Jews" are the representatives of money, which is itself *an apparatus of representation.* For money is a symbolic substance, a pure abstraction that reduces everything to a common denominator; it is at once material and immaterial, it is mental but it is also a mental "thing," it is a mediator of social relations, and it represents social in-teraction. Money creates "reality"[2] and reduces everything to merchandise; every-thing can be bought, everything has a price, above all that which is priceless.

"The Jews" in "the anthology" have *the language and the sex of money:* another nation, another language, another sex (or no nation, no language, no sex). They represent money as the other of truth, of "the nation," of language, and also of sex. A logical scandal, representing money and at the same time the margin and exclusion?

The Politics of Money

A theory of money (and of "the Jews" as its representatives) *would be at once a theory of the sign and a theory of fiction, power, and desire.* And also *a theory of the state* and the coups d'état in relation to the economic crises of the periphery. The represen-tation of "the Jews" in "the anthology" would be defined by its relation to the state.[3]

"Jews" as usurers, simulators, madmen, effeminate men, who sexualize money and power (and who are linked to prostitution)[4] hide in the shadows, in the caves, and from there they carry out a clandestine invasion of society, a conspiracy against "the nation." They are active in opposing political parties, like Eleazar de la Cueva; later they will be communists and capitalists at the same time. They are enemies of the state ("the enemy who infects the political body," according to Hitler), and when they congregate it is to hatch a conspiracy, a secret "plan," and to constitute *a state within the state.*

The center of the stories of Jews of the anthology is always political, but it al-ways involves *a specific type of politics:* that of the double agent and the conspiracy (which brings us to Arlt's Astrologer, with his communist and capitalist speeches, accompanied by the Jew Bromberg in his suburban estate). A type of politics that articulates state and beliefs, the sick, the mad, homosexuals and prostitutes. The discourse of the anthology is one about political enemies and also a rhetoric of hatred, which is the condition for the acceptance of homicide. In it we would see how the Argentine "Jews," from 1880 until their assassination by Gregorio and Emma, have embodied in literature the politics of money, the politics of the two sides, and "the plan," the politics of language and the effeminate physique, the politics of the secret society and the state within the state, and the politics of the "Jewish invasion" in Argentina.

In the anthology of Argentine literature, "the Jews" are the antithesis of the "high culture" of "the aristocracy" (and of "the nation"), and they are invariably contrasted with a figure of "truth" (nobility, honor, transparency, nation, religion, even poetry). They are opposed to the gentleman in *La gran aldea* (Cueva and Cristal); to the son of the Englishman in *La Bolsa* (Mackser/Glow); to the man of science in *Los simuladores de talento* (Moisés in Ramos Mejía); to whiteness and the nation in *Divertidas aventuras del nieto de Juan Moreira* (Eulalia Rozsahegy/María Blanco) and to "spirituality" in the Eucharistic Congress at the end of *Oro* (Gold).

They are opposed and they are also accompanied by other "enemies" or "guilty parties": the adulterous women of Lucio V. López, the immigrants and speculators of Julián Martel, the Moreiras of Payró, the liberals of Wast. In the anthology it would be seen that racism consists not of more or less abstract or individual prejudices, but rather of a specific social relation in a historical situation.

The anthology would be made up of fragments of the following Argentine texts:

Lucio Vicente López, *La gran aldea*, 1884

Julián Martel (pseudonym of José María Miró), *La Bolsa*, 1891

José María Ramos Mejía, *Los simuladores de talento*, 1904

Roberto J. Payró, *Divertidas aventuras del nieto de Juan Moreira*, 1910

Hugo Wast (pseudonym of Gustavo Martínez Zuviría), *El Kahal*, 1936, and its sequel *Oro*, 1936

Movimento Nacionalista Tacuara, *El caso Sirota y el problema judío en la Argentina* (The Sirota case and the Jewish problem in Argentina), 1962

Walter Beveraggi Allende, *El Plan Andinia o El nuevo estado judío* (The Andinia plan or the new Jewish state), 1965

It would also be made up of "characters" composing a "gallery" of "Jews":

Don Eleazar de la Cueva from *La gran aldea*, the old Jewish simulator who "goes bankrupt" and benefits, or who benefits from bankruptcies, who has neither honor nor patriotism, and who acts on opposing political sides; the Barón de Mackser in *La Bolsa*, "the king of finances in the River Plate," "the secret envoy of Rothchild," who displayed "a hypocritical humility" even as he prepared "the invasion"; Moisés T. from *Los simuladores del talento*, a madman with his "rapacious instincts intact," who gives up praying in favor of appraising gems in psalmodic tones; Estanislao Rozsahegy, the banker with neither nation nor language in *Divertidas aventuras del nieto de Juan Moreira;* and Blumen, Kohen, Migdal, Silberstein, and the other bankers who form the secret Jewish government in *El Kahal* and *Oro.*

But the anthology would close with a leap into the "reality" of the 1960s and 1970s in the two final texts, where we would read the politics of the two political parties and "the plan" preceding the coups d'état. *It would close as follows:*

From *El caso Sirota y el problema judío en la Argentina:* "The politics of the Israelite Collective in Argentina constitutes an intent to *create a State within our State.* The Jew is an Argentine citizen and an Israeli citizen: he swears allegiance to both flags, he recognizes two territories, *he affiliates himself with two political parties,* he obeys two executive powers, he is represented by two legislative powers, he is defended by two judicial powers" (22; italics added).[5]

From *El Plan Andinia o El nuevo estado judío:*

> They are always the "advisers" of all governments in economic matters and matters of internal and international politics . . . "the Jews" squander the Nation's revenues, encourage administrative corruption ("shady deals and embezzlement of State funds"), unleash speculation and graft, and impoverish the nation, agitate the climate of discontent among workers, and prepare the social revolution. (19)
>
> They aspire to make Argentina the capital of the great Latin American Jewish nation. *The plan* implies the concession of sovereignty over a portion of the land surface to the "Society of Jewish" [*sic*], because Theodor Herzl's *original plan* included two Jewish states, one in Palestine ("the historic homeland") . . . "the majority of Argentines are unaware of this *conspiracy,*" which would take control of Patagonian petroleum . . . the plan will provoke "the intervention of international armed forces in our territory, which the present Argentine Government is secretly and rapidly preparing. On one hand it submits the country to total *North American* hegemony, and on the other it facilitates *communist* takeover throughout the Argentine territory." (20–33; italics added)[6]

And in the April 1975 issue of the magazine *El Caudillo,* the following text by Gabriel Ruiz de los Llanos appears, bringing "the anthology" to a close.

> We must now break everything. Nine o'clock in the evening is a good time for it. You are summoned to destroy the enemy strongholds. When it really starts, you will see the flames. Let fire mingle with shouting, shouting with night, night with smoke, smoke with the barrio, flame with flame. Let us be the fire. The world remembers only the brutal and the great. Let us be that brutality and that greatness. For each *usurer* running terrified, a prize is promised. Let us generously unfurl our *hatred,* multiple and multicolored. Let us give way to our black and white hatred. Fire and fire. Let us raise our red *hatred.* That masterful *hatred* for

driving the *merchants* from the temples. So that they never again enter anywhere. Today our prayer will be a blandishing of crowbars. It will be a multiplying of ruins. They have sucked our blood and wrung us dry. It is just that they should pay with blood. Cordon off the barrio. No one leaves without prior notice, without subsequent permission. We authorize pillaging, seizure, whatever is called for. Those who discover the businesses of *the speculators* can opt to shoot again. You already know the place: the *Barrio of Usury*. A thousand clubs are swung, a thousand heads bloodied . . . let everything be devastated. (4; italics added, ellipses in original)[7]

The notes and the coda are already written; only "the literary anthology" remains to be compiled.

.

conclusion

.

The Crime Story of the Very Much Read

In the *corpus delicti* there would also be "programs" or theoretical fictions: stories made solely of symbols, differences, orders, spaces, powers, truths, and justices. Today, in the "terminal station," I have the honor of presenting to you one of those geometric and virtual stories: "the crime stories of the very much read." It is the story of some of the most often published and filmed Argentine texts of the twentieth century, texts taught in secondary schools and featuring crimes.[1] And it would be one of the central "programs" of that second, modern, and progressive culture which appeared on the frontier of the century as the "other" of the high "aristocratic" Argentine culture of the subjects of the liberal state. We now characterize it as a culture that attacks the state in the institutions of state and combines international celebrities with local "monsters," and as a culture founded on "collections"—nearly always missing a volume—and on chronicles and confessions. This theoretical fiction allows for a certain reflection on some Latin American cultural formations (positions, crossings, spaces, and final solutions) that form the basis of one of the fables of identity of the progressive culture, always demanding a transformation of the state in the name of justice and truth.

Our very much read story is built on the guilty subjectivity of the criminal, the representation of political-state power, the absence of state justice for the criminal, and the crime of truth. And it tells both crimes of passion and political crimes because it contains, besides the representation of the criminal character, some representation of the national state as itself criminal. These facts are important for differentiating this story from others centered on exclusively economic and social representations, rather than political-state ones, and wherein the guilt for the crime is not subjectivized.

The protagonists of the "story" are the criminal, who is the narrator and also a second man (it can also be a woman); a first man (who generally represents the state); the victim and his space; and the truth, sometimes embodied in a chronicler to whom the criminal confesses his crime, and who writes it: the "truth" of writing. The story of the very much read is generally told in the form of chronicle and confession, which are two "discourses of truth." And also, finally or at the end, we find "justice." It is a "great story" of Latin American modernity, with universal values and representations of the national state: a story of fictions of exclusion and dreams of justice.

The constellation of the story of the very much read articulates criminal and victim (and this means that it articulates subjects: voices, words, cultures, beliefs, and bodies), and it also articulates law, justice, truth, and state with those subjects. It contains a universe of beliefs, a system of differences, and an epistemological discourse because at its center are the symbolic differences (which are not seen), empirical differences (appreciable, which are seen), and beliefs in the crimes of those who are different.

The Criminals

In the "story," the criminal is the central character, the place of subjectivity, he who speaks and confesses his crime. This criminal is marked by two types of differences: differences of order (hierarchical or numerical) or differences of name or title. He narrates his entry into a space previously occupied by another (saying either that he is a younger son or a dependent) and thus appears from the outset as a second, he who comes after the principal: his field is that of social, economic, political, military, familial, or sexual secondariness. He may also have a lack in name or title in relation to the other names of the fiction. If the other characters have a name, he has only a nickname; if they have two names, he has only one, and he may also have no name whatsoever.

The criminals of this story are minors, seconds, "illegitimate" because of their names or titles, or they are subject to an authority capable of punishing or annihilating. They represent a zone of absence of status and right, which is delimited by opposition to a zone of sovereignty: by means of this representation they symbolically invert power from outside and below. They are situated outside of productive labor and often beyond class divisions, and they thus represent that division. *But they have "something more" that differentiates them from their equals:* they may be artists, scientists, or writers. They circulate like money and beliefs, and they cross society to divide it between rich and poor, legitimate and illegitimate, credulous and incredulous. They move in the interstices (spatial, economic, social, linguistic: they can represent new social groups), and in that movement they define flows (for example, from the country to the city at the beginning of the century,[2] or from the barrios to the center in the twenties and thirties, or from the center to the international scene after that) in a time of change, convulsion, ambivalence, and Latin American "modernization."

In the story of the very much read we would encounter two types of crimes or legalities: one determined by the state according to its laws, and another determined by beliefs (traditional remainders, diffuse ideologies often inscribed on bodies, with blood, and in names) or cultural representations of difference. And in the "theoretical fiction" we would see the way in which sexual, linguistic, religious, national, racial, and familial differences are inscribed in literature from the point of view of its "crimes." For example, the belief in the crimes of those who speak another language, in female crimes, in the crimes of those who are in contact with money, or who manage it, and the crimes of "the Jews" . . . Or the belief in the crimes of the illegitimate and the seconds, which is the belief in "crimes of name and honor." The apparatus of state and the cultural apparatus of beliefs regarding differences of legitimacy and crimes that constitute the subjects of that state are correlative, but this correlation is tense and contradictory: the beliefs are not synchronous with the state division, but rather drag with them previous and sometimes archaic stages. The story of the very much read exhibits this correlation and stages two dramas or two passions: that of the belief in the crimes of those who are different (the drama of a culture) and the drama of the Latin American state at each historical juncture. The agents of articulation between state and culture would be the guilty subjectivities of the criminals with their mark of secondariness (social, economic, familial) and their "something more."

The First Men

In the story, the criminal narrates his relation to what could be called some first man who has what he lacks, a mark of power in his name, another name or title added to his own. He can be a representative of the state and appear as a politician, a judge, a police chief, a priest, a physician, a soldier; but he can also represent an institution linked to the state. The theoretical fiction establishes from the outset the proximity, alliance, supplement, or complicity between the criminal and the first man or institution (the bracketing of work, a constant in the story, allows for this relation without mediation): *they are united by a semantic field, that of simulation or fraud.*

Everything takes place on the other side of justice and law in the crime story of the very much read: the representative of the state is a criminal; the state is a criminal state. Because the first man commits religious, political, military, medical, judicial, or economic crimes that accompany and complement the thefts or murders of the main character.[3] Inasmuch as the reason of state is the rationality linked with truth and legitimacy, the crime of truth is the way in which the criminal state of the story governs and administers justice: with discourses, acts, and ceremonies identical to the "true" ones, but in another, different place or time, or with another, different subject or protagonist. Or they may be accompanied by a different, opposite discourse or act. As justice is identified with truth, a generalized illegality is produced in the story: farces of education and marriage, of political discourses and projects, the fiction of the story puts the criminal into relation to the criminal Latin American state: it puts the "second man" into alliance, supplement, or complicity with the first man. They share the field of fraud, the crime of truth and fiction.[4]

The Victims and the Corpus Delicti: Fictions of Exclusion

The victim of the theoretical fiction is situated, socially or economically, above or below the criminal, and he or she often belongs to the political opposition (to what could be called the antistate or the counterstate: to those political opposition forces with possibilities of gaining power). He or she has his or her own space and a supplement or additive, another mark of difference, visible or audible: another language or another gaze. The supplement may be fused with the victim (who may be squint-eyed or blind, or who may speak Italian, Guaraní, Arabic, or Yiddish) or it may be separate, but in alliance or contact with him.[5]

That appreciable, supplemental difference of the victim in the story of the very much read, the other voice or gaze, evokes beliefs relating to the crimes of stigmas: the evil eye (evil of seeing or being seen) and the malediction (from *maledictus*, badly said). These are the most archaic beliefs, in "evil," which are sometimes associated with gender difference. The clash between the symbolic differences (of order and name) of the criminal and the empirical differences (visible or audible) of the victim is the clash between signs of alterity in a specific social, political, and state power relation. So the criminal commits the crime in order to vacate that space and to curtail the production of descendants; the victim can be a man; if it is a woman, she is never a mother. Annihilation implies a violent change, the end of a type of association, the erasure of a space, and a change of place for the criminal.

In the place where the criminal enters into contact with the victim we find, finally, a *corpus delicti*: the other voice and gaze, which in beliefs appear "evil" and which are superimposed over social and political differences. Since the victim could represent a danger or a threat to the state at a given juncture, the cultural construction of difference and its collusion in the crime appears as a supplement of the criminal national state. It is a specific sexual, social, political, and at times racial relation (*each field with its own logic: the cultural is situated on the frontier of social cat-*

egories) between two sets of differences, symbolic and empirical, at the pole of evil. And so the alliance between the first and the second makes sense: the state would make use of the criminal, and with him the cultural apparatus of belief in the crimes of those who are different, in order to eliminate the social, economic, or political space of the "enemy," the space in which the body of evil resides: the criminal would be an agent of the criminal state. The theoretical fiction says, at times: when the state is a farce of truth, the seconds execute fictions of exclusion. And the exclusions are read *from a double politics:* they can be the murders of Jews, foreigners, women, workers, or representatives of the oligarchy.

For this reason, the story of the very much read is linked with specific junctures either of strong threats to the state on the part of the opposition, or of state change. By this I mean that the place (and the body) of crime always includes, in the story of the very much read, contemporary political reality.

The Chronicler and Writing: Dreams of Justice

In the story of the very much read, the criminal narrates his relationship with the first man and with the victim (he moves between them and this movement is the same movement of the narration) in the form of a confession to a chronicler who writes it down (he himself can also write it, in the form of a chronicle-confession). The chronicler is sharply opposed to the investigator or even to the scholar, who can appear in other crime fictions, but he may share some of their features. The chronicler's writing would represent the instance of truth, and thus a possible, just state opposed to the criminal one.

Chronicle and confession are discourses enunciated in order to be believed because they are constituted in the service of the truth of a subject or the truth of the succession of events, located in time and space. The chronicle can function at once as "history" and as the "legal writing" of a culture founded on belief in the truth of confession and on guilty subjectivities.[6]

Chronicle and confession, two genres of truth (and sometimes another genre of truth and justice, the apocalyptic)[7] are the foundational narrative discourses of the story because they sustain the narrative pact of truth and justice, the central values of this line of Latin American culture. (Chronicle and confession appear at the same time in reality because they occupy judicial, scientific, medical, journalistic, psychoanalytic, and literary spaces that are occupied and have been occupied by the representatives of the culture of the very much read.) The pact between chronicle and confession is a temporary, limited pact between the oral truth of a subject and the written justice (of time), between a second and a first, which is at the base of the fables of identity and which forms a diptych, a matrix with two entries. The criminal can say everything because he says it from the lowest edge and from outside the law. The criminal and the chronicler, and their pact of discourses, constitute the frames and the spaces of representation of the story. They are its two frontiers (*its two "I's"*), the lower and the upper; between the two, the territory of the state and the territory of those who are different, and thus the set of beliefs regarding their crimes which lead to the fictions of exclusion.

The criminal is an accomplice to the state's crimes of truth, but in the confession, which is the moment of truth, he denounces the state as criminal and illegitimate because of its crimes of truth. Or better still: the criminals of the story are double agents and execute two sets of politics at once: the criminal politics of the state (the fictions of exclusion of those who are different) and, in their confessions, the politics of criticism and truth in opposition to the criminal state (the dreams of justice). The criminal appears as an internal supplement to the criminal national state and also as its critic, and as a supplement to the justice and truth of the chronicler. He appears as the "second man" of two "firsts." This type of second criminal, double agent, and guilty subjectivity, the type of representation of the state as criminal in relation to truth, justice, and legitimacy, the absence of state justice and the chronicler who writes truth and justice, only occurs in the crime story of the very much read, and it defines a zone of Latin American culture: the modernizing progress of the end of the nineteenth and beginning of the twentieth centuries through, perhaps, the last globalization or the last reformulation of the Latin American state. This was its literary and political textuality, which represented itself in the direct relation between the state (the specific Latin American state) and also in the direct relation between that position and the truth and justice of a chronicler.

The chronicler also represents justice because he contains a supplementary time in relation to the criminal, and he narrates what occurs following the crime and the confession. Since the criminal in the story does not receive punishment on the part of state justice, the textual-temporal justice of the chronicler relates that he has died, killed himself, or left the country, which is to say that he has surpassed the temporal or spatial frontiers. In this supplement of time the chronicler can also narrate the criminal's reward (he can question the category of criminal). The temporal interval reestablishes "justice."

The supplemental temporality is the specific temporality of the very much read, the temporality necessary for truth and justice, and it leads us into the future. Something else can occur in the story, something that escapes the chronicler and the truth and justice of the fiction and which returns us to reality. Something like a future justice or truth outside the story but within the *corpus delicti* and overflowing in all directions: beliefs, realities, fates, professions, past and future states. If the criminals of the story have not died, if they have not gone into exile (*if the chronicler did not apply justice following the crime*), they can reappear in the "real" political future at the side of the ruler or as *seconds of state*. Here we read the anticipatory function of literature in a world configured by the relation between state and culture. The story of the crime of the very much read (a strange cultural remainder in the heart of the political) could thus embrace the future histories of the state and the history of the successive contemporary counterstates.

The Laws of Those Who Are Different

The theoretical "fiction" would include a series of cultural formations with a proliferation of times and realities. Because with the story of the very much read, it is possible to formulate not only a "theory" of victims and criminals, of the real state and the possible state, but also a "history" of specific junctures and correlations: with the political opposition, with breaks and reformulations of the state, and, perhaps, with future states.

Because the story always displays something more, it signals a specific relation between literature and the law of the state in Argentine culture. Belief in differences and their crimes, the resulting fictions of exclusion, and the dreams of justice which they produce are ever more linked to laws regarding "those who are different" in the progressive, modernizing culture: prostitutes, farm workers, Peronists, just as belief in honor and names, and their crimes, are linked to laws regarding the private or corporative justices of the military and the oligarchy. From the Law of Residence or expulsion of "undesirable aliens" (1902) to the closing of brothels and the Law of Prophylaxis (1935–1936), the Statute of the Farm Worker (1945), the prohibition of Peronism and the imposition of martial law (1955), and the laws prohibiting duels (1921) and private justice for offenses to "honor." Each one of these laws has its punctual correspondent in the representation of differences and beliefs in the story of the very much read, which always excludes or includes one of "those who are different." The history of the story would also follow the history of electoral laws and coups d'état, and the changes in the national state, its transformations, falls, and democratizations, which are always accompanied by laws regarding those who are different or the different justices of the progressive modernizing culture. And once again we can read two sets of politics: on the one hand, prostitutes, Peronists, and farm workers, and on the other, the military and the oligarchy.

Envoi

The history of the crime story of the very much read (a judicial, political, linguistic, literary, and cultural text that always includes a network of symbols and differences and "something more" in order to speak of justice and truth) also narrates the struggle for literary power, and not only for state power, in this line of Latin American culture.

Throughout its history, our story of the very much read regulated a certain aesthetics, a certain relation of literature with society, and a certain literary politics. As it went, it put aside the "unread" capable of deciphering it, leaving behind a literary residue that signified "excess," "cruelty," "hardness," "pessimism," or "destruction." And through all its republications and film adaptations it sowed fodder for the used bookstore and the library, the spaces that have loaned a certain entertainment to our "Manual of Curiosities."

From here on, only questions and possibilities.

Is it possible to say that the story of the very much read needed these exclusions (needed the unread) in order to win one of its wars, the war of the second culture to become the first, that of the lesser or second against the greater? And that this triumph coincides with the dissolution of the high culture, which appears to have succumbed to the advance of the very much read in the era of globalization?

Is it possible to say, in the theoretical fiction of the very much read, that the story "won the place" of the high culture from 1880, and that this "triumph" coincides with the transformation of the cultural into the economic, and with the almost total separation between culture and state produced by the market and globalization? One transnationalized, the other "national-regional." And could this separation between culture and state (which implies an almost total literary autonomization) and this triumph be capable of producing dissolution of frontiers between the different levels of culture? Would they be capable of erasing the limits and fusing all the lines in a national-regional culture?

And, thus, in this situation, how would crime be transformed, after having served us in this manual as an instrument for separating cultures and cultural lines, an instrument of division and exclusion?

How will the story narrate this new situation? How will the crime story of the very much read be written? Will those fictions of exclusion and those stories of justice still need the Latin American national states, or while they remain only for "literature"?

Who will be the criminal? Of what languages and discourses will it be made? How will it write its temporal supplement with its chronicler, its justice and its media? Will it have to undertake an internal self-critique and show the meaning-lessness of its story as an emblem of the second culture? Will it attempt to refor-mulate it with the scraps of the first culture and those of its own story? And who will be the first men and the victims?

And in that globalized culture, and in those states, and in that fusion of the dif-ferent levels of culture, and in that literature, who will be the future unread? Which best-sellers of globalization will be left to languish in used bookstores or the uni-versity library?

At this precise point, this Scheherazade of the modern stories dreams of taking a well-deserved vacation . . . and bids farewell to those who have accompanied her so patiently in this long and sinuous voyage in search of the *corpus delicti*. Of the evidence of what is not known . . .

notes

Introduction

1. *Theory of Surplus Value*, pt. 1 (Moscow: N.p., 1963), 387–88; italics added.

•

2. "El no delito: ¿Tan sólo una ilusión? Entrevista a Juan Carlos Marín," *Delito y Sociedad: Revista de Ciencias Sociales* (Buenos Aires) 2, no. 3 (first semester 1993): 133–52. Marín maintains that crime is not an "abnormality," but rather the opposite; what is normal, *what is dominant as a mode of social normalization is crime*. This is what we receive as dominant information in the press, in literature, and in communication in general, says Marín. The discourse of the normal is violence and crime, and the discourse of the ideal is the absence of crime. There is, then, an *absence of polarity*.

Marín also says that *crime is a theorization;* the "crime and punishment" relation is a theory of the use of force and power in the human race and in society. The crime and punishment scheme is a fallacy, he says, of those who attempt to confer upon it a use and an absolute value which it does not possess. *It has historicity, and it forms part of the modes of a culture that legitimize a dominant class.* And this has been the case ever since the construction of social order. The crime and punishment scheme is a legitimizing scheme, which passes from one dominion to the next. He adds that *culture maintains sin, transgression, and crime separate in law and united in consciousness.* So far, Marín.

In their essay "Reflections on Realism," in *Rethinking Criminology: The Realist Debate,* ed. Jock Young and Roger Matthews (London: Sage Publications, 1992), 1–23, Roger Matthews and Jock Young introduce us to the new English school of "radical realist" criminologists (so called because they are post-utopian radicals). They maintain that crime must be understood on a square graph of relations (a scheme in which it appears as the intersection and articulation of a series of lines): at one corner the offender, at a second the victim, at a third the state, and at the last, society. The nature of relations within the square and the construction of different "crimes" are functions of the relations of forces in its interior, say the new criminologists, recognizing that "the relation between state and civil society and victim and criminal are of a different order and a different magnitude." The square is complex, say Matthews and Young, and it serves as "an important reminder of the various processes through which 'crime' is constructed" (19).

The authors speak of the emergence of alternative approaches to the problem of crime, and of the necessity of constructing a criminology at once "radical" and "realist." There are "new realists" on the right, who have certain contacts with the "radical realists": "They share a concern with the corrosive effects which crime can have on communities and with the formulation of workable policies, but they are ultimately oppositional and competing positions" (5). "New realists and radical realists differ with respect to the causes of crime: those on the right see it as "ultimately a function of trans-historical 'human nature.' As a result their analysis lacks a social economic context and is excessively individualized" (5). Realists of the right thus "embrace essentially punitive policies aimed at controlling the 'wicked'" and "prioritize order over justice," resorting "to genetic and individualistic theories to blame the 'underclass.'" In contrast, "left realists prioritize social justice" and "point to the social injustice which marginalizes considerable sections of the population and engenders crime. If the two realisms share anything in common it is the rejection of utopianism" (6).

These new radical realist criminologists not only differ from the new realists, but also from the postmodernists—the radical realists defend modernity as an "as yet unfinished project,"— and they adopt an element of "standpoint feminism," according to which "knowledge is a function of the 'standpoint' or the location of the collective subject" (15). The various social groups speak from different positions and social experiences.

"One theme which remains central to both realists and feminists," say Matthews and Young, "is the *definition of crime*. The definitional issue has always been a stumbling block within criminology. Often criminologists have relied on simplistic definitions of crime and seen it as an 'act' or claimed that it is a function of the 'reaction.' In attempting to move beyond these limited oppositions, realism has begun to examine the processes of action and reaction through what has become termed 'the square of crime.'" The authors explain the square as a shorthand "designed to serve as a reminder that *'crime' arises at the intersection of a number of lines of force*. It is therefore an important antidote to those who see crime solely in terms of victims and offenders and ignore the role of the state and public opinion. And at the same time it serves as a critique of those who see the process of 'criminalization' as a wholly state-generated process" (17; italics added).

In their conclusion, Matthews and Young say that radical realism

> does offer a distinctly different approach to the analysis of the processes through which crime is constructed, one which avoids the excesses of idealism and essentialism. Realism argues that previous criminological theories have been partial. That is, they only focus on one part of the square of crime: the state (as in labelling

theory, neo-classicism), the public (as in control theory), the offender (as in positivism) or the victim (as in victimology). One of its major aims is to provide an analysis of crime on all levels. . . . Realism is critical of the extremely simplistic notions of causality implicit in traditional social democratic theory. (19–20)

Finally, they say, "left realism involves the *repoliticization of crime* . . . crime reduction requires . . . an appreciation of a wide range of political and structural processes which go beyond the boundaries of conventional criminology. . . . crime control must inevitably become part of a comprehensive political programme" (21; italics added).

•

3. Sigmund Freud, *Totem and Taboo: Some Points of Agreement between the Mental Lives of Savages and Neurotics* (New York: W. W. Norton & Co., 1989).

•

4. In the seventies, Howard Zehr, *Crime and the Development of Modern Society: Patterns of Criminality in Nineteenth Century Germany and France* (London: Croom Helm, 1976), showed the correlation between crime and modernization and a certain "functionality" of crime, and said that *"crime is inherently political. If crime often does imply a rejection of or a protest against society or its norms, it is obviously a political act on the part of the offender. But crime is also highly political from the vantage point of society. It is of course often the result of political decisions, such as the decision . . . to use unemployment as a means of combating inflation. But the political nature of crime goes deeper than that, for crime by its very definition is political. . . . Crime—its commission, its causes, its definition, its enforcement—is a political act"* (144; italics added). The conservative position, says Zehr, is that the responsibility is the criminal's; the liberal position absolves the criminal.

Returning to the ideas of Émile Durkheim in his 1951 study *Suicide: A Study in Sociology*, Zehr concludes that "Crime is normal; it plays a definite role in society, and it involves behaviour not so dissimilar from that of non-offenders," above all in a modernizing society (144). This, from the seventies.

In the sixties Hans Magnus Enzensberger said, "Between *murder* and *politics* there exists an old and close dependency. This dependency pervades the foundations of all power. He who can render dead his subjects wields power. The one who governs is the survivor."

•

5. In the nineties, David Lloyd and Paul Thomas, "Culture and Society or 'Culture and the State?'" *Social Text* 30 (1992): 27–56; this article by Lloyd and Thomas is reelaborated in their book *Culture and the State* (New York: Routledge, 1998), *does*

not directly relate *culture with society, but rather with the state.* They are interested in the function of culture in its intersection with the state and in the basis of what Althusser calls "ideological state apparatuses." They revise Raymond Williams's *Culture and Society, 1780–1950* and say that Williams thinks neither about the state nor about the relation between the state and cultural theory. He places more emphasis on an intellectual history or a history of ideas than on the relationship between "industry, politics and culture," and this prevents him "from grasping more radical possibilities" (28). In the "high" tradition running "from Burke through Coleridge to Mill and Arnold which is ultimately most important to Williams," there reappears a series of concerns: "concern with the fragmentation of the human by the division of labor, concern with mechanization, deracination and the cultural impoverishment as well as the exploitation of the mass of the population" (29).

Lloyd and Thomas maintain that the "discourse on representation, which was always implicit in the idea of culture" (53) must be understood in connection with the debates over representation within the press and the socialist movements of the period, and in connection with the debates over representation and education, and with the type of subject formed by or against the emerging state.

I. From Transgression to Crime

1. This work is nothing more than an attempt to reorder one of the fundamental critical fields of Argentine literature established by David Viñas and Noé Jitrik (that of the writers of 1880 and liberalism), according to the categories of state, culture, and subject positions, which I consider to be fundamental to thinking about Latin American literatures today. See Viñas's classic works, "El escritor *gentleman,*" "Infancia, rincones y Mirada," "De la sacralidad a la defensa: Cané," in *Literatura argentina y realidad política: De Sarmiento a Cortázar* (Buenos Aires: Siglo Veinte, 1971). And "Cané: miedo y estilo," "'Niños' y 'criados favoritos,'" in *Literatura argentina y política: De los jacobinos porteños a la bohemia anarquista* (Buenos Aires: Sudamericana, 1995). And by Noé Jitrik, *El '80 y su mundo: Presentación de una época* (Buenos Aires: Jorge Álvarez, 1968), and *Ensayos y estudios de la literatura argentina* (Buenos Aires: Galerna, 1970).

This work, then, is simply a "school paper" for my beloved teachers of the *Contorno* group. An exam for *Contorno* on the "coalition's stories of education and marriage," dedicated to the memory of Ramón Alcalde.

2. It is clear that in 1880 modernization was carried out from within the state in Latin America (as generally occurs on the peripheries); the state rationalized society from above in the absence of a powerful autochthonous bourgeoisie.

In discussing modern Greece, Gregory Jusdanis, *Belated Modernity and Aesthetic Culture: Inventing National Literature* (Minneapolis: University of Minnesota Press, 1991), refers to "many modernities" and says that peripheral societies "internalize the incongruity between western originals and local realities as a structural deficiency" (xiii). Necessarily "imposed from above through centralized planning," belated modernization remains, for Jusdanis, necessarily incomplete. He suggests that modernization from within the state generates two processes: resistance from the church and contradictions between state and society. Jusdanis analyzes the enduring weight of the family and kinship ties in the body politic in Greece as the result of "political modernization without industrialization" and "the incorporation of bourgeois institutions without a polity of citizens" (105–6). In peripheral countries the state dominates civil society, Jusdanis says, and he underscores that tension: the state penetrates civil society and erases the distinctions between the private and public spheres: *there are no frontiers between state and culture.* Judanis also points to the "over-politicization" of society and the clientelistic networks "produced by the imperfect integration of western prototypes and the autochthonous infrastructure." Modernity is installed on the basis of "traditional kinship patterns" integrated and transformed in the new context, rather than eliminated (106). So far, Jusdanis on peripheral modernity.

Julio Ramos, *Desencuentros de la modernidad en América Latina* (México: Fondo de Cultura Económica, 1989), argues that uneven modernization in Latin America would imply the impossibility of the complete institutionalization (autonomization) of literature; before the turn of the century, men of letters were both politicians and men of the state. My analysis merely continues that of Ramos, in that sense, with a greater emphasis on the processes of literary autonomization produced by political autonomization (the constitution of the state): an emphasis on the depoliticization of literary representations beginning with the threshold of 1880. Paradoxically, the fictions written by the cultural coalition for the state require a depoliticization, which implies a certain autonomization, of literature.

In Argentina, modernization from within the state in 1880 represented a literary break because this literature was constituted as completely different from the previous literature, to the point where we can imagine the nineteenth century encompassing two universes: one beginning with independence, and another beginning in 1880.

In the first phase, that of the civil wars, literature revolved around a phantasmic national space, as a utopia of unification. Literature was *almost fused with politics* because all of the voices or verbal representations were politicized and all cultural difference was political difference.

The other universe arose beginning with the break in state formation in 1880, in which *representations were depoliticized* and made purely social and cultural. With the constitution of the state the political was autonomized and constituted as a sphere separate from cultural and literary space. This break put an end to the discourse of war, and the literature of the cultural coalition of the liberal state drew a social, cultural, national, racial, and sexual map of the depoliticized society of 1880. That autonomization of the sphere of literature and culture, visible in the coalition's "stories" (which represent a political past in the "education stories" and a purely cultural present in the "marriage stories"), produced a total change in literary history, or simply in history. For the coalition's "purely cultural" literary representation, arising in 1880, "invented" or generated other sequences, forward and backward.

In the first place it founded the language and the literary representation of the high, "aristocratic" culture, the culture of domination in Argentina: the voices of the Teatro Colón, of the Recoleta cemetery, of the Jockey Club, with their quotes in the original European languages, with their creolisms and their encyclopedias, and with their aesthetic of simplicity. Second, the independence of literature and politics opened another sequence backward because it unified the torn and polemical political-cultural voices of the previous nation, in the new sequence of "national literature." In other words, the independence of spheres of "literature" and "politics" permitted the *nationalization* of the warring voices and cultures of the previous phase (and to this end, the cultural coalition constructed alternative versions of the previous warring nation in its education stories).

•

3. The so-called "generation of '80" was formed by "minor" writers of classics within national frontiers and unknown beyond them because peripheral cultures only transcend frontiers with a quota of two or three "masterpieces" for each nation, or for each century of each nation. The inverse relationship is interesting: the writers of secondary classics in the dominant cultures are, for the most part, read and admired in peripheral countries, and this is one of the signs of "high culture." Borges was one of the Argentine writers who advocated the reading of the secondary classics of the dominant cultures.

These founding writers of Argentine high culture were diplomats, deputies, ministers, senators, and they wrote political speeches, memoirs, stories, fragments, travel notes, and cultural chronicles. We will refer to two of them at this first juncture of the coalition; their texts are relatively little known outside Argentina but canonical in national culture: they are read in secondary schools, and they are permanently in print.

Miguel Cané (1851–1905), author of the classic *Juvenilia,* was born in Montevideo during the dictatorship of Juan Manuel de Rosas and the political exile of his parents, and beginning in 1880 he served as a diplomat in Colombia and Venezuela and later in Vienna, Berlin, and Madrid. His chronicles and accounts were collected in *En viaje* (On my travels) (1884) and in *Charlas literarias* (Literary chats) (1885). In 1892 he became mayor of Buenos Aires. In 1899, as a senator from the capital, he published the book *Expulsión de extranjeros* (Expulsion of foreigners), in which he synthesized the legislation of the principle European nations regarding the right to expel foreigners, and he presented to the senate his bill for another type of law of the liberal state, law 4144 (1902), called the Law of Residence. It allowed the expulsion of foreigners "of bad conduct" from the country (politically, anarchists and socialists). In 1900 he became dean of the newly created Faculty of Philosophy and Letters at the Universidad de Buenos Aires.

Lucio V. López (1848–1894), author of *La gran aldea* (The great village), was the son of historian and Romantic novelist Vicente Fidel López and the grandson of Vicente López y Planes, author of the Argentine national anthem; he was born in exile in Montevideo, like Cané. In 1880 he became deputy to the National Congress, and in 1881 he wrote *Recuerdos de viaje* (Travel memories), the first travel book of 1880. He was also one of the founders, in 1884, of the newspaper *Sud-América* (where he published *La gran aldea,* his only novel, in installments), one of the official organs of the supporters of Roca (*roquismo*) and of the "generation of '80." In 1890, on the eve of the Revolution of '90, which he supported, López gave a famous speech at the graduation ceremony of the law faculty, exhorting a return to the past and a struggle against cosmopolitan advances. In 1891 he published *Curso de derecho constitucional* (Course in constitutional law), and in 1893 he served as minister of the interior for thirty-six days under Aristóbulo del Valle. He died in 1894 in a duel with Colonel Carlos Sarmiento, occasioned by political discrepancies. He expired in the arms of Aristóbulo del Valle, and his last words were: "How unjust, Aristóbulo! That's how these inorganic democracies are!"

•

4. In "L'autobiografia di una nazione" (*L'Autobiografia: Il vissuto e il narrato, Quaderni di Retorica e Poetica,* vol. 1 [Padua: Liviana Editrice, 1986]), Maria Antonietta Saracino analyzes the autobiographies of political leaders of independence and the establishment of the new African states (Ghana, Kenya, Zambia) in the sense of a *double autobiography, individual and national.* These works were pub-

lished on the occasion of the country's independence, and they are emblematic cases. In Ghana, for example, *The Autobiography of Kwame Nkrumah* was published the same day as the proclamation of independence, 6 March 1957. These books were not written at the end of a life; they are not memoirs marking the completion of a human arc; they are written, rather, at the culmination of a career, and the "I" is present in the modulation of historical processes.

•

5. One writes from where one has read. Martín García Mérou was Cané's secretary on a diplomatic mission to Venezuela and Colombia when he wrote *Juvenilia* in 1882. In *Recuerdos literarios* (Buenos Aires: Rosso, 1937), García Mérou explains their acquaintance, saying that "Cané had been my examiner in History, and upon the appearance of my first book, *Poesías,* he wrote a few affectionate words of encouragement in *El Nacional,* which compelled my gratitude" (339). And he recounts:

> Our stay in Venezuela did not exceed four months. We lived together, engaged in intellectual work, in a picturesque little house with a beautiful garden full of tropical plants and trees. . . . When we ate alone, depressed by that unattractive existence, by our solitude and our distance from our homeland, absorbed in thoughts which for neither of us were rose-colored, and after the obligatory phrase of friendly greeting, we would sit at the table each with a book in front of us. . . . Cané was at that time one of the most formidable and tireless readers I know. He would stay hours and hours, from morning till night, with a book in his hand, devouring volumes of criticism, history, political law, philosophy, literature. . . . During that period Cané wrote the glowing scenes of *Juvenilia* which he sent me a few years later. . . . Yes, I saw them being written, day by day, in notebooks whose manufacture was one of my specialties, and which were rapidly filled with his fine, tight and irregular handwriting. During certain hours when the *spleen* let up, he would read me fragments of those delightful reminiscences of his student life. . . . It is impossible to read *the school scenes,* the infantile adventures of that happy and mocking epic of adolescence, without passing from outbursts of the frankest hilarity to moments of touching sweetness. . . . And all of it has a special, typical character, a *coloring which is all ours, a coloring I might call porteño,* and which constitutes another of the attractions of this toy written by a masterful hand. (340–32; italics added)

And one final displacement: *Juvenilia* was written in 1882, when Cané was a diplomat in Venezuela. In 1883 he was sent as a diplomatic representative to Vienna, where he published *Juvenilia* in 1884.

Ricardo Sáenz Hayes, *Miguel Cané y su tiempo (1851–1905)* (Buenos Aires: Kraft,

1955), says that "the first expression of sympathy is that which is closest to Vienna and to Cané's heart," and he cites a letter from Martín García Mérou to Cané when *Juvenilia* appears: "Perhaps without thinking about it and above all without proposing it, you have made the poem of that age which is so interesting and so full of sensations, a complete poem in which the analysis is more than once delicate and profound, in which nothing is lacking: the first and purest love of one's life, the ambition which insinuates flattering promises, infantile poverty full of unsuspected greatness, all this is faithfully recounted in these pages into which you have put the best that there is in every man: his heart!" (317).

•

6. Amédée Jacques (1813–1865) arrived in Argentina in 1852 as a political exile after being expelled from his country along with Victor Hugo. He settled first in Santiago del Estero and later in Tucumán, and despite having studied in the foremost universities of Europe, he was obliged to make his living working as a baker. But someone noticed his abilities, and in 1858 he was invited to run the Colegio Nacional de San Miguel. There he put in motion a pedagogical project that was revolutionary for its time. In 1863, Bartolomé Mitre assumed the presidency and undertook a plan of reorganization and improvement of secondary and university education, and he named Jacques director of the Colegio Nacional de Buenos Aires and professor of physics at the university. Jacques brought new energy to the study of the social and natural sciences and of the arts, and he had the rare virtue of being adored by his students despite his strict and fairly irascible character. Cané describes him as a tall and corpulent man, somewhat careless in his appearance and always dressed in black. He recounts that he would arrive at school at nine in the morning and ask whether any of the professors were absent, in which case he would go to the classroom and teach chemistry, physics, math, history, literature, or Latin without hesitation. His presentation, Cané relates, was so enthralling that the students would close the door so as not to hear the bell marking the end of the period in order to keep listening to him. He was also a man of great idealism, a defender of freedom and justice ("Esto pasó un 4 de julio" [of 1813, the day of A.J.'s birth], *Clarín* [Buenos Aires], 4 July 1997).

•

7. Sylvia Molloy, "A School for Life: Miguel Cané's *Juvenilia*," *At Face Value: Autobiographical Writing in Spanish America* (Cambridge: Cambridge University Press, 1991), 97–107, analyzes Cané's text, "Mi padre," which precedes *Juvenilia* in various editions following Cané's death. Molloy writes that the portrait of the father can be read as a review of Cané's own work, which also includes a number of ephemeral texts and an unfinished national novel, *De cepa criolla* (Of Creole stock). Molloy's

analysis shows the necessary relationship, in Cané, between the father's story and that of the school. The same occurs when she analyzes two other paternal figures, the rector Agüero and Jacques, in relation to Cané's intellectual history. In this chapter we merely continue her hypothesis. Molloy's reading closes with ironic allusion to the current reading of *Juvenilia* in Argentine secondary schools: the descendants of immigrants mock immigrants along with Cané. And we would add that the provincials also mock Cané's provincials. "One would like to think that the irony would not be lost on Cané," concludes Molloy (107).

•

8. And another difference with respect to the provincials, which Cané shares with Goyena and Sainte-Beuve. In chapter 15, Cané says that the philosophy professor Pedro Goyena, echoing Sainte-Beuve, says that a native of Corrientes "lacks the fine golden sand" (81). Cané repeats this phrase of Sainte-Beuve as the epigraph to *Juvenilia*: "Toutes ces premières impressions . . . ne peuvent nous toucher que médiocrement; il y a du vrai, de la sincérité; mais ces peintures de la enfance recommencées sans cesse, n'ont de prix que si elles sont d'un auteur original, d'un poète célèbre" (43).

•

9. In order to continue with this forward jump and to read Cané in the second cycle of the coalition and of the liberal state, see Carlos Sánchez Viamonte, *Biografía de una ley antiargentina: La ley 4144* (Buenos Aires: Nuevas Ediciones Argentinas, 1956). According to Sánchez Viamonte, "The first precedent for the law of expulsion of foreigners number 4144 was a bill presented in 1899 by senator Miguel Cané." He transcribes the bill, which says in article 2, "The President of the Republic, in agreement with ministers, shall be able to order the expulsion of any foreigner whose conduct could compromise national security, disturb public order or social tranquility." (And in these words we read again the history of the liberal state and its future military discourses.)

In *Soy Roca* (Buenos Aires: Sudamericana, 1989), Félix Luna explains that in 1901 and 1902, during Roca's second presidential term, strikes directed by "foreign anarchists" imperiled the property and safety of the population. "For this reason I did not hesitate to promulgate the law authorizing the expulsion of undesirable foreigners which Cané promoted on the basis of a text prepared for him by Paul Groussac, whom, let it be said in passing, I appointed director of the National Library for which he requested and obtained the splendid building which had been built and intended for the Lottery, on Calle México" (345).

The amusing thing about this real adventure is Cané's alliance with the Frenchman Groussac and with the National Library (and we can already hear Borges), which replaces the lottery on Calle México. From his essay and his bill for the expulsion of foreigners, Cané goes on to publish in 1891 his translation of Shakespeare's *Henry IV* and to occupy the post of dean of the recently created Faculty of Philosophy and Letters.

•

10. In Eduardo Wilde, *Páginas Escogidas* (Buenos Aires: Estrada, 1939).

•

11. Nicholas Shumway, "Bartolomé Mitre and the Gallery of Argentine Celebrities," chapter 8 of *The Invention of Argentina* (Berkeley and Los Angeles: University of California Press, 1991), 188–213, poses a series of questions regarding national history which originated in the debate between Sarmiento and Alberdi. For example: "Whose view of the past will become official? . . . Who would be iconized as national heroes? . . . Who, in short, would build the national pantheon?" (188). And he refers to Bartolomé Mitre, defender of *porteño* privilege, rival of Alberdi and Urquiza, as the "chief creator of official history." He says that Mitre put his most ambitious historical projects in motion between 1853 and 1880, and that the most significant was a volume of biographies titled *Galería de celebridades argentinas,* published in 1857. Edited by Mitre with Sarmiento's help, the volume was a collection of biographies; all of them served the *porteño* cause and no biography of any *caudillo* was included. What interests us at the moment is the dispute between Cané and López regarding *mitrismo,* but it is possible that these "celebrities" may reappear alongside José María Ramos Mejía's *Las neurosis de los hombres celebres* (Neuroses of famous men) later in the manual.

•

12. Francine Masiello, *Between Civilization and Barbarism: Women, Nation, and Literary Culture in Modern Argentina* (Lincoln: University of Nebraska Press, 1992), argues that Aunt Medea symbolizes the decadence of Argentina and that her death, watched over by science, is a "metaphor for a narrative flow that cannot be sustained in an old and wasted body" (214 n. 29).

•

13. This hypothesis of the absorption of previous political differences, of their transformation into cultural differences and the simultaneous depoliticization of culture, could measure the history of the successive Argentine liberal states and the cultural coalitions, patrician or otherwise, which almost always accompany them up until 1960. (For example, the liberal-military state of the Liberating Revolution [1955] and the place of *Sur* in its cultural coalition.)

•

14. In *Myth and Archive: A Theory of Latin American Narrative* (New York: Cambridge University Press, 1990), Roberto González Echevarría says that "Legal writing was the predominant form of discourse in the Spanish Golden Age. It

permeated the writing of history, sustained the idea of Empire, and was instrumental in the creation of the Picaresque" (45). According to González Echevarría, the most significant characteristic of the Spanish state that was reproduced in the Americas "was its legalistic make-up," and "its most visible feature was the pervasive meticulousness of its organization and the entanglement of the individual in a complex set of relations with the central power" (48). The position of *cronista mayor* was created, and the person occupying it was charged with writing "the State's version of history" (48). With regard to the *first person account* (a report, deposition, or confession in the penal sense), it is an arbitrary imposition from outside which links the individual and his life history with the state. González Echevarría says that the "I" and the rhetorical conventions of the account will give the novel, from the picaresque onward, its autobiographical and reflexive form (56–57).

•

15. Miguel Cané, "La primera de Don Juan en Buenos Aires" (Don Juan's first in Buenos Aires), *Prosa ligera* (Light prose) (Buenos Aires: "La cultura argentina," Vaccaro, 1919), 89. The text is from 1897 but it again deals with recollections; Cambaceres is already dead.

In *La gran aldea* (Buenos Aires: Eudeba, 1960), we read: "A classic night of opera at the Colón brings together the choicest men and women of Buenos Aires. One need only cast a gaze around the semicircle of the hall: president, ministers, capitalists, lawyers and lions, they are all there" (142).

•

16. Eduardo Rinesi, *Ciudades, teatros y balcones: Un ensayo sobre la representación política* (Buenos Aires: Paradiso Ediciones, 1994), analyzes the conception of liberal politics as theater and representation. He says that the theatrical metaphor is constitutive of the modern way of thinking about politics because politics and theater have in common the attribute of representing what is "offstage," and this representation appears as a masking and also as a staging of a Text which precedes it and speaks through it (42).

His fundamental thesis is that the "theatrical metaphor for thinking about politics is absolutely integral to a certain philosophical-political tradition of enormous importance in Modernity: the liberal tradition" (63). Rinesi analyzes the logic of the privatizations that accompany this metaphor, and he criticizes the theatrical, representationalist paradigm because there is no appearance in contrast to reality or truth; the appearance does not hide anything, it is the reality (106). Therefore, "to think against the analogy between theater and politics is to think in favor of democracy" (65).

Theater for Rinesi is the metaphor of the political model of a liberal, representative democracy that restricts its citizens' right to deliberation and active participation in the administration of their common affairs (in the "scene" of "the public").
Politics is constitutively spectacular (the theatrical model has now been replaced by
the "phantom scene" of cinema and television, Rinesi says). See also his *Mariano*
(Buenos Aires: La marca, 1992).

Matei Calinescu provides another look at theater and democracy in modernity
in *Five Faces of Modernity: Modernism, Avant-Garde, Decadence, Kitsch, Postmodernism*
(Durham: Duke University Press, 1987). Calinescu reviews Friedrich Nietzsche's
diatribe against "theatrocracy" in *The Birth of Tragedy* (in the "Attempt at a Self-
Criticism," written for a new edition in 1886) as follows:

> Wagner's perversion of music does not represent [for Nietzsche] an accidental
> deviation from the specificity of an art—it is expressive of the whole crisis of
> modernity, which manifests itself by what Nietzsche calls quite suggestively, *the-
> atrocracy*. Wagner is an "incomparable *histrio*," an *actor*. He is not a musician who
> errs, he is not a poet either, he is only an *actor* of genius—"he became a musician,
> he became a poet because the tyrant within him, his actor's genius, compelled
> him . . . Wagner's music, if not shielded by theater taste, which is very tolerant
> taste, is simply bad music." (191)

Calinescu also cites Nietzsche's claim that Victor Hugo and Wagner, who appeal
to the masses, "signify the same thing: in declining cultures, wherever the decision
comes to rest with the masses, authenticity becomes superfluous, disadvanta-
geous, a liability. Only the actor still arouses great enthusiasm" (192). For Nietzsche,
Calinescu concludes, "Modernity leads to theatocracy because 'the theater is a
form of demolatry' [worship of the masses] in matters of taste; the theater is a revolt of the masses [*ein Massen-Aufstand*], a plebescite against good taste.—*This is
precisely what is proved in the case of Wagner:* he won the crowd, he corrupted taste,
he spoiled even our taste for opera" (191–92).

17. All quotes are from Lisa Dillman's recent translation, *Pot pourri: Whistlings
of an Idler: A Novel of Argentina* (New York: Oxford University Press, 2003). *Pot
pourri*'s few critics do not mention Voltaire's *Pot pourri* (1765), one of his *Stories* in
the form of a pamphlet, which likens Christianity to a puppet-making business.
The main character is Punchinello, who travels with his troupe of bohemian pup-
peteers from village to village staging farces. See Voltaire, *Romans et Contes* (Paris:
Garnier, 1960), 408–23.

18. Martín García Mérou's study titled "La novela en el Plata—*Pot pourri (Sil-bidos de un vago)—Música sentimental—Sin rumbo* (estudio) por Eugenio Cambaceres" appeared in *Sud-América* on 7 December 1885 (p. 1, cols. 2, 3, 4, 5). It was reproduced the following year in García Mérou's *Libros y autores* (Buenos Aires: Félix Lajouane Editor, 1886), with the title "Las novelas de Cambaceres" (71–90). Martín García Mérou says of *Pot pourri*:

> it has provoked our judgment and produced our literary sympathy. . . . What originality in this profoundly human book, so vivid and written with such a con-tinuous abundance of humorous paradoxes and colorful reflections! How it pa-rades before us the society, politics, press, and life which bustle around us and which it reproduces like an implacable daguerrotype! . . . The culminating quality in Cambaceres's writings is the strength, the emancipated vigor of his thought and his word! . . . His rough, incisive, cutting paragraphs with their sharp edges have the temper of steel . . . a terrible satire, an almost dithyrambic hatred.
>
> To conclude, let us note two distinctive traits in the works which concern us here. Above all, the setting. The author of *Silbidos de un vago* has *founded among us the contemporary national novel.* . . . Second, the language. It is the true *porteño* slang, as a young critic of shrewd spirit has pointed out. The most familiar phrases, the current terms of our conversation, the jargon of our compatriots such as *the semi-French, semi-indigenous argot of the upper class,* are the remnants that form the weave of this picturesque, deftly handled, *genuinely national* language in which these books are written. . . . Cambaceres is, in sum, an original literary personality gifted with a merit all his own. In our scarce intellectual life he is called to occupy an important post and to clear the path along which the Argentine novel will ex-tend itself in the future. (89; italics added)

García Mérou's article is from 1885, after the appearance of Cambaceres's third novel in which he abandons slang and the satirical tone. It is a fundamental criti-cal text because it very openly marks the adoption of Cambaceres as a figure of the coalition. Three weeks later, on 28 December 1885, Cambaceres in turn pub-lished in *Sud-América* (p. 1, cols. 2, 3) an article titled "García Mérou" about García Merou's recently published novel, *Ley Social*. He says: "I summarize: *Ley Social* has its appointed place, a place of honor in our embryonic literature. Its author, an un-questionable, luminous, solid talent, is one of the Argentine writers called to melt the frost of public indifference in this blessed land, where people read so little and do so many other worse things." Quoted by Claude Cymerman in "Para un mejor conocimiento de Eugenio Cambaceres," *Cuadernos del idioma* (Buenos Aires) 3, no. 11 (1969): 62.

As we see, the writers of the coalition are also critics and write about each other's books. This fabric of mutual references published in the official newspaper was the central fabric of the coalition. *Sud-América* published *La gran aldea* in installments (and García Mérou published a note about *La gran aldea* in 1885). And in 1887 it published, also in installments, Cambaceres's last novel, *En la sangre,* with a prior advertising campaign. Claude Cymerman says that "*Sud-América* advertised the imminent, constantly postponed appearance of *En la sangre* between March and September of 1887, piquing readers' curiosity." The publication rights were bought from Cambaceres for five thousand Argentinian pesos, a considerable sum in that era. (Is the author of the best-seller of '80 also a "professional writer"?)

•

19. Why can't we have "our" dandies? What are their differences with respect to English and French dandies? Are they differences in seduction or in the direction of sexuality? In the violence of their discourse? Or is the difference in the type of "aristocracy," European or Latin American, to which they are related? Or in the type of state? Or in the language and the tones they use? Or in the way they represent "the Creole"? Or in a certain *rastacuerismo* (from the French "rastaquouère" or "rastacuère," meaning "flashy adventurer")?

In *The Dandy and the Señorito: Eros and Social Class in the Nineteenth-Century Novel* (New York: Garland Publishing, 1991), Gloria Ortiz distinguishes between the French and English dandy and the Spanish and Latin American *señorito:* "The quintessential, historical dandy was not a seducer; the *señorito,* with rare exceptions, is. The dandy's legacy to the *señorito* was, therefore, confined to the realms of clothes, appearance, and a leisurely way of life" (17). Spoiled and narcissistic, the *señorito* appears as an active seducer who conquers women to feed his self-esteem. Ortiz adds that he "generally shows a marked aversion to work. When he does work, he tends to dabble at the occupation, which is sometimes a political appointment achieved through social connections, but which in any case requires minimal effort. He places great emphasis on clothes. He relies on them to convey an impression of economic well-being and social distinction which are often waning or nonexistent. He is usually young, though the exceptions are notable. The condition of *señoritismo* seems more a state of mind involving an overall falsification of values than an age-related phenomenon," concludes Ortiz (7).

In "Imagen de Mansilla," in *La Argentina del ochenta al centenario,* comp. Gustavo Ferrari and Ezequiel Gallo (Buenos Aires: Sudamericana, 1980), 745–59, Sylvia Molloy also marks Mansilla's difference with respect to the classic dandies. Molloy says:

His dandyism has often been discussed and it is certain that in the context of '80, [Mansilla] is the outstanding craftsman of his appearance: "I am a man of my look and of my time." . . . One could say that Mansilla intuits the *mots justes* of dandyism—passing for what we are not, falsifying oneself at odd hours, my look and my time—but that at the same time he can't contain himself: the scandalous image is not given free reign. What happens nakedly with Mansilla would never happen with Baudelaire's dandy, "latent fire which one must guess that he could but does not want to radiate." (747)

Molloy speaks of the difference between Mansilla's discourse and that of the dandy: "The dandy's discourse is intransigent, it is a truly one-armed discourse which refuses all contact; in his texts, however, Mansilla needs to touch with the vehemence of *he who aims to please* at all costs" (748).

Nevertheless, the land of the dandy, the theater, the "I," are present in Mansilla: "References *to theater, to simulation,* are frequent in *Una excursión a los indios ranqueles* as in all of Mansilla's writing. A comedian as always, he does not fail to take advantage of dramatic effect" (756; italics added). Molloy continues: "The texture of Mansilla's 'I,' of the *overwhelming person* who dominates his interlocutor and at the same time dismantles himself before our eyes. It is useless to attempt to re-compose an 'I' that finally does not wish to be composed: which prefers—not like a dandy, but rather like an adolescent—to maintain itself in indecision. But it is also difficult to read Mansilla dispensing with this first person which operates as a perpetual screen, as much in its dissimulations as in its epiphanies" (757–58).

So far, Sylvia Molloy and the differences (dandy or adolescent? intransigence or complacency? to radiate or not to radiate?) between European and Latin American dandies. Nevertheless, the fair Mansilla's life in Paris puts him in close contact with several "historical" or "classic" French dandies—for example, the count of Montesquiou. In the "Frontis" which precedes his preliminary study of Mansilla's *Una excursión a los indios ranqueles* (Expedition to the Ranquel Indians) (Buenos Aires: Ediciones Estrada, 1959), Mariano de Vedia y Mitre says that the best portrait of Mansilla's personality was painted by Georg Brandes, who met Mansilla in Paris. Brandes's portrait is included in "In the Bois de Boulogne," *Samlede Skrifter,* vol. 11 (Copenhagen: Gyldendalske Boghandels Forlag, 1902), 153, which describes an "international" luncheon given by Maurice Barrès in the summer of 1896, with the famous dandy the count of Montesquiou also in attendance. I quote De Vedia, who quotes Brandes:

> Above all the Argentine general Lucio Mansilla, nephew of Rosas, the former dictator of his country, a true *adventurer and a most beautiful man,* who with his martial air and his joviality, despite his white hair and beard, could still make a dangerous rival for any young man. He is so handsome with his military bearing,

with his faint characteristics of the *rastacuère* and the mischief in his black eyes, that even his own satisfaction with his physical person "doesn't suit him badly."

In the course of the meal I used the word splendid (*esplendide*). He: "Were you speaking of me with Montesquiou?" "No." "No? When I hear words such as splendid or splendor, I always think that people are speaking of me." And he laughed like a child. But his military campaigns are rightly famous in South America, as are his other more peaceful conquests. . . . Mansilla was accompanied by another Argentine military man. He was young and slender, but the vast personality and the humor of his old compatriot left him totally in the shade. (vii–viii; italics added)

I would like to add something about Montesquiou as a "classic" dandy and his relations with those "splendid," slightly "*rastacuère*" Argentines. (Is *rastacuerismo* our difference? The martial air?) Patrick Chaleyssin, *Robert de Montesquiou: Mécène et dandy* (Paris: Éditions d'art Somogy, 1992), says that Montesquiou (1855–1921), a dandy à la Brummel (which is to say, the very epitome of the dandy), was a friend of Marcel Proust, who took him as the model for his baron of Charlus. But before that he was the model for Jean Floressas des Esseintes in Huysmans's *A rebours*. Montesquiou was a "haughty, impertinent" eccentric and an admirer of Baudelaire, formulator of one of the principles of dandyism: "the aristocratic pleasure of displeasing." He practiced joking and sarcasm, and he was feared. "Arrogant, painstaking in his appearance, he was given not without a certain delight to sometimes violent verbal games," Chaleyssin writes (144). He was a painter, a symbolist writer, and a poet of recognized talent from 1892 onward. Very sensitive to the decorative arts, he was also a generous patron of poets and painters, and above all of Verlaine, who thanked him in verse. "Thanks *to his aristocratic and artistic alliances*," Chaleyssin says, "he was the guest of honor at the masked balls and the elegant *soirées* of the 'Belle époque'" (139; italics added).

Montesquiou and the Argentines. Apart from the "international" luncheon given by Maurice Barrès in the "Bois de Boulogne" in the summer of 1896, where we find Montesquiou and Mansilla speaking of "splendid" things, as later recounted by Brandes (did the patricians Cané, López, and Wilde, for example, attend this type of social event?), another Argentine also appears in Chaleyssin's book in relation to the famous dandy: a "faithful private secretary" and "secret agent." Chaleyssin says that *"Behind a counter at the Louvre*, Baron Doasan had discovered a young man born in Argentina in 1868: Gabriel de Yturri. In 1885 Montesquiou removed him from his post with the Baron . . . Yturri became his faithful secretary and Montesquiou imposed him on his friends. He soon came to share his patron's pleasures and seconded the count in all his social affairs . . . Yturri soon became *his secret agent*. With his marked accent, he called him "Mossou le connte" (29–30; italics added). Diabetes would later kill him, Chaleyssin says.

And the questions continue. Mansilla, Cambaceres, López, Cané: tension between "male aristocrats": between the patrician political exiles of the Rosas period and the heirs to Rosas's economy? They speak the same language and read the same books, but the heirs (the economic power) are, paradoxically, more modern, more French, more audacious, more fin de siècle. And more "Creole." A certain tension, then, between the "ancients" and the "moderns" of the coalition and one that is generally resolved with an "aristocratic" war of mutual ironies: a war between the "national heroes" and the dandies over women ("in female").

•

20. "Paul Groussac referred to that 'lie that was concocted in far-off lands' and then immediately attacked the writer: 'having pretended to be a novelist with the publication of scandalous anecdotes, told, as if sitting around the club, in an *aristocratic-Creole dialect,* he was naïve enough to want to carry on—with the success he imagined—in this literary vein, as artificial as his old-world nobility'" ("Trois pionniers du progrès," *Le Courrier de la Plata,* 16 December 1917, quoted in Cymerman, "Para un mejor conocimiento," 53).

We have taken Cambaceres's biographical data from Cymerman's article and from Rodolfo A. Borello's "Para la biografía de Eugenio Cambaceres," *Revista de la educación* (La Plata), first bimonthly issue 1960.

•

21. "Separación de la Iglesia y del Estado: Discurso del Sr. Dr. D. Eugenio Cambaceres: En la sesión de la Convención de la Provincia para la reforma de su Constitución del 18 de Julio de 1871," *Revista del Río de la Plata* 2 (1871): 275–89. Asking for the most complete liberty in matters of religion, without privileges, Cambaceres says:

> That political miscarriage known as State religion must not be legitimized in the eyes of the Republic!
>
> What is the state? indeed, Mr. President: in its political sense, the state is an assembly of public powers; and since those powers are constituted by delegates, by the leaders of the people, the state is no more than the expression, the manifestation, as it were, of the people themselves. Starting from this point and given that people profess, as they do, different religious beliefs, what right does the Legislator have to declare an official religion? How can the state be legally justified in saying, I am Catholic, Protestant, Jewish or Mohammedan? How can it then, in turn, represent the Catholics, Protestants, Jews and Mohammedans? Clearly, sir, such a declaration presents the most tangible contradictions, and with flawed foundations, the consequences will also be flawed.

If this is not so, then justify supporting the Catholic faith, paying their ministers, building and repairing their temples, etc., with the people's money. Prove
that it is fair and just to tell a Protestant, for example, who is as much a citizen as
a Catholic: you have the power to be Protestant, if you wish, but at the same time
*you must pay taxes and all sorts of contributions that will subsidize a religion that is not
yours;* so, purchase your right to be Protestant by paying the Catholic tab. No, Mr.
President, the very articulation of such a doctrine, consecrated in the same law that
grants each citizen the right to freedom of worship, is itself the most eloquent
refutation that one could provide.

And he concludes: "Based on these considerations and adhering to a deep conviction, I propose to the Honorable Convention an amendment to the article under
discussion, adding the following words, or words to this effect: 'the State neither
has nor subsidizes any religion.'"

Cymerman says that this bill "made him the enemy of the whole Catholic
party headed by Estrada and Goyena" to such an extent that its press organ, the
newspaper *La Unión,* demanded on 1 November 1885 that *Sin rumbo* be prohibited
and that its author be fined. And Cymerman quotes from *La Unión,* the Catholic
newspaper: "The Mayor . . . has taken no measures tending to impede the sale of
don Eugenio Cambaceres's new book titled *Sin rumbo,* despite its being a highly
immoral publication" (p. 1, col. 6). The newspaper also demanded that the author
be fined and that "the copies currently for sale in all the bookstores of the Capital"
be confiscated (48).

1885: at the moment when the "Catholic party" demands the prohibition and
confiscation of *Sin rumbo* (and when Cambaceres abandons the satirical tone and
the novel of fragments), the patrician cultural coalition welcomes him openly into
its literary bosom.

•

22. On 15 July 1886, there appears in *Sud-América* (p. 1, col. 5) a description of
Cambaceres's mansion. We quote from Cymerman: the house, which was at the
end of the Calle de Buen Orden, now Bernardo de Irigoyen, where it turned into
Avenida Montes de Oca, "looks exactly like a miniature castle set on a hill":

Its marble staircase leads to a living room covered with rich Gobelins; here a
painting, there a piece of furniture of incalculable value and marked by the seal
of the artist's hand; further along, a splendid mirror of Venetian glass; armchairs
and furniture that incite the visitor to the sweet voluptuousness of a decent lazi-
ness; elsewhere, a window covered with rich and heavy curtains . . . Cambaceres
leads a life which is at once active and comfortable—his tastes are those of a
sybarite and his nervousness that of an enterprising industrialist—; he is a mix-

ture of the great lord and the poor man who battles fate in order to make his fortune. It is understood that the fortune he now seeks is that of renown—which he has already half conquered by means of his previous books, and which he will prodigiously increase with the following ones—. (57; ellipses in original)

23. This gesture is repeated by Marcelo Torcuato de Alvear, another radical/Radical aristocrat and future president of the nation, who in 1906 married the Portuguese soprano Regina Pacini, provoking a scandal in Argentine "society." The newspaper *Clarín* ("Esto pasó un 29 de abril," 29 April 1998) reports that he met her at the Politeama theater in 1899; at age twenty nine, she already enjoyed international prestige, while he, at age thirty-three, was the leader of Radicalism whose fame as a sportsman and a seducer surpassed his political prestige. When the wedding was announced, more than five hundred friends, relatives, and partisans signed a letter imploring him not to marry. At the request of the Alvear family, Argentine newspapers did not publish news of the wedding. Regina abandoned her artistic career, devoted herself to charity work, and founded the Casa del Teatro.

While contemplating an Argentine woman at the elite ball, Cambaceres's dandy says:

> His dance partner was a lovely creature some 15 years of age who possessed all of the charming graces and southern spirits of a native-born girl, but hollow, superficial, and ignorant in the manner typical of Argentinian women, whose intelligence is a veritable swamp thanks to the tender and exemplary concerns of the paterfamilias. . . .
>
> Yet draw closer with the aim of passing but one half hour in her amiable company; either you shan't survive ten minutes, pummeled by boredom as if by a club, or you will be obliged to partake in utter triviality: providing merriments or receiving them of her; prattling on about boyfriends, about who says that So-and-so is courting such-and-such a girl and shall ask her hand; discussing who left some other boy high and dry; or, as a last recourse, drawing out the knife and stabbing it repeatedly into the back of whomever's path it should cross.
>
> And as if woman were as a weed in the park, something well-nigh indifferent that should hold no sway over the family and, therefore, over society and its improvement, this is how we try to raise her moral standard.
>
> What do we care if in other places—in the United States, for example, which we are proud to ape—often with neither rhyme nor reason, monkey-like, they award her the dignity of worrying about her political rights and allowing her to be a lofty public servant, doctor, lawyer, etc.?
>
> It suits us to have her know her place and station, hang it! And that is the way we want to keep it, by god.

Why?

Because. Because routine is a profound vice that flows through our blood-streams and because that was the tried and true custom of our Spanish forefathers. You made your bed, now lie in it; let the dance continue, and long live the revolution! (*Pot pourri*, 21–22)

•

24. Contemporary French comedy gives Cambaceres the theme of adultery and money. In the first travel book of the coalition, the 1881 *Recuerdos de viaje* (Buenos Aires: La Cultura Argentina, 1917), Lucio V. López writes "La Comedia Francesa," dated in Vichy, 19 August 1880: "The school of Molière inspires the modern comedy. . . . *Adultery* has been the muse of Alexandre Dumas and *cocottes* the heroines of Augier." But he criticizes this "dramatic literature of our time" because, he says, the theater of Sandeau, Feuillet, Augier, and Sardou is a "school of moral decadence. These would-be rebuilders of society begin by demolishing what exists without rebuilding anything in exchange." López recounts the plot of Sandeau's *Le Gendre de Monsieur Poirier*, which is very similar to that of *En la sangre*: a "repugnant rogue marries a delicate girl without loving her and counting only on paying for his tricks with Monsieur Poirier's three million." And why, he wonders, attack the bourgeoisie so much, if one wants to fight social and political battles, and not the Jesuits or the red press that eulogize the flames of 1871? (184–86).

There is a problem with the cultural or political "enemies," and there is a problem of morals or good taste in the aristocratic coalition. The patricians or ancients seem to be more moral and more political, and they cultivate good taste; the dandies Cambaceres and Mansilla appear more modern, more depoliticized and "meaner" (*canallas* is Cambaceres's word).

•

25. Parodied: the critics mention the author Suárez Orozco, who published *Música celeste* under the pseudonym "Rascame-Bec" (Paris: José Jola, 1885). See Cymerman, "Para un mejor conocimiento," 51.

Attacked: Cymerman takes charge of the repetitions of the "scarce biographers" and previous critics: Carlos A. Leumann, E. M. S. Danero, and Alberto Oscar Blasi, author of *Los fundadores: Cambaceres, Martel, Sicardi* (Buenos Aires: Ediciones Culturales Argentinas, 1962); he was denigrated during his lifetime with tags such as "mason," "heathen," "atheist." And Cymerman adds that he was surrounded by a "scandalous non-conformism" and "a bad reputation" in the "prudish and bourgeois environment of his era."

•

26. Me, marry?, asks the dandy:

"That is a cross I could not bear!

"To bring a strange being in to my home, some Joan of Arc to share my things, my table, my bath, and, far more serious, my bed, in which—armed with her legitimate title—attempt to sleep every night and every day without my having recourse to kick her out when it struck my fancy were I not in the mood for her company." (71)

•

27. The "actor" in *Pot pourri* presents himself as an authentic "historical" or classic dandy: is this his parody or farce, his "argentinization," his "translation"? Does this importation of a European cultural myth to Latin America attack the model or does it mix with local traits that corrode it from inside? Perhaps its difference lies in Latin America's lack of a true aristocracy, which gives the dandy meaning in Europe.

Let us present some of the dandy's history in order to leave the possible answers to this enigma to the reader. The first dandy seems to be Alcibiades, *arbiter elegantiarum* of Greek antiquity; he later reappears under the names *cortegiano*, courtier, and *honnête homme* in Italy during the seventeenth century, in England during Elizabethan times, and in France in the seventeenth century. But the word "dandy" and the modern history of the nineteenth-century dandies begin with the reign of "Beau" Brummell (George Bryan, 1778–1840) in the English court between 1805 and 1816. Protected and promoted by the Prince of Wales (later he suffered a vertiginous fall and died insane), he displayed a discrete and unmistakable distinction that would become the English ideal of elegance. His principle: he who wishes to dominate (and Brummell was something like Napoleon's other, *and this is something we wish to underscore because of the relationship between the dandy and the state*) should not let himself be dominated by sentiment. According to Ellen Moers, *The Dandy: Brummell to Beerbohm* (Lincoln: University of Nebraska Press, 1978), Brummell was not all that handsome but dressed in an austere and dignified style, and contrary to popular legend he wore neither jewelry nor perfume nor brilliant colors.

As the fashion of the dandy spread, it underwent various metamorphoses: one of the first was its exportation to France, where it mixed with another English export, Romanticism. The French version of the English dandy, Moers says, took its inspiration from books and was therefore more intellectual than the English one. The dandyism of the nineteenth century is above all *an intellectual attitude,* and it appears as the "destiny of the modern artist," according to Hans Hinterhäuser, *Fin de siècle: Gestalten und Mythen* (Munich: W. Fink, 1977).

In the treatises of Balzac, "Traité de la vie élégante" (1830), Barbey d'Aurevilly, *Du dandysme et de George Brummell* (1844), and Baudelaire, *Un peintre de la vie mod-*

erne (1859), this figure appears as the embodiment of social protest and rebellion against hypocrisy and conformism: against the masses hostile to art and the spirit. Although the French dandies of Balzac, Barbey, and Baudelaire differ, we can synthesize their traits in a "philosophy of dandyism" as fixed by these writers and as read in the classic anthology of Émilien Carassus, *Le mythe du dandy* (Paris: Armand Colin, 1971), which contains an introduction and the most important texts about and by dandies—texts by Balzac, Barbey d'Aurevilly, Théophile Gautier, Byron, Baudelaire, Huysmans, Albert Camus, Jean-Paul Sartre, and Roland Barthes, among others. Let us look at the features of this cultural representation.

The Weapons of the Dandy

The dandy is antibourgeois and antiutilitarian; he exaggerates his singularity and has an "aristocratic project" of distinction; his role is that of an actor in perpetual representation and self-creation; he is impassive and imperturbable (a modern form of stoicism); he situates himself beyond good and evil; he produces the unforeseen; he is adept at modulating his impertinence, his irony, and his disdain in a game that has variable doses of cynicism and sadism and which culminates in provocation. But his game is maintaining himself within the bounds of convention: he revolves around himself and does not intend to change the world.

A New Aristocracy?

Baudelaire says that dandyism is "a type of religion" with rigorous laws and *a new form of aristocracy* that appears in times of political transition, when democracies are not consolidated. The dandy's rejection of bourgeois vulgarity (if we understand as bourgeois the love of money and a baseness of spirit) configures a new ideal of personality.

The Dandy and Power

In "Le dandysme: Continuité et rupture," *L'honnête homme et le dandy,* comp. Alain Montandon (Tübingen: Gunter Narr Verlag, 1993), 123–49, Jean-Pierre Saidah says that dandyism proceeds to a rejection of sentimentality and develops *a taste for domination;* a dandy flees from all situations in which he finds himself in a position of weakness or of losing control. *There is a will to power in dandyism.* Was it not said that Brummell *reigned* at the English court? Dandies impose their law and their will. Their blasé attitude, the boredom they exhibit in their pose, deepens the distance that separates them from the world and assures their domination. The mask exhibits a made-up, artificial reality, the product of an acting will and the expression of a *cult of form* (143).

The Dandy and Literature

Saidah says that one of the essential breaks brought about by the dandy was a *literary one:* a break with Romantic ideology and the ideology of mimesis, a break with the dominant discourse in favor of the preeminence of play. Refusing to take himself seriously, *the dandy views the world as a vast stage on which everything is permitted;* the ease of the ever-present narrator and the recourse to figures of distancing refer back to a ludic conception of literature that appears to mask an ardent and wrenching love (148).

The Dandy and the Law

And Françoise Coblence, "Le dandysme et la règle," in Montandon, *L'honnête homme et le dandy,* 169–77, says that the law to which the dandy submits, and of which he is the author, *is the same to which the artist submits.* The dandy *is* the rule, the law he inscribes on his clothing, his body, his character. *The law of political power is helpless against the dandy.* His body thus incarnates the rigor of the law. For this reason, the dandy would testify to the void of the law and the impossibility of an aesthetics and of a modern heroism in the bosom of a world with neither model nor aura (177).

The Dandy and the Social Order

Jean-Paul Sartre, *Baudelaire* (Paris: Gallimard, Idées, 1963), 184, defines the dandy as a parasite of the poet who is also a parasite of a class of oppressors; Albert Camus, *L'Homme révolté* (Paris: Gallimard, 1972), 67–74, makes the dandy a romantic hero who defies the existing order, *limiting himself to the moment of negation and derision* by means of the astonishment and the surprise he provokes; it is an aborted revolt, *respectful of a social order which he does not intend to overthrow.* And his aestheticism appears as a rejection of political commitment.

The Dandy and Fame

Leo Braudy, *The Frenzy of Renown: Fame and Its History* (New York: Oxford University Press, 1986), says that in the nineteenth century, "the question of fame takes on an explicit political aspect that touches everyone in a society. The great expansion of the reading and viewing public . . . ensured that no one aspiring to public recognition . . . could be unaware of the multitude of ways it had been done in the past and was being done in the present" (476). One effect of the new culture of celebrity *was an interest in "the style and sometimes the substance of social marginality. The appeal of the outsider, perhaps our most widespread psychological inheritance from nineteenth-century Europe, seems necessarily generated to salve the wounds of a vast number of individuals who, however successful, still felt left out of the triumphal parade of social and scientific progress. . . . The dandy especially took that alienation and turned it into a badge and style of honor" (477; italics added). *Standing outside social convention and "placing the most ordinary circumstances in a ridiculous point of view* . . . the dandy as *spiritual aristocrat,* whose style was independent of class or genealogy, might share characteristics with *the criminal* who disdained normal social standards as well as with *the sage and the hero* who soared beyond them. . . . In a world becoming increasingly specialized, this new fame was decidedly nonprofessional, especially when it touched on the world of art" (477–78; italics added).

The Dandy, Journalism, and Fashion

Braudy explains that the term "journalism" was imported to England from France in the 1830s in order "to denote *the newspaper's daily processing of the world.* 'Gossip column' had to wait until the 1850s, but in the voluminous pages of caricatures, anecdotes, and commentaries on social events, the attitude existed long before the word" (479; italics added). According to Braudy, nineteenth-century journals also gave birth to modern fashion, "in the general sense of an awareness of dress and style as a form of self-expression available to all those who are interested" (479–80).

The Dandy and Sexual Gender

The misogyny of the dandy is well known. Baudelaire, *Oeuvres completes* (Paris: Gallimard, 1975), 1272: "La femme est le contraire du dandy. . . . / La femme est *naturelle,* c'est-à-dire abominable. / Aussi est-elle toujours vulgaire, c'est-à-dire le contraire du dandy." The "classic" dandy exhibits a marked sexual ambivalence, an androgyny and a misogyny expressed to the point of provocation; woman appears as an involuntary and overdetermined scapegoat. She is accused of incapacity for intellectual and spiritual elevation, and she is reduced to a purely decorative object, in a gynophobia that accompanies the homosexual temptation.

In *Gender on the Divide: The Dandy in Modernist Literature* (Ithaca: Cornell University Press, 1993), Jessica R. Feldman summarizes conclusions regarding the gender of dandies as follows: "For Albert Camus the dandy is a species of the rebel, 'a man who says no.' For Walter Benjamin, it is always the *flâneur*, never the *flâneuse*, who walks about the city, the man of the crowd. Emilien Carassus, in his anthologized excerpts from forty works concerning dandyism, includes not a single female dandy, as if the concept were a contradiction in terms. Perhaps Roland Barthes's statement best summarizes the truth of dandyism; it is, he reports, "un phénomène essentiellement masculin" (9–10).

Feldman says that dandyism "exists in the field of force between two opposing, irreconcilable notions about gender. First, the (male) dandy defines himself by attacking women. Second, so crucial are female characteristics to the dandy's self-creation that he defines himself by embracing women, appropriating their characteristics" (6). Her central point is that in a culture that polarizes gender, dandies "poise themselves precisely upon, or rather within, this divide: the violence of such self-placement generates the energy of dandyism as a cultural form" (7).

Feldman examines the dandies of Théophile Gautier, Barbey d'Aurevilly, Baudelaire, and in the field of North American English, those of Willa Cather, Wallace Stevens, and Vladimir Nabokov, and she shows that "these writers both reject and pursue women because they engage in that most self-dividing of activities: living within dominant cultural forms while imagining new forms taking shape in some unspecifiable 'beyond'" (7). The cultural change can commence, Feldman says, with this type of individual who sees things in a new (and sometimes illogical or even apparently insane) way. "In fact," Feldman continues, "the literature of dandyism challenges the very concept of two separate genders. Its male heroes, artists and their subjects alike, do more than punish women or dally with them—*they relocate dandyism within the female realm in order to move beyond the male and the female, beyond dichotomous gender itself.*" This "requires us to understand the dandy as neither wholly male nor wholly female, but as the figure who blurs these distinctions, irrevocably" (11).

The Dandy and the Anarchist

Michel Onfray, *Politique du rebelle: Traité de résistance et d'insoumission* (Paris: Grasset, 1997), rehabilitates the dandy, together with the cynics of Greek tradition, from a libertarian political perspective. He says that dandyism and libertarian thought function in all those who, far removed from the imperatives of that socialist realism which demands the submission of art to politics, propose precisely the opposite and hope that art will nourish, strengthen, and energize politics. From this perspective, dandyism (contemporaneous with the century of the Industrial Rev-olution) can be read as a reaction against the unidimensionality generated by the metamorphosis of capitalism. Onfray says: "In opposition to egalitarianism, that harmful religion of equality, dandyism vindicates a radical active subjectivity in its struggle against the order of the day: the cult of money and property, bourgeois dogma and family mythologies" (226). Diogenes and Baudelaire, Wilde and Carlyle are reconciled. See the genealogy of the dandy and the anarchist in "History of a Best-Seller: From Anarchism to Peronism" later in this manual.

•

28. Walter Benn Michaels, *The Gold Standard and the Logic of Naturalism: Ameri-can Literature at the Turn of the Twentieth Century* (Berkeley and Los Angeles: Uni-versity of California Press, 1987), establishes a series of relationships between the "I" as property and the female body as "the utopian body of the market economy, imagined as a scene of circulation" (13). In the North American naturalism of the late nineteenth century (for example, in the "corporate fiction" of Frank Norris's *The Octopus*—which can't help but remind us of the octopus that closes Julián Martel's *La Bolsa* [The stock exchange]—or in Theodore Dreiser's *The Financier*), Michaels establishes a series of relationships among capitalism, a specific system of representation—the daguerrotype or photo—and women (or slaves) treated as property. Female sexuality appears as the biological equivalent of capitalism, and the marriage contract, what Michaels calls "the phenomenology of the contract," appears as a strategy for containing (and repressing) its disorder. Michaels invokes Leo Bersani's thesis that "desire is a threat to the form of realist fiction" because it "can subvert social order" (46).

•

29. James Eli Adams, *Dandies and Desert Saints: Styles of Victorian Masculinity* (Ithaca: Cornell University Press, 1995), refers to the hero of Carlyle's *Sartor Resartus* and says that

> the persistence of the *dandy as a shadow of both prophet and capitalist* reflects a par-adox within the regime of what [Max] Weber called inner-worldly asceticism. . . . Like the desert eremite, the Carlylean hero [like the dandy] is constantly on dis-play even in the midst of solitude. . . . Ascetic discipline dictates the presence of an audience . . . from this point of view dandyism is an exemplary asceticism. . . . In Baudelaire's canny description, it is "a kind of religion" governed by discipline "strict as any monastic rule" but one that openly acknowledges a public gaze. . . . And it is for this reason that the dandy is such a tenacious and central presence in Carlyle's writings—as in so many Victorian discourses of *middle class* masculine self-fashioning. (35; italics added)

With regard to the general definition of masculinity in the Victorian period, Adams says that *"The understanding of masculinity as an ascetic discipline forms an* especially powerful continuum between early and late Victorian rhetorics of masculine identity, and between writers who might seem to occupy opposite sides of the (sometimes elusive) boundary dividing normative and transgressive sexualities" (230; italics added). He also notes that "struggles for masculine authority have a still more mundane and pervasive analogue in the incessant Victorian preoccupation with *defining a true gentleman [by] distinguishing between sincerity and performance.* If the status of gentleman is not secured by inherited distinctions of family and rank, but is realized instead through behavior, how does one distinguish the 'true' gentleman from the aspirant who is merely 'acting' the part?" (53; italics added). This was the challenge posed by social mobility, Adams says, given that the role of gentleman presupposed *"a degree of theatricality."*

•

30. Tony Tanner, *Adultery in the Novel: Contract and Transgression* (Baltimore: Johns Hopkins University Press, 1979), says that, "although the eighteenth- and nineteenth-century novel may be said to move toward marriage and the securing of genealogical continuity, it often gains its particular narrative urgency from an energy that threatens to contravene that stability of the family on which society depends. It is thus a paradoxical object . . . a text that may work to subvert what it seems to celebrate" (4). As "an act of transgression" against the family, adultery "can be seen as an attempt to establish *an extracontractual contract, or indeed an anticontract that . . . threatens . . . continuations, distinctions, and securities* (6; italics added). But what is worth exploring, Tanner says, are

> the connections or relationships between a specific kind of sexual act, a specific kind of society, and a specific kind of narrative. . . . Adultery as a phenomenon is in evidence in literature from the earliest times, as in Homer (and indeed we might suggest that it is the unstable triangularity of adultery, rather than the static symmetry of marriage, that is the generative form of Western literature as we know it). It is a dominant feature of chivalric literature; and it becomes a major concern in Shakespeare's plays. . . . But it seems to me that *adultery takes on a very special importance in the late-eighteenth- and nineteenth-century novel."* (12; italics added)

Tanner mentions Jean Jacques Rousseau's *La Nouvelle Héloïse,* Flaubert's *Madame Bovary,* and Leo Tolstoy's *Anna Karenina* and *The Kreutzer Sonata* as prominent examples of the many canonized nineteenth-century novels that center on adultery. For Tanner, "marriage is *the* central subject for the bourgeois novel" because in bourgeois society, "marriage is the all-subsuming, all-organizing, all-containing contract. It is the structure that maintains the Structure, or System. . . . In confronting the problems of marriage and adultery, the bourgeois novel finally has to confront not only the provisionality of social laws and rules and structures but the provisionality of its own procedures and assumptions" (15). He says that "when marriage is seen to be the invention of man, and is felt to be the central contract on which all others in some way depend, . . . adultery becomes, not an incidental deviation from the social structure, but a frontal assault on it. Divorce is, of course, the main way in which society came to cope with adultery, but it is notable that, although the topic arises, in none of the novels I wish to consider does divorce occur, nor is it felt to offer any *radical* solutions to the problems that have arisen" (17–18).

The chapter in which Tanner analyzes the violation of frontiers, hospitality, and the disruption of a previous order is titled "The Stranger in the House." He concludes that the appearance of the artist in a dominant role marks "the decline of the bourgeois novel as such. . . . One is tempted to say that the emergence of the artist-as-hero [seen in the novels of Henry James] is coincident with a sense of the family-as-ruin" (99).

•

31. "In the upper balcony no one was left standing; refuge of old maids and maidens whom luxury and wealth neither favor nor popularize, it became Criterion: there all reputations, whether man's or woman's, were run through the sieve . . . tongues, like so many shaving razors, are not content to shave; they slash, they murder." And immediately thereafter, the authoritarianism of the patricians: "You who have authority, abolish the upper balcony, bring in a male element; unaccompanied women turn to snakes in that aerial den" (144–45).

•

32. To depoliticize is to produce a reformulation of politics. The writers of the coalition, as we pointed out with regard to Cané, depoliticize their representations when they cross, in their texts, the threshold of 1880. The past associated with school is political and is put in 1860, while the present of the marriages of 1880 is purely cultural and social. This operation permits them to announce a new politics: that of the liberal state in the phase of its end-of-the-century dominance.

•

33. The epistemology of the liberal state is positivist-materialist, and it is for this reason that the scientific sector of the coalition includes not only the naturalist writers but also all those who explain the world through science: it serves as a bridge between liberal culture and the new "progressive" culture. In 1896 the Centro Socialista de Estudios was created; Leopoldo Lugones was the librarian and Roberto

Payró the secretary, and he gave a talk titled "On the Relationship between Biology and Sociology."

In *La locura en la Argentina* (Buenos Aires: Paidós, 1985), Hugo Vezzetti marks the difference between socialists and anarchists with respect to the themes of degeneration and criminality and the hygienic mechanism of the state. Individualist anarchism, he says, tended to reject the apparatus of hygienics and to denounce it as an instrument of state domination, although it seemed to replace it with the construction of an aesthetic ideal. Socialism, in contrast, converges with medical thought and, what's more, collaborates actively in the confirmation of the hygienic and criminological mechanism. This is not only because it finds points in common with its own program of reforms, but also because it endorses that positivist utopia which makes science and the progress of institutions the principle engine of social change. From this viewpoint and with their hopes invested in the role of science, socialists took a position of principle according to which the social and moral elevation of the popular masses demanded a struggle against deviation and crime (180–84).

•

34. Mark Seltzer, *Bodies and Machines* (New York: Routledge, 1992), refers to the link in North American naturalist literature between processes of generation and degeneration (or degradation) and also to the relation between the economic and the sexual. These two registers appear contradictory but are connected and coordinated in a "general economy of power," in a "circuit of exchange" between machines and bodies (40). Seltzer says that the subject of the realist novel is "the internal genesis and evolution of character in society" and that "through techniques of narrative surveillance, organic continuity, and deterministic progress, [it] secures the intelligibility and supervision of individuals in an evolutionary and genetic narration." There is a "progress" of subjects "consistent with their determining antecedents." The naturalist novel, according to Seltzer, "involves a mutation in these techniques that consists also in a systematic and totalizing intensification of their effects. This mutation makes for functional shifts in emphasis—thematic and narrative shifts, for instance, . . . from histories of marriage and adultery to case histories of bodies, sexualities, and populations" (43).

The coalition rejected and later accepted literary naturalism. Martín García Mérou, the official critic, says: "It is not possible to examine Cambaceres's novels without brushing up against the eternal question of naturalism. Let us hasten to say that, in our view, he should not be considered a disciple of Zola." And he adds that he was previously opposed to Zola's naturalism (and this rejection is also seen in Lucio V. López's *Recuerdos de viaje*), but "reflection and life, as much as personal experience, have later shown us the profound and devastating truth of those paintings" (in reference to *Nana;* see "Las novelas de Eugenio Cambaceres," *Libros y autores,* 88).

•

35. In his four novels, Cambaceres invents two narrative positions *linked to theatrical representation* in order to embody the new subjects or gazes: that of the dandy and the scientific naturalist gaze. The dandy's theater or spectator's box, where the "I" is distinct and massive, and the scientist's amphitheater, without an "I." They are distant gazes, one aesthetic and the other scientific, which go together and accompany the culture of the state as its autonomized other. The difference lies in what is seen: the dandy looks only at his surroundings, at high life, and the scientist looks down at others. But in both cases these are characters who enter the "private homes" of the ranchers (Juan's secretary and "confidant" in *Pot pourri* and Máxima's husband, Genaro, in *En la sangre*).

Manuel T. Podestá (1853–1918) was a contemporary of Cambaceres and of the empire of Zola and Daudet. He attended the Colegio Nacional familiar from *Juvenilia,* and at age twenty was already the chief of the surgical clinic at the old Men's Hospital. Later he became a national deputy for the province of Buenos Aires, secretary of the Department of Hygiene, director of the San Roque Hospital, welfare director, professor of the Faculty of Medicine, and clinician at the Hospital for the Insane.

•

36. In a chapter of *La locura en la Argentina* devoted to "Insanity and Immigration," Hugo Vezetti refers to Cambaceres's Genaro *in relation to immigration.* He says that in Ramos Mejía there subsists a characteristic of the evangelical immigrant, the ideal laborer, linked to constant work and sanctified by his faithfulness to his patrons. But we also see in Ramos the sign of the degenerative immigrant in his portrayals of the "lout." Vezetti says that other texts draw the opposite face of this biblical immigrant: the idler, the upstart (like Genaro Piazza), the anarchist, with the degenerative reference seen in the literature of the naturalists. Without the mass of foreigners, the series of psychiatric theses about simulation would not be possible, Vezetti says, but *it is evident that this figure of the upstart is constructed in the novel;* in *En la sangre,* Genaro remains a pure and decidedly archetypal form (186).

So far, Vezetti. I think it would be interesting to contrast *Irresponsable* with *En la sangre* on the basis of their *opposing representations of immigrants.* And to be able to glimpse, again, certain differences in the scientific sector of the cultural coalition. Or certain differences between the coalition and a scientific sector that detaches from it in order to install itself in another culture. The dumb "Neopolitan tinker" with the square head, who is Genaro's father in Cambaceres, differs from the healthy, robust immigrants who walk through the Calle Florida with their chubby children and their buxom women in Podestá. The "beasts" in *Irresponsable* are the Creoles at the police station, the policemen "of inferior race" in chapter 11. At the moment of transition from the culture of the liberal state to another "more modern" and progressive culture, the difference between the "inferior races" appears. The choice of "beasts" is crucial and defines various cultural lines.

•

37. A Dispute over the Simulation of Talent

With Podestá and Cambaceres, with their "stories of education and marriage," the coalition (the scientific-fictional subject of the liberal state) defines a madman and a simulator of talent scientifically and through narrative and literature. They appear at the same moment not only in literature but also in science, psychiatry, criminology, and politics. In purely scientific treatises on simulation by José Ingenieros (1877–1925) and José María Ramos Mejía (1849–1914), these two categories are joined at one point. *Both Ingenieros and Ramos begin with simulation and end with crime and insanity.* Hence, the "cases" of Cambaceres and Podestá, united by the exam, are again united scientifically, and they are resolved in crime.

Simulators and the analysis of simulation, the theme which Ramos and Ingenieros develop almost simultaneously, point toward *differences integral to modern society*. At the top of the pyramid, they place geniuses and men of talent, who do not simulate; in the center, the mediocre, who simulate; and on the bottom the brutes or idiots. The "middle" is the problem.

Simulation (a privileged object of liberalism and its double identities) interests us because it can be taken as a "crime of truth" (because it puts the problem of beliefs into motion), and because it is linked with falsification and fraud. But simulation is a privileged object because *it is the place where there is a dispute about representation and also a political debate*. It is a theory of representation and of resistance. And it is here that Ramos Mejía and Ingenieros differ.

In *Los simuladores del talento* (The simulators of talent), which appeared in 1903 (we cite from the Tor edition, Buenos Aires, 1955), José María Ramos Mejía attacks José Ingenieros from the outset. Ingenieros, his disciple, had already published chapters of *La simulación en la lucha por la vida* (Simulation in the struggle for life) in *La semana médica* and in *Archivos de psiquiatría* between 1900 and 1902. (He is one of the first immigrant intellectuals and he entered science through simulation;

Ingenieros's text was presented at the Faculty of Medicine as the introduction to his thesis, *Simulación de la locura*, 1900.)

In the very introduction to his study, Ramos Mejía says that "Ingegnieros" (so written, as an Italian immigrant name) described simulators psychologically and classified them. But Ramos claims the originality and the anteriority of his own specific focus on talent. He says that *no one* broached the theme studied in his book and whose first chapter he had published several years earlier in *Anales de la Facultad de Derecho*. The nucleus for the development of his thesis was the *Argentine caudillo*. This book, Ramos Mejía says, studies the *"defensive faculties" which the caudillos applied in their political administration*. (In Ramos Mejía we find "the Creole" and "the encyclopedia": the national as represented by "aristocratic" Latin American culture.)

And in note 5 of the eighth edition of *La simulación en la lucha por la vida*, Ingenieros says, "Ramos Mejía has studied in particular *Los simuladores del talento* in a book with *political projections*." And toward the end: "The thesis of this book is paradoxical: it is necessary to possess true talent in order to carry off such a simulation of talent successfully" (Ingenieros, *Obras completas*, vol. 1 [Buenos Aires: Elmer Editor, 1956], 87).

Ingenieros simply and plainly denies the thesis of Ramos's book at its very foundations: he says that it is *a political, not a scientific, book* and that there is no simulation of talent because talent is not representable: one must have it in order to "simulate it." This dispute is crucial and separates them radically, and it is possible that it also separates two lines of Argentine culture. Or that it separates "a scientific subject of the coalition" from another type of scientist.

Ingenieros, in his remarks on talent, is on the verge of refuting the theory of simulation at the very point at which simulation or representation (performance) would be the "truth" of a subject, *because he politicizes it*. Critiques of successive theories of simulation are accompanied by a critique of the truth that would lie beyond simulation, and also of the politicization of simulation. There is no real and true being against which to exhibit or simulate; there is no truth underneath the fiction at the very heart of the subject; one is what one represents. The theory of simulation can only be refuted from the very heart of the subject called "simulating," and from politics and resistance.

Ramos Mejía and Ingenieros are differentiated and also united because, apart from talent, both agree that simulation is a problem of modernization, and they agree on Darwinism and on simulation as a resource of life itself (and of "the struggle for life"). Ingenieros and Ramos construct a Darwinian and Nietzschean social world, totally penetrated by fiction, by falsification and fraud: a world that will reach its culmination in Roberto Arlt.

But Ingenieros not only universalizes simulation and links it with fraud, he also opposes it to war and violence as a peaceful procedure for avoiding confrontation. He shows it as a means of resistance. Ingenieros says, in the struggle for life, everyone is a gladiator who fights or an actor who recites. And he concludes that with social revolution (and he quotes Marx), with the coming forms of social organization, simulations appear destined to dwindle to the degree that the "struggle for life" eases.

The two coalition scientists agree that there are *dangerous cases of simulation that must be denounced: these are the ones that lead to crime and madness*. Simulators and madmen once again, turning as if in a circle, because the appearance of one immediately summons the other. And between them, crime.

Ramos Mejía says that simulation is cunning or crime, depending on our perspective, and that some simulators throw off the mask, break through the dykes of discipline, and resort *to murder* or simple compensatory aggression (94–95). "This is the type *of the unbalanced aggressor,* the neurotic murderer, *bordering on madness* without being completely within it, but drinking from its golden fountains the inspiration and the irresistible impulse which drives him" (96).

And in his "Classification of Simulators," Ingenieros makes a chart and differentiates between mesological simulators (acquired or through environment: cunning or servile), congenital simulators (deceitful or refractory) and pathological simulators (psychopathic or delusional). Simulators by adaptation to environment include cunning simulators, embodied in the "fortune hunter," but whose cunning may become overly predominant. "The personality of these subjects is grounded on slippery moral terrain. Given the utilitarian purpose of simulation, it arrives at *zones bordering on criminality, engendering a mixed type of "criminal simulator"* (83–85; italics added).

In Ingenieros the study of simulation leads to crime and to penal reform. And for this reason he writes the second part, *La simulación de la locura*. Those criminals who simulate madness are declared not legally responsible; the legal reform proposed by Ingenieros would tend to *put an end to the simulation of madness by criminals:* with the deception of the state.

Simulators, madmen, criminals: a field shared by José Ingenieros in *La simulación en la lucha por la vida* and Roberto Arlt in his treatise on the simulations and crimes of madmen and monsters (*Los siete locos* [The seven madmen] and *Los lanzallamas* [The flamethrowers], 1929 and 1931). Ingenieros's series (or the limits of simulation and its combinations) persists in Arlt: madness can be simulated, and simulators can go mad and arrive at crime. In fact, Ingenieros defines certain of Arlt's characters: the Astrologer, the Espilas, and Erdosain.

The Astrologer

We met numerous simulators among individuals professionally dedicated to the propaganda of *political ideas,* religious ideas, social ideas, etcetera. There exists in them the obligation, as a *modus vivendi,* to simulate political, religious and social passions at set times and in front of the most varied audiences, passions which in some cases are at odds with their mental and organic state at that moment; but if they were not opportune simulators, they would compromise not only their prestige, but also the daily bread they earn by means of simulation. They constitute *the disagreeable antithesis* of that other, extremely sympathetic figure, the individual full of faith and conviction who sacrifices himself for the propaganda of any idea, noble or absurd, which he considers good or just. (Ingenieros, *La simulación en la lucha por la vida,* 90–91)

Ingenieros's Brechtian and capitalist world of Chicago with its *simulating beggars* is also present in Arlt in the figures of the Espilas, whose simulated condition is that of beggars and "victims of science":

The *mise en scène* of these subjects is usually flamboyant and refined. In Chicago, according to the press, the police discovered a beggars club a few years back on West Adam Street. They found there a group of subjects, very healthy and happy, who used to eat, drink, play, and smoke there, and who possessed a library of ancient philosophers with which to pass their leisure hours. During the day, all of them would pretend to be lame, blind, mute, stupid or deaf, and they would beg in the streets of the city; at night they would gather at their club in order to enjoy the profits of their daily "work" in peace. In one of the rooms the police found a large number of cripple's carts, crutches, wooden legs, shoes simulating deformed feet, eyeglass cases and bandages for the eyes, canes for weak old people, false beards, boxes of paints used to simulate all kinds of wounds and pustules on the skin, a specialty to which two members of the club, true artists of the brush, dedicated themselves. There were numerous *signs* with appropriate inscriptions: "blind from birth," "deaf mute because of fright," "Civil War invalid," "have gotten leprosy caring for other lepers," etcetera. After their arrest, they were found to be in an excellent state of health and fit for work; for a long time they had been associated in order to exploit the charity of philanthropists, to the detriment of the real poor.

Cases such as this one—which attained a certain fame due to its magnitude—occur in all big cities. In Buenos Aires, false mendicancy has not yet attained vast proportions. We do know, however, a professional thief who told us of *having worked as a blind person for five years;* he performed his job "honorably" with discrete earnings until the police discovered his fraud and arrested him. In prison he met various professional thieves; when he was released he couldn't return to his former trade, and so took up professional *robbery* in the company of his new friends. (Ingenieros, *La simulación en la lucha por la vida,* 112–13; italics in the original)

Ingenieros also leads us to the *thieving cashier:* to Emma Zunz's father in Borges's "Emma Zunz" and to Erdosain, Arlt's *thieving bill collector:*

"Persecutory observation." He is a fairly learned cashier, a gambler, who has no neuropathic heredity, but who stole money from the cash register to meet *gambling debts.* The owners noticed the embezzlement, they have him arrested, and when he is called to testify his attitude is suspicious, he answers with difficulty, he presents *delirious ideas* of a persecutory nature, accompanied by aural, visual, and olfactory hallucinations and *suicidal ideas.* There are no physical signs of illness. The defense attorney asks that he be declared not responsible due to mental condition. But his simulation was discovered and he was convicted. In jail his false melancholia didn't disappear suddenly, Ingenieros says, but "it was gradually normalized." His moral sense was retained. (199)

Arlt transforms Ingenieros's theory of simulation from 1900 into a politicized fiction of the twenties: simulation, madness, and the crime with money, the plan and "the revolution."

Ingenieros and Arlt also share one last field. According to Elías Castelnuovo in his *Memorias* (Buenos Aires: Ediciones Culturales Argentinas, 1974), Arlt

felt a morbid attraction for everything macabre. I recall that one morning we visited the municipal crematorium together in Chacarita, *with purely journalistic objectives.* Immediately, he hit it off with *the director of the institute, a doctor of hygiene* and fervent partisan of cremation, whose proselytizing zeal on this point made him more than a little suspicious. More than a report on the technique of the procedure, he gave us a master class incorporating his knowledge of the putrefaction of cadavers, and the objective of this catechizing propaganda was to convince us that when it was our time to depart this vale of tears, we should not allow the worms to savage the remains of our corporal covering. For this purpose, he had at his disposal a folder containing a register where we could put down our signature to declare our intent.

Arlt reacted with enthusiasm:

"Stupendous!" he exclaimed, opening his eyes wide, "To see a two hundred and fifty pound mastodon with his pockets full of money reduced to three pounds of dust! *It's fantastic! Great!"*

This doctor's friendship finally cost Roberto Arlt dearly. Whether out of conviction or out of condescendence, the fact is that he finally put down his name and surname, thus sealing his agreement. What happened after his death is already known. The sad end to which he came: he ended up occupying an urn in the Chacarita columbarium along with José Ingenieros, another partisan of cremation. (142–44)

Simulation Today

From Simulation to Cybernetics

In 1981 Jean Baudrillard declared "the era of simulation" open, announcing the suppression of the referent and the substitution of the signs of the real for the real. With simulation, according to Baudrillard, *Simulacra and Simulation,* trans. Sheila Faria Glaser (Ann Arbor: University of Michigan Press, 1994), "It is no longer a question of imitation, nor duplication, nor even parody. It is a question of substituting the signs of the real for the real, that is to say of an operation of deterring every real process via its operational double" (2).

Baudrillard says: "To dissimulate is to pretend not to have what one has. *To simulate is to feign to have what one doesn't have* . . . pretending, or dissimulating, leaves the principle of reality intact: the difference is always clear, it is simply masked; whereas *simulation threatens the difference between the 'true' and the 'false,' the 'real' and the 'imaginary'"* (3; italics added). He opposes simulation to representation, which "stems from the principle of the equivalence of the sign and the real (even if this equivalence is utopian, it is a fundamental axiom). . . . Simulation, on the contrary, stems from . . . the sign as the reversion and death sentence of every reference" (6).

Baudrillard continues: "The transition from signs that dissimulate something to signs that dissimulate that there is nothing marks a decisive turning point. The first reflects a theology of truth and secrecy (to which the notion of ideology still belongs). The second inaugurates the era of simulacra and of simulation, in which there is no longer a God to recognize his own, no longer a Last Judgment to separate the false from the true, the real from its artificial resurrection, as everything is already dead and resurrected in advance" (6). For Baudrillard, cybernetic models or simulacra

no longer constitute either transcendence of projection, they no longer constitute the imaginary in relation to the real, they are themselves an anticipation of
the real, and thus leave no room for any sort of fictional anticipation—they are
immanent, and thus leave no room for any kind of imaginary transcendence.
The field opened is that of simulation in the cybernetic sense, that is, of the ma-
nipulation of these models at every level (scenarios, the setting up of simulated
situations, etc.) but then *nothing distinguishes this operation from the operation itself
and the gestation of the real: there is no more fiction.* (122; italics in original)

From Simulation to Transvestites

In *La simulación* (Caracas: Monte Ávila, 1982), Severo Sarduy refers above all to
transvestites and to the baroque, and he separates the copy from the simulacrum.
He discerns in transvestitism "an *intensity of simulation* which constitutes its own
end, outside of what it imitates: what is simulated? Simulation" (11). "The transvestite does not copy; she simulates, since there is no norm which invites and mag-
netizes transformation, which decides the metaphor: it is more the non-existence
of a spoiled being which constitutes the space, the region and the basis of that simulation, of that concerted imposture: an appearing which regulates a Goyaesque
drive: between laughter and death" (13).

Sarduy says that in the transvestite's simulation there would be *a drive toward
metamorphosis, toward transformation,* that is not reducible to the imitation of a real
model, but rather strives to cross the limit, going beyond womanhood. Citing
Roger Caillois, *Méduse et Cie* (Paris: Gallimard, 1960), he attempts to demonstrate
that "animal mimetism *is useless* and represents nothing more than a desire for ex-
penditure, for dangerous luxury, for chromatic splendor, a need to display colors,
arabesques, filigrees, even if they serve no purpose—numerous studies demonstrate this" (16). Sarduy says that the transvestite confirms the existence of an identical desire for the baroque in human behavior, and he invokes Caillois's formulation
of "*a law of pure disguise in the living world, a practice which consists of passing for another,* clearly proved, and which is not reducible to any biological necessity derived
from the competition between species or natural selection" (16; italics added).

According to Sarduy, the simulator does not copy but rather makes a simulacrum, gives the illusion of the model (and he cites Deleuze's *Logique du sens*).
Icon copies (linked to an Idea) attempt to duplicate the truth of the model, whereas
*phantom-simulacra add to the model, they are "against the father," they do not pass for the
Idea* (18).

Sarduy's main idea would be that *simulation appears as a mockery, as a travesty* of
a model and implies "laughing at authority, insulting the model, impugning the

inquisitors, sullying, staining . . . what is untainted, what is perfect, what is unattainable in its clarity and harmony." He reclaims "iconoclastic energy, subversion of the classical figure, agitation, blasphemy" and says that "the model and its disfigured copy, the monument and its parody, the operation and its blasphemy" alter the "sacramental charge" with which "Power" invests its "Culture," writes Sarduy (123).

From Simulation to Resistance

In *Domination and the Arts of Resistance: Hidden Transcripts* (New Haven: Yale University Press, 1990), James C. Scott refers to simulation as resistance and to masks, gestures, performances, and acting always in hierarchies of gender, race, caste, and social class. The practice of domination creates what becomes hidden in subordinate groups, engendering a subculture and opposing its own form of domination to that of the elite. There will always be, according to Scott, "a hegemonic public conduct and a backstage discourse consisting of what cannot be spoken in the face of power" (xii).

38. Vezzetti finds the notions and the fundamental focus of positivist criminology (as finally constituted by Ingenieros and de Veyga) announced in Alejandro Korn's 1883 doctoral thesis, *Locura y crimen* (Madness and crime). The thesis concludes as follows: "From a philosophical point of view we will agree, then, that between madness and crime there exists only a difference of degree" (quoted in Vezzetti, *La locura en la Argentina*, 118). Vezzetti later adds that 1902 marks the beginning of the publication of *Archivos de criminología y psiquiatría*, under Ingenieros's direction. The journal's editorial committee included not only Ramos Mejía (who had published *La locura en la historia* [Madness in history] in 1895), but also Francisco de Veyga, Manuel Podestá, and Pietro Gori, an Italian criminal lawyer who resided in Argentina from 1898 to 1902 and who played an important role in the diffusion and organization of anarchism. In 1898 Gori founded *Criminología moderna*, whose editorial board featured professors from the Faculty of Law and the Faculty of Philosophy and Letters, national deputies, madness specialists such as Manuel Podestá, and police officials such as Juan Vucetich (180–81).

Criminology has a history which runs parallel to that of the state, according to Marie Christine Leps, *Apprehending the Criminal: The Production of Deviance in Nineteenth-Century Discourse* (Durham: Duke University Press, 1992). "The intertextual circulation of criminological discourse has coincided with periods marked by civil unrest: during the great depression of the end of the nineteenth century, when movements fighting for the rights of the working classes in general or women in particular were increasing their momentum, and toward the end of the twentieth century, during the 1960s and 1970s . . . the concept of 'criminal man' . . . must present specific ideological advantages warranting the emergence of criminology, the science of 'criminal man,' when authority structures are threatened" (43).

Leps says that *criminology is an intertextual science,* a bricolage of "medicine, physiology and psychiatry, anthropology, zoology and botany, linguistics and philosophy" (44). As an intertextual science, it is an amalgam of ideological principles regarding deviance determined by prevailing notions of nationality, "race, sex, class and morality" (47). Leps adds that "By denying the notion of free will and posing that illegal acts were biosocially determined, criminology changed the rules for the administration of justice" (58).

•

39. Jonathan Cott, *Thirteen: A Journey into the Number* (New York: Doubleday, 1996), says that some believe that the number thirteen brings bad luck and others that it brings good luck, and he explores the many curious facets of this "maligned number." He recounts how the composer Arnold Schoenberg numbered sounds up to twelve and how he became so terrified after turning seventy-six ($7 + 6 = 13$) that he "took to his bed, depressed, on Friday the 13th of July, 1951, and died thirteen minutes before midnight" (6).

The number thirteen (or *the law of luck in the field of numbers*) generated an "industry" which will not be long in imposing itself among us, says our dandy Lucio V. Mansilla in his *Causerie* titled "Superstición y puntualidad," published in 1890 in *Entre-nos: Causeries del jueves,* and reproduced in *Humorismo argentino,* ed. Luis Alberto Murray (Buenos Aires: Ediciones Culturales Argentinas, 1961), 29–32. I am indebted to Marta Palchevich for this text:

> Yesterday was Tuesday; a bad day to embark, marry, submit requests, borrow money with interest, or commit suicide.
>
> In addition to it being Tuesday, this letter had to bear, as it does, the number thirteen, a number of bad omen, mysterious, enigmatic, symbolic, prophetic, fateful, in a word, cabalistic.
>
> Things that come in thirteens are always bad. Between thirteen people, misfortunes always occur. When thirteen eat together, sooner or later one of them is hung, dies suddenly, disappears inexplicably, is robbed, shipwrecked, ruined or wounded in a duel. Finally, there is usually a traitor among them.
>
> It is a fact that has been proved infallibly time and again since that famous supper at which Judas gave Jesus his perfidious kiss.
>
> For this reason, *there exists in France, that most refined nation, an industry which*

will not be long in introducing itself in Buenos Aires, where the plagues of civilization in-
vade us every day with terrifying speed. . . .

The industry of which I speak takes its name from those that practice it, commonly called *quatorzième* (fourteenth). . . .

When someone has invited various friends to eat at their house, in a restaurant or in a hotel, and it turns out that due to the absence of one or more only thirteen arrive, and when the quarter hour grace period conceded to the less than punctual has expired, recourse is made to the *quatorzième*. (29–30; italics added)

And our ineffable Mansilla goes on to describe the functioning of this French "cultural industry."

•

40. *Exam Stories: Notes for a Possible Anthology*

The physics exam of 1880 as a "story of education and marriage," as a liberal exam of social truth founded on the abstract science of bodies, opens cycles and carries us into the future: it brings us to Roberto Arlt, 1920. *It marks a unit of cultural time, between two changes or mutations.* A unit of time between Genaro Piazza and "the magnet fellow," on the one hand, and Arlt's Silvio Astier and Augusto Erdosain on the other; the cultural unit of the physics exam stories with simulators, madmen, and criminals (and with "Jews"). For what does the autobiographical character of *El juguete rabioso* (Mad toy) undergo at the School of Aeronautics, where he was sent by *a Jewish* neighbor, if not a physics "exam"? He passes the exam but it does him no good: we don't need people who know things here, they tell him, only brutes to do the work. And what is the plan Erdosain submits to the Astrologer at the end of *Los lanzallamas* (before *the blood of the Jew* is spilled) if not a "written exam" in physics and chemistry? In this cultural cycle, which is the time between the physics exam and the physics "exam," the story disperses (it could reach as far as Peronism to include Julio Cortázar's *El examen*) and generates other exam stories "with laughter." These are the ones that would form the "possible" anthology. The physics of the liberal state, like so many other things, is inaugurated by our (Cané's) beloved Amédée Jacques, and it appears at our starting point, in *Juvenilia*. And it is associated with a grammar exam. In chapter 16 of *Juvenilia*, Cané says in reference to Amédée Jacques: "One thing displeased us: that Jacques did not belong to us completely and exclusively. We would have given a great deal to see him resign his chair in *physics* at the University." And he goes on to recount his exam in Spanish grammar, which is "the grammar of translation" typical of the "aristocratic" culture of the coalition:

In order to get into the first-year Latin class, I had to take an impalpable exam in *Spanish grammar*, in which I was ignominiously failed by the committee composed of Minos, Aeacus and Rhadamanthus, in the form of Larsen, Gigena and Doctor Tobal. They gave me a passage from Laren's translation the *Aeneid* to analyze grammatically; it was an invocation which began with: "Goddess!" "Possessive pronoun!," I said, and that was enough, because Larsen shouted at me in a thunderous voice: "Out, you animal!" (84)

Other exam stories with laughter. The physician-writers are profuse in their *exam stories with madmen at the Faculty of Medicine*. Let us look at one that appears in the first volume of *Libro extraño* (Strange book) (Barcelona: Granada y Cía. Editores, 1910), by the physician and writer Francisco Sicardi (1856–1927). Here again a "madman" and loser is defined. Don Manuel de Paloche, at age forty, takes the anatomy exam for the second time:

> Doctor Polifemo coughed, pointing to one of the examiners.
> "The brain," he said very seriously.
> "Organ of thought," Don Manuel answered quickly, "although this doctrine is not in accord with the Christian religion."
> "That is not what you were asked," said the professor, wrinkling his brow . . . "Continue . . . anatomy of the brain."
> "And seat of the spirit, which the sages locate . . ."
> "I repeat—anatomy of the brain . . ."
> "That is what I am answering, sir," replied Paloche, irritated.
> Repressed laughter was heard.
> "Because I am not one of those," he continued, "who resigns himself to accepting opinions without discussing them, and in the end I believe that one should at least be given freedom to speak."
> The laughter became more pronounced.
> "Reconsider, Mr. Paloche, and restrict yourself to the question."
> "I am restricted, professor sir. But before delving deeply into the matter, I will point out that an organ of such importance deserves due psychological consideration."
> "Don't digress . . . to the point, to the point, sir."
> "Psychology is not a digression," Paloche answered forcefully.
> "Enough," roared Polifemo, and then coughed. *The laughter multiplied into something of a muted seguidilla.* (119–20; italics added, ellipses in original. This first book is from 1894; the five volumes were completed in 1902.)

Sicardi was José Ingenieros's professor in the Faculty of Medicine, and Ingenieros wrote an article about *Libro extraño* titled "La psicopatología en el arte" and published in *Archivos de criminología y psiquiatría* in 1903. Let us look, then, at one of Ingenieros's exams with laughter, as recounted by Manuel Ugarte in *Escritores Iberoamericanos de 1900* (México: Editorial Vértice, 1947):

> On a certain occasion Ingenieros subtly mocked scholastic truth while examining a student.
>
> "Do you believe that the earth is round?" he asked point-blank.
>
> The young man hesitated until, recovering his senses, he gathered the courage to answer:
>
> "Yes."
>
> "And do you also believe that the earth revolves around the sun?" he continued with increasing violence.
>
> The victim, terrified, trembled as he made an affirmative gesture.
>
> "So then," Ingenieros thundered, striking the table, "how does it not fall? Explain to me, how does it not fall?"
>
> Sensing the student's terrible anguish, the executioner abruptly changed his tone, and in a soft voice, he threw a lifesaver to the shipwrecked boy.
>
> "Have you ever seen a map?"
>
> The answer was a sigh:
>
> "Yes, sir . . ."
>
> "And have you noticed the lines which mark latitude and longitude on the map?"
>
> "Yes, sir . . ."
>
> *More and more smiling and cordial,* Ingenieros stood up to shake the hand of the young man who was coming back to life.
>
> "If you have seen those lines, my friend," he told him, "you can answer my question. Always remember what you're hearing now. Those lines are the wires that hold up the world."
>
> After which, he gave the young man the highest grade, explaining by way of an epilogue:
>
> "At least this one answers when he knows and holds his tongue when he doesn't." (151–52; italics added)

The "Ingenieros" and the "Moreira" figures are mortal enemies in the *corpus delicti* and in Argentina: they define two lines of culture. Let us go then to the province where one of the Moreiras recounts his exam with laughter in *Divertidas aventuras del nieto de Juan Moreira* (Amusing adventures of the grandson of Juan Moreira) (Barcelona: Maucci, 1910). The author, Roberto Payró, belongs, like Ingenieros, to the socialist and progressive line. "Juan Moreira's grandson" says:

I didn't understand a word of the mystifying interrogations suffered by the boys who went before me, and questions and answers sounded to me like a bothersome buzzing of formless things, the grumbling of an unknown litany. But anxiety weighed on my chest, the aplomb I had felt in Los Sunchos now completely lost, and when my turn arrived, I shook as I approached the chair in the middle of an empty space in front of the green tablecloth. It looked to me like the dock of the accused, if not death row . . .

What did they ask me first? What did I answer? Impossible to reconstruct it! I only recall that Don Prilidiano leaned over to Don Néstor's ear and mumbled, not so softly that I couldn't hear with my senses sharpened by fear:

"But he doesn't know a word!"

"Bah! That's why he's here, to learn. He's Gómez Herrera's son," Don Néstor said.

"Oh! Well then . . ."

Doctor Orlandi interrupted the aside, asking me:

"Whad is-a da biggis gondinende in-a da world?"

"The Argentine Republic!"

The three of them burst out laughing [. . .] Don Néstor came to my assistance, saying haltingly:

"That's not exactly right . . . but it's always good to be patriotic . . . Don't you learn geography at school in Los Sunchos? . . . That's a good one! . . ."

I started to get up, considering my martyrdom to have ended in moral death, but the Latinist stopped me with this sudden and devastating question:

"What is the function of the verb?"

Half standing, with my right hand resting on the back of the chair, I steadied my frightened eyes and stammered:

"I . . . I've never seen it!"

Don Prilidiano's rage was stifled by *the Homeric guffaws* of the other two, between whose outbursts I heard Don Néstor repeating:

"That's fine, sit down! That's fine, sit down!"

Completely trapped, I sat back down in the dock, telling myself that this torture would end only with my death, material this time; but the rector managed to contain himself and he said to me more clearly, with mocking kindness:

"No, no. Go to your seat. Go to your seat."

My ears were buzzing, but as I passed the benches, I thought I heard: "He's an ass," and I thought about fleeing all the way back to Los Sunchos, but I didn't have the strength. I collapsed into my seat. *How the professors and the students had laughed at me! At me, Mauricio Gómez Herrera, at whom nobody in my town would have dared to laugh!* (76–78; italics added)

In order to close the scientific circle of the exams and of simulation (Ingenieros's circle), or to close for now the "possible" anthology, let us point out that after Ingenieros's death, Roberto Payró wrote about him and about his "simulation" in the magazine *Nosotros* 199 (1925). There Ingenieros appears as an Italian immigrant and *as a simulated porteño,* more Argentine than the Argentines:

> He was small and slight, gesticulative, restless. His high-pitched and rather sour, unpleasant voice accentuated the sarcasm and irony which were his favorite modes of expression. He used to talk as if in successive explosions, with abrupt leaps in tone, but always in abundance. . . . Nevertheless, he seemed more of a hothead, unsuited to cold scientific investigation, and more of a destroyer than a builder. Some, ill able to distinguished content from form, came to consider him a fool and took his positive knowledge as garrulous patter. Appearances deceive, and one might say that Ingenieros strove to multiply and complicate these deceptive appearances. Why? For what purpose? A mystery. . . . But among the causes that, outside of his always youthful and playful character, compelled him to these attitudes, *his southern Italian ancestry* must figure along with his evident desire to mingle, to alloy himself with us—he finally overcame the "g" in Ingegnieros— *and to be as porteño as the best of them, adopting and exaggerating some of our ways,* among them our levity, our spiritual and epigrammatic skepticism.
>
> He even pretended not to take seriously some of the works in which he invested the greatest effort. I recall that one afternoon in his study at 1131 Calle Cuyo, when I congratulated him on his recently published *Simulación de la locura,* he responded by gesturing carelessly toward the books in his *well populated library* and saying:
>
> *"Bah! That's what all this is for!"*
>
> And a few days later, he wrote to me in regard to a note published in *La Nación:*
>
> "Dearest Payró: Many thanks for the benevolent recollection of my book, which I have just read in your newspaper. *In view of its success, I shall continue simulating.* Yours always, Ingenieros."
>
> This, which at first glimpse seems a mere witticism, has nevertheless a positive content, since by his own admission, if he did not simulate, he at least dissimulated, and, what's worse, exclusively to his own detriment, depriving himself of admiration and perhaps affection. *To state my thoughts frankly, I believe he "was too clever for his own good."* (76–77; italics added)

Is this not the moment (a circle appears to close) to leave the "stories of scientists," of exams, of madmen, of simulators? The moment to leave "the coalition," with the parody of the *porteño* and his library?

II. The Frontier of Crime

1. Eduardo A. Zimmerman, *Los liberales reformistas: La cuestión social en la Argentina, 1890–1916* (Buenos Aires: Sudamericana-Universidad de San Andrés, 1995), 11–16, says that in this period, and as a consequence of massive immigration, urbanization, and industrialization, the so-called "social question" became prominent: problems of health, housing, urban criminality, and protests by workers. It was a process of social conflicts and intellectual transformations; new ideological currents challenged the validity of the existing political and social institutions and instituted a debate over the capacity of classical liberal institutions to provide solutions to the new problems. The clamor for social and political reforms coincided with the appearance of a reformist liberal current in the government and in the opposition (Radicals, socialists, Catholics), which included professional groups (above all lawyers and doctors) in search of a middle road between orthodox laissez faire and state socialism. Their orientation was legalistic, scientific, and internationalist. Zimmerman demonstrates that in this period a new "inclusive" political language was constructed, culminating in the 1912 Sáenz Peña law which introduced universal male suffrage and a compulsory, secret ballot (the principle of citizenship was consolidated).

•

2. It seems that these transmutations occurred biographically in the cases of Leopoldo Lugones (from revolutionary socialism to fascism), Horacio Quiroga (with his retreat to Misiones province), and Juan José de Soiza Reilly (with his abandonment of satire in the twenties).

About the frontier, see *Border Theory: The Limits of Cultural Politics,* ed. Scott Michaelson and David E. Johnson (Minneapolis: University of Minnesota Press, 1997), especially Alejandro Lugo's article, "Reflections on Border Theory, Culture and the Nation," 43–67. Renato Rosaldo, in *Culture and Truth: The Remaking of Social Analysis* (Boston: Beacon, 1993), defines culture in terms of frontiers. Edward W. Soja also refers to the logic of the frontier in *Thirdspace: Journeys to Los Angeles and Other Real-and-Imagined Places* (Cambridge: Blackwell, 1996). And as Guillermo Gómez Peña says in *Warrior for Gringostroika: Essays, Performance Texts, and Poetry* (St. Paul: Graywolf Press, 1993), the frontier is a place of boycott, conspiracy, illegality, a new cartography, and a new internationalism.

About mutants: In *The Imperial Archive: Knowledge and the Fantasy of Empire* (New York: Verso, 1993), Thomas Richards says that toward *the end of the nineteenth century,* "a new form of monstrosity arose to outwit Darwin. These new monsters were essentially mutants, capable of sudden and catastrophic changes of form, a kind of change outlawed and virtually unknowable under the Darwinian system. Even at the height of Darwinism in late Victorian Britain, writers began to imagine a great variety of monsters that fell outside the sureties of lineage enshrined in morphology" (48–49). They were threats to Darwinism's universal pretensions because they interrupted the very order of things and even threatened to bring about the end of the empire. Richards says that the British monopoly of knowledge ends in Bram Stoker's *Dracula* (1897), where a *colonial alterity*, the vampire, refuses accommodation within the scheme of historical-morphological development. "The narrative of *Dracula* makes it clear that there are some species whose origins cannot be understood using the Darwinian model, and these originless species, impossible according to Darwin, had become the archetypal monsters of the twentieth century" (49).

Citing H. G. Wells's *The Island of Dr. Moreau* (1898) as another major and contemporaneous mutant narrative, Richards relates those phenomena which break "forms" to an imperial trajectory of "colonization, occupation, and decolonization." His study "reconstructs the central position the notion of form occupied in pre-imperial discourse and considers Lewis Carroll's *Alice's Adventures in Wonderland* (1865) and *Through the Looking Glass* (1871) as an anatomy of the problem of positive knowledge of exceptional forms within mid-Victorian morphology. The Alice books are about a little girl dropped into a world of monsters, monsters whose world changes in accordance with the dictates of logical form" (49–50). Richards follows his examination of *Dracula* with an analysis of J. G. Ballard's *The Crystal World* (1966), "a text that links African decolonization with the rapid spread of an unknown crystalline form" (50). Richards says that "the search for the positive knowledge of form passed, as was the case with so many other positivist projects of comprehensive knowledge in the late nineteenth century, first from the domain of science into the domain of myth, and last into the domain of ideology" (50).

In *Great Themes of Science Fiction: A Study in Imagination and Evolution* (New York: Greenwood Press, 1987), John J. Pierce says that the concept of the mutant appeared in North American science fiction in 1885, in "Old Squids and Little Speller" by Edward Page Mitchell, and in 1895 in "Another World" by J. H. Rosny (26–48).

•

3. Eduardo L. Holmberg, *Cuentos fantásticos* (Buenos Aires: Hachette, 1957), 170–236. The volume includes a preliminary study by Antonio Pagés Larraya.

Between 1870 and 1890, Eduardo Holmberg invents the fantastic, detective, and science fiction genres in Argentina. He founds the literature which accompanies realism and naturalism, that of *the limits of science* in mental phenomena (telepathy, spiritualism). Holmberg wrote about the inspirational processes of an artist who speaks with his dead sister in "El ruiseñor y el artista" (The nightingale and the artist), from 1876. There he dramatized telepathic phenomena: the action of one spirit on another, mental suggestion, and remote communication. He also wrote about automatons in 1879 in "Horacio Kalibang o los automatas," dedicated to José María Ramos Mejía. The idea of this *nouvelle* is that of an independently functioning brain, and it also introduces robots at a time when Cibernius had not yet been born, according to Antonio Pagés Larrea in his preliminary study of the *Cuentos fantásticos*.

Bernard Gooden identifies Holmberg as a science fiction pioneer in "De quelques thèmes originaux dans la SF espagnole et hispano-américaine du XXe siècle," in *Just the Other Day: Essays on the Suture of the Future,* comp. Luk De Vos (Antwerp: Restant-Exa, 1985), 143–60. Gooden says that Holmberg's novel *Viaje maravilloso del señor Nic-Nac* (Mr. Nic-Nac's marvelous journey) appeared in 1875 in installments in the Buenos Aires newspaper *El Nacional,* and that this marks the true starting point of Hispanic science fiction. There the author develops the themes of metempsychosis and inhabited extraterrestrial worlds.

But we are interested in marking Holmberg's frontier character. In his preliminary study, Pagés Larrea refers to the fin de siècle climate to which the author belonged and suggests to us that Holmberg provides the perfect link between the "subjects of the liberal state" and those of "the new culture." He belongs to two groups at the same time, to the patrician state coalition as well as to the bohemia of the *modernistas,* hence his ambivalence. The "subjects of the liberal state" recognize him as one of them because of his family, his "blood." And on the other hand, the new subjects (and media) associated with Darío, Lugones, and Ingenieros recognize him as one of their own.

Pagés Larraya provides us with the following information:

On the Patrician Side

In a chapter of his *Recuerdos literarios* (1937) titled "La cultura popular," Martín García Mérou says that "Holmberg is the strange product of an exotic genius in our civilization. Although his grandfather, the Baron of Holmberg, a direct participant in the Independence campaigns, was a compatriot of Humboldt, his heredity is such that *the blood of patriots and Argentines* runs through his veins" (cited in Pagés Larraya, 9).

And Miguel Cané, in *Ensayos* (1877): "The first time our eyes happened upon the name Holmberg was on a glorious page of the epic of our Independence. The Baron of Holmberg commanded the artillery of the patriots at the battle of Tucumán, under Belgrano's orders. The grandfather *ennobled his name* on the fields of that holy struggle; the grandson enters life dignifying his with the pure reflection of a beautiful intelligence" (cited in Pagés Larraya, 9).

On the Modernista Side

Pagés Larraya says that Darío's visit in 1893 was followed by the proliferation of the literary gatherings, circles, and cafés that Holmberg frequented. When Holmberg appeared among the many Argentines immortalized in *Las caricaturas contemporáneas* by the cartoonist Cao (*Caras y Caretas,* 23 June 1900), he was introduced with the following epigraph:

> D. Eduardo L. Holmberg
> Although he pays no heed / to the progress of French fashion, / and attaches no importance to his suit, / he proved his elegance with his pen / in "La bolsa de huesos." // To Natural History / with exceptional talent / he dedicates long hours, / among the beasts he studies / he's one more intellectual beast. (Cited in Pagés Larraya, 30)

In his "Versos de Año Nuevo" (New Year's verses), also published in *Caras y Caretas,* Darío himself portrayed Holmberg among his *porteño* comrades: "Our wise German fellow / told us profound things / and in picturesque language / he gave out laurels and gave out thrashings" (cited in Pagés Larraya, 31). Darío and Holmberg associated with José Ingenieros, Antonino Lamberti, Charles de Soussens, Alberto Ghiraldo, and all of those who constituted literary bohemia at the turn of the century, Pagés Larraya says, and he adds that the scientist's humor, originality, and *interest in esoteric subjects* attracted Darío's attention. Darío says: "I also spent time with other friends who were no longer young, such as that unique spirit, so full of diverse ideas and emanating such a generous and sympathetic current and such contagious vitality and joy, Doctor Eduardo L. Holmberg" (cited by Pagés Larraya, 31).

Pagés Larraya also cites an article by Leopoldo Lugones in *El tiempo,* 18 September 1896, about Holmberg's *Nelly,* in which he remarks on literary knowledge of telepathic phenomena and says that Holmberg is "one of the most complete intellectuals to be found in the country of the Argentines." When Holmberg died on 5 November 1937, *La Nación* published a note that said: "At night, at café gatherings with Rubén Darío, whom Holmberg called 'the last sacred poet of Hellas';

with Roberto Payró, with the astronomer Harperath, he conversed about Germanic poetry, about the religions of India, about translations of Greek and Latin. He spoke with a parsimonious slowness which strongly emphasized his unexpected commentary and his disconcerting paradoxes mixing difficult quotations with the twists and turns of vernacular fluency" (cited by Pagés Larraya, 31).

This material collected by Pagés Larraya locate Holmberg on the frontier, in the passage between the scientific subjects of 1880 and the new subjects of *modernismo*.

    •

4. We are in what has been called the "positivist utopia" or the "religion of science." Consider this speech delivered by Juan Angel Martínez, a deputy from the province of Buenos Aires, in the National Chamber of Deputies on 1 September 1902, in the context of a debate over a bill for a divorce law:

> Science shall teach us how best to educate each man for individual and collective life; science shall correct all the great errors in social organization which have occurred up until now and it shall banish all the great worries; only it is capable of ever realizing the doctrine of Christian fraternity, equality before the law, and human solidarity; only it shall be capable of suppressing the frontiers between peoples; of banishing, of extinguishing the hatreds of the human masses and of bringing us closer, through love and mutual affection, to all peoples, to all men of all faiths and of all nationalities; of creating a single type of currency to serve throughout the world as an intermediary of exchange of the products of the arts, of work and of intelligence; in a word, only it is capable of leading humanity to its highest destinations, under the auspices of this trinity: justice, science and liberty! (Cited in Ricardo Rodríguez Molas, *Divorcio y familia tradicional* [Buenos Aires: Centro Editor de América Latina, 1984], 116)

    •

5. The quotes are from *Las fuerzas extrañas* (Buenos Aires: Manuel Gleizer Editor, 1926). Lugones originally published another of the stories included in *Las fuerzas extrañas*, "Un fenómeno inexplicable" (An inexplicable phenomenon), with the title "La licantropía" (Lycanthropy) in *Philadelphia: Revista de las Ciencias Ocultas*.

Modernismo as a Frontier

Howard M. Fraser, *In the Presence of Mystery: Modernist Fiction and the Occult* (Chapel Hill: University of North Carolina Department of Romance Languages, 1992), says that in "Ensayo de una cosmogonía en diez lecciones" (Essay on a cosmogony in ten lessons), Lugones *attempted to reconcile* literature with the latest scientific discoveries, or *to read science from literature*. There he presents an entire Pythagorean geography from which objects and beings descend. "Lugones communicates his animistic interpretation of life from the point of view of el hombre, *a wise old man of the Andes* who assumes the identity of a *Theosophist Master*. This *guru* speaks to the first-person narrator in epigrammatic sentences, and through his sage pronouncements the initiate learns that all forms of nature have been generated from a single, primeval force. . . . Lugones's narrator can be perceived as *the quintessential modernista*, an initiate who undertakes a spiritual quest" for "the elusive essence of things" (Fraser 75–76; italics added).

Fraser remarks upon *the convulsion brought by the modernization-globalization which accompanies modernismo* (dislocation, confusion, the threat of annihilation and violence) and upon the *resort to occultism as a vehicle of cosmic vision,* a first step toward finding spiritual solutions. The *modernistas "denied the supremacy of reason which was the cornerstone of Positivism* and its attendant glorification of experimental science, industrialization, and material progress as a justification of a new bourgeois and dehumanized social order" (124; italics added). They adopted the classical belief that the "poet," a word that connoted the artist, was the only one able to guide a spiritually blind world. And they placed the *shaman,* who manipulates cosmic forces, alongside the *writer or poet.*

Caras y Caretas (Faces and masks), the popular *modernista* weekly through which the entire "turn of the century" can be read, disseminated the principles of theosophy, occultism, and divination. Fraser cites the articles "La teosofía en Buenos Aires" (no. 157 [1901]); "El mundo de las adivinas" by Carlos de Soussens (no. 84 [1902]), and "Adivinando el porvenir" by Nemesio Trejo (no. 363 [1905]); "La astrología del siglo xx" (no. 489 [1908]), "La forma de los pensamientos" (no. 344 [1905]), and the column "Lo desconocido," which dealt with cases of telepathy. The magazine also published *photos* of spirits in "El espiritismo en Buenos Aires. Curiosas fotografías de espíritus materializados" by Benjamín Villalobos (no. 308 [1904]).

Fraser refers to the founder of the American Theosophical Society, Helena Petrona Blavatsky (1831–1891), who was important in attracting Darío and Lugones to theosophy (69). And Sandra Hewit and Nancy Abraham Hall analyze these relations in "Leopoldo Lugones and H. P. Blavatsky: Theosophy in the 'Ensayo de una cosmogonía en diez lecciones,'" *Revista de estudios hispánicos* 18 (1984): 335–43.

Annie Besant was also important. There is an essay by José Martí, "La oradora humanitaria, Annie Besant" (The humanitarian orator, Annie Besant), in which he hailed Besant's visit to the United States by saying that she discovered and classified acts of the spirit, treating them like scientific facts.

Martí makes use of what is devalued by rationalization, says Julio Ramos in

Desencuentros de la modernidad en América Latina. The opposition to modernization (read as "materialism" or "pragmatism") appears as a definition of the cultural values of Latin America, of "Latin American identity." Before the end of the century, when this process of modernization occurs, Latin American men of letters were political men and men of the state, says Ramos; in Martí there is a place of enunciation *outside the state, on the margin,* and he therefore appears as a critic of the dominant discourses of the state. (He changes *the public space* where literature appears, with the chronicle linked to journalism and the market, another form of modernity, Ramos says.)

They are on the frontier: revolutionary socialism, anarchism, theosophy, modernismo, *and the religion of truth.* The poetry of Ariel Schettini synthesizes these relations in "Capdevila," from the volume *Estados Unidos* (Buenos Aires: La marca, 1994):

> Lugones and Palacios. On Las Heras Avenue, the brilliance of the dark, mute, close night.
> . . . They had gathered, as on so many nights, at the Argentine Theosophical Society; and they left. Mute, together, down Las Heras.
> . . . They were mute because they were conversing about the sign hanging at the ATS:
> The well-known apothegm: SATYAT NASTI PARO DHARMAH (There is no religion higher than truth). (55)

Final Investigations Regarding the Sect and Its Leaders

In *The Masters Revealed: Madame Blavatsky and the Myth of the Great White Lodge* (Albany: State University of New York Press, 1995), K. Paul Johnson argues that this group, a true network, was made up not only of spiritual movements, but also *clandestine political causes:* some were Masons who supported Garibaldi in Italy; others were Hindu political and religious leaders who conspired *against the British empire.* Blavatsky, who loved intrigue as much as the occult sciences, emerges in this book as an *anticolonialist pioneer.*

Blavatsky's fame was based on the pretense that she received her ideas in letters sent through an astral postal system by members of the Great White Lodge, a group of Indian and Tibetan "masters." K. Paul Johnson's hypothesis is that these "masters" were not astral, but rather real people who hid their identities behind "astral" characters.

In *Las ciencias ocultas en la ciudad de Buenos Aires* (The occult sciences in the city of Buenos Aires) (1920), Arlt writes a biography of Madame Blavatsky linking her with "outmoded English imperialism," and he says that Hodgson discovered her frauds. (In 1884, Richard Hodgson of the British Society for Psychical Research went to India to investigate Blavatsky and called her "one of the most successful, ingenious, and interesting imposters in history.") But what Arlt doesn't say is that Hodgson considered her a *Russian spy* with ties to the Russian occultists. The report ended with her career in India, but she revived herself in London, where her admirers included Yeats and Gandhi. She died in England in 1891.

Peter Washington, *Madame Blavatsky's Baboon: A History of the Mystics, Mediums, and Misfits Who Brought Spiritualism to America* (New York: Schocken Books, 1995), said that Blavatsky attracted her followers with a mixture of ecumenical religion and personal eccentricity. She founded the Theosophical Society in New York in 1875, two years after her arrival, and her great prodigy was Jiddu Krishnamurti. But the complex organizations that they founded were *sites of scandal, power politics and sexual imbroglios*. Blavatsky was accused of plagiarism in her letters, and another member was accused of pederasty and ventriloquism. It was said that a spirit had informed Charles Webster Leadbeater that "In other ages Mrs. Besant acquired twelve husbands for whom she roasted rats" (129). In his introduction, Peter Washington says that many of the devotees and their leaders *were woman who defied conventions in radical ways*.

According to Sandra Gilbert's "Heart of Darkness: The Agon of the Femme Fatale," in Sandra M. Gilbert and Susan Gubar, *No Man's Land: The Place of the Woman Writer in the Twentieth Century*, vol. 2, *Sexchanges* (New Haven: Yale University Press, 1990), there is a "link between, on the one hand, the alternative historical and theological possibilities propounded by spiritualism and theosophy and, on the other hand, the possibilities of disorderly female rule" (29).

•

6. A series of antistate topics can be read in *La Montaña*, founded in 1897 under the direction of Lugones and Ingenieros (its twelve issues were reproduced and published in 1996 by the Universidad Nacional de Quilmes). The first issue opens with a manifesto, "Somos socialistas." We are socialists, the editors proclaimed, "because we consider the political authority represented by the State to be a phenomenon resulting from the private appropriation of the means of production, whose transformation into social property necessarily implies a suppression of the State and the denial of all principles of authority." Following the manifesto, the first article is "La sociedad sin Estado" by Gabriel Deville, which continues in the second and third issues.

The most provocative articles in *La Montaña* were those contributed by José Ingenieros in the series "Los reptiles burgueses" (The bourgeois reptiles). The series consists of ardent attacks on the Church and on pilgrimages to Luján (issue no. 2); on "the moral masterminds" of society: storekeepers, public servants, "soldiers who kill in the name of the fatherland," bourgeois politicians, magistrates, judges, "high class" ladies (no. 5); on intellectuals and stockbrokers: "The bourgeois 'intellectual' and the bourgeois 'stockbroker' are beings who do not even possess a psychology of their own; they are pedicles on the great social pubis" (no. 8); and on "The fathers of the fatherland," deputies and senators: "Who can doubt that the Argentine Parliament is a temple of mediocrities?" (no. 10).

I would also like to mention Macedonio Fernández's article in issue no. 3, "La desherencia" (The disinheritance) (where he wonders: *why is so little light shed on the problem of the essential difference between science and art?*); a polemic with the anarchists (who accuse the socialists of authoritarianism) in no. 8; articles in defense of feminism in nos. 4, 6, and 12; and in nos. 9, 10, 11, and 12, a translation of Edward Carpenter's "Defense of Criminals," the last part of which is titled "The Usefulness of Robbery and Prostitution."

In "Los políticos de este país" (This country's politicians), nos. 1 and 4, Leopoldo Lugones accuses the bourgeois politicians of robbery, and in "La moral en el arte" (Morality in art), he argues that the artist must rise up against "eternal morality, eternal religion, eternal property, eternal commerce, eternal imbecility."

For an analysis of *La Montaña*'s discourse, see Marcela Croce's *La Montaña: Jacobinismo y orografía,* Hipótesis y Discusiones, vol. 8 (Buenos Aires: Facultad de Filosofía y Letras, Universidad Nacional de Buenos Aires, 1995).

•

7. *Toward a Literary History of Torture in Argentina*

Sarah Wood, "Writing the Violent State: The Representation of State Violence in Southern Cone Narrative" (Ph.D. diss., Yale University, 1997), refers to the body as "truth" in Arlt, and she quotes Elaine Scarry's *The Body in Pain: The Making and Unmaking of the World* (New York: Oxford University Press, 1987): "at particular moments when there is within a society a crisis of belief—that is, when some central idea or ideology or cultural construct has ceased to elicit a population's belief either because it is manifestly fictitious or because it has for some reason been divested of ordinary forms of substantiation—the sheer material factualness of the human body will be borrowed to lend that cultural construct the aura of 'realness' and 'certainty'" (14).

Sarah Wood traces a literary and political history of bodies in Argentina in their relation to the state. Before the constitution of the Argentine state in 1880, she says, *the female—or feminized—body appears in literature as a symbolic sight of struggle between Federalists and Unitarians, and torture also appears:* in Esteban Echeverría's *El matadero;* Luis Pérez's "El testamento de Rivadavia" (*El Torito de los Muchachos,* 1830); Hilario Ascasubi's "La refalosa" and "Isidora la federala y mazorquera"; and the pregnant body of Camila O'Gorman. (As is well known, Wood says, *Amalia* and *El matadero* mark the foundation of the narrative tradition in Argentina.) The politicization of the body and of torture, which corresponds to moments of crisis and violence, appears in the twentieth century in Arlt's Melancholy Pimp (who in *Los lanzallamas,* following the coup of 1930, is tortured by the police detective Gómez); in the "Russian Bolshevik" Jew of the Peronism of "La fiesta del monstruo" by Borges and Bioy Casares; and in the student Pablo Alcobendas in *El incendio y las vísperas* by Beatriz Guido (published in 1969 but written between 1960 and 1964). All of this, of course, is repeated in the literature of the most recent dictatorship, which is the focus of Wood's work.

•

8. "Folletines de *Caras y Caretas*" (Buenos Aires) 13, nos. 588–93. Our quotations from *El hombre artificial* are from Horacio Quiroga, *Obras inéditas y desconocidas: Novelas cortas. Tomo I (1908–1910)* (Montevideo: Arca, 1967). This collection features a prologue by Noé Jitrik and notes by Jorge Rufinelli.

In his prologue, Noé Jitrik says that Quiroga published a total of six serial novels under the pseudonym S. Fragoso Lima between 1908 and 1913 (one per year), with five appearing in *Caras y Caretas* and "Una cacería humana en África" (A human hunt in Africa) in *Fray Mocho.* Jitrik says that both "El mono que asesinó" (The monkey who murdered) and *El hombre artificial* are linked to the fantastic literature of the early twentieth century. The influence of Quiroga's readings of Poe and of his experience with drugs was already seen in the stories of *El crimen del otro,* according to Jitrik, and he adds that Quiroga had contact with Lugones and Ingenieros. And he cites Quiroga's readings: Ingenios (*La simulación de la locura, La psicopatología de los sueños, Interpretación científica del hipnotismo y la sugestión, Las doctrinas sobre el hipnotismo*), Lombroso (*Hipnotismo e espiritismo*), Flammarion (*Les forces naturelles*), Charcot (*Traité sur les maladies nerveuses*), José María Ramos Mejía (*La locura en la Argentina*), Enrique García Velloso (*Instituto Frenopático*), Rafael Barret (*El espiritismo en la Argentina*), and also Cosme Mariño, Pancho Sierra, and "Mother" María (21–22).

Jitrik's book, *Horacio Quiroga: Una obra de experiencia y riesgo* (Buenos Aires: Ediciones Culturales Argentinas, 1959), includes a chronology by Oscar Masotta and Jorge R. Lafforgue. The following passage refers to Quiroga's return to Buenos Aires from the Chaco, following the failure of his cotton crop and the loss of six thousand pesos: "*1905.* He shares a room with Brignole, who upon returning from

Europe has decided to open a medical practice in the city. The room serves as a bedroom, a library and a workshop all at once, for Quiroga has devoted himself entirely to *galvanoplasty*. The two friends frequently attend the literary gatherings hosted once a week by Lugones and his wife, as well as the group which meets for an evening coffee at La Brasileña on Calle Maipú. The group includes Soiza Reilly, José Pardo, Roberto Payró and Florencio Sánchez, among others" (19).

Quiroga (who acknowledged the impression Darío made on him by naming a son born in 1912 Darío Quiroga), Lugones, Soiza Reilly (and his son Rubén Darío Soiza Reilly), *Caras y Caretas, Fray Mocho:* other literary gatherings and groups, different from the state coalition, populated by the new journalist-poet subjects (the professional writers).

•

9. Beatriz Sarlo, *La imaginación técnica: Sueños modernos de la cultura argentina* (Buenos Aires: Nueva Visión, 1992), says that *El hombre artificial* has its origin in the serial novel tradition and in literature of popular education, and that "science touches a mythological territory when it manages to create life, but at the same moment it reaches a moral limit: can the three scientists infuse consciousness into the inert body of Biógeno, their creature, at the cost of annihilating another human being by submitting him to a paroxysm of physical suffering?" And further on: "Positivism finds its limit in this Faustian parable which raises the question of the relation between knowledge and values, and which again wonders about the institution of a hierarchy qualified to direct science and to define which obstacles are permissible to tackle and which it should not approach" (41).

Beatriz Sarlo does not refer to the parallel drawn in Donissoff's story between science and revolutionary politics in relation to ethics (and to the sacrifice of lives).

•

10. *Scientist Stories*

"La atrevida operación del Dr. Otis" (Dr. Otis's daring operation) by Otto Miguel Cione (*Caras y Caretas,* no. 133 [1901]) features an *Argentine Frankenstein* who transplants a lobe from a normal brain to replace a sick lobe in the brain of his cruel, wicked, and perverse son. But the malignant force of the son's blood poisons the implant and infects the body again. The doctor dies of rage.

In regard to the "wise madman" (for the hunchbacked asylum director of the fourth transmutation operation story goes mad when he realizes that Moreira was transmuted into a madman and not a superman-genius), let us consult the entry "Savant fou" on pages 797 and 798 of Pierre Versins's *Encyclopédie de l'utopie, des voyages extraordinaires et de la science fiction* (Lausanne: L'Age d'Homme, 1972).

The figure is important primarily in science fiction. The "wise madman" is *the man who can do anything,* and his power has no limits other than those imposed by the imagination of the writers who create him. Either blinded by his power or seeking vengeance (his worth having gone unrecognized), he dominates the period between Jules Verne and the Second World War. The prototype of the first variant is Wells's Dr. Moreau, unless one prefers Robert Louis Stevenson's Dr. Jekyll, from *Dr. Jekyll and Mr. Hyde* (1886). Or, even more remotely, Mary Shelley's *Frankenstein* (1817). *They are all surgical doctors.* In U.S. cinema, *Frankenstein's Trestle* appears in 1902, J. Searle Dawley's *Frankenstein* in 1910, and James Whale's *Frankenstein,* the most famous version and the first with sound, in 1931.

For their part, L. Spage de Camp and Thomas D. Clareson say in "The Scientist" (in *Science Fiction: Contemporary Mythology,* comp. Patrick Warrick, Martin Greenberg, Joseph Olander [New York: Harper and Row, 1978], 196–206) that in the United States the diabolical scientist appears in 1871 in William Rhodes's "The Case of Summerfield." The protagonist of Rhodes's tale is left with no option but to kill Summerfield when he threatens to set fire to the world's oceans with a pill of his own invention unless the citizens of San Francisco pay him a million dollars. In *The Sign at Six* (1912) by Steward Edward White, a mad physicist threatens to annihilate New York by cutting off the vibrations that carry heat and light through the ether, unless a notorious capitalist is tried for his crimes.

As we can see, this is a figure closely linked with capitalism and money. Another example from these first works is the "mad" scientist in Arthur Train and Robert Wood's *The Man Who Rocked the Earth* (1914–1915), who unsuccessfully uses atomic energy and threatens to change the earth's axis in an attempt to end a war in Europe.

Roslynn D. Haynes, *From Faust to Strangelove: Representations of the Scientist in Western Literature* (Baltimore: Johns Hopkins University Press, 1994), reviews the history of the representation of the man of science from the medieval alchemist through the present and describes the influence of the fictional doctors Faustus, Frankenstein, Moreau, Jekyll, Caligari, and Strangelove on the popular imagination and on stereotypes of the scientist. Almost all of them are men, "middle-aged or older, either bald or having a large mass of hair like Einstein," and "they are almost always depicted as working alone or in isolated laboratories; and where the object of their research is indicated it is usually conspicuously labeled as 'secret' or 'dangerous.' This deep-rooted suspicion about scientists is not confined to children" (1–2). Haynes suggests that "Fictional scientists are expressions of their creators' response to the role of science and technology in a particular social context and thus are interesting in their own right; but when viewed chronologically they achieve an added historical significance both as ideological indicators of the changing perception of science over some seven centuries and as powerful images that give rise to new stereotypes" (2).

Haynes identifies the six most prevalent stereotypes of scientists as follows:

- The alchemist, who reappears at critical times as the obsessed or maniacal scientist. Driven to pursue an arcane intellectual goal that carries suggestions of ideological evil, this figure has been reincarnated recently as the sinister biologist producing new (and hence allegedly unlawful) species through the quasimagical processes of genetic engineering.

- The stupid virtuoso, out of touch with the real world of social intercourse. This figure at first appears more comic than sinister, but he too comes with sinister implications. Preoccupied with the trivialities of his private world of science, he ignores his social responsibilities. His modern counterpart [is] the absentminded professor of early twentieth-century films . . .

- The Romantic depiction of the unfeeling scientist who has reneged on human relationships and suppressed all human affections in the cause of science. This has been the most enduring stereotype of all and still provides the most common image of the scientist in popular thinking, recurring repeatedly in twentieth-century plays, novels, and films. In portrayals of the 1950s there is an additional *ambivalence about this figure:* his emotional deficiency is condemned as inhuman, even sinister, but in a less extreme form it is also condoned, even admired, as the inevitable price scientists must pay to achieve their disinterestedness.

- The heroic adventurer in the physical or the intellectual world. Towering like a superman over his contemporaries, exploring new territories, or engaging with new concepts, this character emerges at periods of scientific optimism. His particular appeal to adolescent audiences . . . has ensured the popularity of this stereotype in comics and space opera. More subtle analyses of such heroes, however, suggest the danger of their charismatic power as, in the guise of neoimperialist space travelers, they impose their particular brand of colonization on the universe.

- The helpless scientist. This character has lost control either over his discovery . . . or . . . over the direction of its implementation. In recent decades this situation has been explored in relation to a whole panoply of environmental problems . . .

- The scientist as idealist . . . sometimes holding out the possibility of a scientifically sustained utopia with plenty and fulfillment for all but more frequently engaged in conflict with a technology-based system that fails to provide for human values. (3–4; italics added)

With regard to the extremely influential image of Victor Frankenstein, invented by Mary Shelley when she was eighteen years old, Haynes observes that "Frankenstein's problems begin with his isolation, which lead directly to his suppression of emotional relationships and aesthetic experiences and the delusion that his work is being pursued in the interests of society, when in fact the real goals are power and fame" (4–5).

As Peter H. Goodrich, "The Lineage of Mad Scientists: Anti-Types of Merlin," *Extrapolation* 27 (1986): 109–15, points out, the *mad scientist* has a long history prior to Frankenstein, in black-and-white magic, the alchemists, and satirical and religious attacks on science. Mary Shelley's work incorporates contradictory elements of this tradition. On one level, we find *the Faustian man of science* who has divine aspirations: not content with being merely a man, he seeks to prolong life eternally or to revive the dead (he creates a creature who is the counterpart of Mephistopheles). On another level, Frankenstein has a basis *in alchemy*. In the novel, Waldman's lecture connects alchemy to the occultists and to the modern man of science, and in this way Mary Shelley marks the importance of the tradition.

The symbol of power in *Frankenstein* is the capacity to revive the dead, but the modern man of science is also a male violator of female nature. Here we see a third level of the tradition, which refers back to Francis Bacon and his program for the investigation of nature. The result of these multiple levels is a visible thematic tension in *Frankenstein* and in other gothic tales of mad scientists. As a result, *Frankenstein is full of interpretive indeterminacy.*

•

11. *Cosmópolis* was the title of one *modernista* publication in Venezuela and another directed by Enrique Gómez Carrillo in Madrid (Ricardo Gullón, *El modernismo visto por los modernistas* [Barcelona: Labor, 1980], 36).

•

12. The "stories of international celebrities" appear in Argentine culture with the modernizing leap of the late nineteenth century. Until recently these stories were sold in Argentina under the generic title "Los hombres" and before that as "Hombres célebres": *La neurosis de los hombres célebres* by José María Ramos Mejía, the first Argentine psychiatric text, is from 1879–1882.

Celebrity is a typical mass phenomenon arising at the end of the nineteenth century and related to the professionalization of journalism; it is one of the cultural industries of journalism, the industry of desire. In Argentina celebrity interviews appear in *Caras y Caretas*. Celebrity is also related to a change in social structure and to the expansion of the reading public (*Caras y Caretas* sold 200,000 copies a week).

Joshua Gamson, *Claims to Fame: Celebrity in Contemporary America* (Berkeley and Los Angeles: University of California Press, 1994), says that in the United States in the mid-nineteenth century, "a series of dramatic changes in the media of publicity and communication established celebrity as a 'mass' phenomenon" (19). The discourse of fame coincided with the professionalization of journalism, the invention of new technologies of information, and the advancement of consumer culture. In this rapidly changing environment, Gamson says, "publishers fighting for a competitive edge . . . made stories about *people* a central feature of journalism. 'What was vital,' writes Richard Schickel, 'was the symbol.' In particular, newspapermen like Joseph Pulitzer and William Randolph Hearst sought '*human symbols* whose terror, anguish, or sudden good fortune, whatever, seemed to dramatically summarize some local event or social problem or social tragedy.' Names, in short, began to make news. . . . Photography, of course, meant encountering not only a name . . . but also a realistic image" (20). And as P. T. Barnum demonstrated, the subjects of these stories and images could well be freaks. *The logic of monsters* accompanies *the logic of celebrities*.

In the work previously cited, Leo Braudy says that the culture of fame is inseparable from the politics of performance and from visual culture, and that it implies the creation of an international culture. P. T. Barnum *invented fame in the United States*. He was "the impresario of a newly expansive America, intent on collecting and exhibiting everything that was or claimed to be unique—the best—the only . . . he made his first show business coup exhibiting a woman who was supposedly 161 years old and the nurse of George Washington. . . . Barnum . . . marks the characteristically American shift to a conviction that the stage is the proper display for the democratic, the unique, and the natural rather than the hierarchic and the artificial" (498–99). Barnum founded "a democratic theater," Braudy says. "From 1835 to his bankruptcy in 1855, it is the individual visual oddity that attracts audiences; from 1860 to his death in 1891, it is the spectacle" (499). The impresario "became world famous not for anything that he did himself so much as for the way he focused attention on the talents, the peculiarities, and the unique nature of animals, objects, and other people" (500). Through "his ability to use all the powers of the press" to promote his American Museum, Barnum achieved national and international success. He "taught the world about the fame of America as a nation as well as how fame was being created in America" (502).

Leslie Fiedler, *Freaks: Myths and Images of the Secret Self* (New York: Simon and

Schuster, 1978), says that in the nineteenth century P. T. Barnum was a creator as important in his medium as was Dickens in the novel. Together with Hugo, Poe, and Walt Whitman, Barnum helped mold the imagination of the first mass public. Barnum's circus exhibited "freaks and wonders": the world's fattest woman, the living skeleton, the dog-faced boy, giants and midgets, the bearded lady, the snake charmer, and many more. His American Museum was an institution as unique to North American culture as its name suggests: "Originally a storehouse of curios and Freaks [...] it became what Barnum described as 'a vast National Gallery . . . a million of things in every brand of Nature and Art, comprehending a *cyclopaediacal synopsis* of everything worth seeing and knowing in this curious world's curious economy'" (277).

Richard Schickel, *Intimate Strangers: The Culture of Celebrity* (New York: Doubleday, 1985), maintains that "perhaps the least profitable way of studying celebrity [is] through the lives of people who have acquired it as an unearned increment of success deserved or undeserved. It is much more interesting, and much more difficult, to consider it in another way, as the principle source of motive power in putting across ideas of every kind—social, political, aesthetic, moral. Famous people are used as symbols for these ideas, or become famous for being symbols of them. . . . They are turned into representations for . . . inchoate longings" (viii–ix).

Soiza Reilly became famous for his chronicle interviews of international celebrities, which appeared serially in *Caras y Caretas* in 1907 and 1908 and which he collected in 1909 in a book titled *Cien hombres célebres* (One hundred famous men) and subtitled *Confesiones literarias* (Literary confessions), which became a best-seller (the manual's second, after *Pot pourri*).

For the history of *Cien hombres célebres,* let us turn to Alejandro Andrade Coello's "Apuntes biográficos del autor" (Biographical notes on the author) (dated in Quito, Ecuador, 1920), which preceded Soiza Reilly's novel *La escuela de los pillos* (The school of rascals) (Buenos Aires: Tor, 1939). (Does the title *La escuela de pillos* not announce the story of Arlt's *El juguete rabioso,* originally called "La vida puerca" [The filthy life]?)

Andrade Coello says that Soiza Reilly interviewed 533 famous men, and that he is "a sensational journalist. He knows how to write a gripping article, one that cannot go unread. He attempts to show that news should read like a novel" (11). Pragmatically, Andrade Coello continues:

> Title of his first book: *En el reino de las Cosas* (In the realm of things). Price of each copy? Two pounds sterling. *The only copy of this 32 page pamphlet sold* was bought by the author himself.

He later produced *Cien hombres célebres*. This *strange* book was published in
Barcelona by Maucci. It features a prologue by Paola Lombroso, who amiably
calls the Argentine critic pedantic and rash. She then adds that his spirit is "sharp
and agile, full of irony and impertinence." *The first edition of 20,000 copies earned
its author five thousand pesos in royalties*. It is now in its fifth edition and has been
widely read by students and novice journalists in Ecuador, and some have even
imitated its style. It has been translated into French and Italian. (13; italics added)

It is worth noting that here Andrade Coello, like the boys in *El juguete rabioso,* puts
a price on books.

In this period Soiza Reilly also published *Crónicas de Amor, de Belleza y de Sangre*
(Barcelona: Maucci, 1912). (Quiroga's *Cuentos de amor, de locura y de muerte* is from
1917.) These chronicles are dedicated "To my companions in labor at *Caras y Caretas*" and are preceded by "Palabras interiores" (Inner words), dated in Buenos
Aires, 11 June 1911. There he says:

For many years I have been living in the environment of *famous men*. At present,
I am the writer who has most closely seen the greatest number of illustrious men
. . . My books *Cien hombres célebres. Confesiones literarias, Hombres y mujeres de Italia*
(Men and women of Italy), *El alma de los perros* (The soul of dogs), and *Cerebros de
París* (Brains of Paris) contain the description of *my thousand and one visits with the
world's greatest geniuses and its most insignificant popular men* . . . I was the first man
of letters who *undressed* the great men of Europe in South America. With my
books, I have helped to make known many talents who, despite being already consecrated in the old world, were unknown in America. One more book read is one
more man educated. *I have educated many.* (7–9; italics added, ellipses in original)

The celebrity collection or best-seller for Latin American youth shows that along
with the new media there appears a new politics of culture. *These series of celebrity
biographies help found the "new" culture* because they embody ideals and values and
also a political and cultural struggle over models for youth.

The celebrity interview—or report—is typically "North American" as a form,
function, and "educational" theme. Marta Varela, *Los hombres ilustres de Billiken:
Héroes en los medios y en la escuela* (Buenos Aires: Ediciones Colihue, 1994), says that

Unlike prestigious literature, which resorted systematically to European fashions
and models, journalism in Argentina, from the nineteenth century on, took as its
point of reference the North American press. This is a moment of modernization
in which the polemic and political prose that had characterized the nineteenth-
century press loses currency, and in which the figure of the professional journalist
arises. It is a process that culminates in 1905 with the creation of *La Razón* and in

1913 with *Crítica*, which follows the North American line of "yellow" journalism. In the case of magazines, this process is carried out by *Caras y Caretas* from 1898 on. . . . This disparity of sources remains evident until much later in Argentine literature and journalism. And this is why we must search for the models of the *Billiken* biographies in the North American press. There also exists a "national tradition" in the genre, but the format—one-page biographies in a periodical publication—repeats almost without variations that of North American publications of the same period. (47)

But let us return to Soiza Reilly's *Cien hombres célebres* (which applies the North American model of fame to famous Europeans and local freaks), because there we can clearly see a position, a subject that has journalism as its way of life (and to be a journalist is to be modern) and that writes about new human symbols. In some interviews, Soiza Reilly announces his journalistic aesthetics, which is that of the intimacy of fame. What matters are not so much the words of the interviewed celebrity, he says: the business of citing the interviewee textually (mere stenography) and showing him the interview before its publication is better left to "idiots who go by the manual." What matters about the celebrity is precisely what he does not say, his world, his setting, his gestures; what matters about the celebrity is "the intimacy of fame," and his job as a journalist is to invent "a soul" for the celebrities (271, 388, 418, 415). Soiza Reilly says: I created this *system of intimacy* with the physical portrait, the environment, gestures, smiles, in order to know what "celebrity" really means (389).

For the journalist who interviews celebrities is, in reality, a *modernista* poet and not merely a journalist. Soiza Reilly dedicates his collection "to the Countess of Requena, Doña Gloria Laguna" and, like Rubén Darío, he addresses her as follows: "A woman of your hauteur, of your caprices, of your sins, is worthy of deserving the book of a poet without morals and without faith. . . . From my American jungle I dedicate this book to you. . . . Lend me your ear" (7–8).

The countess of Requena, an "artist" and "an aristocratic bohemian," is a "woman dandy" opposed to conventions: she smokes, she drinks *mate,* and she divorced her husband, and Soiza opens the collection with his interview of her. This poet's muse is an aristocratic outsider who embodies the aristocratic-anarchist aesthetics of *modernismo*. From here, we could trace a genealogy of dandies beginning in 1880 with Cambaceres and Mansilla, passing through *modernismo,* and ending in this transmutation into a Spanish countess and Soiza Reilly's muse; the link between them (with Manuel Ugarte in the middle) appears later in the manual, in "History of a Best-Seller: From Anarchism to Peronism."

But the most important aspect of the chronicles of the hundred celebrities is that they distinctly register in Argentina the *apparent antagonisms* produced by the popular culture of fame: *they are encounters with geniuses and men of talent, and also with marginal characters, bohemians, madmen, and criminals.* The central celebrities are located abroad *in Europe* (men of Spain, Italy, France, the pope, princes, socialists, anarchists, bullfighters, singers, painters, sculptors), and the marginal celebrities are located *in Argentina and Uruguay* (these are the freaks: bohemians, defeated men, neurasthenics, madmen, criminals, drug addicts, and even bootblacks and beggars).

There are also women on both sides, and I can't resist telling you in passing what happened in the interview with the "Almodovaresque" serial novelist Carolina Invernizzio (who is read by Arlt's "Lame" Hipólita). She is famous, Soiza says, and everyone knows her, but no one mentions her or refers to her by name. She writes unforgettable novels about love affairs, kisses, and crimes: they are macabre novels, with dark scenes of passion: they are horrible and full of murders!, says our Virgil (427). He also says that they are novels for dressmakers, romantic books that have nothing to do with literature or ideas, books for "people who don't know any better." But he adds: let us speak respectfully and affectionately of Carolina, because she has disciples in America.

For she *in person* belies her books, she's just the opposite, there's nothing tragic about her: her husband is "a military hero who displays medals and crosses for bravery." Carolina says that she writes all day and never crosses anything out (just the opposite of Matilde Serao, who also gets an interview): "I write what occurs to me, I don't know what's going to happen, I let it flow." And then Soiza compares her not to a popular writer of Argentine serial novels, but rather with an Argentine "apostolic figure": her descriptive system, he tells her, is exactly like that of Joaquín V. González. This pleased Carolina so much that she promised to visit Argentina soon.

But let us return to our theme, because otherwise we could go on indefinitely. In Europe, Soiza Reilly interviewed the celebrities who were cited by Ingenieros in the same period: Enrique Ferri, Felipe Turati, Max Nordau, Camille Mauclair, and also Edmundo D'Amicis, Menéndez y Pelayo in his library, and even a messiah (who preaches a new world that is neither above nor below us, with neither Satan nor Christ; his holy city is Nature: we must shed our clothes and feed on plants).

In contrast, the range of Argentines and Uruguayans interviewed or narrated is as follows: a poor Argentine student who killed himself in Paris over an "aristocratic" cabaret singer; a bootblack from Plaza Lorea (who later became a famous painter in Italy); the "lyrical vagabond" Martín Goycochea Menéndez, who died in Mexico; the bohemian madman Florencio Parravicini; the "aristocratic poet" Julio Herrera y Reissig, whose "martyrdom" consists of living alone and taking drugs to write (and the photo from *Caras y Caretas* shows him shooting morphine!); the "neurasthenic poet" Zuviría, from Uruguay; Father Castañeda, who shares *the blood of Moreira,* according to Soiza (372); the "dog philosopher"; and the beggar woman of the Paseo de Julio, a famous dancer who murdered the son of a European banker.

This combination of geniuses and famous European talents with local oddities, madmen, bohemians, neurotics, and criminals "forms" and gives order to the collection of the hundred celebrities; *it is its principal principle of organization.* Would it be too bold to think that this "combination" constitutes, in modern progressive culture, the equivalent of the Creole element and the encyclopedia in high culture? (In Arlt this is clearly seen in *Los siete locos* and *Los lanzallamas:* the mixture of international celebrities in the Astrologer's speeches with the novel's local "madmen, simulators, and criminals," who dream of becoming international celebrities.)

But there is a second antagonism in the logic of fame which also serves as a principle of organization of the best-seller about famous men and which shows another "combination": that of the subtitle, *Confesiones literarias.* (*Cien hombres célebres* combines chronicle and confession, two founding "discourses of truth" in Latin American culture.) In the confessions we find the writer's position of intimacy in relation to celebrity culture, the debate between "the popular" (he writes for an audience of 200,000 in the first edition) and the literary (he writes for himself). In other words, the intimate debate between the journalist and the poet. (Aníbal González, *La crónica modernista hispanoamericana* [Madrid: Ediciones José Porrúa Turanzas, 1983], 81–82), says that journalism was a source of employment for writers and a means of publishing, but that journalism questioned the notion of the "author.")

In the "Confesión inicial," Soiza says that he does not belong to the crowd, that it is repugnant to him, and that he writes in public for himself. *He is an antipopular writer who scorns the masses, and he is the journalist of celebrities.* This apparent paradox between a real function linked to the popular, with an economic basis that Paola Lombroso emphasizes in the prologue, and an antipopular, aristocratic-anarchist aesthetic of individuality is what interests us in the relation between the chronicles and the confessions of *Cien hombres célebres.* (Around 1890 the tendency toward a union of *modernismo* and anarchism became stronger, as Iris M. Zavala explains in *Colonialism and Culture: Hispanic Modernisms and the Social Imaginary* [Bloomington: Indiana University Press, 1992], 112. The new aesthetic was repeatedly defined as an "anarchist aesthetic," "literary anarchism," and a "socialist aesthetic," since it problematized hegemonic rationalism.)

In the "Confesión inicial," Soiza *also complains about the hostility of the world:* he says that hostile dogs bark at him and chase him because he is a feline, that he is *an error from the asylum* who thinks about things in his own way and speaks accordingly, and that this is a grave sin *in America*. Leo Braudy, again in *The Frenzy of Renown*, says that fame is accompanied by *the complaint of the artist, by his position as victim* of a hostile and indifferent world whose conventions (except for fame) he wholly rejects, and also by the belief that artistic value is inconsistent with popular approval.

Cien hombres célebres exemplifies the functioning of a *dual logic of fame* in Argentina and Latin America: in the distribution of centers and margins (the European and the local) and also in the position of the "artist" or the poet-writer. Celebrities and their logic of fame, journalistic chronicle, poetic confession, and "crime." This specific conjunction is found in *Cien hombres célebres,* and it is in this figure that I imagine the utopia of my search: one of the initial points of that modern, progressive culture which is my own.

The anarchist aesthetic of the destruction of the celebrity is seen in the "crowning interview" of *Cien hombres célebres,* which is titled "La vida artística de Gabriel D'Annunzio" (The artistic life of Gabriel D'Annunzio). The interview is central not only because Arlt recalls it in 1930 and in 1917 (he refers to Soiza as "the man who saw D'Annunzio") and because Paola Lombroso cites it in her prologue, but also because it opens "in crime," with an offense which will close the text as "criminal" (falsifier of papers, false name, antipatriot):

> "It's a crime. It's a crime to destroy that legend."
> "You're right. It is a crime . . . But is there anything more beautiful than committing a crime? Imagine feeling the enchantment of a crime in your veins. Not of an ordinary crime. Not of an artless crime . . . A wise crime! Imagine the delight that runs through your marrow when you destroy anything: a woman, a doll, a piece of candy. Anything at all . . ." (86; ellipses in original)

Soiza will enjoy the destruction of a "poet's legend."

> My heart suffered no few pains when the philosophy of the old dogs came to sink its teeth into the legends of my youth. Therefore, for the consolation of wounded souls, vengeance was sought. Is there any better consolation? It is delightful . . . To take revenge! To scornfully injure any heart which blocks our way. To trample. Oh! To sink knives into young flesh! Into flesh that vibrates with the fear of waning rage. To destroy is one of the most divine virtues of nature . . . *It is good to destroy. And to destroy works of art.* We must destroy all false legends . . . throw rocks at the monument . . . Above all when the works of art are made of clay. Any monument is bad because it serves as an example to the men who pass by. And

examples must be avoided. Bad examples. And also good ones . . . Examples are like advice . . . Youth which follows advice is flesh destined for death. (Ellipses in original)

Do not ascend to the pulpit in order to preach good advice or morality, he advises. *"Ascend to the pulpit of print in order to tell youth not to believe in the enchanting, sacred, sweet nonsense of ingenious men,"* says Soiza to his muse before going to destroy the famous D'Annunzio and reveal to us the tensions generated by the logic of fame, as well as the particular combinations of this "new culture of the frontier."

•

13. *Genius Stories*

The physician-writer of *La bolsa de huesos* sought "success" with his novel; the monstrous physician of *La ciudad de los locos* wants to become famous by transmuting his stepson into a superman-genius. We already spoke of success, fame, and celebrities as key points in the new culture industry; now we turn our attention to geniuses and, specifically, to stories of geniuses (and their differences from madmen) in more learned and scientific media. Let us listen to José Ingenieros, a real doctor famous for his expertise in madness, in a lecture at the Faculty of Philosophy and Letters in 1911. He, who also went in search of Argentine genius, will perhaps explain for us this desire for celebrity, which is so intense in the hunchbacked physician of *La ciudad de los locos* that it leads him to commit a crime with the protection of "his laws."

The text appears in volume 3 of *Anales de psicología* (Buenos Aires: Talleres Gráficos de la Penitenciaría Nacional), 521–40, published by the Sociedad de Psicología de Buenos Aires in 1914 and including work from 1911, 1912, and 1913. It opens with a presentation:

The evening organized by the Psychological Society in honor of the wise Florentino Ameghino took place before an audience overflowing the conference room at the Faculty of Philosophy and Letters and filling the anterooms and the hallways.

All the most significant representatives of our university and intellectual world attended the ceremony, accompanied by the Society's president, Doctor Ingenieros, the dean of the Faculty of Philosophy and Letters, Doctor Matienzo; the president of the Universidad de la Plata, Doctor Joaquín V. González; the vice president of the same, Doctor Agustín Álvarez; and a large part of the teaching staff of both universities. (521)

Ingenieros's lecture is titled "Ameghino y el problema del genio" (Ameghino and the problem of genius), and it opens as follows:

A sage and a philosopher, Ameghino was a pupil able to see in the night, before dawn broke for the rest of us. He created: it was his mission. Like Sarmiento, he arrived in his own climate and at his own moment. By a unique coincidence, both were school teachers, autodidacts, without a university degree, educated outside the metropolis, in direct contact with nature, far from all the external complications of the worldly lie, with their hands free, their heads free, their hearts free, their wings free. One could say that genius blooms better in the solitary mountains, caressed by storms, which are its natural atmosphere; *it withers in the hothouses of the state, in domesticated universities, in their well-paid laboratories, in their fossilized academies and in their hierarchical bureaucracies.* Genius has never been an official institution. (525; italics added)

This totally antistate posture (is it the same as that of *La Montaña?*) opens and closes the "genius" lecture given before the authorities of the faculty founded by Miguel Cané. Here is Ingenieros's militant position, his separation from the liberal coalition, and another feature of the new progressive modernizing culture.

Following his attack on the "hothouses of the state" at the "domesticated" state university, and in front of its "hierarchical" officials, Ingenieros develops a general discourse on "genius" from a materialist perspective. "Of what does it consist? Is it not divine inspiration, a demon, an illness? Never. It is both simpler and more exceptional. Simpler, because it depends on a complicated *histological structure of the brain and not on fantastic entities;* more exceptional, because the world is teeming with sick people, and rarely does an Ameghino appear" (531).

But in addition to innate gifts, Ingenieros continues, genius requires effort, creative imagination, and a morality or ethic which *"cannot be measured by precepts current in our catechisms;* no one would measure the height of the Himalayas with pocket-sized measuring tape." This unofficial ethic is defined by Ingenieros as faith in a human ideal: in beauty, in truth, in good. The genius embodies the highest point of humanity: of the virtues and gifts of man. (Ingenieros refutes the assimilation of "genius" and "madman": "No one was ever a genius because of his madness; some were geniuses despite it; many were submerged in shadow by sickness" [534]).

With the antistate genius at the summit, Ingenieros enunciates a division of men *into hierarchical classes according to intelligence:* the genius and men of talent, the "common" and middling men (who may possess certain abilities and a certain shrewdness), and the idiots. The middling types are the subordinate, narrow spirits, *the mediocrities;* envious, hypocritical, debased men who depend on the judgment of others and on circumstance and who sustain orthodoxies and fanaticisms. Also included among the mediocre are those who lack an ideal: the unbalanced, those preoccupied with success, and simulators always hungry for power. *These are the ones who make up the state and constitute mediocracies*, says Ingenieros in front of the presidents, vice-presidents, and deans of the state university.

Ingenieros continues: "In the face of the *leveling tide* which threatens us on all sides in contemporary mediocracies, every homage to genius is an act of faith: only it holds out the prospect of the perfection of Humanity. When a generation becomes *fed up with ignorance, with duplicity, with servility,* it must turn to the geniuses of its race for the symbols of thought and action which will temper it for new efforts. . . . Teaching the admiration of genius, holiness, and heroism, they prepare for themselves a climate propitious to their advent" (540; ellipses in original).

Between the genius that "withers in the hothouses of the state" at the beginning of the lecture and "the contemporary mediocracies" at the end, *in an antistate posture at a state institution,* Ingenieros lays out not only certain basic ideas of progressive modernizing culture, but also *its cultural politics.* From this posture, he addresses youth in order to advocate idealism, faith in dreams of glory, liberation, and access to a higher realm.

Let us move quickly from the faculty in 1911 to the library to consider some of the problems that Ingenieros raises in this curious lecture in front of the university authorities and which informs us somewhat about the history of this "progressive culture" with its attacks on the state and on mediocracies in relation to "Ameghino's genius."

The Idea of Genius

Penelope Murray, editor of *Genius: The History of an Idea* (Oxford: Basil Blackwell, 1989), says in her introduction (1–8) that the modern notion of genius arises in the eighteenth century with *rationalist aesthetics;* that it passes through *Romanticism* (the Romantic cult of genius) and arrives at "an ambiguous status in the twentieth century" (5).

"By the end of the eighteenth century," Murray says, "the genius, and in particular the artistic genius, comes to be thought of as the highest human type, replacing such earlier ideal types as the hero, the saint, the *uomo universale* and so on" (2). She adds that genius is not only difficult to define, but also

> perforce elitist, not only in that it privileges certain individuals, but also because
> it elevates certain kinds of activity above others . . . the notion of genius raises

questions about the role of the creative individual and his place in society. . . . Does the possession of genius . . . allow the individual complete license to disregard all the rules of the society in which he lives, to be judged by standards quite different from those which are applied to his fellows? . . . a belief in the alienation and otherness of the creative individual was an essential aspect of the Romantic cult of genius, in which suffering was the inevitable price the genius had to pay, not only for his superhuman powers, but also for the total freedom which it was his duty and privilege to exploit. This complex of ideas is also expressed in the Faustus legend, which, from Marlowe to Thomas Mann, provides the earliest and most continuous example of the Mephistophelean view of genius, epitomized in the cry of Busoni's Faust: "Give me genius with all its pains." (6)

Murray concludes that "the study of genius is ultimately the study of human creativity . . . (which is no doubt the reason why psychology and psychiatry are the only intellectual disciplines in which the analysis of genius still flourishes)" (6–7). Today the term "genius" has fallen into disuse, replaced by references to "eminent" figures, and distinguishing between artists and men of science, she says.

The Mad Genius

G. Becker, in "The Mad Genius Controversy," in *Genius and Eminence: The Social Psychology of Creativity and Exceptional Achievement,* ed. Robert S. Albert (Oxford: Pergamon Press, 1983), 36–39, states that the

tendency, common in the mad genius literature, to link certain types of artistic and intellectual expression with various forms and degrees of pathology, deserve[s] to be seen as an attempt to control or monitor the direction of intellectual change and innovation . . . [. . .] The start of the mad genius controversy toward the middle of the nineteenth century [. . .] appears tied to the revolutionary unrest of the period and, more specifically, to the recognition that those identified as geniuses often tended to occupy a central position in fermenting social, political and intellectual unrest. The evaluation of the men of genius in terms of sanity and madness constituted one response to the perceived influence of many of these individuals. (37)

The Genius, Agent of Transcendence

"Almost every theory of genius expects a violent end to the realm of alienation," argues Robert Currie in *Genius: An Ideology in Literature* (London: Chatto & Windus, 1974). "The transcendental realm is the work of a transcendental agency, humanly speaking, a genius," he says, adding that genius represents an image of God in the human realm (45). *Secular culture* began with the conviction that human alienation could be transcended; geniuses are the protagonists of this transcendence.

In chapter 7, "The Ideology of Genius: From Romanticism to Modernism," Currie refers to what Ingenieros calls the middling or mediocre social elements, also known as philistines. Currie says that the modern usage of the word "originates from the jargon of German university students who called their enemies (and creditors) among the townsmen, *philistines*. Thereafter, the term was adopted by Romantics such as Hoffmann or Marx who used it to described the urban many, equated first with the legal-administrative bourgeoisie and, later, with the commercial classes" (201). "According to this ideology," Currie continues, "the genius transcends the alienated condition of the philistine many by introducing a higher or other order," a realm of signification distinct from that of mere life (208).

A culture without genius, Currie adds, "ceases to be transcendental and can only be assessed in this-worldly terms. Culture without genius might therefore be understood simply as entertainment" (214).

And a Dig at "Geniuses"

In his 1907 preface to *The Sanity of Art: An Exposure of the Current Nonsense about Artists Being Degenerate,* (London: Constable and Company, 1932), 281–332, George Bernard Shaw says that "it is necessary for the welfare of society that genius should be privileged to utter sedition, to blaspheme, to outrage good taste, to corrupt the youthful mind, and, generally, to scandalize one's uncles" (289).

"Three Argentine Cases with Geniuses": José Ingenieros, Macedonio Fernández, and Roberto Arlt

(1) In *Evocaciones de un porteño viejo* (Evocations of an old *porteño*) (Buenos Aires: Quetzal, 1952), Roberto Payró refers indirectly to this homage to Ameghino's genius on the part of Ingenieros. He says that although Ingenieros was a destroyer who constructed,

> he preferred to show himself in another light, at least externally, affecting selfish impassivity, skeptical nonchalance, a cynical contrariness and even—at times—a *voluntary abstention from the discovery of some truth which didn't square with his outlook.* Thus, for example, when he was speaking with one of our sages about *certain disputed theories of Ameghino,* and when his interlocutor invited him to study

them in depth and in his texts on the bone fragments he discovered by Ameghino in the south, a task for which he was sufficiently prepared, Ingenieros answered:

"I won't do it. I'm afraid of arriving at the same negative conclusions as you . . ."

Whoever stops to ponder this detail for a moment will soon see that it is not lacking in beauty, and that these words are not those of a demolisher or a skeptic. At issue was one of the country's greatest men, regardless of whether he might have committed errors in his extremely vast and fertile work. Also at issue was the necessity of erecting to him a well deserved moral monument, the popularization of his admirable works, and *it was not fitting to diminish the homage with objections and arguments* which are not suppressed by being postponed: when the spring sun shines upon us, we pay no mind to its spots. Furthermore, the theories we might call suspicious could have no currency except in the scientific world, where the controversy had already been underway for some time. (77–78; ellipses in original)

(2) "Carta de Macedonio Fernández a Ingenieros a propósito del genio" (Letter from Macedonio Fernández to Ingenieros on the subject of genius), *Papeles antiguos (escritos 1892–1907): Obras completas*, vol 1 (Buenos Aires: Corregidor, 1981). I am indebted to Horacio González for this text.

Distinguished Director of the Archivos de Criminología *(Dr. José Ingenieros):*

With best wishes for the success of the Archivos, *I the undersigned, as inexperienced in the field as desirous of overcoming my inexperience, and taking you up on your benevolent invitation, dare to propose a cordial controversy over a certain matter, in my judgement the most fascinating of all to ponder.*

I refer, Mr. Director, to the problem of genius.

This is a matter which could mitigate the somber environment of criminological studies and which, nevertheless, falls within the vast framework of Psychopathology.

This is also a matter that is not the object of special study, or even summary study, in either of the two liberal careers to which all of us, as collaborators of this magazine, probably belong. This being so, I, at least, would not consider it useful for myself or for others to undertake an isolated personal study of a matter so profoundly complex and so relatively ignored by contemporary science.

In view of this, it is easy to imagine the mutual benefit which would redound to those of us who might intervene in the change in ideas which I propose, as well as the good sense of not attempting isolated studies in a field so little cultivated among us.

As a starting point, I could, for my part, formulate this question, to which I personally would anticipate a negative response:

Has contemporary science, or more accurately, the reigning tendency toward physiological study of the spirit, made any advancement in clarifying the problem of genius?

I would recommend the advantages of studying the spirit spiritually, of practicing

psychological psychology (if you will allow me the designation) in the first place, without
excluding the use of physiological information.

I hope that this project will be received with the enthusiasm I anticipate. Its benefits
would be felt before long.

With sincere and enduring friendship,
Macedonio Fernández
January 14, 1902

A note in the text says that after transcribing the letter, the editors of the journal added that *"Archivos* warmly welcomes Doctor Fernández's idea. We hope that he himself will initiate such an interesting controversy by demonstrating the anti-physiological thesis he upholds; he can be sure that he will not lack for adversaries. The Editors."

When *Argentina libre* (4 April 1940) reproduced Fernández's letter to Ingenieros, then director of *Archivos de criminología, medicina legal y psiquiatría,* it noted that "Apart from constituting a curiosity, the controversy which the letter proposes over the problem of genius reveals an *anti-positivist* position which can now be appreciated in its full implications. As for the polemic, it was not possible to establish whether it took place."

(3) Elías Castelnuovo recounts the following about Arlt in *Memorias* (Buenos Aires: Ediciones Culturales Argentinas, 1974):

Roberto Arlt was not unaware that there were doubts about his sanity, but, far from letting them hurt his feelings, he took them as flattery since they identified him with the great madmen of history, from Friedrich Nietzsche to Vincent Van Gogh. He was so convinced that a true artist could never be a normal person that when I told him that *Los siete locos,* his greatest work, besides being a novel, *was a clinical testimony and that the only madman in the romance was him, since he had distributed himself generously among the seven in the novel,* he was so pleased that I was taken aback. His conviction that a genius was obliged to be crazy was so deep, so sincere, that he once confessed bitterly to me:

"Do you know what Emil Ludwig says? That a genius never goes mad!"

This undermined his belief that geniuses were mentally ill.

"Don't believe it," I consoled him. "Geniuses never go mad because they are already mad. And besides, why do you want to be a genius? You're not satisfied with the suffering and the setbacks your talent already causes you, and you're determined to add more? Don't you see that geniuses, who are always born at the wrong time, end up in jail or in the insane asylum? Remember what happened to Dante Alighieri. Or Galileo Galilei. Or Tommaso Campanella. Or Edgar Allan Poe. Please. Don't go asking for your own ruin." (145–46; italics in original)

14. I wrote that on the frontier there were at least four transmutation operations, and after I had written about them, Sylvia Molloy sent me an article of hers, then unpublished, titled "La violencia del género y la narrativa del exceso. Notas sobre mujer y relato en dos novelas argentinas de principios de siglo," which later appeared in *Revista Iberoamericana* 64, nos. 184–85 (July–December 1998): 529–42. The article deals with two novels by the Argentine Atilio Chiáppori, *Borderland* (1907) and *La eterna angustia* (Eternal anguish) (1908). Quoting me, Sylvia Molloy refers to what I have called "the cultural coalition" of the late nineteenth century, and writes that *Borderland* is "a frontier tale which explores the edges, tensions, and deviations of the coalition" (531). But Sylvia was not familiar with "my frontier," and I was not familiar with "hers." And there are more coincidences in this dialogue between critics, because *La eterna angustia,* Molloy says, returns to *Borderland* to broaden the tale and resolve enigmas, and it narrates a "surgical experiment" featuring "the violence of a man against a woman who rejects him"! The "medical revenge" of Doctor Biercold, son of immigrants and "the foremost women's specialist" who, under the pretext of operating on a cyst, "desexed her at her very root, in her entity of origin," as the doctor confesses in a letter before committing suicide (534). "Medical penetration" empties the subject. After gynecology, "one could say led by gynecology," Molloy says (538), Biercold becomes a psychiatrist and ends up impersonating the devil. Molloy marks this itinerary and also the encounter, in Chiáppori, among medical intervention, narrative intervention, and female gender: "the tale of gender, both at the level of the narrator and at that of the author, does not differ much from the surgical intervention" (541). Molloy reads these texts as excessive because, she says, they say what "good" *modernismo* represses and border on parody (535). And I add to "the frontier" this fifth story, that of "excess," of Sylvia Molloy's "female transmutation operation."

•

15. José Joaquín Brunner, *Cartografías de la modernidad* (Santiago: Dolmes Ediciones, 1994), says that modern Latin American culture *is not the offspring of ideologies,* whether liberal, positivist, or socialist, *but rather* the product of the spread of universal education, the electronic communications media, and *the constitution of an industrially based mass culture.* The Córdoba university reform, certain elements of the Mexican revolution, or the ideas of Mariátegui and Martí represent momentary interruptions of the traditional cultures by new elements, but they themselves, Brunner argues, do not found modernity. There must be a social, technological, and professional base on which to found modern Latin American culture (165).

•

16. As is well known, the paradigmatic text in this regard is José Enrique Rodó's

Ariel (1900). On the cover of the 17 December 1904 issue of *Caras y Caretas* (no. 324), "El peligro yankee" (The Yankee danger) appears, with a drawing of Uncle Sam, Monroe Doctrine in hand, taking control of all of Latin America. According to Howard M. Fraser in *Magazines and Masks: "Caras y Caretas" as a Reflection of Buenos Aires, 1898–1908* (Tempe: Arizona State University Center for Latin American Studies, 1987), Theodore Roosevelt's presidency "was perceived as imperialistic despite his guise of protecting the Americas by means of the tenets of the Monroe doctrine" (244). Fraser says that in the magazine's first decade, "the vision of the United States is that of a 'careta' which veils the unpleasant 'cara' beneath it. *Caras y Caretas* shows an admiration for U.S. might and achievements while disparaging unethical business practices and excessive nationalism" (243). Among the abuses denounced by the magazine were "the inhumane aspects of capital punishment by electrocution" in the U.S. (243). *By around 1890 the role of the United States is clear, as is its insatiable appetite for wealth, its rapacity, and its desire to dominate the world.*

In a text entitled "Sueños, espíritus, ideología y arte del diálogo modernista con Europa" (Dreams, spirits, ideology, and art in the *modernista* dialogue with Europe), which appears as the introduction to his edition of Rubén Darío's *El mundo de los sueños* (San Juan de Puerto Rico: Editorial Universitaria, 1973), Angel Rama says that *the United States was the center of dissemination of new theosophical currents* (28). In 1875 Madame Blavatsky founded the first Theosophical Society in New York. And Rama adds that *the continental center of Europeanist politics was Buenos Aires,* which had created the most powerful instruments of communication and ideological persuasion ever known in Spanish America up to that time: *La Nación* and *La Prensa.* *La Nación* sends Rubén Darío to Spain in 1898 to report on the situation in Spain after its defeat by the United States and to offer a view of Europe. It sent Martí to New York as a correspondent in 1882. *It seems that there was an attempt to intensify links with Europe in reaction to the hegemony of the United States,* Rama says. Propaganda about European customs, the superior values of its culture, dissemination of its languages (French more than English), constant information about its technical discoveries under the guise of scientific interest, transmission of its rigid social hierarchies and of its daily life: *the great journalistic organs of Spanish America carried out the task of European culturalization* through their correspondents, European information services, or translations of articles from foreign newspapers. In 1898 Darío became *La Nación's* man in Spain and Europe (39–41).

For Walter Benn Michaels, "Race into Culture: A Critical Genealogy of Cultural Identity," *Critical Inquiry* 18 (1992): 655–85, the key date is 1898, "the year in which the United States annexed Hawaii, went to war in Cuba, seized the Philippines from Spain, and emerged as an imperial power" (655). Michaels refers to the anti-imperialist novels written in the United States in this period, such as *Red Rock* by Thomas Nelson Page (1898), and *The Leopard's Spots* (1902) and *The Clansman* (1905) by Thomas Dixon. The response to the question "Nation or Empire?" Michaels says, "placed anti-imperialism at the heart of an emerging discourse of American national, racial, and, eventually, cultural identity" (658).

17. The new genres show the interpretive indecision they produce in relation to the law: they show the ambivalence of the frontier. Both the detective tale and satire have given rise to polemics about their ideologies.

The Detective Novel

In *Form and Ideology in Crime Fiction* (London: Macmillan, 1980), Stephen Knight attempts to analyze the *ideological nature and function* of crime fiction: the function is to provide the audience with a "consoling" resolution of its anxieties. Detective fiction, he says, can "appear to deal with real problems but are in fact *both conceived and resolvable in terms of the ideology of the cultural group dominant in the society.*" The form and the content are in accord "with the audience's beliefs in dominant cultural values," and they therefore *contribute to hegemony* and produce "a pleasing, comforting worldview." The "ultimate realities," Knight says, remain "ideologically obscured" (4–6; italics added).

John Docker responds to Knight in *Postmodernism and Popular Culture: A Cultural History* (Cambridge: Cambridge University Press, 1994), saying that Knight's is a "Late-Modernist" perspective which disparages popular genres, and he argues that "Ideology does not issue from the detective genre itself, but rather from the historical character of individual texts . . . form cannot be identified with ideology, cultural conventions are not the same as discourse. Genres are open fields of possibilities" (221).

The "postmodern problem," for Docker, is that of private life: how to insert private life into a literature of public life and of public men. One way was by means of crime, because through crime private passions burst into public life. He also says that in U.S. fiction the detective confronts the law, which is linked with power and money (the case of Chandler's Marlowe).

In satire we find the same ideological ambivalence (with the same interpretive indecision on the part of the critic) as in the detective novel and in many *modernista* stories (as well as in *Frankenstein*).

Brian A. Connery and Kirk Combe, "Theorizing Satire: A Retrospective and Introduction," in *Theorizing Satire: Essays in Literary Criticism* (New York: St. Martin's Press, 1995), 1–15, say that satire is "less an identifiable genre than a mode" (9); it is seen in modernist and postmodernist texts accompanied by a "resurgence of historicism" and a "reconsideration of the power of literature and the literature of power" (11). Some writers, such as Pope and Swift, considered satire "a supplement to the law" (recognizing "satire's relation to law and its capacity to discipline and punish"); for them, its "habitual construction based on thesis and antithesis" creates "the potential for satire as a site of resistance to cultural and political hegemony— as well as for satire's implication within hegemonic discourse" (11).

In *Satire: A Critical Reintroduction* (Lexington: University Press of Kentucky, 1994), meanwhile, Dustin Griffin argues that the current interest in satire derives from our sense over the last ten years that satirical works, like all of literature, reflect and in a certain sense constitute the system of relations (political, economic, and legal) that govern a culture, distribute rewards, and control access to power. Satirical writings are implicitly directed at the enemies of society (such as they are defined in these writings) and at the custodians of the laws of society.

And Steven Weisenburger, *Fables of Subversion: Satire and the American Novel, 1930–1980* (Athens: University of Georgia Press, 1995), says that in the twentieth century the purpose of "degenerative" satire was to *delegitimize:* "it functions to subvert hierarchies of value and to reflect suspiciously on all ways of making meaning, including its own," to interrupt the transmission or inheritance of culture (3). Weisenburger sees degenerative satire as a postmodern phenomenon, and he cites Jean-François Lyotard's affirmation that the Latin *saturae* relied on "values without 'truth value' and justice without doctrine." In contemporary satires, Wisenburger says, *all* structures are suspect, "including structure of perceiving, representing, and transforming." And the definition he gives is this: degenerative satire is a way of interrogating and subverting "*all* kinds and of codified knowledge," revealing them as "dissimulations of violence" (5).

•

18. In *El alma de los perros* (Buenos Aires: E.D.E.A., 1950), 31–36. Soiza Reilly also became famous for this "literary" and fragmented book first published by Sampere in Valencia in 1909. The prologue was by Manuel Ugarte, another Argentine writer of Parisian *modernista* chronicles (*Crónicas del boulevar*, 1902, with a prologue by Rubén Darío) who lived in Paris and published his books there or in Madrid, never in Argentina.

In my chapter in this manual, "History of a Best-Seller: From Anarchism to Peronism," when I review the history of the editions of *El alma de los perros*, I will draw a genealogy of Ugarte and the dandy Mansilla. There, through the "story of the submission of the first manuscript to the master," the enigma of "Arlt and his precursors" will be resolved.

•

19. Joel Black, *The Aesthetics of Murder: A Study in Romantic Literature and Contemporary Culture* (Baltimore: Johns Hopkins University Press, 1991), analyzes two different representations of modernity, or better yet, of two modernities, that of Romanticism and that of modernism (as understood in English). The two representations are that of the criminal as artist and that of the artist as criminal. The first is the Romantic representation of the artist frustrated because he cannot communicate a sublime aesthetic experience that the criminal, who would be the real artist, shows through destruction. That is to say, the first representation is that of the criminal as artist, which becomes visible in the eighteenth century and culminates in Romanticism. The second, that of the artist as criminal, appears in the second half of the nineteenth century and culminates in the twentieth, and is, Black says, a modernist representation. Let us follow Black for a moment in his travels through the two modernities and the two relations between crime and literature.

> Cultural historians agree about dating the modern phenomenon of crime from the late eighteenth century and finding its first literary appearance during the romantic era. . . . And what Albert Camus has called "metaphysical rebellion," or crimes commited as deliberate acts of protest against the human condition, "does not appear, in coherent form, in the history of ideas until the end of the eighteenth century—when modern times begin to the accompaniment of the crash of falling ramparts." The eighteenth-century connection between literature and crime is particularly significant when we consider that the modern concept of "literature" itself—of literature as *art*—also dates from this period. . . . The romantics introduced the modern idea of literature as an autonomous art form. . . . This recognition of literature's artistic autonomy—the romantic author's self-image as someone whose detachment from human laws and conventions gave him privileged access to supermundane realms—dialectically coincided with society's recognition of the author as a mundane, social being. The introduction of copyright laws in the late eighteenth century established the legal identity of individual literary works as well as the institutional identity of literature itself. Michel Foucault has drawn attention to the emergence of these laws. (30–31)

The first representation of the criminal as artist is found in Thomas De Quincey's essay "On Murder Considered as One of the Fine Arts" (1827). Black says that it was De Quincey who carried Kant's concept of the sublime to its logical conclusion by proposing the relation between crime and the aesthetic experience of the sublime, and also *the murderer as an artist, or anti-artist, whose specialty is not creation but destruction.* In an essay titled "Crime," also from 1827, De Quincey says that the most brutal crimes can be appreciated as works of art if they are seen from an *amoral, disinterested, aesthetic perspective.*

Perhaps the most important aspect of De Quincey (and his revision of Kant's aesthetics), Black says, is that he describes "the disparity between ethical and aesthetic experience: the act of murder is the correlate of the violence with which the artist breaks with the conventional world, the opium trance is the correlate of the artist-assassin's state of aesthetic suspension from the world" (55). This awareness led De Quincey "to contemplate writing the *Confessions of a Murderer* as a sequel to his *Confessions of an English Opium-Eater.* Although never written, this project anticipated such psychological studies of homicide in nineteenth- and twentieth-century literature as that of Raskolnikov in *Crime and Punishment,* Lafcadio in Gide's *Les Caves du Vatican,* Meursault in Camus's *L'Étranger,* the terrorist Chen in Malraux's *La Condition humaine*" (61).

Black continues:

No topic so readily exposed the inherent contradictions in the ideas of aesthetic disinterestedness and of artistic creativity as that of criminality, and especially that of murder, as demonstrated by De Quincey's essays on the subject. . . . Not only was murderous violence a logical subject for later romantics in search of sublime effects, but the psychology of the murderer—his passionate spirit of rebellion, his unfulfilled fantasies and desires, his overworked imagination—was a superb object for aesthetic (dispassionate, disinterested, value-free) contemplation. Theodore Ziolkowski's insight that the "criminal mind rather than the criminal act" came to be recognized "as a worthy object of aesthetic contemplation" in "works of romanticism . . . concerned with crime" is exemplified in De Quincey's essay on *Macbeth* and in the spate of psychological studies of the criminal in nineteenth-century literature. (81)

Descriptions of crimes achieve artistic value when the focus changes from the point of view of the victim to that of the criminal, which is to say, when they are aestheticized.

The phenomenon of the criminal as artist is evoked in the work of other Romantic writers such as E. T. Hoffmann ("Der Sandmann," 1816), Poe, and later Marcel Schwob. These writers present themselves as *frustrated artists* who attempt to communicate an aesthetic experience lived by someone else who is the true artist: the criminal.

In the meanwhile, according still to Joel Black, there has occurred a radical subversion of Kant by Nietzsche, aesthetics *against* ethics, interpretation *against* truth, rhetoric *against* philosophy. For Dostoevsky and Gide, crime is not only a moral transgression and an artistic performance, but also a cognitive and creative act. The second literary modernity, then, which represents *the artist as criminal,* appears in the second half of the nineteenth century and extends into the twentieth. Toward the end of the nineteenth century, says Black, "modernist artists appropriated the murderer's disinterested state of mind for themselves in what I've called the artist-as-criminal phenomenon" (81). Black cites Wilde's *The Picture of Dorian Gray* (1891) as "a good example of a transitional work that bridges the romantic criminal-as-artist and the modernist artist-as-criminal traditions" (39). A "modernist discovery" visible in the works of Gide, he adds, is the "idea of a motiveless crime" that "becomes a crime against reason itself" (93). Sartre's works on Genet are also "modernist" in this sense. "Literary narratives or films that describe murder in a manner that evokes an aesthetic response in the reader or viewer are actually metafictions—works of art about art" (40), and they thus mark the shift from autonomy to self-reference seen in modernism.

Black concludes: "modernist representations of murder typically reinforce the sense of a clear-cut difference between art and life. Murder is presented in the great modernist works of literature (Gide, Musil, Eliot) and surrealist painting (Magritte) in a formalized, de-realized guise. . . . Once murder was aestheticized in modernist works of art, actual murder in all its brutality was free to flare up on an unprecedented scale in the form of fascist genocide" (93).

•

20. José Bianco, *Las ratas: Sombras suele vestir* (Buenos Aires: Siglo XXI Argentina Editores, 1973). The first edition of *Las ratas* was published by *Sur* in 1943. Manuel Mujica Lainez, *Los ídolos* (Buenos Aires: Planeta, 1991). The first edition was by Sudamericana, 1953.

•

21. Ernesto Sábato moved personally, biographically, from the physical and mathematical sciences to literature, and in 1948 he moved from painting to literature in *El túnel,* which also takes a painting as its starting point (in this case, one titled "Maternity"). The novel was first published by *Sur,* and the most current edition in English is *The Tunnel* (New York.: Ballantine, 1988), translated by Margaret Sayers Peden.

In *El túnel* the painter murders his upper-class lover (the only one who "understood" the painting he showed in the Salón Nacional) after accusing her of being a prostitute, and he ends up mad in an asylum writing his confession, as in *Las ratas,* and he says: *now I'm famous.* He also says: "There are times when a person feels he is a superman," and he refers to Einstein and Christ (3).

This complex of art, celebrity, madness, passage from one art to another through crime, chronicle, confession, truth, and "oligarchy" is *El túnel*. We are far from the subjects of the liberal state, but the scientists (and the artists of *modernismo*) led us to the frontier. The oligarchy in decadence (which is also present in *Los ídolos* and in *Las ratas*), "blind" like Allende (or myopic like Mimí Allende) is now "the victim": the painter Castel kills María Iribarne at the ranch.

El túnel is a novel (like "El pozo" [1939] by Juan Carlos Onetti) centering on the spirit's descent to "the depths"; the antecedents to which it refers are Dostoevsky (*Notes from the Underground*), Tolstoy (*The Kreutzer Sonata*), Kafka (*The Metamorphosis and The Castle;* the character is named Castel). Woman is a mystery, a darkness (Castel's lover is married to a blind man): she appears as a "chaste adolescent" and also as a mature prostitute, with no happy medium. Is the mystery of kinship and of María's names the "mystery" of woman or that of "the oligarchy"? And is this the feature that differentiates *El túnel* from the bildungsromans of Bianco and Mujica Lainez? An apparent confusion of names leaves us wondering whether María Iribarne Hunter is single or married (Hunter is the cousin of her blind husband Allende, which is the name of the train station near the ranch). We do not know what her "kinship" is, and therefore whether there is incest with "the blind man" or with Hunter.

The criminal artist, who is outside of social classes and who moves between his studio, a low place ("I got drunk in a small café in El Bajo"), and high places (Recoleta, San Martín plaza, and Allende's ranch), crosses society in order to arrive at the "mystery" of woman, of the upper class, and of his "detective novel" at the ranch. For there again, as in *Las ratas* and *Los ídolos,* the characters talk about art and literature, but in the mode of farce. Mimí Allende speaks with a French accent about Dostoevsky and Chekhov (and Russian appears as another metaphor of incomprehension because there is no access to the original; it is only read in translation), and she also refers to Georgy (Borges) and his detective novel collection, "El séptimo círculo." Hunter talks about the detective novel as a family novel. In *El túnel* the "literary theories" of the ranch are staged: *translation, the national writer as a person ("of the family"*: Georgy, Martincito), and *the detective novel as a family novel,* oedipal and self-referential, in which the investigator discovers that he is the murderer. The murderer-detective "I" (or the detective "in crime") refers back to the story of Oedipus and will reappear in Alain Robbe-Grillet's *Les Gommes* (1953), one of the manifestos of the *nouveau roman*.

El túnel supports various readings derived from the figure of the artist as criminal: a metaphysical and symbolic one, and another strictly literary one (autonomy and accursed modernism). But the readings of most interest to us at this moment (although we lack space and time to develop them) would be those relating to a specific political context (right at the beginning the novel alludes to Nazi violence; the *Sur* coalition was liberal and antifascist) and, perhaps, an *economic reading:* the problem of the art market during Peronism (can this woman of the oligarchy who "understood" my painting buy it from me? Should I seduce her? Her husband is blind). *And the political reading:* a marginal "artist" (outside of all academies, all orthodoxies, and schools), but one who shows at the Salón Nacional, could represent, or better yet, if we prefer, could be "an agent" of the Peronist state who "kills" the oligarch at her ranch (the place of a possible "counterstate" at this moment; at the ranch there is talk not only about literature but also about a 1945 Peronist law defending the rights of rural workers).

In 1952, during Peronism, León Klimovsky adapted *El túnel* to the cinema in a film starring Laura Hidalgo and Carlos Thompson. The dialogue and the screenplay were by Sábato himself, but the novelty is that the film is framed by a *medical discourse;* two psychiatrists discuss the paranoia of Pablo Castel, the painter.

•

22. Translation as a literary genre in the Argentine "high" culture of 1880 continues in the 1930s and 1940s with the journal *Sur,* the organ of the cultural coalition of the military-liberal state of 1955. José Bianco, for many years the secretary of *Sur,* was one of the most important translators in Argentina. In this culture divided between those who spoke foreign languages and those who did not, and between the national and the imported, the translator and the cultural importer are key figures. Although translators of literature can appear as privileged cultural importers, there is another type of importer-translator who is persistent in Argentina. This is the intellectual who embodies the system of some philosopher or theorist of prestige (or of the avant-garde) and who explains it, glosses it, teaches it, and disseminates it. As the "specialist in . . ." or the local "representative of . . . ," this importer figure has enjoyed great prestige in Argentine culture. "Theoretical" importers and "literary" translators, then, can appear as similar figures but they are not; in fact, they belong to different lines of culture: one to "high" culture, and the other to "progressive modernizing" culture.

In "La secreta tradición de los traductores argentinos," an article published in the "Cultura y Nación" section of *Clarín* (16 July 1992), Luis Chitarroni says that in the 1940s and the 1950s, Emecé's "Cuadernos de la Quimera" collection (directed by Eduardo Mallea) published Aurora Bernárdez's translation of Baudelaire and Haydée Lange's translation of Henry James, with a prologue by Borges (Bianco's *Sombras suele vestir* also appeared). Angel Battistessa's translation of Paul Valéry's "La politique de l'esprit" appeared in the collection "La Pajarilla de papel," directed by Guillermo de Torre.

José Bianco selected and translated short stories by Henry James for Ediciones del Mirasol; he also translated Jean Genet and Samuel Beckett from French, and he recommended the translation of John Berger; his version of *G.* was published by Sudamericana in 1973, one year after it appeared in English. He also translated Stendhal's *La chartreuse de Parme* in the 1970s for a collection by the Fondo Nacional de las Artes, while Manuel Mujica Lainez translated Racine's *Phèdre,* and Enrique Pezzoni, another great Argentine translator, rendered *Moby Dick* into Spanish.

•

23. Everything in *Las ratas* and *Los ídolos* revolves around a portrait. Or everything begins with a portrait (the "picture" is also present in "Historia de un espíritu" and *El túnel*). In *Outsiders: A Study in Life and Letters* (Cambridge: MIT Press, 1982), Hans Mayer refers to *The Picture of Dorian Gray* and says that the really scandalous aspect of Wilde's novel is "the image of the world reduced to a purely aesthetic totality," but he also notes that in the novel, "all those guilty of aesthetic idolatry succumb to suicide and loneliness or are murdered" (224). Mayer relates this aestheticism to the "existence of the homosexual outsider in the bourgeois society in the nineteenth century" which "is conceivable only as an aesthetic experience" (225). *The Picture of Dorian Gray* is for Mayer the "first consistently homosexual novel" (229), and he says that "Oscar Wilde in *The Picture of Dorian Gray* has attempted to describe an . . . aesthetic intermediate realm where one has neither to wear the mask of respectability nor opt for scandal. . . . It is from this vantage point that Wilde's novel must be understood as a homosexual creation. *And to this extent it also has a programmatic intent,* as outlined in Wilde's famous preface. *It is a program of total aestheticism and immoralism on principle*" (225; italics added).

The novel presents the typically homosexual dilemma of the double life, Mayer says, and it incorporates literary motifs ranging "from Wagner's Tannhäusser to the pact between Faust and Mephistopheles. . . . Yet the dominant symbolic motif is Wilde's own creation: the picture that grows old in place of him depicted in it. The literary sources in Poe and Balzac's *The Fatal Skin* are well known. Yet something new and original is at play" (228–29).

But the fundamental issue, for us, is crime: Dorian kills the painter of his portrait, Basil Hallward, and he himself is supposed to be murdered in a pub which is also an opium den. (Mayer reminds us that drugs and crime are linked in a tradition extending back to De Quincey.)

In the chapter "Los sueños del inventor" (The inventor's dreams) in Roberto Arlt's *Los siete locos* (1929), Erdosain dreams of beta rays and electromagnetic waves, and he also dreams that he could age without aging "like the *absurd character in an English novel*" (he doesn't say that it's Dorian Gray). And so he links, in "dreams," the two autonomous and criminal spheres, science and literature.

24. *Coda on Encyclopedias and Collections*

In Borges's "Uqbar, Tlön Orbis Tertius," *Collected Fictions,* trans. Andrew Hurley (New York: Penguin, 1998), 68–81, the combination of the Creole element with the European encyclopedia or order, which is the mark of Argentine "high" culture, reaches its culmination. The point of departure is the pirated *Anglo-Americana Cyclopaedia* which *reproduces* the *Encyclopaedia Britannica* and whose volume 46, which only Bioy has, includes an alphabetical supplement and four additional pages (from 917 to 921) where the "unreal" territory of Uqbar is found. The story begins, as we recall, in the Buenos Aires suburb of Ramos Mejía with Bioy Casares's reproduction of a quote about mirrors and copulation (which in the *Cyclopaedia* is transmuted into "fatherhood").

These points of departure lead vertiginously to the reproduction of encyclopedias and of territories, and also of the "Creoles" who accompany them. Uqbar is an entry and a few "additional" pages in the "pirated" "American" *Cyclopaedia,* and it is also a territory ("a false country"). This territory of the encyclopedia "reproduced" by Bioy is the entryway into the universe of Tlön (which is the *imaginary region* of Uqbar and later an invented planet) and into its encyclopedia, which already contains Orbis Tertius. Tlön *exists* in volume 11 (the number one duplicated, and it has 1001 pages) of another encyclopedia in English, *A First Encyclopaedia of Tlön,* which is also *North American.* The *Britannica* is the "measure" of other encyclopedias: the North American *Cyclopaedia* pirates it and the North American encyclopedia of Tlön duplicates it. The series of encyclopedias would be an increasing series of territories (geography was the queen of imperial sciences in the nineteenth century) arriving at the third one, Orbis Tertius, the empire that closes the story. In Borges the high culture turns back on itself to reproduce imaginary encyclopedic orders (a territory, a planet, a world) beginning with the *Britannica,* and it concludes them in the "reality" of the "Empire."

The planet Tlön, then, is found in volume 11 of the first encyclopedia, which was unknowingly received from Brazil by an English engineer, a friend of Borges's father, who resided at a hotel in Adrogué and who died before opening the envelope. He had been working with different number systems and "transposing some duodecimal table or other to sexagesimal" as commissioned by a Norwegian. Borges writes: "We spoke of the bucolic rural life, of *capangas,* of the Brazilian etymology of the word '*gaucho*' (which some older folk in Uruguay still pronounce as *ga-úcho*)" (71). The combination of the Creole element and the encyclopedia, invented by the subjects of the liberal state of 1880 as a mark of high culture, is shown here in relation to the volume of the *First Encyclopaedia of Tlön* which the Englishman received but never saw. There Tlön is no longer an imaginary region of Uqbar but "a vast and systematic fragment of the entire history of an unknown planet, with its architectures and playing cards, the horror of its mythologies and the murmur of its tongues" (71), wherein a new, third world, Orbis Tertius, is prefigured.

The story of the first and second encyclopedias and of the expanding territories is divided into two parts and two times; the first is assigned to the *Anthology of Fantastic Literature,* and the second is postulated as "reality." The first part is dated in Salto Oriental in 1940 (and it closes with the "reality" of Tlön, where real objects duplicate themselves: *the reality of Tlön is reproduction*), and the second part is a postscript from 1947, in which the complete encyclopedia of Tlön returns to reality as an empire, as Orbis Tertius. After two or three imaginary territories, there is an intrusion of the fantastic world in the real one (as in the case of the Rosicrucians who were imagined by Andreä in the seventeenth century and who later came into being in reality). Tlön returns to reality twice, and Borges situates himself as a witness both times in order to reproduce the combination of the "Creole" and the "aristocratic French element." To the first he lends the weight of religion, situating it *on the frontier,* where the three territories of the gaucho (Argentina, Uruguay, and Brazil) meet. The second arises in Buenos Aires, where the French princess Faucigny Lucinge receives a silver table service sent from Poitiers and with it a compass with letters on its dial belonging "to one of the alphabets of Tlön" (79–80). Let us look at Borges's Creole episode.

> This event took place some months later, in a sort of a country general-store-and-bar owned by a Brazilian man in the Cuchilla Negra. Amorim and I were returning from Sant'Anna. . . . we were kept awake until almost dawn by the drunkenness of an unseen neighbor, who swung between indecipherable streams of abuse and loudly sung snatches of *milongas*—or snatches of the same *milonga,* actually. . . . By shortly after daybreak, the man was dead in the hallway. . . . In his delirium, several coins had slipped from his wide gaucho belt, as had a gleaming metal cone about a die's width in diameter. . . . I held it for a few minutes in the palm of my hand; I recall that its weight was unbearable, and that even after someone took it from me, the sensation of terrible heaviness endured. . . . Amorim purchased it for a few pesos. No one knew anything about the dead man, except that "he came from the border." Those small, incredibly heavy cones (made of a metal not of this world) are an image of the deity in certain Tlönian religions. (80)

The Creole element (with obvious allusions to the place where José Hernández, the author of *Martín Fierro,* was exiled) combined with the real presence of the encyclopedia of Tlön. The "Creole element" of the frontier and its heavy religion (and the light "French element" of the compass and the alphabet of Tlön) *is a fantastic organization of knowledge and power*. Tlön and the encyclopedic order return as "the imperial archive": "Handbooks, anthologies, surveys, 'literal translations,' authorized and pirated reprints of Mankind's Greatest Masterpiece filled the world, and still do" (81).

This story is a fiction of encyclopedic order (or the encyclopedic order of fiction) and not only a fiction of its relation to "the Creole element." For encyclopedic order is not only alphabetical or numerical in "Uqbar, Tlön, Orbis Tertius." It is an order of knowledge: a positive knowledge, ordered in parts, and also a conception of knowledge as a totality encompassing the parts. In the territory of Uqbar, information is divided into zones or "sciences" (geography, history, language, and literature), and a philosophy organizing this information is also enunciated in the planetary "territory" of Tlön. This is a fiction of encyclopedic order because all encyclopedias function on the basis of *organization* (in this case, of Tlön), As Jay David Bolter writes in *Writing Space: The Computer, Hypertext, and the History of Writing* (Hillsdale, N.J.: Lawrence Erlbaum Associates, 1991): "The key to any encyclopedia is . . . its organization, the principles by which it controls other texts. And the choice of organizing principles depends upon both the contemporary state of knowledge and the contemporary technology of writing" (90).

This encyclopedic order is also a utopian order with secret societies and with mental countries and universes: "The splendid story had begun sometime in the early seventeenth century, one night in Lucerne or London. A secret benevolent society . . . was born; its mission: to invent a country. In its vague initial program, there figured 'hermetic studies,' philanthropy and the Kabbalah" (78). The encyclopedic vision was that the great book would contain all knowledge. An alphabetical and numerical order, a territorial order, an order of knowledge, a utopian order . . . Finally, a "real" order, in which the encyclopedia returns as an empire, as Orbis Tertius (with the post-English of Tlön, *which Borges will resist* by devoting himself to a useless and "indecisive translation in the style of Quevedo of Sir Thomas Browne's *Urne Buriall*" (81): a translation between previous empires and their languages).

In "Uqbar, Tlön, Orbis Tertius" the encyclopedias ironically show an unfamiliar face, and they appear finally as one of the fantasies of imperial power (and of colonial power, with the "Creole element") of "aristocratic" Argentine culture. Borges seems to have taken the fiction of the imperial archive and the "total knowledge–total power" equivalence from the English-language literature of the British empire of the end of the nineteenth century (or from the *Encyclopaedia Britannica*) in order to bring to its culmination (and to its "truth") one of the marks of Argentine high culture of the cultural coalition of 1880.

Thomas Richards says that he wrote *The Imperial Archive* "to try to understand what it means to think the fictive thought of imperial control" (2) and to explain why British literature of the late nineteenth century "was so obsessed with the control of knowledge" (5). ("The administrative core of Empire," he says, "was built around knowledge-producing institutions like the British Museum, the Royal Geographical Society, the India Survey, and the universities" [4].) According to Richards, the narratives of the end of the nineteenth century are full of fantasies about an empire united not only by force but also by information, and they were more concerned with the control of knowledge than with the control of the empire: "never has the alliance between knowledge and power been more clearly presented than in turn-of-the-century [British] fiction" (5). Richards analyzes Rudyard Kipling's *Kim* (1901), Bram Stoker's *Dracula* (1897), H. G. Wells's *Tono-Bungay* (1909), and Erskine Childers's *The Riddle of the Sands* (1903). "Each of these novels," he finds, "equates knowledge with national security. . . . And each goes so far as to see knowledge itself not as the supplement of power but as its replacement in the colonial world. . . . These novels and others like them . . . go so far as to create a myth of a unified archive, an imperial archive holding together the vast and various parts of the Empire" (5–6).

"This archive was neither a library nor a museum," Richards continues, but rather "a fantasy of knowledge collected and united in the service of state and Empire. . . . The myth of imperial archive brought together in fantasy what was breaking apart in fact, and it did so by conjoining two different conceptions of knowledge that may at first seem contradictory. These are the ideas of a knowledge at once *positive* and *comprehensive*. The familiar Victorian project of positive knowledge divided the world into little pieces of fact. . . . Comprehensive knowledge was the sense that knowledge was singular and not plural . . . that all knowledges would ultimately turn out to be concordant in one great system of knowledge" (6–7). In sum, the basic project of the imperial archive was the organization of all knowledge into a coherent imperial whole, Richards says.

I am trying in utopian fashion to find in the body and on the frontier of crime one of the points where another line of modern Argentine culture could be clearly seen to emerge. At specific moments I imagine it in certain collections, in the very idea and image of the collection, which is different from the idea and image of the encyclopedias of high culture.

A group of objects is moved from one place to another and it acquires a new meaning as a result of its recontextualization in a "collection." The collection is linked with displacement because it is the gathering of scattered or serialized works into a new whole, endowed with its own identity. In his drafts of "The Collector," *The Arcades Project*, trans. Howard Eiland and Kevin McLaughlin (Cambridge: Belknap Press, 1999), 203–11, Walter Benjamin notes that "What is decisive in the art of collecting is that the object is detached from all its original functions in order to enter into the closest conceivable relations to things of the same kind" (204). The object is organized in a new way, in a new historical system, the collection, and it is placed under *the logic of completeness*, Benjamin says. And this is perhaps what is interesting about "collections" as the point of emergence of something utopian which I seek on the frontier of the *corpus delicti*: its logic, because if a single piece or specimen is lacking, we are left with only a fragmentary series.

The collection, says Susan Stewart in *On Longing: Narratives of the Miniature, the Gigantic, the Souvenir, the Collection* (Baltimore: Johns Hopkins University Press, 1984), founds a new order that erases the past. A collection does not attempt to preserve or constitute a memory, but rather seeks to forget the past and found a universe from scratch (151–54). This "new order" of knowledge without a past, and its logic of completeness, could separate collections from encyclopedias. It could clearly separate the aristocratic Argentine culture of the encyclopedias (and its imperial fantasies with Creoles) from this modern culture whose birth I seek on the frontier and in the best-selling "collections" of international celebrities (with the order of fame as the new order of knowledge revealed in its combinations). For it is there that I imagine the utopian point within the *corpus delicti* where the progressive modernizing culture emerges as a second culture: that of the children of immigrants, of journalists, of the new middle classes, my culture.

Between the British encyclopedia of the high culture and the complete or incomplete collections of the second culture, two concepts of knowledge are defined. Let us engage our instrument of crime in order to return to the "collection stories" as they culminate in 1926 in Roberto Arlt's *El juguete rabioso*, available in English translation by Michele McKay Aynesworth as *Mad Toy* (Durham: Duke University Press, 2002). As a bildungsroman, it is precisely one of the fables of identity of the second, progressive modernizing culture. In the first chapter, "Los ladrones" (The thieves), which recounts the famous robbery of the school library by the "Club of the Midnight Horsemen" (a secret society of three), the boys from a barrio of Buenos Aires review the books and the money that they will get for them. Initially, in the planning stage, they had talked about the possibility of stealing the "ency-clopedic dictionary" because *it would be the most profitable,* but it was ruled out as too heavy: "And what are we going to carry twenty-eight volumes in? You're nuts . . . or were you planning to hire a moving van?" (37; ellipses in original).

The encyclopedic dictionary is rejected because it is like a piece of furniture or like a territory. So the three boys chose books to steal and construct a series, to which Enrique later adds a few volumes of Malte-Brun's *Geography* ("I'm keeping it for myself") when he returns to the library to "close the door." The total haul of *twenty-seven books* has exactly *one volume less* than the encyclopedia of twenty-eight. (It includes Lugones's *Las montañas de oro,* which they intend to sell, a biography of Baudelaire, which the narrator keeps for himself, Lebon's *The Evolution of Matter,* and manuals of organic and inorganic chemistry and infinitesimal calculus.) The total haul of twenty-seven volumes is divided into "sellable" ones and "expropri-able" ones for personal use. And it is equitably divided into three parts (nine for each of the "Midnight Horsemen"); the encyclopedic dictionary, with its twenty-eight volumes, was indivisible by three. Are collections perhaps defined by the com-bination of a scientific manual (such as Malte-Brun's geography, which Enrique expropriates for himself), with the biography and poems of Baudelaire (which the narrator expropriates for personal use)? Or is the culture of collections defined by the one volume always lacking?

This bildungsroman of the barrio provides the perfect cultural counterweight to Ricardo Güiraldes's "Argentine" bildungsroman of the ranch, *Don Segundo Sombra,* also from 1926. (Güiraldes in fact named both novels, having suggested to Arlt the title *El juguete rabioso.*) Arlt's novel opens with Enrique's collection of figures of national flags, presenting once again the drama of the collection. He is missing one, the Nicaraguan flag (which evokes Rubén Darío), so he falsifies it "using India ink and blood" in order to reproduce it "so skillfully that no one could tell the original from the copy" (24). (Enrique will come to no good, ending up in jail, as the nar-rator informs us at this moment.) Two crimes are committed: *the robbery,* which discards the encyclopedia and forms a series with one book or volume less, and *the forgery* of the "missing volume" that completes the collection of figures and there-fore obtains the prize (a rifle that Enrique sells). These two crimes will define this specific position with regard to collection as fundamental in a new order: that of the fables of identity of this second culture which emerges on the frontier and which reaches its culmination in the 1920s. It is a culture "one figure" shy of com-pleteness, the encyclopedia and encyclopedic "order."

In *El juguete rabioso* the boys are not only book thieves and collection forgers but also "inventors." Enrique offers: "Che, if you need some scientific data, I have a collection of magazines at home called *Around the World* that I can let you borrow" (26). In the libraries of the new culture of the frontier, the "scientific" collection is the equivalent of the encyclopedia.

III. The Moreiras

1. Eduardo Gutiérrez, *Juan Moreira* (Buenos Aires: Centro Editor de América Latina, 1987), 13. All subsequent references are to this edition.

•

2. For example:

> We have taken *a trip* ex professo to collect information in the areas where this gaucho first lived and which he later terrorized, without finding any cowardly action in his life which might throw even a single shadow on the appeal of our account. (13)
> We have spoken with the policemen who fought with Moreira, all of them now disabled, and we have conversed at length with the captain of the Lobos and Navarro parties, who is also now disabled, and they have all conveyed to us the deep impression made by Moreira's gaze in combat. (31)
> We are not writing a novel, we are narrating facts which can be verified by Mr. Correa Morales, Mr. Marañón, Mr. Casanova, then Justice of the Peace, and many other people who are familiar with these facts. We state this clearly because such are the events in Juan Moreira's life that they surpass any novel or fantastic narration written with the sole object of entertaining the reader's spirit. (83)

Or: "An event which we would not dare to narrate if Mr. Nicolás González, then Justice of the Peace, could not *testify* to this novelesque event, worthy of the strong souls who figured in the Middle Ages" (115). With regard to *scientific statements,* Moreira is diagnosed with "profound melancholy": "Moreira let out a curse that sounded like a clap of thunder, and then he stood still and mute, so still that he seemed to have fallen into that frightful and crushing madness which science has classified as profound melancholy, a state very like death, which we will discuss elsewhere" (136). Vicenta is diagnosed as "idiotic": "Her lips had stopped moving and she was static, with her gaze fixed on Moreira and the idiotic expression characteristic of the microcephalic" (157).

In the second chapter of *El discurso criollista en la formación de la Argentina moderna* (Buenos Aires: Sudamericana, 1988), Adolfo Prieto clearly showed the modernity implied by Moreira in relation to Martín Fierro. He says that modernization can be read in Juan Moreira: railroads, hotels, pool halls, brothels, the new campaign settlements, and the internal migrations to Buenos Aires. And the fact that the narrator is a journalist who interviewed Moreira is a clear sign of modernity (91).

•

3. Jorge B. Rivera, *Eduardo Gutiérrez* (Buenos Aires: Centro Editor de América Latina, 1967), says that Gutiérrez nationalized the truculent serial novel and that the critics of 1880 censured what they read "as an attack on 'social culture' (that is to say, on the covering up of zones of conflict)." He shows that Martín García Mérou (the official critic of the state cultural coalition) condemns him in *Libros y autores* when he writes that in Gutiérrez's works "all categories of rabble rub elbows, from the highly schooled thief, to the artistic pickpocket who works in miniature and who makes a science of prestidigitation. . . . Reduced to their simplest expression, these *police dramas* are the epic of robbery and murder" (29).

Rivera speaks of "Moreirism" as a mythic-populist elaboration of the attributes of *guapeza,* or courage, and he links it to immigration and the paternalism of the liberal oligarchy, "which tolerates and implements the forms of marginality" and prepares the rudiments of what will be the paradigmatic gaucho, "a character who justifies a certain type of agricultural and livestock production seen in Güiraldes."

Anarchism, socialism, liberalism, Darwinism, cultural nationalism, and populism: Rivera shows all possible perspectives on Moreira and also his projections in literature, cinema (for example, Moglia Barth and McDougal's 1948 *Juan Moreira*), opera (Arturo Berutti and Guido Borra's 1897 opera *Pampa*), and in the two comic strips drawn by Walter Ciocca and published in *La Razón: Juan Moreira* and *Hormiga Negra* (45–46). Many of the facts I use to construct the genealogy of "The Moreiras" are taken from Rivera's book, which is my main source for the chapter.

•

4. It was, of course, Borges, so linked to Moreira, who first saw the visibility of the hero. In "Eduardo Gutiérrez, escritor realista," which appeared in the magazine *El Hogar* in 1937, Borges says that Gutiérrez's serial novels were tearjerkers written in a prose "of incomparable triviality," but that they "are saved by a single fact that immortality is accustomed to favor: they resemble life." He adds, "I have forgotten Gutiérrez's words, but the scene remains. Two countrymen fight with knives on a street corner in Navarro. . . . Is this invention of a walking, silent fight not memorable? Does it not seem imagined for the cinema?" (*Textos cautivos: Ensayos y reseñas en "El Hogar" (1936–1939)* [Buenos Aires: Tusquets Editores, 1986], 47).

Borges inherited Moreira through his ancestor who appears in the chapter "El último asilo" (The last refuge) in *Juan Moreira* as "the brave Colonel Borges."

Daniel Balderston, "Dichos y hechos: Borges, Gutiérrez y la nostalgia de la aventura," *La Torre: Revista de la Universidad de Puerto Rico. Nueva Época* 2, no. 8 (October–December 1988): 595–615, exhaustively explores the relationship between Borges and Moreira. Balderston says that the mythology of the sheath knife and the cult of bravery in Borges have their most important precedent in the works of Gutiérrez, where the knife fight is codified and acquires mythical dimensions. He adds that Borges's first published version of "Hombre de la esquina rosada" (Man on pink corner) appeared in the magazine *Martín Fierro* in February 1927 with the title "Leyenda policial" (Police legend), after Gutiérrez's crime dramas.

Balderston quotes Borges himself as confirming Gutiérrez's importance in *El idioma de los argentinos* when he comments on his first readings and evokes Gutiérrez first: "I suspect that Eduardo Gutiérrez's crime sagas and a Greek mythology and *El estudiante de Salamanca* and the ever so reasonable and not at all fantastic fantasies of Jules Verne and Stevenson's grandiose serial novels and the world's first serial novel, *The 1001 Nights,* are the greatest literary enjoyments that I have known" (in Balderston, 596).

I should add that Borges also wrote the story of Billy the Kid in *Crítica* in 1935 with the title "El asesino desinteresado Bill Harrigan" (The disinterested killer Bill Harrigan), included in *Historia universal de la infamia.*

•

5. Hannah Arendt, *On Violence* (New York: Harcourt, Brace & World, 1969), says that "violence—as distinct from power, force, or strength—always needs *implements* . . . the revolution of technology, a revolution in toolmaking, was especially marked in warfare. The very substance of violent action is ruled by the means-ends category" (4).

Arendt maintains that much can be learned from George Sorel, "who at the beginning of the century tried to combine Marxism with Bergson's philosophy of life—the result . . . is oddly similar to Sartre's current amalgamation of existentialism and Marxism . . . Sartre, who in his preface to Fanon's *The Wretched of the Earth* goes much farther in his glorification of violence than Sorel in his famous *Reflections on Violence* [1906]—farther than Fanon himself, whose argument he wishes to bring to its conclusion—still mentions 'Sorel's fascist utterances'" (12). Arendt adds that "Fanon, who had an infinitely greater intimacy with the practice of violence . . . was greatly influenced by Sorel and used his categories" (71).

Arendt *relates violence to the state.* There is a tradition of political thought, she says, which depends on an "old notion" implying violence: that "of absolute power that accompanied the rise of the sovereign European nation-state, whose earliest and still greatest spokesmen were Jean Bodin, in sixteenth-century France, and Thomas Hobbes, in seventeenth-century England" (38). She cites Max Weber, who in *Politics as a Vocation* (1921) defined the state as "the rule of men over men based on the means of legitimate, that is allegedly legitimate, violence," and also Trotsky, who remarked that "Every state is based on violence" (35).

Arendt also *differentiates between power and violence*. She says that "power always stands in need of numbers, whereas violence up to a point can manage without them because it relies on implements. . . . The extreme form of power is All against One, the extreme form of violence is One against All. And this latter is never possible without instruments" (42). "Power and violence," Arendt continues, "though they are distinct phenomena, usually appear together. Wherever they are combined, power, we have found, is the primary and predominant factor" (52). She concludes: "politically speaking, it is insufficient to say that power and violence are not the same. Power and violence are opposites; where one rules absolutely, the other is absent. . . . This implies that it is not correct to think of the opposite of violence as nonviolence; to speak of nonviolent power is actually redundant. Violence can destroy power; it is utterly incapable of creating it . . . violence cannot be derived from its opposite, which is power" (56).

•

6. Alberto Gerchunoff clearly saw this in the theater, and he wrote that it was "an essentially anarchic drama. In effect, Juan Moreira is a rebel in a society organized on the basis of political privilege. . . . Is there any difference, then, between the drama of Juan Moreira and the current anarchist dramas portraying the injustices of the political and economic order in which we live?" ("La vuelta de Juan Moreira," *El hombre que habló en la Sorbona* [Buenos Aires: Manuel Gleizer Editor, 1926], 167–75).

•

7. With regard to the relation between violence, justice, law, means and ends, Walter Benjamin writes in "Critique of Violence," in *Selected Writings*, vol. 1, *1913–1926* (Cambridge, Mass.: Belknap Press, 1996), 236–52, that the task of such a critique "can be summarized as that of expounding its relation to law and justice" (236). For Benjamin, the question of "whether violence, as a principle, could be a moral means to even just ends" remains open, and to resolve it, "a more exact criterion is needed, which would discriminate within the sphere of means themselves, without regard for the ends they serve" (236). He refers to the prevailing current of legal philosophy, natural law, which distinguishes "between violence used for just ends and violence used for unjust ends" (238), and to positive law, which distinguishes between legitimate and illegitimate means of violence ("so-called sanctioned force and unsanctioned force" [237]). But what is fundamental, he says, is that "there is a lawmaking character inherent" in all violence (240). The state, he says, "fears this violence simply for its lawmaking character, being obliged to acknowl-

edge it as lawmaking whenever external powers force it to concede them the right to conduct warfare, and classes force it to concede them the right to strike" (241).

"All violence as a means," he concludes, "is either lawmaking or law-preserving. . . . It follows, however, that all violence as a means, even in the most favorable case, is implicated in the problem of law itself" (243).

Jacques Derrida analyzes Benjamin's text in "Force de Loi: Le 'Fondement Mystique de L'Autorité,'" *Cardozo Law Review* 11, no. 5–6 (1990): 919–1045.

•

8. In Argentina, liberal populism is sharply differentiated from the populism of Rosas. The novel recounts that the dictator sent Juan Moreira's father to the police chief Cuitiño with a letter that he thought ordered Cuitiño to hand over some money he had been promised, but which actually ordered Cuitiño to shoot him.

Addressing the relation between populism and popular criminals in the United States, Paul Kooistra, *Criminals as Heroes: Structure, Power and Identity* (Bowling Green, Ohio: Bowling Green State University Popular Press, 1989), says that "Social bandits such as Jesse James and Billy the Kid in the 1870s, the Daltons and Butch Cassidy in the 1890s, and 'Pretty Boy' Floyd and John Dillinger in the 1930s emerged concurrently with agrarian political organizations that proved quite effective," such as the Populist Party of the 1890s (29).

> Considering that agrarian groups perceived laws as little more than crimes and invoked religious metaphors such as crucifixions as ways of expressing the impact such statutes [as the Coinage Act of 1873] had on them, it is not difficult to understand how certain criminals could become transfigured into heroic figures symbolic of justice for portions of the agrarian population . . . the victims of the outlaw were identical to the alleged oppressors of the farmer. . . . The heroic criminal and organized agrarian political movements, such as the Populist movement in the United States, seem to find their genesis in the same cause: agrarian discontent with existing political and economic practices. (31)

Kooistra continues: "One of the most striking facts about the American Robin Hoods is that they do not emerge randomly. As we have already noted, they appeared, like their counterparts throughout the world, in a rural agrarian setting. In the United States, these outlaws roamed the Midwest and West. But they also appear in clusters at particular times" (32–33). Kooistra points to the 1870s, 1890s, and 1930s as "three periods [that] have something in common: an economic depression that was widespread throughout the country" and in which "The middle-class merchant or more affluent farmer . . . may suddenly find his modest economic holdings swallowed up by taxes or interest rates he can no longer afford to pay" (33).

Kooistra signals the *importance of the late nineteenth century press* in the construction of these heroes in the United States. The press, playing fast and loose with "the facts," treated crime as entertainment, and so began the fiction of the heroic criminal. His physical features are reconstructed, charitable acts are attributed to him. A typical example is Jesse James, whose glorifications overlooked his crimes against women and children. The same happened with Billy the Kid. Jesse James, Billy the Kid, and Butch Cassidy are the American Robin Hoods, Kooistra says, but there are others such as Bonnie and Clyde and "Pretty Boy" Floyd, for example, who have been presented as heroic criminals. Although they lived in different places and times, the legends are basically the same: driven to a life of crime as victims of injustice or for having committed an act that the state, but not the community, considers criminal. They are considered honorable by many; they break the law but they represent a "higher" justice, robbing the rich and giving to the poor. They do not defy the legitimacy of the state, but rather the corrupt practices of the oppressors of the people. And their victims are enemies of social justice. They are constructed in such a way that their social roles are inverted: the hero is seen as a man with whom we may easily identify. These are the attributes of the heroic criminal in the press, and so is the legend created and perpetuated.

In his introduction to *Bandidos: The Varieties of Latin American Banditry* (New York: Greenwood Press, 1987), 1–9, Richard W. Slatta recalls Eric J. Hobsbawm's characterization of rural banditry in *Primitive Rebels* and *Bandits* as a prepolitical form of protest, but he adds that in order to study social bandits in Latin America, models other than Hobsbawm's are required, "including the political bandit and the guerrilla bandit" (2). Slatta finds that, on balance, "the social reality of banditry in nineteenth- and twentieth-century Latin America exhibits far more divergence from than convergence with Hobsbawm's model" (8). In an article in the same volume ("Brazilian *Cangaceiros* as Social Bandits: A Critical Appraisal," 97–112), Billy Jaynes Chandler suggests that in Brazil, as elsewhere in Latin America, the culture of violence was linked with "rugged individualism, an exaggerated sense of personal honor, and an extreme concept of manliness" (107). Slatta adds that the rural masses in Latin America "clearly used banditry more for economic gain than for pre-political protest" and that ties between bandits and the oligarchy "appeared much more frequently than the peasant-bandit union posited by Hobsbawm" (8).

In his conclusion (191–99), Slatta observes that in much of rural Latin America,

Outlaws, whether deserters, bandits, or worse, could sometimes count on protection from chronically labor-short ranchers. . . . These ties between rural elites and bandit gangs also lent a degree of legitimacy to the outlaws. . . . The elite-bandit relationship also illustrates the fluidity between legal and illicit actions by bandits. In nineteenth-century Mexico, yesterday's bandit could become tomorrow's rural policeman with relative ease. . . . Hoping to use Lampião against rebellious army personnel (tenentes) marching through the backlands in the 1920s, the Brazilian government commissioned the famous bandit as an army officer. Politicians in need of strong-arm men also might lend aid to known criminals. The famous bandit of the Argentine pampas, Juan Moreira, worked as a bodyguard and "enforcer" for a national political party. The same fluidity between criminal and official ranks could be observed in Bourbon Spain and czarist Russia. . . . (193)

Some Latin American bandits, such as Juan Moreira, Silvino, and Lampião, enjoyed the reputation of invisibility and invincibility of Hobsbawm's noble robber . . . peasant folklore uses a "selective memory" that remembers bandits as class champions, even if historical reality was otherwise. (196)

In another article in the same volume ("The Oligarchical Limitations of Social Banditry in Brazil: The Case of the 'Good' Thief Antônio Silvino," 67–96), Linda Lewin finds clear evidence of cooperation between bandits and the plantation oligarchy of the Brazilian backlands. Silvino began his career in 1899, and his "incredibly prolonged survival as a cangaceiro is explained by the fact that his most reliable protection derived consistently from his connections with the powerful rather than with the humble in rural society" (77). Nevertheless, Lewin says, the images that appear in the *literatura de cordel* exalt him as a popular hero of the Paraíba region, and the effect of this treatment of Silvino and other cangaceiros "has been to obscure, even to deny, the cangaceiro's actual historical role as an instrument for maintaining the established order on behalf of local agrarian elites" (69). Silvino was captured in 1914 and imprisoned. He converted to Protestantism in jail, and in 1937, President Getúlio Vargas pardoned him and gave him a minor government post. "According to a frankly admiring witness," Lewin relates, "Silvino had only two personal weaknesses. The first was a fondness for diamonds. . . . The other was his vain addiction to bathing his face in eau de cologne, followed by generous applications of brilliantine to his hair" (76).

•

9. Héctor and Luis J. Bates, *La historia del tango: Sus autores,* vol. 1 (Buenos Aires: Cía. General Fabril Financiera, 1936): "A milonga was first danced on a Río de la Plata stage in 1889, and the honor belongs to Don Antonio Podestá, who wrote 'La estrella' for the first Creole drama to be performed in our theater, 'Juan Moreira,' in the time when the characters of the work did not yet speak, the spectacle consisting entirely of a simple pantomime enhanced with music" (24).

As for Cocoliche, Enrique García Velloso devotes the chapters "José Podestá y

'Juan Moriera'" and "Eduardo Gutiérrez y la verdad sobre Juan Moreira," in his *Memorias de un hombre de teatro* (Buenos Aires: Eudeba, 1960), to recounting the whole process of the passage from circus to theater and the success of the play, and he says that Gutiérrez's preliminary draft of the play included other scenes from the novel *as well as characters who did not appear in the original work.* The most outstanding of these was Cocoliche, "a type comical in his language, in the contrast between his natural abilities and his eagerness to assimilate himself into an unattainable realm of heroic adventures, in his dress, and in his grotesque physique." García Velloso compares him to Hernández's *papolitano,* who went on to become the comical type in gaucho drama and who, in the course of time, he says, gave rise to a prolific theatrical literature. The Cocoliche character was invented by a fan of the Politeama Theater and of the Podestás, a medical student named De Negri who died of tuberculosis. He would sneak out of the hospital at night to go to the theater and would imitate the jargon of foreigners, and one delirious night he went out on stage dressed outlandishly and invented Cocoliche. The audience members laughed themselves silly, and his debut was a success. The character appears in later works culminating in Carlos M. Pacheco's *Los disfrazados,* performed by Florencio Parravicini. Cocoliche is an everlasting type, the origin of a whole comedic literature in Argentine theater, says García Velloso.

•

10. According to Roger N. Lancaster, *Life Is Hard: Machismo, Danger, and the Intimacy of Power in Nicaragua* (Berkeley and Los Angeles: University of California Press, 1992):

> Machismo is not a set of erroneous ideas that somehow got lodged in people's heads. Rather, it is an organization of social relations that generates ideas. Machismo, therefore, is more than an "effect" produced by other material relations. It has its own materiality, its own power to produce effects . . . machismo is more than a "reflection" of economic practices. It is its own economy. . . . Nor can the question of machismo be fully addressed as a matter of relations between men and women. It is that, but it is also more. . . . It is a means of structuring power between and among *men.* . . . Machismo, then, is a matter of constantly asserting one's masculinity by way of practices that show the self to be "active," not "passive." (236–37)

Lancaster differentiates between sexual practices and genders in the universe of English and Anglo American culture and those of Nicaragua—I would say Latin America—through this active-passive correlation in masculine relations. Masculinity is defined as activity, and only the passive *cochón* is stigmatized as a homosexual.

In Nicaragua, Lancaster says, *cochón* is a term that "marks and delimits a set of sexual practices that partially overlaps but is clearly not identical to our own notion of the homosexual . . . it is the passive role . . . that defines the cochón. . . . It is typically a noncochón male who plays the active role in sexual intercourse: a machista or an *hombre-hombre,* a 'manly man'" (238–39).

The active *hombre-hombre* affirms precisely his masculinity not only with women but also with the *cochón.* "The one who initiates action, dominates, or enters is masculine; whoever is acted upon, dominated, or entered is feminine. This relationship holds as the ideal in all spheres of transaction between the genders . . . when one 'uses' a cochón, one acquires masculinity; when one is 'used' as a cochón, one expends it" (242). The *cochón* is a product of machismo: he founds the system of machismo and keeps it in place, just as machismo founds the *cochón* and keeps it in place.

•

11. Ricardo Rodríguez Molas, *Divorcio y familia tradicional* (Buenos Aires: Centro Editor de América Latina, 1984), refers to the state of family legislation at the end of the nineteenth century in Argentina. He says that the codes *penalized female adultery with arrest.* Article 247 of the penal code then in force in the province of Buenos Aires (where the drama of Moreira and Vicenta takes place, I would add) stipulates that "the woman who commits adultery shall be punished with two years in prison and her accessory with the same period of exile. The husband guilty of adultery shall suffer the same period of exile" (81). In his thesis *Del divorcio,* from 1880, Enrique Parodi writes that "adultery by women is more serious than that by men. In effect, the dishonor of the woman affects the family as well" (81). This in relation to Vicenta's "crime."

In regard to her suffering, Rodríguez Molas elsewhere (*La Argentina: Del Plata a la Cordillera de los Andes* [Paris: Fasquelle, n.d.]), cites a French witness, Jules Huret, who comments on the Argentine wife of the nineteenth century: "Such force of resignation and sacrifice scandalizes North American women who reside in Argentina or find themselves passing through. It drives them up the wall. I recall the contemptuous gesture one of them made when she said to me: 'Do you know what the women here do when their husbands cheat on them? They stay at home and spend their time weeping.'"

In the article on the depenalization of adultery in Italy, the Argentine newspaper *Clarín* (30 June 1997) reports that adultery ceased to be a crime in Argentina in February 1995. Until then, the penal code imposed from a month to a year of jail on adulterous spouses. The betrayed party was required to denounce not only their unfaithful partner but also his or her lover. However, very few people appeared before the courts to request that their spouses be prosecuted: the last conviction was in 1918. Law 24452, which removed the word "adultery" from the penal code, was introduced by Augusto Alasino, a senator from Entre Ríos.

Clarín reports that in Brazil a group of deputies from the Workers Party had proposed six years earlier to delete the duty of conjugal fidelity from the civil code. Reactions were so hostile that the proposal was scrapped.

•

12. Néstor Perlongher, *Alambres* (Buenos Aires: Ediciones Último Reino, 1987). The mute legacy to Julián: "To you, he said, I leave the sky-blue kerchief that I used to wrap my balls / when that half-breed wounded me out on the frontier; and the chestnut horse; / and the moles that you thought were yours, but that are mine . . . [. . .] and I also leave you these carousels, with their cardboard horses that / spin trapped in the mud [. . .] and also that greasy grass where I lost that silver / brooch, if you find it, it's yours."

•

13. In César Aira's *¡Moreira!* (Buenos Aires: Achával solo, 1975; the text is dated 31 December 1972), the "bad" aspect of the popular, that of violence, is the sign of the literary avant-garde and of revolution, and the death in the brothel is the Socratic moment of the text: the moment of literary, political, and psychoanalytic truth. The back cover bears the following inscription: "In this novel the most famous of *bad subjects* returns. Surrounded by his disciples, Juan Moreira awaits the advent of *death;* in the meantime, they argue about the immortality of production. (Moreira always speaks the truth.) The novel glides along and transfigures itself in multiplying scenes, but the curtains of Mother Nature impede the view of its ending." In the text Moreira quotes Freud and exhorts: "Be Marxists" (61). He defeats four hundred soldiers while Felisa, the prostitute, speaks on the telephone in German: *"Wo es war, soll Ich werden"* (If she's going, I'm not going) (76). The soldiers disperse, first in "patrols," then in "hoards." And the novel closes without narrating Moreira's death.

The Moreiras lead us to the avant-gardes, but in 1997 the "postcybernetic" Moreira appears in Buenos Aires in Eduardo Blaustein's *Cruz diablo* (Buenos Aires: Emecé, 1997). He appears in a future in which times are fused and identities mutate, because Moreira, the mutant who always was, is now a computerized business traveler, a cybernetic tracker, who deals with local *caciques*. He is pursued by indigenous people from whom he has stolen the cadaver of the famous singer Carfi, which contains a secret sought by those who govern through screens from Ciudad Central, an artificial island between Buenos Aires and Colonia. Moreira operates today as the future protagonist of a ruinous Argentina, waging a war of Indian raids and guerrilla tactics. *Cruz diablo* is something more than science fiction; it gathers elements of our immediate culture in order to place us in a distant future.

•

14. Allen Feldman, *Formations of Violence: The Narrative of the Body and Political Terror in Northern Ireland* (Chicago: University of Chicago Press, 1991), describes "the cultural construction of violence, body, and history in Northern Ireland between 1969 and 1986." He draws a correlation between "symbolic forms," violent "material practices" (both spatial and corporal), and "narrative strategies": together they form "a unified language of material signification, circulating between and formative of antagonistic blocs" (1).

Feldman says that "oral history emerges as a representational artifact of violence and the body" (4), and he treats "the political subject, particularly the body, as the locus of manifold material practices" (1). These practices point toward spatial constructions that mediate between economic structures, class formations, and ideologies. Within an urban system, violence appears as an important factor in the modeling of spatial structures of segregation and territoriality. "The cultural construction of the political subject," Feldman says, "is tied to the cultural construction of history" (2).

•

15. José J. Podestá, the actor who played Moreira in the circus, reproduces the *Sud-América* article in a chapter of his *Memorias (Medio siglo de farándula)* (Buenos Aires: Río de la Plata, 1930). The chapter is very well titled, considering that it deals with a sort of canonization: "La crítica levanta bandera blanca" (The critics raise the white flag). Teodoro Klein also exhumes the article in "El público de Moreira in Buenos Aires," *Revista de Estudios de Teatro* 5, no. 13 (1986): 49–53.

Also in the 1890s, Eduardo L. Holmberg, the scientist linked with the liberal state and the avant-garde writer who invented science fiction, fantastic literature, and the detective story in Argentina, places the Juan Moreira of the circus, nationalized by the liberal male elite, alongside *La verbena de la paloma* as a classic of popular theater in Spanish. In the dedication of his story "Nelly" to Professor Baldmar F. Dobranich, Holmberg makes reference to his directorship of the Zoological Garden of Buenos Aires, a post which he held from 1888 to 1903: "Will the fact that I have professed the doctrine of evolution and that I now wrestle with cages, walls, plants and animals at the Zoological Garden make me so unfortunate as to miss attending a performance of *Juan Moreira* or *La verbena de la paloma?*" (*Cuentos fantásticos*, 242. I am indebted to Octavio Di Leo for this reference). According to Antonio Pagés Larraya's preliminary study in *Cuentos fantásticos*, "Nelly" appeared as a serial in the newspaper *La Prensa* from 27 January to 6 February 1896.

•

16. In this process, Blas Matamoro, *La ciudad del tango: Tango histórico y sociedad* (Buenos Aires: Galerna, 1982), links the acceptance of tango with liberal politics in relation to the opposition of the Radical "rabble." He says that Radicalism chose subversion in 1890, 1893, and 1905 with adverse results, but that each time it was fortified by the lack of perspective of the exclusivist liberal government. The governing class was left with a choice: either push the Radicals toward a total subversion or agree with them on a middle ground that would leave certain essential mechanisms of power in the hands of the regime. The oligarchy opted for an accord. The political opening which occurred little by little had repercussions in the treatment of marginal culture. There was a tendency to make tango a public institution and to neutralize its pernicious content. Just as Radicalism accepted the accord and became a liberal party, the tango accepted its rehabilitation and left the urban margins, Matamoro says (73–76).

•

17. Rubén Darío, "La novela americana en España," *España contemporánea* (Paris: Garnier, n.d.). Composed of articles published from 1898 to 1900, the book appeared in 1901. In reference to *Juan Moreira* and Eduardo Gutiérrez's other texts, Darío says, "This copious, *barbarous* and hair-raising serial novel, this *confusion of legend and national history* written in an uninhibited Creole style, marks the sign of the times in our literature. This gaucho literature is the only thing up till now which can attract European curiosity: it is a natural, autochthonous product, and its savage ferocity and poetry carry the soul of the land" (336; italics added).

That in regard to the exportation of the novel. In regard to the play, let's consider the opinion expressed by the Argentine writer Manuel Ugarte (a *modernista*, a socialist, a Latin Americanist, and an anti-imperialist) in Paris in 1902. Ugarte published "El teatro argentino en Europa" (Argentine theater in Europe), in his *Crónicas del Bulevar* (Paris: Garnier, 1902), 251–63, which features a prologue by Darío. In that article he writes about the idea of South America prevalent in Paris: that South Americans produced a lot of wheat and amused themselves by playing at civil war. And Ugarte reports that "speaking of a certain unfortunate, a Parisian writer said: he killed himself because he was left with no other option than begging on the street or sailing from Marseilles in hopes of getting himself appointed as a general in some South American republic." But Ugarte also reports and translates a news item that had just appeared in a *boulevardier* newspaper: "a Creole theater company (specializing in scenes of the Pampa) is soon to disembark in Bordeaux, and a certain bold impresario proposes to exhibit them in the middle of Paris with all the indispensible *mise en scène*."

Ugarte says that *we still do not have theater for export.*

They have already made this perfectly clear to us in Spain. A few months ago when a theater company, perhaps this same one, disembarked in Barcelona, *La Vanguardia* said that "nothing is cruder or more rudimentary than Argentine theater," adding that *Juan Moreira* was written "without any regard for literary considerations." . . . It should be clear to everyone that if our theater has had difficulty winning acceptance in Spain, it will certainly not do so in Paris. *It would be an anomaly* to perform *Juan Moreira* in the French capital. Its savage and rude gestures will suffice to alienate everyone. The Parisian public is among the most refined and cultured; they will not be able to understand the brutal legend of our pampas, where man was transformed into a sublime and criminal beast. . . . It matters little that Juan Moreira may *think* he is acting justly; to an enlightened public, he is nothing more than a likable bandit leader. (259; italics added)

•

18. *Misas herejes* (Buenos Aires: Establecimiento Gráfico de A. Monkes, 1908), 95. Borges says that Carriego narrated the death of Juan Moreira, "who went from passionate brothel play to police bayonets and bullets" (*Evaristo Carriego* [Buenos Aires: Emecé, 1955], 39. The first edition is from 1930.) Borges places his Carriego in 1889, ten years before his own birth: "I want to write about that Palermo of 1889": the barrio of farms, general stores, coal yards, tenements, lumberyards (20). Creoles and gringos, native ruffians, guitars, unreality: Carriego, Borges says, was the discoverer, the inventor of Argentina's poor barrios (100).

Carriego links tango, Moreira, and the margin-dwellers, and Borges quotes the poem "El alma del suburbio" from *Misas herejes:* "to the rhythm of a tango, 'La morocha' / two margin-dwellers show off their agile knife-thrusts."

After reading the anarchist Carriego, Borges concludes: "The Argentine finds his symbol in the gaucho and not in the soldier, because the value encoded in the gaucho by the oral traditions is not in the service of any cause and it is pure. The gaucho and the *compadre* are imagined as rebels; the Argentine, unlike North Americans and almost all Europeans, does not identify with the State."

Moreira, anarchism, *modernismo*. María Bonatti, "Juan Moreira en un contexto modernista," *Revista Iberoamericana* 104–5 (1978): 557–67, links *modernismo* and anarchism with Juan Moreira and River Plate theater. Criticism seems to have limited itself to a single aspect of *modernismo*, she says, that of learned or elite prose, but there are other aspects *in the River Plate region* that merit attention. For example, *the Americanist tradition* of *modernismo* (which is crucial for Rodó) and also the relation between *modernismo* and anarchism. Bonatti says that the circus drama permitted the founding of theater in the River Plate region in the works of Florencio

Sánchez and Ernesto Herrera, which were both very successful in Montevideo and Buenos Aires. Both were impregnated with the anarchist ideas of Malatesta, which were then in full expansion in the region. "In a certain sense, it is the realist current infused with an imprecise sentimental-anarchist state that drives them to insert into their works elements of rebellious spontaneism taken from the Moreirist theatrical tradition," Bonatti says (562).

•

19. In his prologue to *Rubén Darío: Poesía* (Caracas: Editorial Ayacucho, 1977), Angel Rama says that in Buenos Aires in 1896 (three years after Darío's arrival there), "The learned read *La Nación* and the latest foreign works; the popular classes read the illustrations and brief articles of *Caras y Caretas,* the first successful example of a modern mass magazine" (xxiv).

In his introduction to *Magazines & Masks,* Howard M. Fraser says that the spectrum of readers attracted by *Caras y Caretas* was the broadest in the whole *modernista* period. It attained a print run of 100,000 copies in its first decade, and it was addressed to men, women, and children, with cartoons, articles on love and marriage, popular culture (soccer matches), and a good deal of advertising. "In fact," writes Fraser, "*Caras y Caretas* might itself be called an exposition of Argentina during the turn of the century" (9).

Fraser says that *Caras y Caretas* is the magazine of the "Belle Époque" (1880–1910) during which Buenos Aires harbored "the illusion of Cosmopolis" (Fraser compares it with Chicago rather than Paris or Madrid). It was a magazine for everyone, one that assimilated "several major trends in nineteenth-century journalism in Argentina," among them "the spirit of free inquiry emblematic of political liberalism from the first years of the nineteenth century and an encyclopedic curiosity about the peoples and cultural activities of the world" (4). Fraser also says that *Caras y Caretas* can be considered a *modernista* literary magazine, although it was not as exclusively *modernista* in character as *La Revista de América* or *El Mercurio de América.*

•

20. In his "Estudio preliminar," *Fray Mocho desconocido,* ed. Pedro Luis Barcia (Buenos Aires: Ediciones del Mar de Solís, 1979), 295–303, Barcia says that Fray Mocho wrote *Galería de ladrones de la Capital (1880–1887),* 2 vols., published by the Imprenta del Departamento de Policía de la Capital Federal (1887). It was a book of photographs of thieves with the characteristics of each one.

According to Barcia, Fray Mocho (a pseudonym of José S. Alvarez) was a contributor to *La Patria Argentina,* the newspaper that published Eduardo Gutiérrez's *Moreira* in 1879. *La Patria Argentina* not only traded in the popular heroes of violence, but also in madmen. It published interviews with madmen of Buenos Aires, for example, "Cuadros extraños (Manicomio de Buenos Aires)" (Strange scenes [The Buenos Aires asylum]), an anonymous serial novel from December 1879. Barcia says that in 1883 the newspaper returned to these profiles of the "mentally unbalanced" with the help of Fray Mocho and Eduardo Gutiérrez (82). The two writers agreed in their preferences, which included depictions of popular Buenos Aires customs, shiftless types, and "ragged potentates." (In this, I would add, they also coincide with Soiza Reilly.) In 1879, when a new cycle began, Moreira (violence) appeared alongside the madmen in the same journalistic space of *La Patria Argentina* and in its writers Eduardo Gutiérrez and Fray Mocho, and thus marked the popular relation between madness and violence.

Sander L. Gilman, *Disease and Representation: Images of Illness from Madness to AIDS* (Ithaca: Cornell University Press, 1988), refers to "the interrelated history of madness, violence, and the body" that underlies "the construction of the image of the insane as violent." Gilman says that popular images of the insane reveal "the dichotomy perceived by the general public between two basic states of 'madness' —the passive state and its active antithesis. Both are understood to be highly exaggerated states of being and therefore indicative of 'madness.'" Gilman defines the first state as one of melancholy, depression and lethargy, in which the mad are characterized "simply as lazy." The second state is that of the "violent insane": "It is the 'mad' as maniacal, out of control, running amok. In this state the mad are perceived as unable to control their own actions, limbs wildly waving, slavering, and, most important, violently aggressive. It is the popular image of the mad, found everywhere from medieval religious art depicting the objects of Christ's cure to contemporary comic strips illustrating uncontrolled rage, and underlies the paradox inherent in understanding the popular notion of the mad as criminal" (11).

•

21. In October 1910, Ingenieros gave a lecture at the Sociedad de Psicología de Buenos Aires titled "Psicología de Juan Moreira" (a summary of the oral presentation was published in *Anales de psicología* 2 [1911]: 149–50, and in *Archivos de criminología* 9 [1910]: 630). Ingenieros says that he is going to reveal the true Juan Moreira, the real identity concealed behind the Argentine popular hero, and that he has all the documents at hand. It is odd that he never wrote out this lecture applying Lombroso's theory to Moreira. After demonstrating with the documents that Moreira, like many criminals, served the highest electoral bidder, that he was a thief, and that he lacked national sentiment, Ingenieros concludes that Moreira was *congenitally amoral, that is, a born criminal,* with the characters imprinted on the type by the gaucho environment. Such an individual is not, therefore, an exponent of the psychological qualities of the Creole, but rather his antithesis, and the cult of such

a character is baneful for our collective morality. With regard to popular heroes and the inculcation of values in the people, Ingenieros says that "it would be preferable to educate the people in the cult of less atavistic forms of courage, for there is more courage in *the teacher* who instructs, in *the worker* who produces, in *the wise man* who studies and in *the woman who is a good mother* than in the human beast trained only to sate himself with the blood of his fellows."

Enrique García Velloso comments on Ingenieros's lecture in his *Memorias de un hombre de teatro*:

> Years ago, in a university session in honor of Ferri, Doctor José Ingenieros gave a lecture about Juan Moreira. The erudite psychiatrist had obtained from the archive of Mercedes courts a copy of all the cases brought by the authorities of Buenos Aires province against the famous bandit and his henchman. Ingenieros was generous enough to allow me to review those most interesting documents, and I have searched Gutiérrez's work in vain for any fact extracted from the truth of those events reviewed by the authorities in the declarations of those prosecuted. Only in the chapter referring to the hunt for Moreira in the brothel of La Estrella does the novelist reproduce details which agree with the official report submitted by Captain D. Francisco Bosch, leader of the party, on 1 May 1874 to D. Eduardo Martínez, temporary Justice of the Peace in Lobos, informing him of the death of the fearsome bandit and of the capture of his companion Julián Andrade. (117)

The problem is what to do with the "real" material and empirical violence and with the imaginary cultural and literary violence of the Moreiras. It is possible that violence itself may be what poses *the problem of reality and fiction:* the problem of the criminal and the hero. One is the real Juan Moreira, attested to by documents and witnesses. The other is literary and mythical. *Real and "literary" violence* separate in Moreira. This duality has been studied in the United States in relation to Billy the Kid.

Kent Ladd Steckmesser, *The Western Hero in History and Legend* (Norman, Okla.: University of Oklahoma Press, 1965), says, "There are two Billy the Kids in legend. The first is a tough little thug, a coward, a thief, and a cold-blooded murderer. The second is a romantic and sentimental hero, the brave and likable leader of an outnumbered band fighting for justice" (57). *Both are legends,* Steckmesser says, and like other nineteenth-century outlaw biographies, those of Billy the Kid "reveal less about frontier life than they do about the literary techniques and moral ideas of the period in which they were written" (32).

Jon Tuska, *Billy the Kid: His Life and Legend* (Westport, Conn.: Greenwood Press, 1994), adds that in the historical romance, "Billy can be either a villain whose death stresses the ultimate victory of the forces of good against evil or he can be a 'tragic' hero whose death emphasizes the injustice of society, of fate, of circumstances" (237).

Finally, Stephen Tatum, *Inventing Billy the Kid: Visions of the Outlaw in America, 1881–1981* (Albuquerque: University of New Mexico Press, 1982), concludes that we must "view myth and legends not as distortions or perversions of the truth—but, rather as in fact different forms of reality and different forms of truth" (175), for "no historical narrative duplicates reality" (174).

In sum: there are not two opposite Moreiras, one "real" and the other "mythical"; both are at once reality, truth and legend. And it is *violence* that doubles them.

•

22. Alicia Dujovne Ortiz, *Eva Perón*, trans. Shawn Fields (New York: St. Martin's Press, 1997), refers to Perón's genealogy: "His father, Mario Tomás Perón, was the son of Tomás Liberato Perón, a doctor, chemist, and senator who was sent to Paris by President Sarmiento . . . for services rendered during the yellow fever epidemic that had decimated Buenos Aires's population—mostly the black population —around 1870. The famous grandfather, the son of a Sardinian merchant who had arrived in Argentina in 1830 and a Scottish mother, Ana Hughes Mackenzie, had married a Uruguayan woman, Dominga Dutey, the daughter of Basques from Bayonne" (66). This Uruguayan grandmother, I would add, is the one who held Moreira's skull in the photograph in *Caras y Caretas*.

Juan Domingo Perón's prestigious grandfather, Tomás Liberato Perón (1839–1889), distinguished himself in the war against Paraguay when he was still a medical student. He met Leandro Alem, Eugenio Cambaceres, Pedro Goyena, Carlos Pellegrini, and Federico Tobal, who wrote Perón's obituary in *La Nación*. He was also remembered in Ezequiel Ramos Mejía's *Memorias*. As a physician, he cured the young Luis de Elizalde, Rufino de Elizalde's son, in almost miraculous fashion (Francisco N. Juárez, "El abuelo ponderado," *La Nación* 3 May 1998, Enfoques, 2).

•

23. José Sebastián Tallón, *El tango en sus etapas de música prohibida* (Buenos Aires: Instituto Amigos del Libro Argentino, 1964). In the chapter "Intimidad de 'El Cívico' y 'La Moreira'" (37–53), Tallón adds that "Everything about 'El Cívico,' as in others of his kind, was erotic. Sexuality was for him a passionate and exclusive vocation. He was a lover and a pornomaniac—I'll allow myself this neologism—by temperament" (52).

A note in Tallón's book attributed to "Juan (Julián) Porteño" says that the first publication of this chapter in 1959 inspired the play *La Moreira* by Juan Carlos

Ghiano, which was debuted by Tita Merello's company in the Presidente Alvear Theater on 19 March 1962.

•

24. Marta E. Savigliano, *Tango and the Political Economy of Passion* (Boulder: Westview Press, 1995), 50–55. But there are other female Moreiras besides Savigliano's "La Moreira," who fused tango with prostitution and abandoned "El Cívico" in order to begin her mutations. For example, Juanita Moreira in *Doña Juana Moreira,* a rural *sainete* in two acts by Alberto Novión, first performed on 7 April 1934 in the Teatro Buenos Aires by the Olinda Bozán Company (*Argentores* 2 [1934]). Doña Juana Moreira is a cook who works for the Italians Luigi and Rosa and their children in a humble house in the countryside. She makes noodles, empanadas, and garlic soup, and the household revolves around her, around food. She is an energetic woman who speaks as a Creole and sends Miguel, one of the children, to a store run by the Italian Don Culín to buy her raisins and olives. Miguel comes back with the order and also a letter in which Don Culín proposes marriage to Juana Moreira. In the house, a drama about marriage unfolds when the family sits down to eat and Virginia, a daughter who had moved out, returns home with a baby. The father rejects her and throws her out of the house; Juana defends her aggressively and takes Virginia and the baby to her room to care for them. Juana is good and has a big heart, Virginia says. Just then Don Culín arrives to ask for a response to his letter and to ask for Juana's hand. But Juana responds: I can't leave Virginia, who is like a daughter to me. And Culín: why don't she and the baby come, too. Juana Moreira and Don Culín are very good people, and someone remarks that there are good and bad Italians, as with all nationalities. Juana Moreira leaves with Culín, intending to get married the following day. Virginia is to be the maid of honor; she has meanwhile made up with the boyfriend who came looking for her and cleared up the misunderstanding. As she leaves, Juana Moreira says to the old Italian couple to keep their anger and their dogs, and she shouts "Mussolini!" She also says, "poor Culín, what a shame that you have that name"! Thus she becomes Doña Juana Moreira de Culín.

•

25. The August 1916 issue of *Fray Mocho* (5:223) features a chronicle by Soiza Reilly titled "'Fray Mocho' en la guerra: Las aventuras de un corresponsal de guerra. Tito Livio Foppa" ("Fray Mocho" at war: The adventures of a war correspondent. Tito Livio Foppa). There are various photographs and one of his son, the amusing *Rubén Darío Soiza Reilly,* teaching Foppa's daughter how to fire a cannon.

•

26. So states Alejandro Sux in an interview done in Paris around 1909 and included in the chapter "Uruguay" of his book *La juventud intelectual de la América hispana,* to which Rubén Darío contributed a prologue (Barcelona: Biblioteca Científico-Literaria, n.d.), 121–23.

In his chronicle, Sux recounts how he found Soiza Reilly in his house on the Rue Clichy: "surrounded by a true gallery of photographs, irreverent little statues, rare books. . . . Skulls and Japanese monsters grimaced on his desk, performing domestic functions. His impertinent little glasses and his Volterian smile peeked out from behind a mountain of papers" (123).

With respect to Soiza Reilly's career, Sux recalls that

He began by making himself known in Buenos Aires through *Caras y Caretas.* In each issue of that magazine, Soiza Reilly told us of his interview with some strange, interesting and unknown character whom he had discovered with his magic lantern in the nooks and crannies of the great metropolis. He showed us that our capital contained a ruined aristocrat who worked as a porter, he spoke to us of the novelesque life of one of our popular comic actors . . . And so on. Soiza Reilly had admirable tact and a marvelous eye for describing the "rich types" of Buenos Aires. (122; ellipses in original)

Sux's chronicle concludes as follows: "After all, Soiza Reilly is irreplaceable for a great magazine like *Caras y Caretas,* and I am sure that there is no other man in the Americas with his talent for the big article. If we were nephews of Uncle Sam, we would say that he is the king of the reporters" (123).

Alejandro Sux (1888–1959) is one of my favorite writers of crime stories. He is also one of the few Argentines who figure in Pierre Versins's *Encyclopédie de l'utopie, des voyages extraordinaires et de la science fiction,* with his novel *El asesino sentimental* (1924), in which murder is justified. Sux's entry in the *Encyclopédie de l'utopie* says that "*El asesino sentimental* is a utopian novel translated from Spanish in 1926, in which a man is a true natural antenna and can act according to 'messages' received from a transmitter who is also human, in this case the woman he loves" (849).

•

27. *Crónicas de Amor, de Belleza y de Sangre,* 2d ed. (Barcelona: Casa Editorial Maucci, 1912). The book is dedicated to "My companions in labor at *Caras y Caretas*" and includes texts written between 1905 and 1911.

•

28. The chronicle gives no indication as to what type of newspaper *El eco de las Mercedes* is. Soiza Reilly wrote two chronicles for *Caras y Caretas* titled "La utilidad de la locura" (The utility of madness) and "El arte en el manicomio" (Art in the in-

sane asylum), which were reproduced in the 1920 novel *La escuela de los pillos,* 8th ed. (Buenos Aires: Editorial Tor, 1939).

In the first chronicle Soiza says that "El eco de las Mercedes" was a magazine founded in 1906 by the director of the Hospital de las Mercedes, "the learned psychiatrist and teacher Dr. Domingo Cabred," in which the madmen wrote. He reproduces some verses by Juan Mendilaharzu about madness as "false judgment" (82–83), and he cites Charcot, Voltaire, Max Nordau (who identifies madmen with geniuses), Swift (*A Modest Proposal,* 88), and Ramos Mejía (89).

In the second chronicle Soiza recounts his visit to the Hospicio de las Mercedes, where the madmen paint, draw, and make sculptures, and he refers to madness as progress and creativity, with quotes by Nietzsche and Poe, among many others.

Like the Moreiras, madness in the history of Argentine literature relates the history of certain political processes that accompany the path of modernization and toward democracy in this cycle. (Later, with *Los siete locos,* it marks the path toward the first coup d'état in 1929.) It relates this history because in the "madmen" (in the series of stories of madmen) all institutions are represented, for madness is defined in this cycle as the opposite or the negation of the institutions of the liberal state, whether in 1889 with Antonio Podestá's *Irresponsable,* in the crisis of 1890 with Julián Martel's *La Bolsa,* in 1905 with Gregorio de Laferrèrre's *Locos de verano,* in 1914 with Soiza Reilly's Locopolis, or in 1929 with *Los siete locos.*

•

29. Alphonse Daudet wrote *Les Aventures prodigieuses de Tartarin de Tarascon* in 1869 and published it in 1872 to offend the local pride of Tarascon, a region of southern France "where the sun magnifies everything." Tartarin "the intrepid," "the great," "the incomparable," is "the king" of Tarascon, "the hero" who represents a small world with a big imagination, because he submits to the sporting and artistic exaggerations of the people. At age forty-five he gets bored and decides to go to Algeria "to kill lions in the land of the Turks." Tartarin is the hero with two faces: Don Quixote and Sancho converse within him. In Algeria his money is stolen and the only lion he finds is a blind one who has been tamed by two black beggars and who wags his tail when someone throws him a coin. Tartarin kills him, and the beggars bring him to court, where he is fined 2,500 francs. He has to sell his weapons to pay the fine, but gets to keep the lion skin, which he sends back to Tarascon. Upon return to his homeland, all of Tarascon welcomes him back and acclaims him as a hero, and at the end of the book, Tartarin begins the narration of his adventures: "one night, in the middle of Sahara. . . ."

Tartarin de Tarascon is a Cervantean satire (a deconstruction) of the invention of a local or regional hero of the nineteenth century as a product "of the sun of southern France." A hero of the era of colonialism and of the extinction of lions, invented by a community that makes a hero out of a petit bourgeois Frenchman from the provinces.

•

30. The first Argentine cartoon character, Don Goyo Sarrasqueta y Obes, was created by the Spanish illustrator Manuel Redondo and appeared in *Caras y Caretas* in 1913. "This character *adopts any profession,* to the point of becoming a painter of pictures because it's less demanding than shining shoes; he will become a war correspondent in 1914 and a fashion expert in 1927" (Oscar E. Vásquez Lucio [Siulnas], "El primer personaje de historieta," *Historia del humor gráfico y escrito en la Argentina: Tomo I—1801/1939* [Buenos Aires: Editorial Universitaria de Buenos Aires, 1985], 263).

There is a rather significant change in Moreira's variable "professions" from the chronicles in *Caras y Caretas* in 1907 and 1908 to *La ciudad de los locos* in 1914: Soiza Reilly does not reproduce the second chronicle, "El diputado Tartarín Moreira (Psicología popular)"; he replaces it with chapter 3: "Un historiador americano" (An American historian). There Agapito finds Moreira on the Calle Florida and, as always, Tartarín invites him to his house, which is full of "portraits of heroes, forefathers, warriors, patriots, soldiers" (30). Agapito asks: "Is it possible that you, Tartarín Moreira, that famous dandy whose reputation as a brawler, a fancy man, and a hell-raiser was known from the Club of Progress to the tenements of Calle San Juan, is it possible that you could have become one of those historians who when they walk down the street seem to be listening to the national anthem?" Moreira answers: "The profession of historian is in fashion. First, becoming a lawyer was in fashion. I got a law degree . . . Then being a sportsman was in fashion. I became one . . . Then came politics. They elected me deputy . . . Next thing I knew, one had to go to Paris. I crossed the sea . . . Then, one had to go up in a balloon. I went up . . . And at the present time, finally, history is the only honorable, beneficial, and *chic* career the rabble has left us" (31; ellipses in original). Note the substitution of "deputy" in the changing series of fashions, which opens with the dandy and ends with "the nationalist historian."

•

31. *The visibility of violence in comics* (and in Moreira): fragmentary, partial, mutating, and rapid, with compressed dialogues and pictorial pantomimes. The satirical and literary trajectory from Cosmopolis to Locopolis reads like a comic strip in *La ciudad de los locos,* just as Nathanael West (1903–1940) intended his novel *Miss Lonelyhearts* to be read in 1933. "Miss Lonelyhearts" is the female pseudonym used

by a male journalist who writes a sentimental advice column: again an organic journalist is at the center of a violent text written "in the form of" a comic strip.

The plot of *Miss Lonelyhearts* is a sequence of vignettes which feature an "almost bald" violence, as in comic strips or the films of Charlie Chaplin: yelling, noises, blows (*Bam! Bam!*), and the invariable "slam ending."

In "Some Notes on *Miss Lonelyhearts*" (first published in *Contempo* on 15 May 1933), West comments on the conception of his novel: "As subtitle: 'A novel in the form of a comic strip.' The chapters to be squares in which many things happen through one action. The speeches contained in the conventional balloons. I abandoned this idea, but retained some of the comic strip technique: Each chapter instead of going forward in time goes backward, forward, up and down in space like a picture" (cited in Thomas Strychacz, *Modernism, Mass Culture, and Professionalism* [New York: Cambridge University Press, 1993], 176). The comic strip model, Strychacz says, appealed to West not only as a means of evoking "a culture in which violence is so gratuitous and endemic as to be barely noticeable" (176), but also as a means of bypassing "the linearity of prose" and conventional literary coordinates of space and time (179). Strychacz considers West's *Contempo* article "to be one of the more provocative little-known manifestos of the twentieth century" (179). West's view of violence as "idiomatic" and "daily" in America is also elaborated in "Some Notes on Violence," first published in *Contact* in October 1932, and reproduced in Alistair Wisker's *The Writing of Nathanael West* (London: MacMillan, 1990), 155–56.

Steven Weisenberger, *Fables of Subversion: Satire and the American Novel, 1930–1980* (Athens: University of Georgia Press, 1995), says that West's work exemplifies a radically subversive mode of satire that "functions to subvert hierarchies of value and to reflect suspiciously on all ways of making meaning" (3). He considers this "degenerative" satire a postmodern phenomenon and compares West's novels with those of Thomas Pynchon. There is no progress in West's narrative, he says, but rather regression to a *primordial violence* that poses problems of control and domination, of "reality" itself as a performance, and of the degradation of symbols that are changed in each new "script." West's imagery is grotesque, and it goes from cartoonish fantasy to zero degree of description, with the juxtaposition of high culture and popular materials.

And if we were to "apply" the discourse of and on Nathanael West to our "unread" J. J. de Soiza Reilly in *La ciudad de los locos*? A U.S. modernist discourse from the thirties to an Argentine *modernista* discourse linking Cosmopolis and Locopolis? Both are "in the form of a comic strip" and center on a journalist, and everything in them revolves around the relation between violence and the journalistic fictions associated with two modernisms.

•

32. As in the 1902 play *Canillita* by the Uruguayan writer and anarchist Florencio Sánchez, whose title character is unjustly accused of theft and who inadvertently caused another crime: the good Catalonian immigrant from the tenement (who loved Canillita's seamstress mother "well") killed the abusive ruffian (who lived with the poor, good mother, robbing her and punishing her). The happy Canillita who sings and shouts out the headlines of *La Nación, La Prensa, Patria,* and *Standard,* is arrested just as he shouts "Revolution in Montevideo!" He was accused by the ruffian of robbing a brooch that his mother had pawned in order to buy medicine and food for his sick younger brother. The good Catalonian immigrant kills the ruffian and says to Canillita, whom he got out of jail: "It is better for me to end my days in prison than for you to begin yours in jail!"

Florencio Sánchez invented the figure of the paperboy "in crime" in Argentine culture, just as Carriego invented the barrio and the newspaper sellers: both were anarchists. In this cycle the paperboys represent the proletarian suffering of the poor and pure childhood, and *canillitas* became a permanent and affectionate name for paperboys in Argentina.

Beginning with Florencio Sánchez, the paperboy is linked with crime, with the satirical violence of Tartarín Moreira, and with a grotesque and ever greater violence; it passes through *Larvas,* by the anarchist Elías Castelnuovo, and culminates in "El niño proletario" (The proletarian boy) by Osvaldo Lamborghini.

But today our story is that of Tartarín Moreira, who smashes the paperboy's head in the fourth *Caras y Caretas* chronicle. Several years later, Soiza Reilly writes two tales about paperboys unjustly accused of murders they did not commit, in the tradition of Florencio Sánchez, but this time with a grotesque twist resembling that of Castelnuovo. The first is *La escuela de los pillos,* from 1920. The text is a "reproduction" of the memoirs of Cachito, a newspaper seller who spent almost his whole life in prison, and who is unjustly condemned to death for a murder he didn't commit.

Soiza's other tale featuring paperboys and crime is "El dolor de un niño" (A boy's pain) from 1926 (*No leas este libro. . .* [*El amor, la mujer y otros venenos*] [Buenos Aires: Librerías Anaconda, 1933], 75–114), and it is also narrated in the first person by the fourteen-year-old paperboy accused, again unjustly, of murder. Finally, after spending almost his whole youth in jail and living through unspeakable horror, he says that he changed his name and his shirt, that he learned to be a thief, and that today, at age fifty, "I am the most honored man, I appear on the social page of the newspapers, and I have factories which manufacture food products that are making the world's physicians rich. My boyhood pain has become an old man's venom."

And if we follow Soiza Reilly (along with Moreira) in our cycle, we find that the gangs (the Moreiras) attack not only paperboys but also journalists and the "bohemian poets" of *modernismo*: in both the 1913 *sainete La patota* (The gang) by Carlos Mauricio Pacheco (author of a previous work about gangs, *La indiada*, in 1908) and in the 1911 chronicle "Las aventuras de un poeta bohemio," again by Soiza Reilly, this time from his *Crónicas de amor, de belleza y de sangre*. But it so happens that the poor bohemian provincial poet, who aspires to join the editorial staff of some newspaper, takes out a revolver and kills one of the aggressive gang members in the "Café de los 36 billares." Soiza's ending introduces the mothers of the dead gang member and the imprisoned poet: "Poor old ladies! they are the ones who pay."

Stories of bohemian poets and stories of paperboys: they are connected by newspapers as sites of work and by the violences to which the Moreiras subject them.

•

33. The same year Ingenieros presented his Moreira at the Sociedad de Psicología and Güiraldes took the tango to Paris, a grandson of Moreira was reincarnated in Pago Chico. *Divertidas aventuras del nieto de Juan Moreira* was written by Roberto J. Payró in Brussels in 1910. The grandson, Gómez Herrera, descends from Moreira to represent the national literary institution of political "Moreirism" or "Creole politics." "Moreirism" is ignorance, *caudillismo*, and the use of violence, corruption, fraud, and cynicism in politics: it is Latin American backwardness and political barbarism.

Moreira's grandson:

> As ignorant and as dominating as his grandfather, he was born in a remote corner of the provinces, and he grew up there without learning anything but love of his person and adoration of his own vices.
>
> He got from his grandfather a reverse atavism, and just as Moreira fought, often wrongly, against the police party, his grandson fought always wrongly with the police party and against everything else. [. . .] He inherited leadership from his father, and wearing civilized clothing, he was from an early age the essence of a gaucho and of a thug, stripped along with the leggings and the poncho of anything resembling virtue. [. . .]
>
> It is time to do away with *gauchismo* and thuggery, to renounce worship of those ghosts of the past, to respect culture in its best forms, and to prefer modest merit over the pursuit of success at any cost. . . . Let Juan Moreira's grandson represent us in Europe! Why not, then, let Facundo govern us, since he was the same?

From the Sociedad de Psicología and from Brussels, in the mode of realism, the socialists of 1910 say: enough of Moreira, nationalist *gauchismo,* barbarism, and political corruption. Moreira not only connects popular culture with the liberal oligarchic male culture, but also delimits, through exclusion, the socialist, scientific, progressive, and modernizing culture: every time that a Moreira appears, civilization and barbarism are again at stake.

How to confront both the language of violence and the language against violence? By inventing a language of counterviolence?

•

34. To put it another way: the history of Moreira, that of tango, and that of the gangs go together from 1890 onward, but also before that, from Moreira's birth, alongside tango, at the end of the 1870s. It is the history of violence related to territories, tribes, marks of identity, foundings, and exportations in "From Cosmopolis to Locopolis." Let's try to recount something of this history bibliographically.

Héctor and Luis J. Bates (*La historia del tango: Sus autores*) say that the first tango appeared shortly after 1870; around 1880, "Dame la lata" was popularized, and thereafter, in 1885 and 1886, it spread through the nightclubs and the dance halls like a grease stain.

> In those years the gangs had not yet made their appearance. *The upper-class gang, a genuinely porteño institution* was a dangerous toy invented by the "well-to-do" boys of "bad" society, in order to make it easier to get into the halls where tango was then danced. Since they did not have the fighting skill of those who dominated those environments, the doors of those halls were closed to them until they began to put an old refrain into practice: "There is strength in numbers." And one night, determined to get a close look at those famous dance halls without grave risk to themselves, they burst right into the establishment firing shots. The method paid off, since the conquest was achieved on the basis of numbers, and the gang became an "institution." (28–30)

And I would add: a doubly "male" institution, like that of the Moreiras, because on 7 February 1903 a photo of two entwined men appeared in *Caras y Caretas* with this inscription: "In *the earliest times* the tango was danced only by men."

Andrés Chinarro, who reproduces this photograph in *El tango y su rebeldía* (Buenos Aires: Continental Service, 1965), 36, says that except in "dance houses" (brothels), "the tango was danced exclusively on the outskirts of the city and the couples were exclusively male. . . . The place chosen for these exclusively male dances might be the back room of a store or an inn, *the successor of the pulpería,* or the broad patio of a lumberyard" (27; italics added).

But our gangs did not go there, but rather to the "dance houses" or brothels, Chinarro says, and "there Troy met San Quintín. They raised some tremendous commotions, breaking the lamps that illuminated the place, and throwing tables, chairs, and any other blunt instrument until shots rang out and they beat the retreat. . . . The 'leader' of one of these gangs, perhaps the most resolute and 'punishing' one, was the great sportsman Jorge Newbery" (52–53).

José Sebastián Tallón (*El tango en sus etapas de música prohibida*) says that gangs like Moreira's did not go to La Boca because it was "a barrio of drunken multitudes and brothels," and there "the number and the criminal dangerousness of the enemy counseled prudence." Tallón continues:

> When it came to playing at war with the ruffians, the gang members were better off in the brothel zone around Junín and Lavalle, in the steak house in the Palermo woods, in Hansen's place or in the café of *La pajarera* stud farm, across from the lower side of the racetrack. When boxing was not permitted, they practiced it on the Delcasse estate, along with Roman wrestling and fencing. Precursors of great resonance in the history of Argentinian sport—Lenevé, Jorge Newbery—were seen going with the gangs who *amused themselves by administering modernist beatings to the ruffians.* (66; italics added)

Roberto Selles and León Benarós, *La historia del tango, primera época* (Buenos Aires: Corregidor, 1977), refer to "Hansen's place" in the 1890s as "the greatest and most enduring myth among *porteño* tango locales," and they say that beginning at eleven o'clock at night it was full of "handsome men and dangerous gangs, which made it a very popular place." People from the outskirts of the city didn't go there because it was expensive and there was police surveillance.

The gangs of rich and idle *porteño* "boys" also went into the poor quarters of the city, where they "gave free reign to their elementary desires," according to Domingo F. Casadevall, *Buenos Aires: Arrabal. Sainete. Tango* (Buenos Aires: Compañía General Fabril Editora, 1968), 76–77. "Descendants of ranchers, spoiled by wealth, they found a world of primitive emotions and stimulating risks just a short distance from their opulent and refined homes." These boys *confused enjoyment with excess and bravery with brutality;* the gold in their pockets, their aristocratic surnames, and the leverage of their influential friends and relatives guaranteed that the public authorities would indulge their abuses."

Once the cycle of violent incursions concluded, Ricardo Güiraldes exported the tango to Paris in 1910, and there it caused a sensation and took the city by storm: tango revolutionized clothing and even the way Parisians walked.

In 1912, *following the sensation in Paris,* "Baron De Marchi organized a famous party in the Palais de Glace to see whether high *porteño* society would be able to embrace the tango. 'Maco' Milani and Carlos Herrera bridged the gap between the forbidden tango and the decent folk on whose doors they knocked. They were skill-ful and subtle ambassadors and packaged the article attractively, in order to facilitate its expedition" (Selles and Benarós, 279).

This same Baron De Marchi and his gangs will reappear as protagonists of an-other of the "Argentine stories" of the *corpus delicti*. Juan José Sebreli, "La cuestión judía en Argentina," *La cuestión judía en la Argentina* (Buenos Aires: Tiempos Con-temporáneo, 1968), says that in 1910:

> Leftist terrorism is met with terrorism from the right. *For the Centenary,* Luis Dellepiane organizes the Civil Police Auxiliary on an *ad honorem* basis, and it is made up of *young men from the upper classes,* with the pretext of cooperating in the celebrations, but with the true objective of intimidating the workers. Gathering at the very exclusive *Argentine Sporting Society* in the days leading up to 25 May 1910, *young gang members* under the leadership of *Baron Demarchi* and with the partici-pation of Juan Balestra, among others, set out to ransack union buildings, set fire to the offices of the newspapers *La Protesta* and *La Vanguardia,* and attack militant workers. *These same young men are the perpetrators of the first Argentine pogrom. On 15 May* a group of them arrive in the Jewish quarter, in the former ninth district. They ransack a Jewish store on the corner of Lavalle and Andes (now José E. Uriburu) and go so far as to rape women. These events are recounted by the vic-tims themselves to the editors of the C.O.R.A. bulletin (Confederación Obrera de la República Argentina). (229–30; italics added)

But let's return to the tango, which becomes fashionable in the salons of the Argentine elite only after conquering Paris. According to Casadevall, upper-class families soon adopted it, with the most valuable support coming from elite families. "Shaw, Tesanos, Pinto, Torres Agüero, Sánchez Elía, Costa Paz, Palacio, Farini, and Tornquist were among the surnames of those families first to adopt it. And so, once the tango had been accepted into the great elite salons and won the sup-port of such distinguished admirers, it soon shed its rags to become a great lord, ennobled by the new environments. Yet it did not forget its old haunts, where the original devotees continued to pay their respects" (50).

This process of acceptance generated a rupture and a dispute between the old families. At the beginning of his study, José Sebastián Tallón says that:

> I belong to an old, middle-class *porteño* family that was divided long before 1910 into a tolerant faction and a prohibitionist faction. My father has yet to reconcile him-self with the tango, which he considers a dance of people of low origin. My uncle

Roberto, his younger brother, was, on the other hand, a man of the tango. . . . To him, being a man of the tango meant simply being a man of Buenos Aires. It was a revolutionary way that the young men of his generation had of feeling thoroughly *porteño*. Sensualism had risen up on the outskirts of the city, and the young people could not remain unfamiliar with the underbelly of the city without being seen as old-fashioned, boring, or nitwits. Ignorance of the secrets of the night was like a painful physical defect. (27–28)

Marta E. Savigliano adds that when the tango succeeded internationally (when it was exoticized, in other words), the Argentine elite was divided in its response.

There were those, the "liberals," who saw themselves positioned so close to the European elite that they claimed to share the joys of exoticism regardless of the nationality of the object. Tango was a part of the culture of their native land (the "popular" part) but their identity was not being threatened. . . . Actually, the members of this "open-minded" sector of the elite had been consuming the tango for a long time. They were frequent visitors to the brothels where women danced the tango in couples in order to create a stimulating environment for the clients. They were the ones who actively participated in the street *carnavales,* mocking the tangos performed by the black *comparsas*. They were the members of the gangs that invaded the bars of the poor and marginals, looking for some spice and violence. This part of the Argentinean elite was precisely the one that contributed to the promotion of the tango in Paris through frequent trips abroad. The opposing sector was made up of those who despised being thrown into the same bag together with blacks, pimps, prostitutes, dock workers, servants, and *orilleros*. They felt that the class boundaries so well known in their home territory were difficult to distinguish at a European distance and hence that their argentino identity was being threatened. . . . they were a colonized elite (an elite susceptible to being exoticized together with the tango). To accept the tango as representative of Argentinean national identity potentially affected both their class identity and their power as legitimate representatives of Argentina. (142)

The violent relations between the Moreira gangs and the tango in "From Cosmopolis to Locopolis" culminate *in reality, in the popular idol, and in the Palais de Glace* on 10 December 1915. On 10 December 1994, an article in the "Sociedad" section of the newspaper *Clarín* recalls that on that date in 1915, a gang member wounded Carlos Gardel with a gunshot as he left the Palais de Glace.

Many "well-to-do boys" frequented the Palais, *true gangs* who amused themselves by *picking fights in the dance halls,* under the protection of their surnames and their family fortunes. Their strength derived from their always large numbers, but above all in their *impunity*, since the Police rarely intervened to restrain them. An investigation later determined that the assailant was *Roberto Guevara*, an adolescent son of the Argentine aristocracy for whom Gardel was nothing more than a member of the rabble. The judge appointed to the case convinced Gardel not to press charges in order not to incur the enmity of a powerful family. (Italics in original)

But let us return to 1910 and to Güiraldes, as he takes the tango to Paris and introduces it not only into society but also into the literature of *ultraísmo* (another modernism or avant-garde) and thus connects "in Güiraldes" the tango, the Moreira gangs, and the second peaceful gaucho, Don Segundo (Moreira's other), who appears in 1926. So one cycle is linked to the next: "in Güiraldes."

Horacio Ferrer, *El libro del tango: Crónica & diccionario, 1850–1977* (Buenos Aires: Editorial Galerna, 1977), says that in 1910 Güiraldes takes the tango to Paris; he calls him Ricardo Güiraldes Guerrico and he describes him as a young Argentine gentleman, age twenty-four, educated in Paris and on La Porteña ranch in San Antonio de Areco, who happened upon the Buenos Aires nightlife: "living it up like so many other young men of his class, Ricardo loves and practices the nocturnal rites of the poor quarter."

Ferrer recounts that Güiraldes is in Paris in 1910 with three friends, and that they dive headfirst "into the nightlife: bistros, concerts, wild French women, cabarets, camambert, baguettes, opera, champagne, even wilder French women. Scientific bohemia" (71). And they dance the tango "El entrerriano." The following year, Ferrer says, Güiraldes writes the poem "El Tango," which appears in *El cencerro de cristal* (The crystal cowbell) in 1915.

Fernando O. Assunção, *El tango y sus circunstancias (1880–1920)* (Buenos Aires: El Ateneo, 1984), confirms this but goes farther with regard to the gangs of well-to-do boys:

These bad boys from good families constituted another important ingredient in the formation of tango, with aptitude from their elegant training in the stiff dances of the aristocratic salons. When they appeared in the dim mirror of the brothel and the suburb, at once dazzled and out of place, like fugitives or voluntary recruits in some sordid conscription of twenty year olds, they found embraces, punch-ups, drunkenness, dancing, love for sale, nausea and spleen, but they also became *active subjects of a new culture*. . . . For the loutish behavior of the gang members was another ingredient in the *world of tango* or its circumstances. . . . Ricardo Güiraldes became famous in the River Plate region for his literary efforts and particularly for *Don Segundo Sombra*, which is on par with or perhaps superior to *Martín Fierro* as a paradigmatic view of the landscape and the inhabitant of the pampa, but he can also be situated as the archetype of the young gentleman immersed in the underworld of the tango. (104)

Silvestre Byrón, "Ricardo Güiraldes y el tango," *La historia del tango. Tomo 3: La guardia vieja* (Buenos Aires: Corregidor, 1977), 503–10, recounts more of Güiraldes's adventures and says that he bases his version on an oral account by Victoria Ocampo. Victoria evokes the ranches of the late nineteenth century and also Ricardo, who was born in 1886 at the home of the Guerricos, his maternal grandparents, and then taken to Paris a year and a half later. When he returned to Paris in 1910 he was twenty-four years old. Victoria says that at that time the tango, "a low-class thing," was not danced in distinguished salons, and that Ricardo introduced it in Paris with the help of Vicente Madero. Ricardo was considered a *poseur* and a decadent, Victoria tells Byrón. The exalted, almost *ultraísta* tone adopted by Güiraldes is evident in the poem "Tango," written in Paris in 1911 and published in *El cencerro de cristal,* which Victoria describes as a failure.

To finish with Güiraldes: Borges speaks with Sábato about literary success and failure in relation to the value of the work. Borges says that he knew people "who took success very seriously. But I think that failure is no guarantee either. When Güiraldes published *El cencerro de cristal* it sold few copies. Disappointed, he threw the unsold books into a lake at his ranch. It was such an unattractive idea, a lake full of books" (*Diálogos Jorge Luis Borges-Ernesto Sábato,* ed. Orlando Barone [Buenos Aires: Emecé, 1976], 80–81).

Here ends the oral history. But anyone who wishes to pursue this particular process of the cycle which leads from Cosmopolis to Locopolis, from the violence of the gangs to *the cultural exportation of national and popular signs* and to their later importation, returning us to the beginning (as with Moreira, the tango, Güiraldes, and the peaceful gaucho) should see how Marta E. Savigliano clearly posits the problem of cultural exportation of symbols of identity in the case of Argentine tango and from the perspective of the relation between "colonies" or neocolonies and imperialism. She describes a "capitalist production and consumption of the Exotic" on the part of imperialism which isolates and categorizes the practices of the colonized: "'exotic' objects have been constituted by applying a homogenizing practice of exoticization, a system of exotic representation that commoditized the colonials in order to suit imperial consumption. . . . The colonizer constitutes his own 'progressive' identity—Civilized, Enlightened, Democratic, Postmodern— on the basis of this confrontation with exotic, colonized (neo- and post- as well) Others" (2).

The allocation of "exotic Passion" to the colonized Others thus provides "a locus of identity" for the colonizer, and Savigliano adds that when the Exotic is "exported to the (neo)colonies of 'origin,' practices of autoexoticism develop conflictively as a means of both adjusting to and confronting (neo)colonialism . . . the exotic/exoticized representations end up becoming symbols of national identity. Such is the case of the *tango argentino*" (2).

IV. The History of a Best-Seller: From Anarchism to Peronism

1. This "story" originated as a dated "author reading," which reads in literature the place of a writer subject with its literary initiations, betrayals, definitions, and weaknesses. This anachronistic critical style, which I would have liked to imitate, searches for fables of identity in literature: it reads "writer stories." My "author reading," however, had a precise intention: that of providing Roberto Arlt with a national past and some Argentine literary father, as a departure from the well-known Russian novelists and the serial novels translated in Spain which almost everyone assigns as his fate, and also as a departure from the pure present to which they assign him as a condition of his foundational and anticipatory function. "Arlt and his precursors" (as this "story" was originally called) implied the introduction of another type of textuality and another past in the chain of national literary history. But the author reading broke apart into "library stories" and "city stories," and "Arlt's precursor" Soiza Reilly gradually increased in importance to the point where he became our Virgil, leading us back to his own precursors. The result is a succession of "stories of submission of the first manuscript to the master" (or "stories of literary initiation in crime"), which tend to construct, backward, a virtual genealogy and to play with the continuity of Argentine culture between anarchism (and perhaps *rosismo*) and Peronism.

☙

Las ciencias ocultas en la ciudad de Buenos Aires, one of Arlt's first texts, appeared in *Tribuna Libre* on 28 January 1920. (I cite from Arlt's *Obra completa,* vol. 1 [Buenos Aires: Planeta-Carlos Lohlé, 1991], 527–53.) In it, Arlt refers to Juan José de Soiza Reilly's novel *La ciudad de los locos,* from 1914.

Las ciencias ocultas assembles a list of literary celebrities in order to recount an initiation into the mysteries of theosophy and occultism. It resembles (or it is) a turn-of-the-century *modernista* chronicle, with references to Darwin, Le Bon, Ingenieros, Darío, Lugones, Nervo, Wells, Oscar Wilde, Valle-Inclán, D'Annunzio, Ibsen, Tagore, Ángel de Estrada, Gómez Carrillo, and many other French, English, and North American poets. Arlt not only assembles celebrities, but also encyclopedias, dictionaries, bibles, and bibliographic exoticisms: the text originates in a library that the author discovered at age sixteen. *Las ciencias ocultas en la ciudad de Buenos Aires* uses the first person to recount an initiation into literature, sex, and politics. It is the first of Arlt's "library stories" and also the first of his "criminal initiations."

The chronicler presents himself at age sixteen as a victim of his love for Baudelaire's poetry. *Les fleurs du mal* had captured his imagination "to the point where I can say that he was *my spiritual father*" (531; italics added). So he dreamed of being a great poet, a literary *genius*, but this dream led him to a situation of extreme emergency, *to hunger* ("the poet as victim") and therefore to the struggle for life: he had to go to work in a used bookstore.

A "ruined marquis," a "strange" and "hyperaesthetic" character, arrived one day in this "dive" (as the narrator calls it) in search of a certain *History of Mathematics*. He was an attractive and seductive young man; when he returned to the bookstore, he discussed *occultism* and *theosophy* with the narrator, and he finally invited him to his home. There he introduced the young man to a library of magic, alchemy, occultism, and astrology (the marquis who initiates him is the Astrologer in embryonic form). This is the immense *exotic library* of the other face of science.

Let's look at the movements of this fable of identity in order to see exactly where Arlt locates its origin. The subject is situated at the exact point of *modernismo* and decadence, in the poetic climate of the turn of the century, with Darío and Lugones, for he recounts that he is initiated in a library of astrology and occult sciences belonging to a ruined marquis. He is initiated into the phantasmagoria of the *modernista* library, which promises him "marvelous powers" (534). But what he felt was a "gray solitude" populated by *hallucinations*: frightful pygmies, hunchbacked, whitish, and obscene apes making disgusting gestures, magnificent naked women "who terrorized me with the implacable flashes of their vicious cruelties," as well as Egyptians and Mongols (534–35). The initiation into drugs and sex appear to fuse with the initiation into the marquis's *modernista* library and into the sect: a world of "particular passions, *the wisdom of the opportunistic astrologers,* and the dubious honor of *certain equivocal women*" (537; italics added).

The chronicler of *Las ciencias ocultas* then recounts that he was the victim of two literary initiations inscribed as "hallucinations." The first was the hallucination of genius inspired by Baudelaire's poetry, which led him to hunger (to the struggle for life: to the Darwinist limit), and therefore to the hellish dive of the used bookstore. From there he went on to the marquis's library and to the sect, where he found the hallucinations (familiar from the *modernismo* of Lugones) of apes, vicious women, and exoticisms.

The problem of initiations (one of the problems of the bildungsroman as a literary genre) is that they require a return from transgression in their conclusions. The chronicler must leave the occult city of the turn of the century and of the sect, in order to say that *he comes from there* and to be able to conclude the movements of the hallucinations and also the account of his initiation. So Arlt recounts his literary initiation in the marquis's library and in the theosophical and *modernista* sect of the occult sciences, and then he denounces it as an almost "criminal" group of delirious madmen who live in sexual promiscuity and who are agents of an expired English imperialism. He places the hallucinations "in crime," "in madness," and "in politics" (he places limits on them) with the help of quotes from sexology, criminology, and politics: with Ingenieros's scientific, materialist, and socialist *library*, to which he refers twice. The first time is in a "scientific" footnote: the *hallucinations of the melancholic* lead *to crime,* according to doctors [*sic*] Kraff-Ebing, cited by Ingenieros. The second time he refers to Ingenieros, it is to refute the irrational affirmations of the feminine sect, which lead *to madness,* "as Mr. Ingenieros has said, referring to work of Madame Blavatsky."

I won't dwell on the dialectic of Arlt's notes in *Las ciencias ocultas* because I want to arrive at the final movement of this bildungsroman, culminating, in its return, *in repression.* After quoting Nordau, the chronicler says that *"some restraint or law"* must be imposed on these groups, which are breeding grounds for future "degeneration" (550; italics added). And then "the reformer poet" *applauds the police* in a note on "recent happenings" in 1920: "The attitude of the police, who not long ago shut down a Magic School situated on the corner of Calle Callao and Corrientes, is worthy of applause" (550 n. 37).

In order *to close the text,* Arlt returns to the sect and to its leaders:

> The presidents and directors of this institution [the Theosophical Society] present themselves as superior and infallible beings. They have lived many lives, they have been the leaders of humanity on this or some other planet, they know the secrets, they have gazed upon God's designs, and they have received their inspiration from Pleroma, like the Gnostics.
>
> What would become of humanity in such a state, in accordance with their desire? I can't help but *recall* Soiza Reilly's "The City of Madmen." (552–53, italics added)

At the very center of the occult city and of the marquis's library, *in the desire for power* of the "superior beings," a memory, a past, an image, *another city* springs to Arlt's mind in 1920: Soiza Reilly's Locopolis of 1914.

Arlt's *El juguete rabioso,* from 1926, is dedicated to Ricardo Güiraldes (who suggested the title). As is well known, *El juguete rabioso* (like the *Quixote*) relates or fuses bandit literature with life, and again it recounts, in the first person, an initiation in crime and in literature. Again it includes used bookstores, theosophists, and sixteen-year-olds; again it features a descent into hell, libraries, and engineers. And, like *Las ciencias ocultas,* it closes with a denunciation or betrayal: this time that of a lame friend nicknamed *el Rengo* in *the engineer's library.* (It was a lame Spanish anarchist shoemaker who initiated the narrator in "bandit literature"; it is a lame Creole thief who is betrayed in the final library scene. The treacherous translation of the Spaniard into the Argentine frames the text.)

In the fourth and last chapter of *El juguete rabioso,* the subject defines himself with the title of "Judas Iscariot" because he chooses the "verbal crime" in order to escape from a plan to rob the engineer, thus "originating" for the second time "in crime," from the other face of the city of Buenos Aires: this time, from Soiza Reilly's "dark Buenos Aires." For in the first chapter, "Los ladrones," shortly *before* the robbery of the school library, we read this: "Graphic photographs accompanying Soiza Reilly's article on the French apaches who had found refuge in Buenos Aires would prompt Enrique to announce, 'The president of the republic uses four apaches for bodyguards'" (*Mad Toy,* trans. Michele McKay Aynesworth [Durham: Duke University Press, 2002], 29).

In Arlt's *Las ciencias ocultas en la ciudad de Buenos Aires,* a modern journalistic chronicle, Soiza Reilly appears "in fictional mode" with his novel *La ciudad de los locos.* Six years later, in the fiction of "Los ladrones" in *El juguete rabioso,* Soiza appears with his column "Buenos Aires Tenebroso" (Dark Buenos Aires) and his modern chronicles of "Los apaches." (The first of a series of articles by Soiza on the Apaches appeared on 17 May 1912 in his column "Buenos Aires Tenebroso" in *Fray Mocho: Semanario Festivo, Literario, Artístico y de Actualidades* 1, no. 3.) In Arlt's *El juguete rabioso,* Soiza's Apaches are transformed into "the president's bodyguards."

Let's descend, for a moment, to *Fray Mocho,* to 1912, and to the Apaches of "Dark Buenos Aires." The chronicler Soiza Reilly recounts how a "chief police investigator" asked him whether he would like to see Apaches in Buenos Aires and invited him to take a stroll through "the barrio of shady characters." There he interviewed the Apache Antonio Mysula, the perpetrator of a robbery at an agency on Calle Reconquista 52, who initiated him *into his language.* The Apaches are pimps and they are called *maquereau*; each Apache has his woman, his accomplice, his "cover": his *gigolette*. He exploits her, he corrupts her, he hits her and then kisses her, Soiza says. He has an enemy, the *béguin*, who is also an Apache, and who the *gigolette* loves. The *miché* is the client (our "paganini," the chronicler says) who is generally robbed by the woman or the pimp. The Apaches are pimps and assassins because they not only live off their women's work, they also kill in order to steal: they murder with a horrible dagger in the shape of an awl. In earlier times they would flee to the colonies, to Algeria or Morocco, but since the *French comedians discovered the Argentine Republic in their "vaudevilles,"* Soiza Reilly says, the tribe of Apaches flees to Buenos Aires. They operate in the downtown zone of Corrientes-Lavalle-Suipacha-Cerrito, and they use Parisian slang, while the *gigolettes* speak Spanish.

In this interesting simultaneous cultural exchange between "low" Buenos Aires and "low" Paris (thanks to the "vaudevilles") the incredible appears, for Soiza Reilly says that, in Europe, the Apache is almost a hero: *what is incredible is the criminal as a hero in the media* of 1912. "The newspapers devote columns of attention to him. When the police find the corpse of a murdered victim, Paris does not hesitate. It exclaims: "It was the 'Apaches.'"

Even when they go to the guillotine, "a cloud of glory precedes them," reports the chronicler of the dark city in *Fray Mocho,* whose subtitle ("Seminario Festivo, Literario, Artístico y de Actualidades") is the same as that of *Caras y Caretas,* founded by the same Fray Mocho.

Soiza Reilly in Arlt: in the occultist sect's "city of madmen" and in the "Dark Buenos Aires" of the "Midnight Horsemen," the secret society of *El juguete rabioso.* Arlt's narrator of initiations found in Buenos Aires the hidden side of literature and of the *modernista* chronicle: he entered through it and he originated in it, in the writings of Soiza Reilly, an "unread" writer.

Arlt's first text, *Las ciencias ocultas en la ciudad de Buenos Aires,* from 1920, closed with the image of the Theosophical Society which recalled Soiza Reilly's *La ciudad de los locos,* from 1914. The fact that Arlt concludes the first day of his second novel, *Los siete locos,* in 1929, with Erdosain's simulation of madness in a tree, refers us again to *La ciudad de los locos* (chapter 10, "El discurso del árbol" [The speech from the tree]), in which Tartarín Moreira climbs a tree at the asylum and gives a speech which marks the turn from madness to genius, through the transformation (redefinition) of the word "mad." Tartarín Moreira removes "evil" from madness, he affirms it as a gift from God, and he defines it as a dynamic force, as *mania,* vocation, innovation, and contradiction. He defines it as "desire," as the impossible desire which landed them in the asylum, since it is not socially accepted: the desire of the teacher who questions all education from its root, for example. Tartarín

Moreira says that science calls this force a "mania" or a "desire" at odds with "the logic of humanity" and that the doctors try to kill it: the "ignorance of the wise men" keeps them locked up in the asylum. Tartartín Moreira is the liberator and the founder because he asks that each madman be allowed to exert his will, and he invites them to burn the asylum and flee to the seaside, where they will found "the New City, the glorious city of the mad, Locopolis, which will be more famous than Athens, Rome, Constantinople, Paris, because the soul of the city will be madness" (70–83).

•

2. *Nuevas aguafuertes porteñas* (Buenos Aires: Hachette, 1960), 221–23.

•

3. Omar Borré, *Arlt y la crítica (1926–1990)* (Buenos Aires: Ediciones América Libre, 1996), records a chronological list of all of Arlt's stories between 1916 and 1942, including one manuscript, and thanks to him we learn the original title of Arlt's first manuscript published by Soiza Reilly, as well as the exact date of his visit: "Jehová. Published in *Revista Popular,* December 1916. Director: Juan José de Soiza Reilly. The date appears on the cover of the first edition of *El juguete rabioso*. A fragment of this text was reproduced in 1968 in *Entre crotos y suicidas,* published by Edicom. The text seems like a fragment of a future novel" (196).

With regard to "artistic prose" or the "crime of the 'dictionary words'" in Arlt's first novel, Rubén Darío says in his prologue to Manuel Ugarte's *Crónicas de Bulevar* that Ugarte is a poet and a journalist (a "new subject"), that he is a person of means and a naturalized Parisian. And Darío adds: "Being young, he has managed to escape various dangers which have wrought havoc among us here in America, dangers such as exaggeration and 'artistic writing,' as it was called" (vi). The same can be said of Soiza: his travels in Europe in pursuit of famous men for importation freed him of this (South) "American" scourge, which surely beset Arlt's first "ultramodern" text.

•

4. Consider the following titles and publishers of some of Soiza Reilly's works from the 1920s:

Carne de muñecas (Doll flesh) (Buenos Aires: Tor, 1922).

No leas este libro . . . (El amor, la mujer y otros venenos) (Don't read this book . . . [Love, women, and other poisons]), 4th ed. (Buenos Aires: Librería Anaconda, 1933; 1st ed., 1926). This book includes a prologue by the Uruguayan writer and journalist Alberto Lasplaces, who says that the good times that he owes to Soiza Reilly date from *his early youth;* everyone awaited Soiza's article in *Caras y Caretas,* with its accompanying photographs and its "short, nervous, absurd, anarchist paragraphs."

"We were also anarchists and accepted no superiority other than that of talent. Soiza fueled our ambitions, he introduced us to famous men, and above all he inspired us to dream a lot."

La muerte blanca: Amor y cocaína (White death: Love and cocaine) (Buenos Aires: Biblioteca Literaria Argentina Floreal, 1926). Dedicated to Rudolph Valentino!

¡Criminales! (Almas sucias de mujeres y hombres limpios) (Criminals! [The dirty souls of clean women and men]) (Buenos Aires: Casa Editorial Sopena, 1926). In the prologue Soiza writes: "There are other criminals even more savage than knife- and revolver-wielding convicts. There are others more fearsome. Terrible. Horrible. . . . They are delinquents which no one yet dares judge. The multitude has no awareness of the just justice that God places in the teeth, the feet, and the hands of the people. . . . For this reason, those criminals live in the most heavenly impunity. Criminals!" (7; ellipses in original).

And (to continue on the road from anarchism to Peronism) let's read what Clarín had to say about the 1930s on 19 May 1998.

On 19 May 1880, Juan José de Soiza Reilly was born in Concordia, Entre Ríos. He became an extremely popular journalist and hosted one of the most famous of early radio programs.

In the 1930s, his hoarse voice, speaking at an inimitable speed and almost without slip-ups, was heard on every radio in Buenos Aires. By then, he was already widely known as a magazine and newspaper journalist. After studying at the teachers' college and working as a history professor, he began to contribute to the famous magazine Caras y Caretas, while sharing café tables with porteño intellectuals and bohemians. His real aspiration was to be a writer, but his books were not successful. Instead, he developed a special skill for interviews, which he put into practice beginning in 1907, when he was sent to Europe as a correspondent and took up residence in Paris. He managed to interview the most important personalities of his age and to extract extraordinary personal confessions from them. His interviews of writers such as D'Annunzio, Maeterlinck, Anatole France, Edmundo D'Amicis, and Juana de Ibarbourou, actresses such as Lola Membrives, or Alphonse XIII, the king of Spain, among many other names on an interminable list, were eagerly awaited by readers. During the war of 1914 he was a correspondent for the newspaper La Nación, and later for La Prensa. When radiotelephony began to take its first steps, he began at Radio Stentor and later moved to Belgrano. There he created a program in which he provided direct help to people, receiving letters in which they told him of their health and work problems and responding by sending the anxiously awaited medicine or sewing machine. This program, the forerunner of many others on Argentine television, ended with a slogan which was very popular: "Arriba los corazones." He worked in radio until shortly before his death in 1959. (Italics added)

(The *Clarín* article states that Soiza Reilly's books were not successful, ignoring "the history of the best-seller," but even so it leads us, by way of the radio, to Eva Perón.)

•

5. In his chronology of Arlt's life and work in the study already cited, Omar Borré refers to this first short novel published in Córdoba: "That same year [1921] *Diario de un morfinómano* appeared with a prologue by Soiza Reilly. This very brief novel has not been located. José Marial states that *El juguete rabioso* was not Arlt's book since he had already published 'the Cordoba novel,' *Diario de un morfinómano,* in 1920" (120).

Borré quotes from César Tiempo's *Manos de Obra* (1980):

Once many years ago when I was in Cordoba in the company of Luis Reinaudi, I found a copy in a secondhand bookstore on Calle Rivadavia. I didn't give it a second thought. On the same table, I saw something else equally unobtainable which interested me more: the Segundo Libro de Loco Amor by the fabulous Bernabé de la Orga, and I chose it over the booklet which contained Arlt's novella. Shortly thereafter, in Buenos Aires, I happened to mention it to Arlt.

"You don't know how happy you've made me. You missed your big chance to spend your whole life blackmailing me with the threat of republishing it." (Italics added)

Again, an initiation "in crime" with a prologue by Soiza Reilly.

In the case of *El juguete rabioso,* it was Elías Castelnuovo who took it upon himself to recount Arlt's odd behavior, his spiritualism, his cremation, and his tribulations in publishing his first novel, *La vida puerca* (The filthy life) (the title suggested to Castelnuovo), later called *El juguete rabioso* (Güiraldes's suggestion, according to Castelnuovo). In the twelfth part of his *Memorias,* titled "El aprendiz del brujo" (The sorcerer's apprentice), Castelnuovo recounts one of Arlt's initiations and in doing so reinforces, from the position of the Boedo literary group, the theory that Arlt wrote very badly and that he imitated *in his excesses* the abominable but best-selling Colombian author, Vargas Vila.

Castelnuovo recounts that Arlt used to visit the garret where he lived, which was the meeting place for the Boedo group of writers. He provides no dates, but says that Arlt "had just been cured of tuberculosis in the mountains of Cordoba and was still recovering from his ailment." Castelnuovo continues:

Knowing that I was the director of the *Los Nuevos* collection, in which the leading lights of the Boedo group, from Álvaro Yunque to Enrique Amorim, were to make their debut, he brought me a work titled *De la vida puerca* in hopes *that I would publish it.* It was a very uneven and scabrous novel which, following a suggestion by Ricardo Güiraldes, was finally called *El juguete rabioso.* Arlt had staked his future literary career on this first attempt, so when I rejected the manuscript, he saw all his hopes go up in smoke and was left so dejected that I had to give him all sorts of explanations. Without mentioning *the mistakes in spelling and composition,* I pointed out no less than twelve words of high etymological voltage, *incorrectly placed,* and for which he could give no explanation. There were, moreover, in their context, two antagonistic styles. It displayed, on the one hand, the influence of Maxim Gorky, and on the other, the presence of Vargas Vila. I also pointed out this contrast to him. *He then confessed, with some embarrassment,* that in Cordoba he had in fact published *a brief novel with a prologue by Soiza Reilly and written in the style of Vargas Vila,* using the semicolon instead of the period, and adding a few pompous terms of his own to the master's logorrhea. Finally, I told him that *De la vida puerca* was unpublishable in its current state. (133–34)

This proliferating "History of a Best-Seller: From Anarchism to Peronism" cannot fail to touch upon the best-selling Colombian writer José María Vargas Vila (1860–1933), who appears as a "delinquent influence" in the "lost booklet" of *Diario de un morfinómano.* He appears as another missing link also leading us from anarchism to Peronism.

In his prologue to José María Vargas Vila's *Diario secreto,* ed. Consuelo Triviño (Bogotá: Arango Editores and El Ancora Editores, 1989), 9–12, Rafael Conte says that we never know why something is read or why it ceases to be read; Vargas Vila "was a best-seller seventy-five years ago; his sixty-eight volumes were published in Colombia, Spain, and Paris: twenty-two novels, three volumes of stories, eleven of literary essays, seven books of philosophy, seven of historical essays, six volumes on political themes, one of lectures, and one tragedy. His most famous and popular publisher was Casa Ramón Sopena in Barcelona" (9). Everything about Vargas Vila seems excessive, Conte says, including his success, the silence to which he was subsequently relegated, and the author himself. In his lifetime "he was resisted almost to death," and critics of Latin American literature rejected him. But since the publication of Luis Alberto Sánchez's book, *Proceso y contenido de la novela hispanoamericana,* he has been more objectively evaluated, Conte says. All that remains, Conte suggests, is for someone to reprint at least Vargas Vila's most significant works, which he suggests might include the novels *Aura o las violetas; Flor de fango;* and *Ibis,* his book on Rubén Darío; two history books (*La muerte del cóndor* and *Los Césares de la decadencia*); and the odd political text such as *Laureles rojos, Clepsidra roja,* or *Ante los bárbaros* (10).

Conte goes on to say that at the moment when Vargas Vila could have been reread, the Latin American boom of the 1960s arrived and changed literary sensibilities and ways of writing. And he adds (for our purposes) that the Boom served to rescue Arlt, whose prose, "now so indisputable," was no "wiser or more correct" than Vargas Vila's. "The bad thing, however, was that Arlt abused his prose to the point of achieving a clear expressive intensity, while Vargas Vila caressed it too much, succumbing at times to fits of sentimentalism" (11). His models were Darío and D'Annunzio, and "he carried them beyond themselves, almost doing away with them entirely" (11). Rafael Conte continues: "In Vargas Vila's overflowing prose, which strives for luxury, there are tons of linked adjectives, verses spilled without the slightest discretion, enjambment of paragraph after paragraph of rhetorical, baroque, descriptive prose in which the pleasure of the word swells to the point of exasperation; words become balloons which either rise into the stratosphere and disappear from view or explode and deflate. What he lacked in measure he made up for in passion: the lack is irremediable, but passion was good, don't forget" (11). Conte says that Vargas Vila "vacillated between almost all currents. At first he was a Frenchified writer . . . in the style of Enrique Larreta, another forgotten writer . . . who was his ideological opposite" (12). Vargas Vila wrote sentimental novels and also political ones, and he was "kitsch."

In her introduction to the same edition of Vargas Vila's *Diario secreto* (13–37), Consuelo Triviño says that "No writer was ever so harshly punished by his compatriots as this radical who earned a distinguished place in our literature by railing against the clergy, by insulting Spanish American tyrants, by vociferating against Yankee imperialism" (13). The fact that he was censored in his country and disdained by Colombian intellectuals only increased his popularity, she says. Vargas Vila enjoyed a good deal of prestige in Spain, and *old anarchists* have testified to the inspiration his pamphlets provided; in Spanish America, he was more widely known among popular sectors: "without even having read him, *students, peasants and workers recited his terrible attacks* on President Rafael Núñez and the conservatives" (14).

Triviño points out that the growth of *the publishing industry* in this period played an important role in the history of the readings of Vargas Vila, for it

enabled broad and traditionally illiterate sectors of society to become familiar with books. The serial novel—as this literature was called—occupied the leisure time of the popular classes and made true myths of certain writers, in the image of Victor Hugo and D'Annunzio. In Cuba, for example, Vargas Vila was the favorite writer of the cigarette girls. *Ante los bárbaros* was the creed on which various generations of anti-imperialists were raised in many Latin American countries.

Romantic novels such as *Aura o las violetas* attained a mass readership and elicited floods of tears from the girls of the time. The speech *Ante la tumba de Diógenes Arrieta* spoke movingly to those radical liberals who, whether living in exile or marginalized in their countries, felt the weight of conservative oppression. (14–15)

And indoctrination by Vargas Vila was not only political but also erotic, explains Triviño. "At the beginning of the twentieth century, many Colombians were sexually initiated by the unbridled eroticism of *Ibis* or *El alma de los lirios,* books which present a deplorable image of women. In their pages, Latin American machismo ran riot, and whether consciously or unconsciously, Vargas Vila used machismo as a hook for catching his readers" (15).

Triviño notes that in his political writings Vargas Vila "showed himself to be a radical and even, apparently, an anarchist. His pamphlets produced an immediate effect in the diffusion of these ideas, a mixture of Nietzsche, Shopenhauer and Emerson. . . . *Journalism played a fundamental role in the transmission of these ideas*" and "*contributed to the growth of his fame*" (21; italics added). Meanwhile, the author "lived shut up in 'complete solitude,' among visions of art and dreams of grandeur. . . . He admired Darío" and "celebrated his genius, but lamented his deplorable conduct," depicting him as an alcoholic (22). Triviño says that Vargas Vila "spent his dark life in *turn-of-the-century Barcelona, a city shaken by general strikes and anarchist bombs*" (22; italics added). His only friend was Ramón Palacio Viso, "an unknown Venezuelan poet who accompanied him in his travels through many countries from the time he was young, and who lived with him for nearly thirty-five years." Vargas Vila called him his adopted son and "attempted to leave him his only fortune: his books, and his diary" (22).

Triviño concludes her reading of Vargas Vila's success, which depended on the publishing industry, journalism, and politics: "Until five years ago, it was thought that Vargas Vila's diary was in the custody of *the Mexican government.* However, in a 1985 interview, Fidel Castro revealed that *the Cuban government* was carefully keeping not only the diary, but also several novels and documents which, according to the Comandante, would be duly catalogued and handed over to experts for study" (23–24).

Malcom Deas includes an essay on Vargas Vila, which he says is his third and last, in *Del poder y la gramática: Y otros ensayos sobre historia, política y literatura colombianas* (Bogotá: Tercer Mundo Editores, 1993), 285–301. He says that his second essay on Vargas Vila appeared in Sergio Bagú's compilation *De historia y de historiadores: Homenaje a José Luis Romero* in 1983. Romero had attended a lecture by Deas on Vargas Vila in Buenos Aires in 1975 and had shown enthusiasm for the

great bad writers of many literatures. His vote for Argentina's equivalent to Vargas
Vila went to Hugo Wast. When Vargas Vila passed through Buenos Aires in 1923,
Wast said that the visitor's books were the kind of thing his cook read. Vargas Vila
responded by saying that in second-rate cities like Buenos Aires, cooks were naturally more intelligent than critics.

Deas says that Vargas Vila's novels were never good, and that today they're un-
readable; the same goes for some of his political prose, which is empty, menda-
cious, and tiresome in style. "It seems to me," he says, "that what is salvable, what
is readable, are the three pamphlets of *Pretéritas*, which, without providing a reliable account of the war of 1885, retain a certain *naïf* appeal . . . certain pages of *Los
Césares de la Decadencia*, which reveal a talent for insults . . . the *Discurso ante la
tumba de Diógenes Arrieta*, for declamatory purposes; . . . a good deal of his *Rubén
Darío* . . . ; some pages of *Laureles rojos* and less of *Ante los bárbaros*. This much is
readable, I'm not saying it's admirable" (295).

*And now Deas with what interests us most in this "story of the best-seller from anar-
chism to Peronism":*

> Vargas Vila was very widely read in Mexico and Argentina, and a *notable case is
> that of Juan Domingo Perón*. While I was exploring this suspicion, I found that the
> phrase "force is the right of beasts"—the title given by Perón to one of his most
> widely known texts, and which seemed to me very much in the style of the "di-
> vine" Colombian—is a quote from Cicero used by Vargas Vila in *Laureles rojos*
> (Paris, 1906. The prize for tracking this down goes to Rafael Maya). I don't believe
> that either Perón or his ghost writers were reading Cicero. In Chile, a great deal
> of Vargas Vila persists in Neruda's most political work, and also, I would say, in
> his literary work. Neruda recounts his reading of Vargas Vila in his book of
> memoirs, *Confieso que he vivido*. (297; italics added)

Finally, Deas refers to "the story that Fidel Castro has the diary," and he says
that Fidel isn't the only Cuban who read it, because "Carlos Franqui's book, *Retrato
de Fidel en familia* is wholly written, from the first page to the last, in the unmistakable style of the master" (299).

So far, Malcom Deas. But I don't want to deprive the readers of the manual of
a sample of this "unmistakable style" of the master Vargas Vila (who also leads us
with his best-sellers to Perón): this one is found in *Odisea romántica: Diario de viaje
a la República Argentina* (Romantic odyssey: Diary of travel to the Argentine Republic) (Madrid: Biblioteca Nueva, n.d.). The preface is dated in Paris, in May 1927,
but the trip occurred in December 1923 and January 1924.

On board the ship, he speaks of the Argentines:

they dress as sportsmen in the morning and play tennis on deck; here, of course, as everywhere else, the Napoli-Argentines take First Prize in ridiculous affectation; when it comes to international displays of Puerile and almost Illiterate Snobbery, no one can compete with them;

they are the Legions of *Rastacuerismo;*

the word was invented for them in Paris, many years ago, when the first invasions of Millionaire Cattlemen appeared on the Boulevards, on *Via Chiaggia, Rectifilo* or *Partenope,* speaking their Neapolitan *patois,* their hoarse shouting and contorted gestures which make the multitudes so picturesque;

but these Argentinized Italians lose all the beauty of their native qualities when they adopt a hybridity of gestures and tastes which are not theirs:

above all in Clothing, when they copy the fashions of London and Paris to the maximum, managing only a caricature of those fashions or of themselves. (39)

Later he vents his hatred of Lugones and *La Nación:*

in this plagiaristic and miserable age, in this diminished and contemptible age in which Poets are no more than the stable boys of Success, jockeys in the pay of Publicity agencies, acrobatic clowns in the Circus of Venality, like Leopoldo Lugones, the jingling Clown of *La Nación,* that Nubian Slave, drunk on the Urine from the stables of the Press, Filibuster of Reaction, in the pay of all despotisms, auctioneer of his Passions, since he has no Ideas to sell, this Ass for hire, who leads the Lyric Muletrain of Versifiers of the Pampas through that Oasisless Desert which is current Argentine Literature, whose Libyan aridity is escaped only by those strange, aggrieved condors who dwell in the heights of the Cordillera and contemplate the cowardly Aridity of the plain, where parasitic ferns dream of attaining the size of oaks, and where skittish goats graze in the brambles, acting as if they were panthers roaring in the reeds of Java, those Condors of whom I speak feel a shudder of Shame in their wings when they contemplate the Mental Pauperism of the Herd which grazes on the silent sand, enjoying its Solitude. (107–8)

The condors are Ricardo Rojas, "the Foremost Writer of Lyric Prose, not only in Argentina, but also in all of our America" (108).

José Ingenieros, "the Great Popularizer who never vulgarizes, the Torch Man to whom Our Continent owes the most of the ideological Light which it currently possesses" (108);

And also Antonio Herrero, Alfredo Palacios ("the Argentine Bayard, the Orpheus Hypnotizer of Multitudes"), Adolfo Espinosa and Martín Fonts.

Vargas Vila says of his visit to Buenos Aires that he does not go

like so many other writers, who go begging for Celebrity or money, in search of a pittance of Consecration, an obol of Alms . . .

at the height of Literary and Political Celebrity at which I have arrived, I consecrate, no one consecrates me;

Buenos Aires can offer me Hospitality, but not Glory; I bring Glory to it. (127)

And parading in all his Glory, he writes:

a Great City of the second order, with aspirations and on its way to becoming
a Great City of the first order;

with appreciable and moving effort, its citizens strive to achieve their dream,
and they deserve to achieve it, such is their scattered and busy determination;

paraître is the motto of this City, and of this People;

ostentation, puffery, show;

Cardboard Babylon, determined to make us think that the *Papier Maché* with
which it builds its palaces is real marble, extracted from the mountains of Carrara
[137–38];

the Absolute Lack of Originality is the characteristic that defines Buenos Aires
in everything from its Writers, to its Sculptors, to its Painters, to its Architects,
and to its Revolutionaries, even its Bootblacks . . .

nothing original, nothing new, nothing of its own;

everything imported, everything transported, everything imitated . . .

imitation is the Muse of that City, which all Creative Spirit is lacking, but where
Simian Souls abound, aping European gestures;

it is the Country of Plagiary;

and it is undoubtedly, for this reason, the Country of Lugones;

here the Copy is the Reigning Norm;

and for this reason, that City without Genius, Home of migrant Artists, incapable of creating anything, copies everything, and from its Letters to its Arts, it is
nothing more than a vast *Museum of Reproductions*. (139–40; ellipses in original)

And in conclusion, as he leaves:

and Argentina has not produced the Great Poet, the Master of Inspiration and
Rhyme who inscribes Models and creates Norms for the Poets of America or of
Spain . . .

nothing . . .

nothing . . .

nothing . . .

sterility . . .

fragility . . .

fatuousness . . .

these are the distinguishing characteristics of:

Cosmopolis,

Bluffopolis,
Snobopolis. (259–60)

(I should clarify that we are not including Bluffopolis and Snobopolis in our travels in this Argentine manual.)

In *Escritores Iberoamericanos de 1900,* Manuel Ugarte devotes chapter 15 (231–42) to Vargas Vila, and he speaks of his vanity: "The inventor of prose without capital letters, of the book in a single ingot, made to be devoured—false hope—in one gulp and without pausing for breath, spoke exclusively of himself, and in the third person. Having lost all perspective, he succumbed blindly to egomania." But this egoistic exaltation, Ugarte says, was the product of a reaction against the hostility of his environment. "Few men were as vilified as Vargas Vila." And his novels, written in a special style, without capital letters and with only the final period ("conceived with the certainty that it was possible to inhale four hundred pages in one breath") "achieved *an astounding popularity between 1900 and 1914, and served as a romantic primer for a whole generation of youth.*" Ugarte continues:

> The opinion of Vargas Vila's literary merit which has become widespread in recent years is so categorically hostile that we ought to reconsider it. Not to accept it, but rather to react against it. Such sudden unanimity in the Americas always arouses suspicion. Leaving passions aside, we understand that Vargas Vila's work, far from being inferior, as some would have it, stands as one of the most complete achievements of its time. Despite the arabesques of bad taste and the odd uncomfortable reminiscence, it contains solid and durable elements. Rejection stems from prejudice or from superficial consideration.

Ugarte speaks of Vargas Vila's vanity and even excuses it: why should the writer and the artist not become conceited, if everyone else becomes conceited about cars and clothing? He recounts an anecdote about Blasco Ibáñez, the best-selling Spanish novelist who published *El alma de los perros*: "'There's only one other automobile like mine,' he used to say, 'and it belongs to the king of England.'" Or: "I've got money coming out my ears." To which Alejandro Sux, then very poor, responded by running up to Blasco, half serious and half joking, yelling: "Let me see!"

Alejandro Sux was the author of *Bohemia revolucionaria,* which was first published in 1909 with a biographical sketch written by Juan José de Soiza Reilly (Barcelona: Maucci, n.d.). *Bohemia revolucionaria* is an autobiographical novel recounting the life of a group of young anarchists and bohemian writers who meet at the Café de los Inmortales. The main character is Arnaldo Danel, who returns to Buenos Aires from exile in Montevideo. They write for *La Protesta* and work on a manifesto against the Law of Residence, they get arrested after a May Day demonstration and spend time in jail before being released, and finally Arnaldo, who has published a book of poems and also articles in *La Protesta,* finds love with another anarchist, the "little Russian" Lelia Merchenky.

Vargas Vila, Alejandro Sux, Manuel Ugarte, Soiza Reilly: all *modernistas,* anarchists, anti-imperialists, and "Peronists," forming a literary genealogy "in crime."

•

6. In 1920 *El alma de los perros* is a famous best-seller, and so it appears in "Apuntes autobiográficos del autor" by Alejandro Andrade Coello, dated 1920 in Quito, Ecuador, and included in *La escuela de los pillos,* Soiza Reilly's novel of the same year. Andrade Coello says: "The most successful book was *El alma de los perros,* which was translated into English, Italian, and Czech. Do you remember that little volume that came from Casa Sempere in Valencia, with the author's portrait in a tiny oval? What you couldn't help but notice was the signature of the prologuist: Manuel Ugarte. *The fourth edition* of El alma de los perros was published in Buenos Aires by the renowned magazine *Nosotros,* in an edition of *ten thousand copies, which sold out.* It was augmented with a brief evaluation by Professor Rodó" (12–14).

In *La juventud intelectual de la América hispana* (Barcelona: Biblioteca Científico-Literaria, n.d.; prologue by Rubén Darío, dedication to Juan de la Presa dated 1911 in Paris), Alejandro Sux said that *"El alma de los perros,* which has given rise to so much discussion among critics in the Americas and also in Europe, is 'strange book' in form, spirit, and motive." And he quotes some of Ugarte's prologue and adds:

> I believe, along with him [Ugarte], that those who greeted Soiza Reilly with rocks in hand have yet to see the end of him . . . I believe that this writer is the creator of *a new form,* about which one may say this or that, but which must be recognized; it is a still imprecise form, one which is in the process of being corrected, of acquiring more plasticity and elegance and losing a good deal of its primitive severity in certain stories in *El alma de los perros,* and for this reason I trust that Soiza Reilly will soon have created a modern, logical and beautiful way of writing. (123)

Writers of the *corpus delicti* in a specific network: they all wrote novels of crime and criminals in new forms between 1920 and 1930: Ugarte's *El crimen de las máscaras,* Sux's *El asesino sentimental,* Soiza's *¡Criminales!* and Arlt's *Los lanzallamas.*

•

7. A word about the "anarchism" of Ugarte and Soiza Reilly. In the prologue to Manuel Ugarte's *Crónicas del Bulevar,* Rubén Darío says that in Paris:

> We have attended socialist and anarchist meetings together. I left with my libertarian daydreams somewhat diminished. . . . I have not been able to endure the outbursts of rudeness, stubborn stupidity, and ugliness in a place of ideas, of

transcendental initiatives. . . . I have not been able to endure the howling of a scruffy madman when a talented artist came out to recite, simply because the artist had been decorated with the Legion of Honor; or the grotesque cry of incomprehension interrupting a serious and noble speech; or the furious cripple named Libertad vociferating against the poet Tailhade, and threatening with his crutch in the middle of a celebration in Tailhade's honor . . . , or a mournful Sévérine, disposed to make peace yet beset by four enraged, gesticulating "anarcos." . . . No, I have not been able to endure it. . . . And, yet, Ugarte, convinced, apostolic, has never failed to excuse these excesses, and he's even taken the side of the unreasoning mob, speaking to me of the coming regeneration, of the universal light of the future, of peace and work for all, of absolute equality, of so many dreams . . . Dreams. (v; ellipses in original)

In Escritores iberoamericanos del 1900, Ugarte says:

Around 1900, the world seemed like a scaffolding promising new construction or demolition projects whose confusing, sometimes esoteric, plans could not but make an impression on youth. The intellectuals of Europe reached out to workers, they translated their anxieties, they supported their claims. False apostles, of course, were not lacking. Neither were lyric apostles. Anatole France presided solemnly over the devastating lectures of Jean Jaurès. The most prominent novelists—Tolstoy, Gorky, Zola, Mirbeau—launched their literary grenades in all directions. Pacifist societies multiplied, as did leagues of defenders of the rights of man. A rebellious fervor, more negative than affirmative, stirred up ideas to the point where our friend Laurent Tailhade—of whom Rubén spoke in his chronicles —came to refer to the deadly bomb of the irresponsible anarchist as a "beau geste." (258–59)

Soiza Reilly's Crónicas de Amor, de Belleza y de Sangre (Buenos Aires: Maucci, 1911), contains a chronicle titled "Los anarquistas," in which he reproduces his response to a survey by La Vanguardia about the Law of Social Defense. The chronicle is dated in Montevideo, 1 May 1911. Soiza says that he speaks as a poet and that he is of aristocratic blood, that his parents were "rich noblemen," but that in his painful and bitter life he has suffered with the masses and that rebellions are born of injustice. Instead of passing laws that aggravate these people's pain, the government should pass laws to pardon them and to help them. The anarchists suffer and their pain comes from the wealth enjoyed by others; everywhere they are expelled without being given the opportunity to become useful beings. Instead of imposing this law of defense, a product of fear, the Argentine Congress should found schools. In Switzerland, there are no anarchists because there are schools, and the jails are empty. But in Argentina, the ideal of legislators is to decrease the number of schools and increase the number of jails. "In sum: the opinion of this sincere poet can be synthesized in a few lines. The Law of Social Defense is one of those laws that, according to Plutarch, appear made by blind men to regulate the use of light. Some of its provisions could be applied to those who passed it . . . (On the island of Barataria, Sancho Panza was the victim of his own laws. The same would happen among us)" (52; ellipses in original).

·

8. It is worth looking at certain aspects of *El alma de los perros:* its literary implementation of political anarchism, the individualism-egoism of the *modernista*-anarchist aesthetic, excess, hatred, blasphemy, destruction, and the hungry and miserable multitudes of "dogs" *who demand justice with their teeth.*

In *El alma de los perros,* there are modern-popular texts about photography of the multitude and the "I" of Italian avant-garde literature; about "Crime Reporting and the Modern Novel"; about "Those without a Country": gypsies and vagabonds; about artists' models in Rome, "Human Dogs"; and about "The Dog Pound," which is the modern jail. There is also a text about old and forbidden books in which a book narrates its own career, telling how it passes from hand to hand, changing according to who reads it and eventually coming into the possession of the old poet of the suburbs, who sells it for ten cents to the narrator-chronicler because he is hungry.

El alma de los perros is a Kafkian serial work composed of fragments and allegorical stories in the form of chronicles (it makes a novel and an allegory out of journalism: it is "modern and popular"), and it contains various layers of reality. It is made up of parables about animals such as dogs and oxen; the words of women, criminals, madmen, aristocrats, vagabonds, bootblacks, philosophers, and criminal artists who aspire to paint "the soul of a generation"; it uses popular cultural artifacts such as Christ and Job ("the great symbols" of the first best-seller) in order to turn them around and mix them with Verlaine (a "famous writer") and with the marginal and failed writers of so-called "bohemia."

Soiza Reilly's "new aesthetic" is evident in his dedication, "A los perros," a literary manifesto whose cries and blows are directed at the multitude and public taste, and at grammatical rules and the academy. He says that he dedicates this book "of forbidden prayers" (like the anarchist Carriego's *Misas herejes*) to "the dogs": "Hatred is the only virtue that has inspired this book. . . . Fortunately, the crowd will excommunicate it as useless and dismiss it with a guillotine-like gesture. Fortunately!" (17; ellipses in original). He also says that "this book [is] infected with blasphemies" (18) and forbidden by the eminent monsignors of the alphabet and grammatical laws, common sense and decency. "I hate humanity with the enormous, terrible, formidable, frightful, sweet, melancholic disdain that it deserves . . . I hate just because," which is "the only reason of the wise and the mad" (18). He continues: "I was not born to write books that delight the multitude. Nor books that make the mangers overflow with alfalfa. Nor books that make tears spill from the eyes and laughter from the mouth" (18).

In their teeth, his dogs hold "the justice with which men should be judged," and these are dogs *which do not attend academies,* consumptive dogs who are brothers to Saint Vincent de Paul, Paul Verlaine, Carlos de Soussens. They are my brothers, Soiza Reilly says religiously: "to you I consecrate this book" (19).

Soiza is an ironic and satirical writer who situates himself clearly in the "canine" tradition, that of the *kyon* (the Greek word for dog) and of the kynic philosophers. (Peter Sloterdijk introduces this spelling in *Critique of Cynical Reason,* trans. Michael Eldred [Minneapolis: University of Minnesota Press, 1987], 101–9, in order to differentiate them from the cynics.) In ancient Greece, the kynic philosophers were the inventors of an *antitheoretical theory.* Sloterdijk recalls parallels drawn by Willy Hochkeppel "between ancient kynicism and the modern hippie and alternative movement" (106), and he says that Diogenes, the original, post-bohemian hippie, pays no attention to proverbs and that his weapon is laughter and satire. *Antitheoretical, antidogmatic, antiacademic: the line runs through Montaigne and Voltaire and leads to Nietzsche* (155). The theory of the kynics is a "low theory" and an uninhibited dialectic, Sloterdijk says, a sort of "embodied theory": a ferocious attack on idealism and a response to the question of how to speak truth. It is the plebeian antithesis of the "great theory" of the truth of seminars, names, and quotes. It challenges the language of the philosophers or "thinkers" with the language of the clown, the materialism of the pantomime, and it discovers another mode of argument that respectable thought has still not learned to manage. "The appearance of Diogenes marks the most dramatic moment in the process of truth of early European philosophy," says Sloterdijk, since he introduces "a subversive variant of *low theory* that pantomimically and grotesquely carries practical embodiment to the extreme. The process of truth splits into a discursive phalanx of grand theory and a satirical-literary troupe of skirmishers" (102).

"Low theory," in Sloterdijk's account, "here for the first time seals a pact with poverty and satire," and *this discourse of truth and poverty* in the tradition of the kynic philosophers *has a specific relation to the state.* The kynic "has to challenge the public sphere because it is the only space in which the overcoming of idealist arrogance can be meaningfully demonstrated" (105); he confronts the state directly, corporally, and uses *his body* (dirtiness, animality) *as a form of argument:* Diogenes urinates in the academy and masturbates in the plaza. And his rebellion is not that of a slave against his master, but rather *that of one power against another:* oppositional power against hegemonic power. Sloterdijk says that society always tells the kynics not to "go too far," *just as the modernistas Ugarte and Rodó tell Soiza in their prologues.* This advice could be a "conscious politics" or "spontaneous regulation of the relation between art and society," Sloterdijk says (109).

After the dedication-manifesto "A los perros," the first text in *El alma de los perros* is titled "Jesucristo: El alma de los perros" (Jesus Christ: The soul of the dogs), and it opens with the lines, "Listen, said the Sheherazade of modern stories. And she began her tale" (which is what Arlt recites to Soiza Reilly from memory). From here on a female voice narrates (we won't dwell here on this new voice: the book also includes various texts about women and "their two souls"). It is the story of a wretched dog, very skinny, sad, dirty, mangy, and miserable, "a Christ named Judas," who will become the furious leader of *the miserable multitude.* The miserable dogs, "Sheherazade" narrates, unite behind the most miserable of them all, who is Judas. This "dog" game of "Jesus as Judas" and as the leader of the wretched of the earth in their endless pursuit of paradise reminds us of the last chapter of *El juguete rabioso,* "Judas Iscariot." This Judas sings "canine songs inspired by the bile of his spirit and the furor of his philosophy," and the dogs grow ever more numerous and traverse endless spaces, eternally territorializing and deterritorializing. Finally a human child kills the old dog Judas with a branch; the mob stops and cries over the death of its hopes, and it hates Jesus for having been as much a dog as the others, and so they divide him up into pieces, which they all eat. The dogs then disperse, never again to unite, "condemned to wander the world with sad eyes, tails between their legs, mange in their fur, hatred in their souls, and a piece of Christ in their stomachs."

Let's turn from Christ as the Judas of the miserable "dogs" to Christ as an anarchist in "La belleza dolorosa de los sueños" (The painful beauty of dreams), where we reencounter the dog poets of the dedication and the aesthetic of destruction ("Destruction was my Beatrice," wrote Osvaldo Lamborghini). In the story three men walk sadly, unable to vanquish their sadness with "daydreams of forbidden things." Carlos de Soussens point out the fountain of Lola Mora and stops there to read a musical sonnet.

(A parenthesis. In *Mujeres de América* [Buenos Aires: Anaconda, 1934], Soiza writes a text about Lola Mora: "Her contemporaries have buried her alive. She was savagely slandered. All manner of zoological weapons were used to wreck the prestige of this incomparable woman, superior to her century. Since they can't deny the exquisite beauty of the Fountain which now stands at the Spa, the slanderous voices cry: It can't be hers!" (56). "But Soiza says that she rose above her detractors and "endured her misfortune proudly. Valiant woman of Tucuman! She could not deny her aboriginal blood. Heroic Indian woman, like those who never knelt before the conquistadors, not even at the crazed moment of death!" (57). "What other woman in history can compare to her? If Lola Mora were North American. . . ." (61). Soiza Reilly adds that "The Fountain of Lola Mora was the first example of fine, brave, intrepid, imaginative art in the city of Buenos Aires. We were fed up with military and equestrian statues. The Fountain of Lola Mora was like a bath of beauty to the youth of my time" (58).

Javier Torre's film *Lola Mora* opened in Buenos Aires in 1996. Leonor Benedetto plays Lola [with no mention of her indigenous blood], and *Soiza Reilly appears as a character, interviewing Lola in Salta!* Here ends the parenthesis.)

In "La belleza dolorosa de los sueños," in the silence that follows the reading of the sonnet at the foot of Lola Mora's fountain, the sad bohemian poets who dream of "forbidden things" and write musical sonnets, hear a vagabond sobbing: "a brother of Job, in Verlaine and in Satan" (97). The narrator befriends the vagabond, whom he calls "the anarchist," and explains why: he is a new and nervous spirit, an emissary of what is to come, he possesses a sadness that is the best element for destroying what is old. The reactionaries call him a failure, but "To fail is to be at odds with and to be defeated by the guardians of the ideal. Everyone who fails, everyone who is sad, everyone who does not laugh, is in truth an anarchist." The winners are peaceful and patient bourgeois; the failures are nervous and full of combative fire. "And we fall. . . . When we fall, the pain saddens us. And the sadness makes us, irremediably, anarchists. . . . Christ was an anarchist" (98–99; ellipses in original).

"The progress of the world requires rebellious fighters, murderers, thieves, drunkards, poets, artists, musicians, singers. . . . In order to construct the new life, we must destroy the old one," the poet-anarchist says (101; ellipses in original), and his words are echoed by those of Arlt's Astrologer, who also leads us from anarchism to Peronism.

David Weir, *Anarchy & Culture: The Aesthetic Politics of Modernism* (Amherst: University of Massachusetts Press, 1997), writes: "The division that emerged in the late nineteenth century between progressive politics and progressive aesthetics reflects the origins and the history of the avant-garde" (158). And he adds that the "politicization of the cultural avant-garde" in the early nineteenth century "did not necessarily imply that politically progressive art would also involve aesthetic innovation. At first, the artistic avant-garde was simply an adjunct to the political avant-garde, an idea that Kropotkin perpetuated when he urged young artists to put their talents to use 'at the service of the revolution'" (159–60). Weir suggests an alternative to the choice "between a politically engaged realist art on the one hand and an apolitical purist art on the other": his argument "is simply that much of modernist art is consistent with the politics of anarchism, and that this consistency extends into the form of the work itself. In this respect, modernism appears as the culmination of the further history of the avant-garde, which began to be identified with radical politics around 1845" (160).

Weir continues: "Although not all artists and writers accepted the designation 'avant-garde' (Baudelaire, for one, did not), the key point here is that avant-gardism and anarchism were closely connected in the late nineteenth century, as shown by Bakunin's choice of *L'Avant-garde* as the name of the journal of political agitation he founded in Switzerland. . . . The historical congruence of avant-gardism and anarchism helps to account for the shape that modernism assumed in the early years of the twentieth century" (161).

Weir clarifies that certain ideas "particular to anarchism were adapted by poets and novelists in such a way that the outcome of those ideas was aesthetic rather than political" (161). These ideas include, in Weir's account, radical individualism or "egoism," the absence of all authority, and a fragmentary and discontinuous style. The phenomenon was very widespread, but few commentators noted its implications. By the early twentieth century, Weir says, when the socialists began to surpass the anarchists as organizers of workers, culture

> was one of the few fields open to anarchist activity. The shift of anarchism from politics to culture was inevitable. . . . Aesthetic practice became a form of political action. The libertarian lessons of anarchism were taken to heart by artists: they were free from all external authority, including the political avant-garde. For many artists the only way to advance anarchism was through culture, not politics, and then only by means of an aesthetic individualism so radical that it could hardly be recognized as specific to anarchism. The irony is that anarchism encouraged the liberation of culture from the political avant-garde. . . . the politics of modernism lies in its aesthetic absorption of anarchism to the point that modernist art can only be political if it does not advertise itself as such. (162)

Weir argues that "fin de siècle avant-garde culture was saturated with anarchist politics" and that "many figures associated with modernism had an interest in anarchism as well," but says that

> The only "evidence" for the ultimate transformation of anarchist politics into modernist aesthetics is the autonomous, heterogeneous, and fragmentary nature

> of modernist culture itself, which appears to manifest or realize anarchist ideology in artistic form. That is, anarchism and modernism are structurally homologous. The problem with this observation is that the culture of modernism can also be explained in other terms. Rather than a transposition of politics into aesthetics, modernism can be understood, for example, as the aesthetic expression of new psychological insights (the "discovery" of the unconscious), as the artistic response to social crisis (the causes and effects of World War I), or as the cultural register of economic forces (the growth of capitalism and consumer culture). Surely all of these factors played a role in the shape that modernism assumed, and, in fact, all of them complement the argument I advance. The Marxist argument that capitalism, rather than anarchism, provides the explanation for the proliferating forms that modernist culture assumed is, paradoxically, the most complementary of all. (165–66)

Many of the representations found in *Los locos* and *Los monstruos* (to revert to Arlt's working titles) are derived from the anarchist cultural tradition: from its *cultural symbols*. For example, the prostitute (Hipólita) as a symbol of exploitation and bourgeois hypocrisy; the *informer* (Barsut) as he who violates the norms of solidarity among the popular classes and is expelled from the political body; the *thief* (Erdosain) as he who extracts revenge for robbery by the bourgeoisie.

All three, according to Richard D. Sonn, *Anarchism and Cultural Politics in Fin de Siècle France* (Lincoln: University of Nebraska Press, 1989), are cultural symbols of the working class *because they situate themselves, as a social category, at the boundaries of the classes*. Sonn analyzes the rhetorical resources that the Symbolists and other French writers of the late nineteenth century borrowed from anarchism, and he says that writers gravitated toward anarchism because they felt excluded from the political order and the official literary system of the Third Republic. Each bomb, and for the Symbolists, each poem, was a prefiguration of the imminent demolition of capitalist society.

Sonn analyzes the turn toward anarchist representation on the part of writers from the perspective of language. In his fourth chapter ("Language, Crime, and Class"), he refers to the relation, also present in Arlt, between *prostitutes* and *argot*.

> Does the prostitute's prominence in argot reflect her increasingly important place in that portion of the society in which argot was spoken? Is there in fact a direct correlation between lexicalization and social role, so that the prostitutes should be considered more central to working-class culture than cobblers or printers? The prostitute clearly was central to argot, but not necessarily to society. It was in fact precisely her peripheral role in the lower-class milieu that made her such a potent symbol, for she existed not at the center but at the boundaries

of that society, at the interface between the classes. Her very marginality defined the perimeters of the lower class far more effectively than could those members located firmly within that class. Although the various terms designated highly specific categories of prostitutes, taken together they signified not the women's social function but rather their cognitive role in defining a critical relationship between the classes. Behind each term for prostitute lay an intimation of a relationship, either between the prostitute and her pimp or her pimp and her customer. . . . Abstract class relations were transformed into illicit sexual relations, thereby familiarizing and naturalizing the exploitive social interchange.

The relation between anarchism and prostitution is less immediately evident than is that between anarchism and crime. Anarchists often praised "individual repossession" as a means of redistributing the bourgeois' ill-gotten gains, yet they did not similarly encourage sexual commerce. Prostitutes and pimps, evidently important and perhaps central to argot, were linked to anarchism symbolically rather than directly. Thieves and prostitutes might both feel victimized by society, but the thief might take satisfaction in getting his revenge through theft, whereas the streetwalker's only hope of improving her status was to integrate herself into society through marriage or by becoming a highly paid courtesan in the manner of Zola's *Nana*. Either of these options—wife or *demi-mondaine*—was rejected by the anarchists as simply substituting one form of exploitation for another. The thief's relation to society was symmetrical and symbolized vengeance; the prostitute's was submissive or complementary and stood for exploitation. . . . Prostitution provided the anarchists with a symbol of bourgeois exploitation of the daughters of the working class, and more generally of a decadent society's perversion of natural passions for purposes of gain. The image of the exploited prostitute thus served the anarchists as a dual symbol of bourgeois domination of nature and of culture. *The thief, the pimp, the whore served as cultural symbols for many in the working class while remaining at the boundaries of that class,* respected for their hostility toward the dominant classes, sentimentalized for their suffering, and reviled when they betrayed their fellows for personal gain. (110–12; italics added)

Sonn also says that the anarchist logic of violence and the Sorelian cult of means over ends "could feed into the radical anti-Semitism expressed during the Dreyfus Affair as well as into anarchism and anarcho-syndicalism" (113). He points out that like contemporary proto-fascist movements, anarchism "moved reluctantly into the modern industrial world, casting a nostalgic glance back toward prepolitical figures of rebellion such as the criminal. . . . Argot provided them with familiar terms and themes drawn from the past and from the underclass, both marginal relative to the social and political realities of the present" (113–14).

Glen S. Close, *La imprenta enterrada: Baroja, Arlt y el imaginario anarquista*, trans. César Aira (Rosario, Argentina: Beatriz Viterbo, 2000), cites Sonn and compares Arlt's novels of revolutionary conspiracy (*Los siete locos* and *Los lanzallamas*) to those of Pío Baroja (the trilogy *La lucha por la vida*, 1904–1905) in terms of their representations of anarchism and culture.

Close says that Arlt's anarchist affinities have been mentioned by some critics, but never thoroughly analyzed. Arlt's novels abolish alienated labor, disperse centralized narrative authority, transgress the norms of linguistic propriety, and denounce a range of bourgeois institutions (marriage, corporations, the army, the state) as perverse and suffocating. Raúl Larra and Rodolfo Ghioldi (representatives of the Communist Party) accused Arlt of petit-bourgeois individualism and of adhering to "the theory of elite minorities" characteristic of anarchism. One aspect of Arlt's leftist "heresy" was his emphasis on the cultural impact of the modern communications media, and, above all, cinema. The Communists accused him of disdaining the masses and of confusing "mythological procedures" with the class struggle or the dictatorship of the proletariat.

Close maintains that for Arlt's characters, who are subjectively penetrated by the cinematic and literary media of urban capitalism, reality becomes consubstantial with cultural representation, and that journalistic discourse produces an interplay between fictional and nonfictional modes of representation. He observes that the two "presses" of the text, that of the anarchists and that of the newspaper which reports Erdosain's crime and suicide (transforming him into a media "celebrity"), are both located *underground*, where they function as the engines of Arlt's text.

•

9. In *Escritores Iberoamericanos de 1900*, Manuel Ugarte recounts another submission of a manuscript story as he traces the silhouettes of two writers:

> First, that of the director of the *Revue Mondiale*, Monsieur Jean Finot, an Israelite converted to Protestantism, short in stature, dynamic, conservative, the author of successful books, and an enthusiastic friend of every original initiative and every new gene.
>
> When I took him *my first article written in French*, he asked me curtly:
> "Who has recommended you?"
> "No one," I responded, a bit uneasy.
> "*A la bonne heure*," he exclaimed, extending his hand. "I'm sick of recommendations. I'll read what you've written, and if I like it, I'll publish it."
> A few days later he called me back to his office, which was located on the Rue Jacob, a predestined name, and on the *rive gauche*, an inevitable location, since he was a Jew directing an avant-garde magazine.

"*C'est très bien, mon ami,*" he told me right off. "I think we'll be seeing a lot of you around here . . ."

And so it was. All the articles which served as the basis of *Porvenir de la América Latina* and *El destino de un continente* appeared in the *Revue Mondiale*, to which I continued to contribute for many years, until Jean Finot's death soon after his fiftieth birthday, not long after publishing *Theory of Longevity*, in which he claimed that we could all live more than a century. (40–41; ellipses in original)

Some information about Manuel Ugarte (1875–1951), who deserves to figure in the manual as the author of the novel *El crimen de las máscaras* (The crime of the masks). We find this information in *Manuel Ugarte* (Madrid: Ediciones de Cultura Hispánica, 1989), an anthology of texts that includes a brief biography of Ugarte by editor Nieves Pinillos Iglesias and a bibliography of works by and on Manuel Ugarte.

Pinillos Iglesias says that Ugarte survived on his paternal inheritance for forty years, first in his career as a writer and later as a political activist. His first three books, *Paisajes parisienses, Crónicas del bulevar,* and *La novela de las horas y los días,* were prologued by Unamuno, Darío, and Pío Baroja, respectively (and we have just mentioned Glen Close's study of Arlt and Baroja). In her biography of Ugarte, Pinillos Iglesias marks two crucial transformations. The first is when Ugarte spends six years in Paris, from 1897 to 1903: he left an Argentine and returned a Spanish American and a socialist. The second is his discovery of imperialism on a trip to the United States precisely in 1898: invasions, annexations, and outrages in Mexico, Cuba, Nicaragua. . . . He returns to Paris a changed man and says: the United States will not stop until it meets with a united resistance from the countries of the south.

In 1903 he returned to Argentina. His contacts with French and Spanish socialists and *his friendship with Ingenieros and Lugones* led him to join the Argentine Socialist Party. In 1904 he participated, at President Roca's request, in the preparation of the Labor Code, which would be the most advanced of its time. When he returned to Europe, he represented Argentine socialism in the Congresses of the Second International in Amsterdam (1904) and Stuttgart (1907), and although the party proposed that he run as a candidate for the National Congress in 1905, he declined all honors. In Europe, he contributed to many Argentine, French, and Spanish newspapers and magazines, and published ten more books. He became radical in his defense of Latin American unity and anti-imperialism, and in 1910 he published *El porvenir de la América española,* where he says that Spanish Americans are compatriots bound by a common origin and a shared language.

In 1911 he began a two-year journey through all the Spanish American countries, and he narrated his travels in *El destino de un continente*. In a lecture at Columbia University, he said: "We rebel against the tendency to treat us as a subaltern and conquerable race."

Nieves Pinillos Iglesias continues: Ugarte's letter to President Woodrow Wilson, urging him to rectify and remedy the mandates and consequences of United States policy toward its southern neighbors, had an enormous impact. But when he returned to Argentina in 1913, he ran up against a wall of silent indifference. He was not invited by the authorities to participate in public forums, and he found the Socialist Party in crisis: he never got along well with Juan B. Justo or with *La Vanguardia*, and *he was expelled from the party in 1913*. He declared himself neutral during the First World War, and in 1915 he founded the newspaper *La Patria*, which closed after three months due to economic difficulties. In *La Patria* he defended neutrality, Latin American patriotism, and the need for social transformation.

By 1918 the family fortune was exhausted; Ugarte returned to Spain and then in 1921 to France. *He lived off his books and his contributions to newspapers and magazines.* In this period he published three books in Spain that form the nucleus of his most important ideological contribution (*and which were not published in Argentina until after his death*): *Mi campaña hispanoamericana, El destino de un continente,* and *La patria grande*.

In 1923 and 1924 he contributed to *Amauta*, the magazine founded in Lima by José Carlos Mariátegui, and to *Monde*, the magazine that Henri Barbusse directed in Paris. But he endured poverty, and his friends, among them Gabriela Mistral, attempted unsuccessfully to help him. In 1929 a group of them, including Mistral, Rufino Blanco Fombona, and Ramón Gómez de la Serna, organized a tribute to him. In 1932, another group including Manuel Machado, Alcides Arguedas, José Vasconcelos, Blanco Fombona, and Mistral petitioned Argentina to award him the National Prize for Literature. He was denied, but France awarded him the Legion of Honor, according to Nieves Pinillos Iglesias.

In 1935, Ugarte sold his library and returned to Argentina, where he attracted no attention. The Socialist Party invited him to rejoin, but his criticism of the electoral results of 1936 provoked *his second and definitive expulsion*. Neutral again during the Second World War, he went to Chile, and upon returning to Argentina in 1946, he was impressed by the national and Latin American appeal of Peronism. He met Perón, and Perón named him ambassador to Mexico. Ugarte remained in Mexico until 1950, when *disagreements with the ministry of foreign relations over political changes in Peronism* brought about his transfer first to the embassy in Nicaragua and then to Cuba. In January 1950, he resigned his diplomatic post. He went to

Madrid, at age seventy-five, and published his last two books, *El naufragio de los argonautas* and *La dramática intimidad de una generación,* which are a fraction of his memoirs. He returned to Nice, where he had lived previously, and on 2 December 1951 he was found dead from gas fumes. In 1954 his remains were returned to Argentina, where *no official act of homage was offered,* Pinillos Iglesias concludes.

Some books by Manuel Ugarte, published in Madrid, Barcelona, Valencia, or Paris: *Burbujas de la vida* (1900); *Estudiantes de París: Escenas del Barrio Latino* (1900); *Mujeres de París* (1900); *Paisajes parisienses* (1901); *Cuentos de la Pampa* (1903); *La novela de las horas y de los días (Notas íntimas de un pintor)* (1903); *Tarde de Otoño: Pequeña sinfonía sentimental* (1906); *Antología de la joven literatura hispanoamericana* (1906); *Nuevas tendencias literarias* (1909); *Cuentos argentinos* (1910); *Poesías completas* (1921); *El crimen de las máscaras* (1924).

In *Escritores iberoamericanos de 1900,* Ugarte, who published his books in Europe, criticizes the fact that for the purposes of national or foreign literary competitions and expositions, only those books printed in Argentina are considered Argentine, thus "systematically excluding from the national account those writers who are published globally, by the great publishing houses of Europe, which is to say, those who circulate as God dictates, without the puerile sham of editions paid for by the author" (17).

Alejandro Sux wrote various articles about Manuel Ugarte: he published "Manuel Ugarte" in the magazine *Gustos y gestos* (Buenos Aires), 1 February 1911; "El porvenir de la América Latina" in *Letras* (Havana), 19 February 1911; and also "Carta abierta a Manuel Ugarte con motivo de su libro *Mi campaña hispanoamericana*" in *Nuestra América* (Buenos Aires), 5th year, 4, no. 35 (October 1922).

Other articles about Ugarte were written by Luis Alberto Sánchez, John William Cooke, in *De Frente* (Buenos Aires), 3 November 1954; Jorge Enea Spilmbergo, Rodolfo Puiggrós, Norberto Galasso, "El encuentro Ugarte-Perón," *La Opinión* (Buenos Aires), 2 September 1973; and Jorge Abelardo Ramos, "Olvido y rememoración de Ugarte," *Amauta* (Buenos Aires), no. 4 (April 1989).

Escritores iberoamericanos de 1900 contains Ugarte's comments on Delmira Agustini (he speaks of the savage spontaneity and the sensual fire of her verses, which created a sort of *cordon sanitaire* around her), Francisco Contreras, José Santos Chocano, Rubén Darío ("A diminished conception of journalism, which only rewards the insubstantial, obliged him to write superficial chronicles from Europe. He admitted it frankly: 'They pay me for what I don't know how to do, or what I do unwillingly; but no one pays me a cent for my verses, which are good'"), Enrique Gómez Carrillo, José Ingenieros ("his first playful and restless gesture in *Siringa* [*sic*], the group he just founded in Buenos Aires, was to solemnly consecrate an obscure provincial poet," and he recounts this "farce" perpetrated in a restaurant on Calle Carabelas). Ugarte says about Ingenieros: "His tendency to fantasize about serious matters discouraged people from taking him seriously. But he was even more inhibited by his tendency to toy with the importance of his own efforts, *in a measured and solemn environment* in which even the biggest dolts puff out their chests and exaggerate their abilities. The lack of responsible opinion among us allows each man to be worth whatever he says he's worth. And since Ingenieros amused himself by stripping away distinctions—starting with those he himself had personally and legitimately earned—he ended up paying for his modesty, that higher distinction, like a *crime,* Leopoldo Lugones, Amado Nervo, Belisario Roldán, Florencio Sánchez (Ugarte recounts what happened to him when he arrived one night in Nice and carried his bags to a plaza, where he sat down on a bench; a ragged woman with two children, one a babe in arms, approached him and offered to carry his bags, left him the baby, which was a bundle of newspaper, and escaped with his two suitcases), Alfonsina Storni, and José María Vargas Vila.

Ugarte speaks of the "Latin American exile of 1900" and of the group of writers he calls "the generation of 1900." He says that this group corresponds, with only a slight variation in dates, to the generation of 1898 in Spain (Azorín, Pérez de Ayala, Marañón, Baroja and Maeztu), a major difference being that the Spanish group developed in its own country while "ours was obliged to bear more fruit abroad." He says that the nucleus of the group, residing in Paris and Madrid, was made up of Darío, Luis Bonafoux, Alcides Arguedas, Juan Pablo Echagüe, Hugo Barbagelata, Gabriela Mistral, Soiza Reilly, Alejandro Sux, the García Calderón brothers, José Vasconcelos, Joaquín Edwards Bello, Rufino Blanco Fombona, and "the author of these lines."

Ugarte's comments on this exile of 1900 could well refer to the Latin American Boom of the 1960s: "The reason for the general exodus is not to be found in any rash admiration of exotic literature, but rather in the suffocating local environment." He criticizes "the cultural illiteracy" of a continent where writers go unrecognized and where people strive only for power or wealth. The writers of 1900 sought a climate propitious for "internal gymnastics," "the warmth they did not find in their native land, in the atmosphere rarefied by the smuggler and the *caudillo*" (20). They "established, more by force of circumstance than by personal will, a spiritual identification between the most diverse parts of Spanish America, an identification similar—and we would do well to meditate on the analogy—to that which at the beginning of the nineteenth century determined, with neither calculation nor obligation, the political independence of these same regions. It is as if equivalent periods, separated by a century, were manifesting themselves in the rotation which marks the evolution of peoples" (16, 18–19).

The final chapter is titled "El destino de una generación" (The fate of a generation), and it is dated in 1942 in Viña del Mar, Chile. There Ugarte says that all the writers he has mentioned were unfortunate, that none escaped economic anxiety, that none achieved a high position in his or her country, and that they lived as expatriates. Six out of twelve died tragically, two murdered and four by suicide. The place of the writer in Latin America is one of discredit: the political, economic, and spiritual metropolis strives toward the elimination of talent. "The flowering of any originality capable of provoking independent thought is avoided" (245).

Ugarte says:

It wasn't for nothing that when we used to philosophize about his issue, Ingenieros would say to me:
"We're like circus animals; the only thing we know while we're alive is the cage and the whip . . ."
To which I responded by completing the simile:
"And the worst of it is that once we they're dead, those same animals serve as luxurious coats for those who destroyed them." (247)

On the theme of cages and beasts, and in order to end the trajectory from anarchism to Peronism, and beyond: in *El arte y la democracia (Prosa de lucha)* (Valencia: Sempere, 1909), Ugarte narrates "Una aventura policial" (139–43), and in a footnote to the title he says: "The author was arrested in Buenos Aires in October 1903, because of his political opinions. It is inevitably painful to return to the country in which one was born, after six years of absence, only to be provided accommodations in the police station. This is a new form of hospitality. We welcome all compatriots who return to their homeland after having glorified the name of Argentina in Europe, in order to whip them and shut them up as we see fit!" And he recounts a socialist demonstration:

From a balcony we watch [socialist leader and congressman Alfredo] Palacios pass, surrounded by a group of policemen. I go down with del Valle Iberlucea, López and some others, and we run to the place where the incident is taking place, we find ourselves swept up in a rush, they trample us and push us into a very small room, where they order us to hand over our money and our watches and to declare our names, professions, and ages, under the suspicious vigilance of the janissaries, still holding their revolvers. All of this, which seems entirely medieval, has occurred at four in the afternoon, in a central street of our town. We protest not our personal treatment, but the system it reflects. (140)

V. Women Who Kill

1. Slavoj Zizek, *Looking Awry: An Introduction to Jacques Lacan through Popular Culture* (Cambridge: MIT Press, 1991), 77.

•

2. Jean Franco has shown the relation between violence and sexual gender in the cultures of Latin America. In her 1992 article, "La Malinche: From Gift to Sexual Contract," *Critical Passions: Selected Essays* (Durham: Duke University Press, 1999), 66–82, she shows the real and epistemic violence occluded by the symbolic appropriation of la Malinche as the "first example" and "the symbol" of the mixture of cultures.

And she also shows the relation between the political violence of the state and sexual gender in Latin America ("Killing Priests, Nuns, Women, Children," 9–17 in the same volume) in reference to the murder of nuns in El Salvador (and priests in Brazil and Argentina), the rape of women in front of their families, the torture of pregnant women, and the "adoption" (kidnapping) of their children by military families in the Southern Cone. Here Jean Franco points out the correlation between the spaces traditionally assigned women in Latin American literature and culture: home for the mother, the convent for the virgin who is not a mother, the brothel for the prostitute, and heaven for the virgin mother of God (13). And she said that feminist criticism based on critique of the patriarchal system and the trafficking of women did not lament the liquidation of the "sacred" figures of the mother, whose domestic power was also servitude. But this critique perhaps underestimated, according to Franco, the potential for opposition inherent in these female territories whose importance as the only sanctuaries became obvious at the moment of their disappearance: the case of the Madres de la Plaza de Mayo.

•

3. The woman who kills is, of course, a close relative of the femme fatale who is one of her possible versions. According to Rebecca Stott in *The Fabrication of the Late-Victorian "Femme Fatale": The Kiss of Death* (London: MacMillan Press, 1992), the femme fatale emerges at the end of the nineteenth century alongside the New Woman, a term which Sara Grand appears to have invented "in an article of 1894 in reference to women who were entering higher education and new areas of employment" (12).

The femme fatale arose in England (and was named in French) in a period of incessant classification and denomination, when normal and abnormal sexuality and perversions were being defined (23). The Victorian novel reveals the fascination of this woman, who appears accompanied by physicians. In *Dracula,* in 1897, we find the physician and the sexually voracious, insatiable woman; the same year, Stott says, "saw the amalgamation of the different suffrage societies into the National Union of Women's Suffrage Societies" (73).

According to Stott, the figure of the femme fatale circulated in conjunction with England's imperial expansion, medicine, criminology, and the press. It was associated with other "danger slogans": "the black peril, the yellow peril, the American peril, even the white peril," that of "decadence" and "degeneration" (21). Stott's central correlation: "the constitution of the *femme-fatale*-as-sign depends upon *what else* (besides Woman) is considered to be culturally invasive or culturally and politically Other at any historical point" (44).

Mary Ann Doane introduces her study *Femmes Fatales: Feminism, Film Theory, Psychoanalysis* (New York: Routledge, 1991) as follows:

> The femme fatale is the figure of a certain discursive unease, a potential epistemological trauma. For her most striking characteristic, perhaps, is the fact that she never really is what she seems to be. She harbors a threat which is not entirely legible, predictable, or manageable. In thus transforming the threat of the woman into a secret, something which must be aggressively revealed, unmasked, discovered, the figure is fully compatible with the epistemological drive of narrative. . . . Both cinematic and theoretical claims to truth about women rely to a striking extent on judgments about vision and its stability or instability. Although her origins are literary and pictorial, the femme fatale has a special relevance in cinematic representation, particularly that of Hollywood insofar as it appeals to the visible as the ground of its production of truth.
>
> The femme fatale emerges as a central figure in the nineteenth century in the texts of writers such as Théophile Gautier and Charles Baudelaire and painters such as Gustave Moreau and Dante Gabriel Rossetti. If, as Christine Buci-Glucksmann points out [in *La raison baroque: De Baudelaire à Benjamin* (Paris: Galilée, 1984), 34], the archaeology of modernity is "haunted by the feminine," the femme fatale is one of its most persistent incarnations. She is associated with the styles of Decadence, Symbolism, and Art Nouveau as well as with the attention to decoration and excessive detail linked to a persistent and popular Orientalism. . . . Her appearance marks the confluence of modernity, urbanization, Freudian psychoanalysis, and new technologies of production and reproduction (photography, the cinema) born of the Industrial Revolution. The femme fatale is a clear indication of the extent of the fears and anxieties prompted by shifts in the understanding of sexual difference in the late nineteenth century. As Buci-Glucksmann argues, this is the moment when the male seems to lose access to the body, which the woman then comes to *overrepresent.* The "working body" is

"confiscated by the alienation of machines" and "submitted to industrialization and urbanization." At the same time, in a compensatory gesture, the woman is made to inhere even more closely to the body. The feminine body is insistently allegorized and mythified as excess in art, literature, philosophy. It becomes the "veritable formal correlative" of an increasingly instrumentalized reason in technological society. . . . It is not surprising that the cinema, born under the mark of such a modernity as a technology of representation, should offer a hospitable home for the femme fatale. She persistently appears there in a number of reincarnations: the vamp of the Scandinavian and American silent cinemas, the *diva* of the Italian film, the femme fatale of the film noir of the 1940s. (1–2)

Doane says that the femme fatale "is an ambivalent figure because she is not the subject of power but its *carrier.* . . . Indeed, if the femme fatale overrepresents the body it is because she is attributed with a body which is itself given agency independently of consciousness. In a sense, she has power *despite herself*" (2). She is also "situated as evil and is frequently punished or killed. . . . Hence, it would be a mistake to see her as some kind of heroine of modernity. She is not the subject of feminism but a symptom of male fears about feminism" (2–3).

•

4. *Caras y Caretas: Semanario festivo, Literario, Artístico y de Actualidades* 1, no. 7 (19 November 1898). I owe this reference to Viviana Hurtado.

•

5. In *Cuentos fantásticos,* as cited in chapter 2. In his preliminary study, Antonio Pagés Larraya says that *La bolsa de huesos* appeared in a 114-page volume published by the Compañía Sud-Americana de Billetes de Banco in 1896.

In Holmberg's *La bolsa de huesos,* we see *the relation between journalism* at the end of the century *and the detective story:*

Two days after this dialogue with my friend, the morning newspapers, in Spanish, French, English, and Italian, offered their readers the following crime report:

A surprise. In a house on such-and-such a street, near the Centroamericana station, a young man who had been passing as a medical student was found dead in his bed. Verifications made by the sectional superintendent have established that the young man was not in fact a student. Upon examining the corpse, the police physician was left perplexed at having found, under a masculine disguise, the most sovereignly beautiful woman ever beheld by human eyes. Removal of a small false moustache adorning her upper lip revealed a delicate mouth modeling all the curves of a kiss. When a pair of large, dark glasses were also removed, all those in attendance were shaken, declaring that they had never in their lives dreamed of such eyes. Black, deep and velvety, they beckoned one in, as if to explore the abyss. She appeared less dead than in ecstasy. "That's how Saturnino looked," said one gentleman involuntarily, and the superintendent asked him for the address.

In her left hand, invincibly tight, she clutched a ruby locket. (235)

We can say that with Clara, Holmberg founds the detective story in Argentina because he is not only the first writer to invent the woman who kills, but also the first who experiments with almost all the literary genres associated with the modernity of the late nineteenth century: fantastic literature, science fiction, and detective literature. But if we take "foundation" in a strictly chronological sense, *La bolsa de huesos* in 1896 had at least one precedent, which is "La pesquisa" (The investigation) by Paul Groussac, from 1884 (first published in 1884 as "El candado de oro" [The golden padlock]), in which the murderer is a man.

Jorge Lafforgue and Jorge B. Rivera, *Asesinos de papel: Un riguroso recorrido por el género policial en la Argentina* (Buenos Aires: Colihue, 1996), say that the first fully documented Argentine detective was Andrés L'Archiduc, whose nickname was "The Linx." He appeared in 1878 in novel *La huella del crimen* (The trace of the crime), written by Raúl Waleis, a pseudonym of Luis V. Varela. Varela was a renowned lawyer and fervent admirer of Émile Gaboriau, the famous French serial novelist who delighted his readers at the end of the nineteenth century with the adventures of inspector Lecoq.

But Holmberg seems to be the founder, because in the same year of "La bolsa de huesos," 1896, he published *La casa endiablada* (The house of devils), of which Pages Larraya writes in his introduction to the *Cuentos fantásticos* (80) that it was the first detective novel written in Argentina and "the first in universal literature in which a crime is discovered by the dactiloscopic system" (invented by the Argentine Vucetich).

1896: foundation of the Facultad de Filosofía y Letras, foundation of the Museo Nacional de Bellas Artes, publication in Buenos Aires of Rubén Darío's *Prosas profanas* and *Los raros*. And also the foundation of the Partido Socialista Obrero Argentino.

In "Zoología: Historia de la ménagerie," *La Jornada* (Mexico City), 21 April 1996, Octavio Di Leo writes a "curious biography" of Holmberg:

The first director of the Buenos Aires zoo was Eduardo Holmberg. He was the grandson of a Tyrolese baron who had arrived in Buenos Aires in 1812 on the frigate *Canning;* on the list of passengers, San Martín, then a lieutenant colonel, also appears. Holmberg's grandfather fought in the wars of independence and commanded the patriotic artillery at the battle of Tucumán. Holmberg's father

accompanied Sarmiento in exile in Chile. The biography of the first director of
the Zoo, as we see, is intimately linked to the history of the nation. In his years
of education, he had Larsen as a teacher of dead languages, the same described by
Miguel Cané in *Juvenilia,* one of the classics of that generation which was called,
for want of a name, the generation of '80. During the yellow fever epidemic of
1871, he took refuge in a provincial town until the plague subsided. Upon Darwin's
death in 1882, a tribute was organized in the capital featuring two speakers:
Sarmiento and him. . . . Holmberg, who had just received his doctorate in medicine with a dissertation on phosgene gas, never practiced it [and here a note
refers to Arlt and phosgene in the war waged with gases]. He wrote "scientific
fantasies" in which Darwin refuted, in the first person, a congress of scholars. He
translated those most English of writers, Dickens and Conan Doyle. And Rubén
Darío, on one of his visits to Buenos Aires, called Holmberg "our wise German
baron." In 1896, the newspaper *La Nación* announced the sale of the second edition of his treatise on mineralogy and the imminent publication of his novel *La
bolsa de huesos,* whose manuscript he reads to a friend in the zoo, while "the light
of the full moon inundated the scene, agitated at intervals by the roaring of the
lions and leopards in their cages."

Octavio Di Leo concludes with the genealogy of directors of the zoo: "Adolfo
Holmberg, the great nephew of the man of science and letters, was in charge of
the Zoo from 1924 to 1943. And Mario Perón, relative of the thrice elected president, was in charge from 1946 to 1955, the year in which Perón was deposed."

☠

But let us follow the traces of our avant-gardist Holmberg a century later. In *La
noche de los bastones largos: 30 años después* (Buenos Aires: La Página, book published
with the Sunday edition of the newspaper *Página 12,* 28 July 1996), Sergio Morero,
Ariel Eidelman y Guido Lichman interview Luis Quesada, a research biologist of
the Fundación Campomar. In 1966 (during "the night of the long clubs") he was a
student at the Universidad de Buenos Aires and he is "still disturbed" by what he
experienced at that time (32). The Center for Students of the Exact Sciences, Quesada recounts, "used to receive science journals that not even the university library
had, since they had to pay for them. We, on the other hand, *exchanged them* for
our own publication, *Holmbergia,* which was named in honor of Eduardo Ladislao
Holmberg, a famous naturalist and Argentine scientist of the past century."
According to Quesada, when the military occupied the Center and destroyed it,
they sold the issues of *Holmbergia* "as old paper, or they burned them" (33).

•

6. The very first were the schoolteachers. Francine Masiello, in "Women, State and Family in Latin American Literature of the 1920s," *Women, Culture, and Politics in Latin America: Seminar on Feminism and Culture in Latin America* (Berkeley and Los Angeles: University of California Press, 1990), 29, says that as early as 1870 there emerged some feminist movements comprised of schoolteachers who formed societies, published newspapers, and worked for the cultural, economic, and social improvement of women. They also organized strikes and acts of sabotage.

Then came the women physicians. Lily Sosa de Newton, *Las Argentinas: De ayer a hoy* (Buenos Aires: Zanetti, 1967), 143, refers extensively to the first women physicians in chapter 5, "El feminismo en la Argentina" (142–59). Cecilia Grierson (1850–1934) was the first: she graduated in 1889 and in 1893 she was in charge of the nursing school. "It was her initiative which founded the Consejo Nacional de Mujeres de la Argentina, an entity whose work was very broad for the era, and which was driven by the desire to elevate the moral and intellectual level of women."

In 1905 only eleven women had graduated from the Universidad de Buenos Aires; between 1905 and 1910 there were twenty-five in medicine, education, and the sciences, and all of them were defenders of the social and economic advancement of women, according to Marifrán Carlson, *¡Feminismo! The Woman's Movement in Argentina from Its Beginnings to Eva Perón* (Chicago: Academy of Chicago Publishers, 1988), 83.

But in order to hear the first Argentine woman physician, we must read Juan José de Soiza Reilly, one of our Virgils in the world of crime in fiction. In "Habla la doctora Cecilia Grierson" (Doctor Cecilia Grierson speaks) (*Mujeres de América*, 95–103), she herself recounts what happened when she showed up to enroll in the medical school in the 1880s. "Imagine the surprise. What a bureaucratic and scientific fright for those grave gentlemen of the School! A little twenty-year-old girl, and pretty to boot, proposing to usurp the science of men!" It is easy to reconstruct the fearful imaginings of the old dons, Soiza Reilly says.

> "A woman doctor of medicine! The world's turned upside down. Where will we end up if all women want to do likewise?"
> It was the first time that female dress invaded the sanctuary of science. At first, ironic smiles. The odd conquering initiative by the odd Don Juan. But, soon, the young men understood that the young woman's eyes announced the strength of her fists. . . . So that her physical appearance wouldn't stand out among the

men, she sacrificed her long hair. One day she appeared at the School with short hair. Cecilia Grierson was the first Argentine woman to anticipate the current fashion, by almost half a century. (96)

Cecilia recounts to Juan José how hard it was for her to get permission to put flowers and plants in the patients' room. "If you knew what I had to go through to convince the hospital directors! They didn't want to! They claimed the flowers harmed the patients! They weren't aware that health often enters through the eyes" (101). Soiza Reilly concludes, at the beginning of the 1930s: "She currently lives out her beautiful old age in the full youth of daydreams. In the summer she takes refuge in her house in Los Cocos, in the mountains of Cordoba, maintaining her refined appreciation of pictorial art. There, in one of her cabins, she offers hospitality to artists who dream and work. An admirable woman! She sacrificed her own love for the love of others. Argentine women owe her a statue. All Argentines should one day kiss her in bronze!" (103).

•

7. Georges Didi-Huberman, *L'Invention de l'hystérie: Charcot et l'iconographie photographique de la Salpêtrière* (Paris: Macula, 1982), in addition to registering these literary crimes, refers specifically to hysteria as a spectacle, as a theater of pain and passion, and he analyzes its relationship with photography as an apparatus of subjectivity, as well as its relationship to "criminality" and to female identity. He works with the "photographic iconography of Salpêtrière," photographs taken of "hysterical women" in the hospital of Salpêtrière between 1875 and 1880, stating that only in 1888 does it provide a photograph of a man (82). The central hypothesis is that the photographic situation was providential for the hysteric phantom, just as the "passionate attitudes" were for the iconographic phantoms (165).

In the chapter titled "The Legend of Identity and Its Protocols," he says: "The physicians of Salpêtrière were like 'scientific policemen' in search of a criterion of difference, understood as *principium individuationis;* that is to say, a recognition, an assignment of identity" (58–59). Like our detective physician with Clara. And he adds that the connivance between Salpêtrière and the police prefecture was "exquisite, tacit and impeccable," because the photographic techniques were the same in both cases. From this subtle medical-police complicity, Didi-Huberman says, a notion of identity was elaborated on the basis of the interplay of signs and scientific or legal research, and of its technical, photographic answers. The photograph was the new machinery of a legend: the compulsory reading of identity in the image (59).

Hysteria as an abysmal and secret force, *as a passion and as a farce or lie:* "that a woman should make her own body lie! How can one practice medicine honestly, if the bodies themselves start lying?" wondered Charcot, according to Didi-Huberman (77). And he shows how Charcot analyzed the hysterical attack: as "spectacle," "illogical movements," "plastic poses," "passionate attitudes" (113); Charcot, he says, *domesticated the most baroque of theatricalities*. It was necessary for Freud to pass through the great theater of hysteria, in Salpêtrière, before inventing psychoanalysis (81).

For hysteria as passion, as "contact between soul and body" (73), is "the illness that has neither lesion nor cause" (74), and it seems "to offer the total spectacle of all illnesses at once" (76). It is a "dramatic reproduction" and the paradox of desire in representation, where the woman shows, acts out, what she cannot achieve (78). It is an extreme imitation, like the photograph and theater, because mimesis is the hysterical symptom itself, and also a tragic mask made flesh, and also simulation, as well as an ingenuous and sincere gift of multiplied identifications. It steals all roles. An actress would never go so far or so deep as a hysteric, says Didi-Hubermann (163).

☠

In "The Image of the Hysteric" (Sander L. Gilman, Helen King, Roy Porter, G. S. Rousseau, and Elaine Showalter, *Hysteria beyond Freud* [Berkeley and Los Angeles: University of California Press, 1993], 345–452), Sander Gilman says: "The image of the hysteric does not simply arise out of Jean-Martin Charcot's personal interest in the visual representation of the hysteric at the Salpêtrière. Charcot did not invent the act of 'seeing' hysteria. . . . it is part of a long-standing European tradition of representing the insane, into which the image of the hysteric must be fitted. Indeed, it is a tradition which is as much popular [and artistic] as it is scientific" (359).

In the same book, Elaine Showalter, "Hysteria, Feminism, and Gender," 286–344, refers to Augustine, the surrealists' hysteric: "She came to the Salpêtrière at the age of fifteen in October 1875, suffering from pains in the stomach and convulsive attacks during the night which sometimes left her paralyzed . . . at the age of thirteen, [she] had been raped by her mother's lover" (311–12). After spending five years at the Salpêtrière, she escaped in 1880 disguised as a man. Showalter adds that "a group of feminist scholars, choreographers and dancers based at Trinity college in Connecticut have produced a performance work about her called 'Dr. Charcot's Hysteria Shows'; and a successful play, *Augustine: Big Hysteria,* was staged in London in 1991" (312–13). This after Showalter wrote about Augustine in *The Female Malady* (New York: Pantheon Press, 1985).

☠

The birth of the detective novel is also linked to photography. In Holmberg's *Clara* we can clearly read the correlation between medicine (and the medical secret), photography, the detective novel, and Argentine jurisprudence at the end of the nineteenth century. It is, according to Jacques Dubois, *Le roman policier ou la modernité* (Paris: Nathan, 1992), a modern correlation that shows the relation between photographic procedures and detective fiction. The police of the belle époque use photographic techniques in their investigations, and so-called judicial photography served to found, through the collaboration of the police and psychiatry, "criminal anthropology," *which is the correlate of the detective literature of investigation,* Dubois says.

And he shows that the detective story plays the same role in the market of fictions that photography plays in the market of images, because the police novel implies *new uses of reading:* it changes the mode of communication and introduces unprecedented relations in the scheme of practices of representations (21). The police story is voyeuristic and fetishistic: the focusing of fiction on the private and even secret life of the characters is consubstantial with the enigma. This focus and the attention to detail, to the trace, link it once again with photography. Photography is trace; the detective novel practices the trace: the two modes of expression refer to the same indicial principal of representation (29).

•

8. Roberto Arlt, "Saverio el cruel: Comedia dramática en tres actos," *Obra Completa,* vol. 3, 289–332. The play was performed in the Teatro del Pueblo on 4 September 1936.

Omar Borré, *Arlt y la crítica (1926–1990),* 208–10, informs us that the film *Saverio el cruel* appeared in 1977, directed by Ricardo Wullicher; it is a free version in which he does not recognize Arlt's work. Alfredo Alcón, Graciela Borges, and Diana Ingro were the principal actors. Alfredo Alcón also played Erdosain in Torre Nilsson's version of *Los siete locos* (1973), which includes some passages of *Los lanzallamas* and which also features Norma Aleandro and Sergio Renán.

In 1984 *El juguete rabioso* was filmed by director José María Paolantonio. Among the actors were Pablo Cedrón (included because of his supposed resemblance to the writer), Julio de Gracia (el Rengo), Cipe Lincovsky, and Osvaldo Terranova. A new version of *El juguete rabioso* appeared in 1998, directed by Javier Torre.

Several of Arlt's other works have been adapted for television, including *Pequeños propietarios* (1974), *Noche terrible* (1983), and *Trescientos millones,* among others.

•

9. In "La personalidad intelectual de José M. Ramos Mejía (1849–1914)" (a speech

delivered at the Ateneo de Estudiantes Universitarios and published in *Revista de filosofía: Cultura-ciencias-educación* (a bimonthly publication directed by José Ingenieros) 1, no. 4 (July 1915): 103–58, José Ingenieros himself speaks of La Syringa as a case of the confluence of science and literature, and he attributes its name to Rubén Darío.

Ingenieros, who declares himself a socialist, recalls that he frequented the Ateneo, where he found the young men's interest was concentrated on Rubén Darío: in 1898 the poet Eugenio Díaz Romero published the journal *El Mercurio de América* under the auspices of Darío and with the collaboration of "almost all the *ateneístas* of the most recent period." Díaz Romero, a librarian at the National Department of Health, used to chat with Ramos Mejía, the president, about Verlaine and D'Annunzio. In the Ateneo there were some (like Obligado, Quesada, Oyuela, Holmberg, and Argerich) insensitive to Darío's preaching, but there were also young men favorable to *modernista* tendencies, Lugones, Jaimes Freire, the Berissos, Soussens, Payró, and Ghiraldo among them. *El Mercurio de América* was in a certain sense the vehicle of these groups. Ingenieros says that "Darío took to calling the youthful circle of *El Mercurio* 'La Syringa,' a name which was spread later when, following the demise of the Ateneo and *El Mercurio,* the nucleus was reformed with the annexation of other young men, who afterward made themselves known in the journal *Ideas*" (134). La Syringa, for Ingenieros, represents that alliance of science with modernist literature; *at no time* does he define it, in this speech, as a "*cachada* club." (Anyone interested in reading a La Syringa "story" somewhat resembling Arlt's, in terms of the military uniform, should see the *cachada* played on the provincial poet, making him believe that he had been "consecrated," in chapter 9 of Manuel Ugarte's *Escritores iberoamericanos de 1900* (144–48), titled "José Ingenieros." Juan José de Soiza Reilly also has, of course, his own "story" about "Pepe Ingenieros," La Syringa, and the *cachada* at the expense of the provincial poet; it is titled "La mujer que pecó" (The woman who sinned), and it is found in his book *Carne de muñecas* (19–40).

Jorge Salessi, in *Médicos, maleantes y maricas: Higiene, criminología y homosexualidad en la construcción de la nación Argentina* (Buenos Aires: 1871–1914) (Rosario: Beatriz Viterbo, 1995), analyzes the Ingenieros of the *Archivos de criminología, medicina legal y psiquiatría* and also the "Ingenieros the joker," and he refers, among many other references, to the previously cited paper on Ramos Mejía, in the context of what he calls the "End-of-the-century proliferation of simulation" and the "Simulations and Put-ons" (133). He says that simulation was used as a strategy of assimilation by immigrants and upwardly mobile social classes, and also that it was used as mockery, as a mechanism of exclusion of the newcomers. And in this double usage it is articulated in the figure, the work, and the life of Ingenieros, and in La Syringa (141). In the chronicles of his contemporaries, Salessi says, Ingenieros appeared as the "chief joker" of La Syringa, along with Darío, and at the same time he was rejected by some intellectuals from families considered traditional. The theorist of simulation declared himself a simulator and was pitiless with other simulators. Simulation as a two-sided weapon, facing "upward" and "downward."

Salessi has worked with almost all the procedures of identity definition in end-of-the-century Argentina: literature, photography, fingerprints, the *Archivos,* psychiatry, criminology, and theater.

And Sylvia Molloy, in "Diagósticos del Fin de Siglo," *Cultura y Tercer Mundo. 2: Nuevas identidades y ciudadanías,* comp. Beatriz González Stephan (Caracas: Nueva Sociedad, 1996), 171–200, refers to La Syringa and the relation between simulation, science, and literature. She says: "La Syringa practices the joke of literature through literature, it is distinguished by its pitiless needling of other literati, by its teasing." According to Molloy, "Ingenieros and the members of La Syringa invent a verb, *lhemisar* or *lemisar,* as an homage to Lémice Terrieux, the famous French simulator, and they employ the expression *lemisar* or *hacer un lemis* to refer to their teasing and the performances with which La Syringa habitually victimizes the unwary," who are, in reality, the different or weak. Molloy points out something fundamental that can also be read in Arlt: the coincidence between the scheme of the teasing and the "therapy" of various clinical cases described by Ingenieros.

10. Arlt's theory of simulation-representation passes through cinema and psychoanalysis, or through psychoanalysis in cinema, and it is for this reason that he approaches the theory of Lacan and the cinema of Hitchcock: to tell the truth by means of fakery. In linking Lacan with Alfred Hitchcock's cinema in *Looking Awry,* Slavoj Zizek refers to "the classical topos of the Lacanian theory concerning the difference between animal and human deception: man alone is capable of deceiving *by means of truth itself*" (73), a logic which Zizek finds prevalent in the plot structure of many Hitchcock films. This simulated "outside," Zizek adds, "is never simply a 'mask' we wear in public but is rather the symbolic order itself. By 'pretending to be something,' by 'acting as if we were something,' we assume a certain place in the intersubjective symbolic network, and it is this external place that defines our true position . . . for in the social-symbolic reality things ultimately *are* pre-

cisely what they *pretend* to be" (73–74). And we deceive ourselves if we pretend to be anything else. To seem, to act as, to simulate, is the same as to be, in Arlt's fiction as well.

☠

With regard to theater actresses in Argentina, Lily Sosa de Newton refers to theater as a profession in chapter 9 of *Las Argentinas* ("El trabajo de la mujer"), and she says that "In the theater women find an appropriate medium in which to exist with a certain independence, on a plane of greater equality with men, and with less subjection to social conventions, even though her own task depends precisely on conventionalisms" (213).

Also in reference to theater: the first and fundamentally "correct" theatrical performance of *El casamiento de Laucha* (Laucha's wedding), Roberto Payró's 1906 novel, was staged by Enrique García Velloso in 1917 at the Teatro San Martín. Alfredo A. Bianchi says in *Nosotros* 96 (1917): "Doña Carolina, in the novel a woman whose life is of little interest and whose misfortunes move us not, appears in the comedy as a type of noble and strong woman, good and trusting, willing to sacrifice herself for one she loves, but unwilling to tolerate betrayal and abandonment. For this reason, *when Carolina kills Laucha at the end of the play after learning that he has married her falsely, her attitude seems much more logical than in the novel, where we see her as a nurse in the Hospital del Pago, following her abandonment*" (*La revista Nosotros*, ed. Noemí Ulla [Buenos Aires: Galerna, 1969], 140).

•

11. The limits of simulation, Ingenieros says, are madness (pathology) and crime. And he is interested precisely in that limit at which the two or three terms meet (the simulation of madness in criminals), because criminals who simulate madness are declared not legally responsible. Given the impossibility of knowing for certain to what degree madness is simulated or not in criminals, Ingenieros calls for *a legal reform* in chapter 5 of *La simulación en la lucha por la vida*. "Since the simulation of madness in criminals is proven to result from the legal criterion according to which punishment is applied according to the responsibility or the lack of responsibility of the subject, its prophylaxis must consist of a legal reform making it harmful to the simulator. Once the criterion of the lack of responsibility of the defendant is replaced by the application of social defense proportionate to his degree of fearsomeness, simulation of madness will become prejudicial to the simulators, thus disappearing from forensic psychology (*Obras Completas,* as previously cited, 117).

•

12. Alicia Dujovne Ortiz, *Eva Perón,* trans. Shawn Fields (New York: St. Martin's Press, 1996), recounts an anecdote told by César Tiempo about Arlt and Eva Perón. (She doesn't provide bibliographic data.)

> One evening, in a bar in Buenos Aires, the famous novelist Roberto Arlt, author of *Seven Lunatics,* was fervently speaking, making big gestures with his hands. At his table, a pale young girl was sipping her café au lait. She was so fragile and coughed so much that she seemed to have jumped out of one of his novels. The girl was Eva, and due to his extravagant gestures, the writer ended up spilling a cup on the girl's skirt. To ask her forgiveness, he got down on one knee with his hand on his heart, at which point Evita got up and ran to the restroom. When she returned, her eyes were red. She calmly sat back down and simply said, "I am going to die soon." "Don't worry, gorgeous," he reassured her, "I will die before you." In fact, he died July 26, 1942, and she followed ten years later, also on July 26. (42)

From this marvelous anecdote which links Arlt with Peronism, let us keep the suggestion that Eva seems to have emerged from *Los siete locos,* because this will be useful to us in our next "Stories of truth and stories of Jews." Arlt is united with Eva in 1940 in a Buenos Aires bar, and also by the date of their early death.

●

13. Jorge Luis Borges, *Collected Fictions,* 215–19. The afterword to *El Aleph* (1949) says: "Aside from 'Emma Zunz' (whose wonderful plot—much superior to its timid execution—was given me by Cecilia Ingenieros) and 'Story of the Warrior and the Captive Maiden' (which attempts to interpret two supposedly real occurrences), the stories in this book belong to the genre of fantasy" (287).

Cecilia Ingenieros appears twice in *El Aleph:* "The Immortal" is dedicated to her. I propose to relate Cecilia Ingenieros, and the Ingenieros family, with that unique genre which Borges attributes to "Emma Zunz," beyond the fantastic and the historical. Between "Emma Zunz" and Cecilia Ingenieros, at that point, Borges writes his specific variant, the other face of the story of the woman worker and the factory owner so characteristic of the social realism of the 1930s and 1940s.

In 1975, in *Diálogos Borges-Sábato,* Sábato speaks of dance as a language, "a form of communicating with gods and men"; "it is probable that dance is the first art, the basis of all the arts. The correlative in spoken language would be poetry."

And Borges evokes her immediately:

"Borges: In the name of Cecilia Ingenieros, I thank you. (*He smiles.*)" (76).

The Ingenieros family, like their mortal enemies, the Moreiras, are everywhere in the *corpus delicti.* Ingenieros and Borges; Ingenieros and Arlt in death; Ingenieros and La Syringa with its provincial poets . . .

●

14. According to Donna J. Guy, *Sex and Danger in Buenos Aires: Prostitution, Family, and Nation in Argentina* (Lincoln: University of Nebraska Press, 1991), "The situation of [female] textile workers is significant because that industry became a major employer of women in Buenos Aires" (69). She adds: "Men became concerned that less expensive female labor would take jobs away from them. They also feared the increased freedom of women who were not economically dependent. . . . By 1935 21,000 women composed 57.3 percent of the textile workforce in large establishments. The expansion of textile production meant that women could compete with men in the industrial workplace" (132).

In reference to the period in which "Emma Zunz" was written, Ronaldo Munck, Ricardo Falcón, and Bernardo Galitelli, *Argentina: From Anarchism to Peronism. Workers, Unions and Politics, 1855–1985* (London: Zed Books, 1987), observe that between 1930 and 1944,

> the position of women in the economic and political structures of the country changed fundamentally. . . . around the time of the First World War, women accounted for one-third of the industrial workforce. By 1939 women represented one-third of the workers in the chemical, pharmaceutical and paint industries, 48% of the workforce in the rubber industry and 58% of textile workers. Cheap female labor-power was thus a prime ingredient in the industrialization of the 1930s. Furthermore, the internal migration of that period was predominantly female, as against the mainly male overseas migration of an earlier era. (123)

•

15. Subsequent references are to Manuel Puig, *Heartbreak Tango: A Serial,* trans. Suzanne Jill Levine (New York: Penguin, 1996). At the moment of Pancho's assassination, Mabel's home is "criminal" because her father is being investigated for illicit business.

Boquitas pintadas is "the serial novel of the 1960s" not only in its ideology of transgression (the metaphoric equivalence of the violation of sexual taboos and the violation of discursive norms that we now associate with the theory of textuality), but also, and above all, because it exhibits the passage from a "library culture" to an audiovisual "media culture" (this is the passage that Manuel Puig clearly represents in Argentine literature). A text about signs and circulation; about the circulation of letters and bodies and their end in the equivalence of cremation/incineration: the letters are incinerated and the dead bodies "burn away" in contact with the linen in which they are wrapped. It is also a strongly framed text, which represents itself constantly in its interior. But it is above all a "serial novel" because of the class justice, popular and moralizing, with which it closes: the children and grandchildren pay for "the sins of the fathers." And also a "serial novel of the 1960s" in its questioning of the category of the "author" and in the proliferation of narrators and chroniclers who deny the existence of a fixed position from which the discourse might emanate.

•

16. Marta Diana, *Mujeres guerrilleras: La militancia de los setenta en el testimonio de sus protagonistas femeninas* (Buenos Aires: Planeta, 1996).
Teresa Meschiatti ("Tina"):

I live in Switzerland and I was a militant of *montonero* Peronism. I don't agree with the term "guerrilla" because it refers to the question of arms. That wasn't the only practice during my nine years of militancy. I prefer the word "militant" because it gives a more complete and finished idea of all the activities that a person can carry out in a revolutionary organization. "Militant" also has a projection of continuity in time. Although I may no longer belong to an organization, or may no longer perform guerrilla tasks, I consider myself a militant when I speak out. (45)

"Peti":

One afternoon when I had to transport some arms. I put them in a bag that ended up being very heavy. I didn't have anyone to leave the kids with so I took them with me. At the Retiro station, when I was getting off the train, fighting with the bag and the kids, a policeman walked up, and even though I tried to give him the kids, he took the bag. The weight was too much for him. He smiled.
    "What have you got in there, miss, guns?"
    "It sure feels like it, doesn't it?" I answered him, smiling back. My legs felt very stiff while we all walked, kids, policeman, bag and all, down the platform to the taxi stand. (75)

"Mariana":

In ESMA [Escuela de Mecánica de la Armada, a detention center], the process of "recovery" of women centered on the exaltation of our feminine feelings. One showed herself to be more "recovered" in direct relation to the interest she demonstrated in dressing, grooming, having delicate manners, etc.
    At the same time, and here I suppose we see one of the keys to the relationships that occurred, they were fascinated by us. We were women totally different from their wives. With us, they could talk about politics, weapons, strategy, movies or philosophy. So that along with the attraction, there was a contradiction, because in order to "recover," we had to be like traditional women, but what attracted them was the very fact that we weren't traditional women. (149)

"Gringa":

With respect to the famous issue of armed action carried out by a woman, I experienced it as a fact situated in the context of an overall struggle, so that it wasn't something that gave me moral problems. Handling weapons is hard for someone who wasn't involved with the issue, and who also belonged to a very hypocritical culture that isn't at all shocked, or doesn't consider it "hard," that a woman should do other things to survive. In the historical moment in which we were living, the arm came to be a prolongation, a form of externalizing the struggle that women were participating in. The case is not isolated. If we go down the map, in Central America we see that there are thousands of cases in which women have shown themselves capable of caring for children, doing housework and taking up a weapon to fight against an oppressor depriving them of justice, or depriving her of food for her children. (181)

•

17. César Aira, *La prueba* (Buenos Aires: Grupo Editor Latinoamericano, 1992). The text is dated 1990. With *La prueba* we arrive at another "reality" because in it the domestic female space is closed and becomes public in the supermarket (public-domestic). The representation of the state disappears and a change in the representation of female crime is marked.

On the cover of the magazine *La Maga* 6, no. 271 (26 March 1997), we read: "A new problem for the year 2000. Women criminals. In the last decade the number of female prisoners multiplied six times. 70% are in jail for robbery or drug dealing. The advancement of women in public life has as its opposite side the growth of female criminality. Nevertheless, as in politics and in business, men continue to occupy the majority of positions of power in criminal gangs."

•

18. For every postulate there exists an opposite: let us see what new meanings appear when the women who kill are in jail. María Carolina Geel wrote *Cárcel de mujeres* (Santiago de Chile: Zig Zag, 1956) from the jail where she is imprisoned for having killed her lover in a Santiago hotel. (The hundred-page text is a chronicle of life in the jail, wherein she describes some of the other prisoners and extols the selfless labor of the nuns who care for them. I owe this text to Raquel Olea.)

But the exception to the rule represented by this text narrated in the first person (a text about the real and the truthful as suffered by the author, a Chilean writer who had already published several books) is that the motives for the murder are obscured, remaining strange to the reader, and knowledge is not forthcoming. The victim's wife had died and the pair was free to be together, but her death led instead to the murder:

I only found out that he wanted to get married when the judge asked me if that's why I'd killed him. I was unaware of that fact just as I was unaware of all the others sensibly cited by those who, in their desire to help me, sought to justify my actions. I knew that I had severed his existence because of a crisis that he provoked, but whose deeper elements came from a more distant past, or rather, which were at the absorbing center of my destiny. Or perhaps they had been situated in time, waiting, even before I came into this life? . . . The morning that he came to tell me of the death which left him free to be with me, that is, a month and twenty-two days before, it so happened that at the very moment he was speaking, the radio was transmitting a piece of music that coincided to the point of the superstitious and the absurd: Mendelssohn's Wedding March. We both heard it and we both fell silent, but in a fraction of an instant I was overcome by the fear that that music was leading to death or emerging from it. And when hours later he spoke of life and of this music as announcing a future together, I had already resolved that those nuptials would never occur. It was so that I wrote to a certain apocryphal friend: "Because all the good that he could give me would not suffice to overcome the horrid moral misery which marriage manages to instill." . . . There commences, then, something nameless, a silent struggle wages in the depths and also on the periphery: there he was with the fixed idea of marriage, and here I was with my horror of it. The absurd plea began to spout from my lips: to leave things as they were. I have never been able to know how deeply a man is hurt when he is rejected upon offering his name. [. . .]

But vain are disquisitions on what might have been. Perhaps everything boiled down to his sudden realization, like mine before, that love is only the mirage of a mysterious aspiration which dwells in the soul and feeds on it. (76–78, 81–82)

She kills him a month later. She buys a weapon, and he helps her choose it! (98)

In jail she feels strange in the brutal company of the other prisoners. They look at her, and she quotes one as exclaiming, "in crude and mature voice, exactly these words: Well, what are you all lookin' at her for? For all she did . . . If it'd been me, I'd have killed all the other men while I was at it" (91; ellipses in original).

In ¡Criminales! (Almas sucias de mujeres y hombres limpios), our faithful Juan José Soiza Reilly titles one section "A Crime Punished with Another Crime."

"One Crime." He tells how he visited the women's jail, attracted by an anonymous note, and he recounts the case of Señora de Livingston, who murdered her husband (a rich and stern man), or, to put it precisely, hired two poor men to stab him to death; the hired murderers were sentenced to death and she to an indefinite prison term. She could no longer see her children because they didn't want to see her, and she wouldn't leave jail alive since she was very sick and dying slowly.

In "Another Crime," he tells of a woman who was very beautiful and who is now a little old woman, who says that she can't wait to die and that her crime was horrible, that when she married she was in love, but that years later her husband started wandering, staying out late and devoting himself to racehorses. He didn't even talk to her, he disdained her, and one day when he shot her a disparaging look, she began to feel a total hatred for him. Then she says that if there had been a full divorce law she wouldn't have had to resort to crime. But she says that no law protects the woman whose husband stops loving her because the law of separation demands proof and witnesses, and only God was witness to her bitterness. She says that public opinion has a special criterion for judging women. If a man kills his unfaithful wife, people applaud because "He killed in defense of his honor!" and the law absolves him, but if it is the woman that kills, people are horrified: "Murderess! You have dishonored your children," and they bury her alive in a jail. At the end, she says that the only defense of decent women is total divorce, which would prevent many crimes: "When that law is put into effect, people will see that I didn't deserve to die in jail. Don't we now consider it unjust that the Inquisition burned women for the crime of having divined the future?" (46–47).

•

19. Ángeles Mastretta, *Tear This Heart Out,* trans. Margaret Sayers Peden (New York: Riverhead Books, 1997). The subsequent page number reference is to this edition.

•

20. Mieke Bal, *Murder and Difference: Gender, Genre, and Scholarship on Sisera's Death* (Bloomington: Indiana University Press, 1988), reads a biblical episode (in two versions: Judges 4 and 5) in which Jael, a married woman, murders Sisera, the chief of a foreign tribe, in order to show how the meaning varies according to whether a man or a woman is the enunciator of the discourse and, in general, according to the codes with which it is read: historical, theological, anthropological, literary, thematic, and generic (125). She also analyzes a seventeenth-century painting, "Giudetta e Oloferne" by Artemisia Gentileschi (Galleria degla Uffizi, Florence) which shows Judith cutting off the head of Holophernes with the aid of another woman; this second woman, an old woman or a servant, she says, appears frequently in the seventeenth century when similar themes are represented, for example, in Rembrandt's and Rubens's renderings of *Samson and Delilah.*

•

21. James W. Messerschmidt, *Capitalism, Patriarchy, and Crime: Toward a Socialist Feminist Criminology* (Totowa, N.J.: Rowman & Littlefield, 1986), quotes Sheila Balkan, Ron Berger, and Janet Schmidt, *Crime and Deviance in America: A Critical Approach* (Belmont, Calif.: Wadsworth, 1980), in asserting that crimes by women

("shoplifting and prostitution in adults, 'promiscuity' and 'incorrigibility' in juveniles") reflect the conditions of women's existence, which "has been male defined and centered around family, sexuality and home" (13). "When they commit violent crimes such as murder, their victims are family members, relatives, or lovers" (14).

Messerschmidt observes that some authors "have attempted to attribute *increasing* female criminality to the effects of the women's movement *on women*. That is, these theorists assume first that women are clearly becoming 'liberated' from masculine domination and second that they are therefore committing more crimes. . . . Moreover, since the women's movement has eroded traditional gender roles, the resulting 'masculinization of female behaviour' leads to substantial increases in crimes of violence by females" (79). But, Messerschmidt says, recent studies tend to indicate that this increase is attributable less to "liberation" per se, than to "the changed attitudes of those who label females criminal—the public, police, judges, and prosecutors" (80).

☠

Claire McNab's, "Killing Women," in *Killing Women: Rewriting Detective Fiction*, ed. Delys Bird (Sydney: Angus & Robertson, 1993), 63–71, says that many women now kill in real life, but above all in fiction: "growing numbers of female writers execute with words," while "women are captivated by murder as entertainment," and they applaud women detectives (63). Women who kill are more exciting and they occupy a great deal of space in the media. Their crimes are "Not obvious, brutal murders achieved in the heat of rage with weapons or beatings, but the subtle killings—the poison in a carefully prepared meal, the incorrect dosage of prescribed drugs, the aforesaid pillow over the face, all occurring in the domestic arena" (66). McNab adds: "In 'real' life, as presented by the media, female murderers receive disproportionate attention. In Australia, for every one woman who murders, there are eight male killers. . . . Those few females who kill their partners, often after years of abuse, break the still-potent concept of gender roles" (67).

•

22. In "Gender, Death, and Resistance: Facing the Ethical Vacuum," in *Critical Passions*, 18–38, an article first published in Buenos Aires in *La Razón*, 31 May 1985, Jean Franco writes that the Madres de la Plaza de Mayo have shown in Argentina

that the discourse on masculinity and femininity is socially constructed. For instance, in a recent incident, the mothers appealed to article 259 of the Military Justice Code, which declares that "a woman whose life is publicly honest can give legal declarations in any domicile that she chose." Claiming to be "publicly honest," Zuleima Leira, one of the mothers who was asked to make a declaration before the military justices in the ongoing trials upheld her right to make the declaration at the headquarters of the Madres de la Plaza de Mayo. Hebe de Bonafini declared, "we do not recognize military justice, and that reference to publicly honest women appears totally anachronistic to us. But in any case, making them come here, looking them in the face, is like winning minor skirmishes." (35)

Jean Franco comments that this shows "the way the mothers' movement has been able to use the symbolic power normally used against women. The incident allowed them to point out that this same military code classifies women as an 'incapaz relativa' [relatively handicapped] along with invalids and those who are not familiar with Spanish. In using the position legally assigned to women while at the same time emphasizing its provisional and socially constructed nature, the mothers go beyond any essentialist definition" (35).

23. Adultery and female crime amid the din of the revolution of 1890! See Vizconde de Lascano Tegui, *Mis queridas se murieron,* ed. Gastón Sebastián M. Gallo and Guillermo García (Buenos Aires: Simurg, 1997). The text of the woman who kills is "Al fragor de la revolución," 121–46, which appeared in *La Novela Semanal* 6, no. 230 (10 April 1922). I owe this reference to Martín Kohan.

Marta kills the poisoned "revolutionary" journalist who knows that she has a lover (and who loves her hopelessly) and who has in his power the letters that betray her relationship with Roberto. The journalist has published an anonymous pamphlet titled "the aristocracy in shirtsleeves." Amid the din of the revolution of 1890, the journalist and the woman's husband meet up with her and her lover, who is a minister of Juárez Celman. Marta is carrying a concealed pistol, and she kills the journalist Dalegri. "The din of the revolution served as a backdrop for their intimate drama . . . She went toward Roberto, who awaited her, safe from ambush, free of all persecution" (146; ellipses in original).

24. Because "Women Who Kill" is also "An Essay on Reality" (on the different layers or grades of reality in reality) based on the video of a "real case" broadcast in Buenos Aires on Saturday, 22 July 1995. "Sleeping with the Enemy (The Demianec Case)" aired on Channel 13 in the series *Justicia para todos* (Justice for all). (I am indebted to Marcela Domine and Martín Kohan for the video.)

Catharina Demianec (a sixty-two-year-old Polish woman, married for thirty-two years) killed her husband Tiburcio Pérez, *a policeman,* in San Miguel del Monte, on 25 April 1990. She shot him repeatedly with a gun while he was sleeping and killed him. Afterward, she left him in the house for about ten days, and finally she dragged him with a chain to a ditch (he weighed 280 pounds), where a neighbor found him, wrapped in a nylon bag, in May 1990. Catharina says that her own mother used to hit her with her father's *military belt* from the 1914 war; that her courtship lasted two months, and that she married in order to leave home, only to suffer more torture.

Both her daughter Noemí Pérez and a niece declare that they never thought that she could kill him. Catharina declares everything in court: *she doesn't know how* she dragged him, she doesn't know how he died, it's all a nebula of nightmare and darkness, she says.

But she recounts how he always mistreated her, from the first year of their marriage: he insulted her, he threw food at her, he blamed her for everything, and he told her that if she left he would kill her. She tried to leave him when her daughter was two and a half years old, but the girl missed him and she returned. The day of the deed he insulted her in front of their daughter and grandchildren, and he threatened, as always, to kill her with the same gun that she finally used to kill him. (Other policemen also declare terrible things about their colleague: he used to put hot sauce on the fruit salad and he had received sanctions.)

Catharina cries, she says that she is remorseful, and she "speaks" to the dead man, to the camera and to women: if your husband mistreats you, don't stay.

Her daughter says that she is a regular old grandmother, and she asks that she not be sent to jail. A woman lawyer defends her. Verdict: Homicide in a state of violent agitation, aggravated by her connection with the deceased. The prosecutor asks for ten years, but the jury declares *veredicto absolutorio.*

VI. Stories of Truth

1. Arlt quotes are from *Obra Completa,* vol. 1 (Buenos Aires: Planeta-Carlos Lohlé, 1991), except in the case of *Los siete locos* (or *Los locos*), available in English as *The Seven Madmen,* trans. Nick Caistor (London: Serpent's Tail / UNESCO Publishing, 1998).

Arlt's *Los locos* and *Los monstruos* are the result of a slight transmutation operation that allows us to put him on even footing with Borges. The operation consists of removing the cabalistic number from the first title and restoring Arlt's original title for the second book, ultimately called *Los lanzallamas* at the suggestion of Carlos Alberto Leumann. Arlt's aesthetic ("La vida puerca," "Los monstruos") restored to its place, free of the titles or aesthetics of Güiraldes and Leumann.

César Aira ("La genealogía del monstruo: Arlt," *Paradoxa* 7 [1993]: 55–71; article dated 1991) does not allude to Arlt's original title, but he reads him within "the logic of the Monster," which is a *formal option of expressionism*.

In this noteworthy critical text, Aira says:

> In Arlt the expressionist world, that of excessive contiguities and deformations due to lack of space in a limited environment, an interior (his world is an interior), is a formal option. It is useless to think of it in psychological or socio-historical terms, or what have you. . . . Arlt's expressionist world is the interior of an organism, of a body. It isn't that it is that interior, but rather that it appears to be, which in representational terms is the same thing. The Monster is an organism. Or the opposite, the organism is the Monster. Later I will try to create the genesis of the Arltian Monster. The gaze that can no longer function due to lack of space annuls all transparency and installs a tactile, obscene and horrible contiguity, red against red, in a medium of blood where everything touches everything. The Monster is a man turned around, one who accompanies us like a terrifying *doppelgänger*. (57–58)

Arlt can make a Monster out of any material, Aira says, and he discusses the "device of monster making": "All the Arltian aporias, that of sincerity, of ingenuousness, of the quality of the prose, are explained in this device of conscience that attempts to attend its own spectacle, the language that it wants to speak to itself, in a word, the Monster. This device itself is the Monster" (61). He says that "Monster" is also "a word" which requires explanation and expression: "The Monster and the explanation progress together toward the infinite. There will always be a need for a supplement of explanation, at least as long as there is time. . . . But it is not the explanation that generates the Monster, far from it. It is too reasonable to do so. The monster is born from the purely novelesque, which Arlt found in the sensational serial novel" (62).

Finally, Aira situates himself (*and situates me*) in relation to Arlt and to the Monster:

> Taking myself as an example of extenuated singularity of time: I climb onto the ribbon of the continuum and run after the Monster covered in the laughable figure of explanation. There I may choose between the possibilities of the real, and I select, for no reason at all, simply to set the "circle of enigmatic factors" spinning, "impressionist criticism." No longer the unfortunate projection of the symbolic, but rather the happy interjection of the imaginary, the reception of Arlt's silent movies, which reaches me in bursts of somber light, in deliciously frightening visions: the mill of the Monsters in its frozen carrousel, the Virgin hanging on the Air: Duchamp called it Perspective, I call it Inspiration. (70–71)

•

2. Information on Milton Sills is available in Sol Chaneles and Albert Wolsky's *The Movie Makers* (Secaucus, N.J.: Derbibooks, 1974), 444; in *Notable Names in the American Theater* (Clifton, N.J.: Jones T. White & Company, 1976), 464; in *Filmarama*, vol. 1, *The Formidable Years, 1893–1919*, ed. John Stewart (Methuen, N.J.: Scarecrow Press, 1975), 232, and vol. 2, *The Flaming Years, 1920–1929* (1977), 488.

But the article that shows the other, philosophical side of Sills (and his library, justifying Borges) appears in *Dictionary of American Biography*, vol. 17, ed. Dumas Malon (New York: Charles Scribner's Sons, 1935), 164–65.

His full name was Milton George Gustavus Sills, the middle part of which he later dropped. He was graduated from the University of Chicago in 1903 with the degree of A.B., and for a year and a half remained there as a scholar and fellow in philosophy. His experiences in college dramatic performances prepared him to some extent for his professional début at New Palestine, Ohio, in 1906. . . . An engagement with Charles Coburn's repertory company gave him valuable experience in Shakespearian plays. . . . In 1914 he deserted the stage for the screen, and in 1916, after preliminary experience in the ill-equipped studios of New York, he went to Hollywood, and there began a new era of success as a motion picture star. . . . He was, it is said, far removed from the popular idea of the film idol when he was outside of the studios. His library contained books in Greek, French and Russian, all of which he read; his chess game was well above the average, and his talk ranged from philosophy or the experimental sciences to the fine points of tennis or golf. . . . He never abandoned his academic studies, and delivered occasional lectures at colleges and universities on various subjects connected and unconnected with the stage; in 1927 he spoke at the Harvard school of business administration on conditions in the motion picture world. He was the co-author with Ernest S. Holmes of a book, published (after his death) in 1932, entitled *Values: a Philosophy of Human Needs,* and he was one of the organizers of the Academy of Motion Picture Arts and Sciences. Unlike most actors, he became a wealthy man and left an estate of several hundred thousand dollars. (164)

That in regard to Milton Sills and his library. For her part, Evelyn Mack Truitt, *Who Was Who on Screen* (New York: R. R. Bowker Company, 1983), 663, informs us about some of the Milton Sills movies that Emma Zunz could have seen (and that Barsut, of course, could also have seen):

Before the crime: *The Rack* (1915); *Patria* (serial, 1917); *Shadows* (1919); *The Week-End* (1920); *The Marriage Gamble, At the End of the World* (1921); *Burning Sands, Borderland, The Woman Who Walked Alone, The Marriage Chance* (1922).

After the crime: *Why Women Re-Marry, The Last Hour, A Lady of Quality, Legally Dead* (1923); *Madonna of the Streets, The Heart Bandit* (1924); *As Man Desires, I Want*

My Man, A Lover's Oath (1925); *Paradise, The Silent Lover* (1926); *Framed, Hard-Boiled Haggarty* (1927); *The Barker, Burning Daylight, The Crash* (1928); *His Captive Woman, Love and the Devil* (1929); *Man Trouble, The Sea Wolf* (1930).

•

3. Torre Nilsson filmed Borges's "Emma Zunz" in 1952, with the title *Días de odio,* situating it in "the present," according to the critics. And he filmed Arlt's *Los locos-Los monstruos* with the title *Los siete locos* in 1972, in the period of the guerrilla movements and the military dictatorship of 1966.

Mónica Martin, *El gran Babsy: Un hombre como yo no debería morir nunca. Biografía novelada de Leopoldo Torre Nilsson* (Buenos Aires: Sudamericana, 1993), refers to *Días de odio:* "In order to demonstrate that Emma Zunz—played by Elisa Christian Galvé—was alone in the world, he makes her into a taciturn woman disgusted with her surroundings. *He sets the story in the present* and has Emma walk through a gray industrial city decorated with pro-Eva Perón graffiti. With these subtle threads he invited the viewer to understand that in Buenos Aires, man was alone in the communitarian conglomerates of *Peronism*" (46; italics added).

Mónica Martin allows Torre Nilsson himself to tell his biography: "Only eighty thousand people saw *Días de odio.* With *Días de odio,* I go back to being in *the minority.* The film was prohibited from being sold abroad and its domestic distribution was severely curtailed. *I don't know whether this was because Borges is an author who is not looked upon favorably by the government, or because it was thought that the subject was too dark or unpleasant, that it doesn't show a very happy Argentina*" (47).

With regard to *Los siete locos:*

"When I really became a filmmaker, that is, when I began to do things with movies that reflected something of my view of the world, filming Roberto Arlt was a sort of grand ambition. As happens with all great creators, he becomes more and more current." . . . When the shooting [of *Los siete locos*] was about to begin, Miguel Paulino Tato burst in with an official order to suspend the movie. Tato was synonymous with Argentine censorship and shortly thereafter he would become Torre Nilsson's greatest enemy and the Salieri of his life. They say that when he found out that Torre Nilsson was intending to film *Los siete locos,* he became sick with envy. *Apparently, he hated Roberto Arlt* since the time when they had been colleagues at the newspaper *El Mundo.* Arlt had died in 1942, but Tato went on hating him. His rancor wouldn't die. No one stood there with their arms crossed. Everyone from Contracuadro went out to challenge the censorship and not long after, the prohibition was lifted. . . . *Los siete locos* cost eighty thousand dollars and was made in seven weeks. . . . It finally premiered on May 3, 1973, in the Gran Rex theater and simultaneously in thirty-nine other theaters. (226–31)

•

4. In *Jewish Self-Hatred: Anti-Semitism and the Hidden Language of the Jews* (Baltimore: Johns Hopkins University Press, 1986), Sander L. Gilman says that in a 1699 work, *Instruction in the Jewish-German Manner of Reading and Writing,* Johann Christoph Wagenseil affirmed that *Yiddish* was the instrument of *Jewish Conspiracy:* "The linkage between the Jews who hide their evil deeds in a language that is not understandable to the powers that be and the idea that Jews lie when confronted by these powers *gives Yiddish, perceived not as a language but as the means for conspiracy, its own hidden power"* (73; italics added). Later in the book, Gilman refers to the United States and to Henry James (one of the writers who practiced the specific type of "fiction" which concerns us here), saying that in *The American Scene* (1907), James "despaired of the future of English because of the 'Hebrew conquest of New York,' where the 'East Side cafes' have become 'torture rooms of the living idioms'" (316).

5. It could be said that between the twenties and the forties the position of Jews in Argentine literature changes; they continue to be represented, as they had been since 1880, as foreign usurers, as misers, and as "feminine" (see chapter 6, "Stories of Jews," note 4), but in Arlt and Borges they are murdered and their murderers perform a farce of truth for the state in order to save themselves from justice. This "fiction" continues "reality," because the first pogrom in Argentina was carried out during the Tragic Week of 1919, with one death (and without state justice); Pedro Wald, an editor of the Yiddish newspaper *Di Presse,* was accused of planning to become president of the nation "following the triumph of the Soviet-maximalist conspiracy" (*Breviario de una infamia,* Cuaderno 1 [Comité de Lucha Contra el Racismo y demás formas del Colonialismo, 1975], 10).

Boleslao Lewin, *Cómo fue la inmigración judía a la Argentina* (Buenos Aires: Plus Ultra, 1971), describes the violent attacks during the Tragic Week of January 1919, which was set off by a strike at the workshops of Pedro Vasena. At that moment, Lewin says, the Jew became disliked because of his Russian citizenship and because of the widespread belief, in the wake of the Radovitzky trial, that Jews were involved in all "subversive" campaigns. (In 1909 the Jewish anarchist Simón Radovitsky assassinated the chief of police, Colonel Falcón.) Lewin says that "despite the efforts of some opportunist Israelite sectors to silence the fact," the Tragic Week brought the death of León Futaievsky, a member of the Jewish socialist organization *Avangard:*

it is also contrary to the truth to deny—as some gentiles and Jews have done— that one of the sad facets of the Week was *the pogrom that lasted from Thursday, January 9 through Tuesday, January 14. Its toll was more than 150 seriously wounded,* hundreds battered and considerable material losses. Neighborhoods inhabited by Jews became the target of punitive expeditions by all sorts of would-be patriots who, besides committing all manner of physical outrages, repeated *the feat of the Centenary year,* burning the books of the Jewish workers' libraries located at Calle Ecuador 359 (*Avangard*) and Ecuador 645 (*Poalei Sión*).

Lewin indicates that *the aggressors were never identified and the victims never indemnified* (171–74; italics added).

What Lewin calls "the feat of the Centenary year" was the first attack, in 1910. See Juan José Sebreli's account of raids by upper-class youths affiliated with Baron De Marchi's Sociedad Sportiva Argentina, previously cited in chapter 3, note 34. We recall that Baron De Marchi and his gangs featured prominently in "The Moreiras" in 1912, in the famous party that the Baron organized at the Palais de Glace, with the objective of convincing *porteño* society to embrace tango.

•

6. There are no indications in the text that the surname Zunz might be Jewish, although Borges plays constantly with *two names* and with the variants between Jewish and German names and surnames: Fain or Fein, Manuel Maier or Emanuel Zunz, Elsa Urstein or the two Kronfusses.

There are no indications but neither is there room for doubt, since a famous Jew named Leopold Zunz figures in the *Encyclopedia Judaica*, vol. 16, *Supplementary Entries* (Jerusalem: Keter Publishing House, 1972), 1235–40. "ZUNZ, LEOPOLD (Yom Tov Lippmann: 1794–1886), historian, among the founders of the "Science of Judaism" (Wissenschaft des Judentums). . . . From 1815–1819 he studied at the University of Berlin and acquired the basis of a scientific approach; he was particularly influenced by the great classical scholar Friedrich August Wolf. . . . he was commissioned by the community [in 1836] to write a treatise on Jewish names as a response to a royal decree banning the use of Christian names by Jews (*Namen der Juden* [1837])" (1236–37).

•

7. The motive is "real," for Bromberg was Barsut's "murderer" in a second order fiction, or a "simulation in fiction," which is "The Wink" of the final chapter of *Los locos.* He believes him because he knows him firsthand as a "criminal simulator."

•

8. A story told by Baudelaire (the starting point of "literary modernity") in "Counterfeit Money" in 1869 ("La fausse monnaie" in *Spleen de Paris: Petits poèmes en prose*) and which Jacques Derrida read as "fiction" in *Given Time: I. Counterfeit Money,* trans. Peggy Kamuf (Chicago: University of Chicago Press, 1992).

In Baudelaire's text the Jew does not appear but rather the beggar, who is another pure incarnation of sign-money and thus of the crimes of truth (and it is possible that the beggar might be another of our guides in the world of crimes of truth). Beginning with "counterfeit money" given to the beggar in Baudelaire's story, Derrida defines falsification as *fiction itself* and introduces the category of literary convention. "Counterfeit Money" is "like" fiction itself because it seems to share with it a trait (passing something off as "truth"), but it is not the same, Derrida says, because convention allows us to know that this is a fiction (93–94). I would say: the crime of truth-falsification-fiction marks the point at which literature and politics meet and separate absolutely in this modern tradition, because the crime of truth is illegitimate in the field of the state, and legitimate in the field of literature, which it may even define.

But in the purely monetary context of Derrida's essay about "the fiction" of the falsification perpetrated on the beggar, Jews suddenly appear *in two footnotes,* first in connection with writing and money through Leon Bloy, and then directly in connection with the library and with Baudelaire's plan for extermination. Let's look at the latter note.

Derrida refers to Baudelaire's anti-Belgian racism and quotes a sequence from *Mon Coeur mis à nu:* "A nice conspiracy to organize for the extermination of the Jewish race. Jews, *Librarians* and witnesses to the *Redemption*" (130 n. 14). Derrida adds that Walter Benjamin "is ready to see in this passage a 'gauloiserie' or prank," observing that "Céline continued in this direction." Derrida concludes that Baudelaire's idea of Extermination "was not so new in Europe. Nor was it the sole property of Nazi Germany" (131). *But he does not relate it* to the metaphor of fiction as falsification.

To put it another way: Derrida does not read the relation between "modernity," "fiction" as a crime of truth and legitimacy, and "Judaism," but he contains it in his book. He involuntarily demonstrates that the metaphor of falsification that allows us to think about certain fiction, the capitalist theory of Baudelaire's fiction, includes Judaism as a fundamental element (whether it is known or not, and whether one is for or against). It either includes it, or "Judaism" is a parallel apparatus, a pair with which it coincides as narration and falsification.

•

9. Other texts written by Borges in the 1940s with names in the title, beside "Pierre Menard," show crimes of truth (false accusations, false identities or names, fraudulent pacts or false oaths, and in the field of writing, plagiarism, and pseudo-epigraphism): "La busca de Averroes" (Averroës's search), "Abenjacán el Bojarí, muerto en su laberinto" (Ibn-Hakam al-Bohkari, murdered in his labyrinth), "La forma de la espada" (The shape of the sword) (which is the translation of the name "Moon" written on the face of the informer and betraying him), "Funes el mem-

orioso" (Funes, his memory), "Examen de la obra de Herbert Quain" (A survey of the works of Herbert Quinn), "Biografía de Tadeo Isidoro Cruz (1829–1874)" (A biography of Tadeo Isidoro Cruz [1829–1874]), and "Emma Zunz." This last story is the only one with a female name, that of a factory worker (apart from "La viuda Ching, pirata" [The widow Ching, pirate] in *Historia universal de la infamia,* which is the matrix text of verbal crimes). Borges's stories with names in the titles revolve around crimes of truth and legitimacy, and they are political or include some political reference. And their politics are also ambivalent. They include other oral or written foreign languages and verbal crimes such as false names, false accusations, and fraudulent pacts that sustain and accompany the fiction. All of them combine chronicle and confession, narrative discourses of truth (as in *Los locos-Los monstruos*).

Other Borges texts with Jews and truths: "La muerte y la brújula" (Death and the compass), "El milagro secreto" (The secret miracle), "Deutsches Requiem," "La fiesta del monstruo" (The feast of the monster), "Guayaquil," "El indigno" (Unworthy). And in Arlt's case: *El juguete rabioso.*

Juan José Sebreli begins *La cuestión judía en la Argentina* with a chronology of the Argentine Jewish community from 1856 to 1967. In 1937 he registers the following: "July: Initial declaration of the Committee Against Racism and Anti-Semitism in Argentina. Jorge Luis Borges serves as a member of the Committee's Governing Council."

•

10. Umberto Eco, "Fakes and Forgeries," *VS.* 46 (1987): 3–30, says that "two supposedly different things are discovered to be the same if they succeed in occupying at the same moment the same portion of space" (5). He refers to Ian Haywood, *Faking It: Art and the Politics of Forgery* (New York: Saint Martin's Press, 1987), and says: "we normally speak of forgeries when something present is displayed as if it were the original, while the original (if any) is elsewhere." For Eco, the definition of forgery raises problems involving "several current philosophical and semiotical notions, for example, originality and authenticity, as well as about the very concepts of identity and difference" (5). He then proceeds to define a forgery as "any object which is produced—or, once produced, used or displayed—with the intention of making someone believe that it is indiscernibly identical with another unique object" (8). "Something is not a fake," he adds, "because of its internal properties but by virtue of a *claim of identity.* Thus forgeries are first of all a *pragmatic* problem" (9). The conditions Eco proposes as necessary for forgery are that an object be different, made by someone else in different circumstances, and that it be "indiscernibly identical" with the first object.

•

11. In *The Origins of Totalitarianism* (New York: Harcourt, Brace & World, 1966; first edition 1951), Hannah Arendt refers to the theory of Jews as scapegoats in times of crisis. "An ideology which has to persuade and mobilize people cannot choose its victim arbitrarily. In other words, if a patent forgery like the 'Protocols of the Elders of Zion' is believed by so many people that it can become the text of a whole political movement, the task of the historian is no longer to discover a forgery. Certainly it is not to invent explanations which dismiss the chief political and historical fact of the matter: that *the forgery is being believed.* This fact *is more important* than the (historically speaking, secondary) circumstance that it is a *falsification*" (7; italics added).

According to Meir Waintrater, "Le mauvais juif de Sion: Antisionisme en anti-Semitisme: les fortunes d'un concepte," *Histoire de l'Antisémitisme, 1945–1993,* ed. Léon Poliakov (Paris: Seuil, 1994), 19–32, the "Protocols" were "pure fantasy" elaborated on a basis of literary plagiarism and police provocation (*exactly like "Pierre Menard," I would add*). Not only was there no conspiracy: the assembly of elders never existed beyond the imagination of the *Czarist officials who published the pamphlet.* But Waintrater adds: "It's not by chance that the first readers of the "Protocols" *confused the secret meeting of the Jews with the first Zionist congress which had met in Basel in 1897.* (They put it in another place and time, and with other protagonists: they put it in the mode of the "crime of truth," *I would add,* so that it would be believed.) In both cases, Waintrater continues, the evocation of Jews is associated with *somber ghosts of domination.* And he adds: the recurring myth of the Zionist conspiracy is sustained by the same sources as that strange superstition which led the *Times* and Henry Ford (*in the 1920s United States, I would add*) to believe, at least for a while, in the authenticity of the "Protocols" (22).

With regard to Argentine falsifications, let's look for now only at a certain Nazi propaganda text that appeared in 1946, following the military defeat of Nazism. It is titled *Un judío contesta a tres argentinos* (A Jew answers three Argentines), and it is published by a certain "Liga argentina por los derechos del hombre no judío" (Argentine League for the Rights of the Non-Jew) and dated *Jüdische Wochenschau,* 2 April 1946. It is thirty pages long.

This is the period in which "Emma Zunz" was written, and here again, of course, we find the "story" told to justice following the murder of the Jews. The frame of the pamphlet is narrative: Roberto, the director of a banking firm, recounts that many years earlier "we formed a circle of four friends: Marcelo, an engineer, Raúl, a physician, Mauricio, a merchant, and myself." They agreed about everything, but on the occasion of the Allied victory, a break in relations occurred because the only one who reacted with enthusiasm was the merchant Mauricio, who "speaks" as follows: "we Jews are the ones that have won the war, and our victory is so decisive that it will lead to our absolute dominion over all the peoples of the earth!" (4).

But the "Jew" not only "speaks" to the three Argentines, but also sends them a letter a few days later, dated July 1945. So a "Jew" "writes," because the text of the letter (whose "quotation" makes up almost the entire pamphlet) contains all the elements of our "stories of truth and stories of Jews," from *the conspiracy and the plan* (it says that the "Protocols" are in effect our "Magna Carta," and it relates the plan to dominate and "devour all the peoples of the world") to the *mechanical reproduction* of the letter.

But what interests us today is the moment at which this Jew places the truth "in crime" (and is believed, he says) when he refers to the Holocaust. What interests us is what the Jew says following the murder of the Jews, his "story."

> In the meanwhile we raised a ruckus about the *supposed atrocities of the German Nazis*. How convenient for us that terrible epidemic of dysentery and typhus at Buchenwald! How we've been able to profit from that phenomenon, only too common in long wars. . . . Today we've transformed that concentration camp for dysentery and typhoid patients into a killing field for several million human beings, and people *again have believed us*. . . . And then there are the mass graves of the hundreds of thousands of dead from the aerial attacks who didn't even fit into the emergency graves, and therefore had to be burned using *flamethrowers,* etcetera.
>
> The greatest enemies of Nazism have returned safe and sound from the concentration camps, for example: the ex-chancellor of Austria, Schuschnigg, then Thälmann, leader of the German communist party, the Protestant bishop Niemoeller, who fought the Nazis so much from the pulpit of his church, and even Leon Blum himself, a Jew and ex-premier of France. It's hard to believe that the Nazis would have killed much less important enemies when they didn't even kill these, their greatest foes.
>
> Nor have they killed or harassed my countrymen, the Jews, merely withdrawing their freedom of action, thus obliging them to leave the country. (23; italics added)

The reading of this "outrage," as the bank director puts it, is followed by a moment of comprehension, and the physician Raúl concludes: "Now I understand everything. They have made us see the Nazi ghost in order to get us hooked and to take away the last shred of independence and national sovereignty we possess" (28). They *print* the "believed" letter of the "Jew," they *renounce* friendship with all "Jews," and they *exhort* everyone to do the same, since "Jews" obey "infernal and subversive foreign regimes."

•

12. My hypothesis of the pairs is that the "modern" correlation (between the

twenties and forties) of "truth" (of the philosophy and aesthetics of truth) with "Jews" is seen clearly if read from the perspective of crime. From the perspective of crime, the pairing of "truth" and "Jews" functioned as a literary story and as a definition of fiction. It also functioned in European philosophy in the twenties and forties, when the questioning of truth appeared as a definition of "thought" or of the philosophy of modernity. And it functioned, again, "in pairs" or "in couples" with the murder of Jews in "reality."

But let's see what happens with poetry. According to Anthony Julius, *T. S. Eliot, Anti-Semitism, and Literary Form* (Cambridge: Cambridge University Press, 1995), what we must examine in regard to Eliot's anti-Semitism (which was in the air in the twenties) are the connections between modernism and anti-Semitism: "what can the history of an infamy have to do with the examination of a major twentieth-century literary movement?" he asks, before responding that these cannot be connections of perspective: "Approaching anti-Semitism from the perspective of Modernism risks trivializing the horror in contemporary Jewish history. Interpreting Modernism from the perspective of anti-Semitism seems both perverse and reductive" (38).

The problem, for Julius, is the idea of "poetic truth," which he explains as

> the belief that while poetry has a different and less direct relation with the world than prose, it is also superior to prose. This is so because while poetry does not make statements about the world, it discloses essential truths about it (or, in the deconstructionist version, about language). . . . These ideas underlie the tenets of both Symbolism, which provided the context for the composition of Eliot's poetry, and the New Criticism, which provided (and to an extent, continues to provide) the context for its reception and study. . . . Eliot wrote out of Symbolism for New Criticism, which "populariz[ed] . . . the modernist idea of literature" and was itself "anchored in non-purposive Kantian-symbolist aesthetics. . . ." The aesthetics of these schools of poetry and criticism did not emerge fresh from a theoretical void. They were related to older views about the constitutive properties of poetry, and of literature in general. (75–76)

Symbolist poetry became the model for all poetry, as distinct from prose (and this is evident in Sartre, Julius says), and it represents the revelation that words can have meanings without having definite referents (97).

Julius asserts that "poetry can be prepositional. . . . Literary works may specifically be written to dramatize and empower a set of beliefs" (76–77). Eliot's poem "Sweeney among the Nightingales," for example, plays with the notion of Jewish conspiracy. "It is an anti-Semitic, Modernist work of considerable complexity and interest. The anti-Semitism and the Modernism go together. Introducing the notion of a narrator entails the misreading of the poem as a puzzle concealing an answer signaled by clues. With ingenuity the answer will be discovered. This misses the point of the poem, which is precisely that there is no answer" (86). Julius continues: "one might suppose that its esoterities, its intangibilities, and its rarefied and personal visions, would make it invulnerable to the conformist vulgarities of anti-Semitism. . . . Too generative of ambiguity, designed to be read with too heightened a sense of nuance, and of the plurality of meanings, surely (someone might insist) poetry demands to be set apart from the flat statements of the bigot?" (92).

Julius acknowledges "the Symbolist possibilities of anti-Semitism, and the anti-Semitic possibilities of Symbolism" but argues that "while Eliot's poetry is Symbolist, and its anti-Semitism is of this kind, the anti-Semitism also represents a crisis in its Symbolism. Anti-Semitism marks the site of the poet's struggle against the non-representation of his poetry" (94). Eliot wrote in 1946 that his own poetry "would hardly be conceivable" without *the tradition that starts with Baudelaire, and culminates in Paul Valéry* (94; italics added). It is a tradition that emphasizes poetry's relation with music, rather than with referential meaning (95). Julius insists that Eliot's anti-Semitism "is evidence of a Symbolism in crisis. . . . The intuitive has become the programmatic, and the vague and suggestive, a fantasy of half-glimpsed conspiracies" (108). Julius summarizes his take as follows:

> It is easy to characterize anti-Semitic discourse in Symbolist terms. Anti-Semitism blurs the distinction between the real world and an imaginary one. It too, when covert, may be vague and suggestive. Like Symbolism, anti-Semitism also posits arrangements that do not correspond to any that obtain in the real world. And while none of this should be taken as contending either that anti-Semitism is inadvertently Symbolist, or that Symbolism is potentially anti-Semitic, there is sufficient congruence between the two to make for the possibility of anti-Semitic, Symbolist poetry. This is a possibility that distinctions between the literary and the non-literary, the fictional and the mythic, cannot frustrate. (96)

VI. Stories of Jews

1. We might well write, like Jean-François Lyotard, *Heidegger and "the jews,"* trans. Andreas Michel and Mark Roberts (Minneapolis: University of Minnesota Press, 1990), in the plural, in lowercase letters, and in quotation marks. Lyotard refers to "the jews" as a place of margin, of exclusion, of radical alterity, obliged to the memory of what cannot be represented. Michel Onfray, *Politique du rebelle:*

Traité de résistance et d'insoumission (Paris: Grasset, 1997), discusses that position which denies the possibility of representation of the horror of Auschwitz. He takes as his point of departure Primo Levi's antepenultimate work preceding his suicide, titled "Buco nero di Auschwitz," which appeared in *Stampa* on 22 January 1986. In order not to close the *black hole*, Onfray says, one must deny Adorno's theses to the effect that the horror was such that it would not be possible, either in the field of thought or in that of writing, to make the tragedy an object of reflection or a moment susceptible to being overcome. In order to do so, one must critique two positions, the "negative theology" and the "theodicy" proceeding from an evil God. The first upholds the impossibility of saying, the ineffable and unspeakable, the impotence of language, and the limits of reason inasmuch as the enterprise of destruction would surpass understanding. Onfray says that "those glossers" who recycle the Hegelian thesis of the "ends," instead of falling silent, publish long obscure pages in order to explain the uselessness of words and the limits of language. The contrary proof is found in the texts of Primo Levi, Jean Améry, David Rousset, or Jorge Semprún, and in Claude Lanzmann's film *Shoah*. The second position is that of "radical evil": a sort of neo-Leibnizian view of Nazisim with variations on horror, hell, monstrosity, and atrocity. *Neither of the two draws on the experience in order to rethink politics in a new way,* Onfray says, and this is the opening of his *Treatise* whose first chapter is titled "On Genesis: To Fill the Black Hole with Memory."

•

2. According to George Simmel, *The Philosophy of Money*, trans. Tom Bottomore and David Frisby, 2d ed. (London: Routledge, 1990), money is the symbol of modernity, the symbol of the dynamic character of the world, the vehicle of a perpetual movement. But at the same time it can embody its opposite because it represents not only a simple economic value, but also abstract economic value in general. Money is the most ephemeral and at the same time the most stable of substances. It symbolizes movement and exchange, and it is "the spider that weaves the social web." Money "represents interaction in its purest form"; it makes the most abstract concept comprehensible; it is an individual thing whose essential significance lies in the transcendence of individualities. . . . Money is the expression of the unity of diverse elements, the "integrating force that upholds and permeates each element"; "it connects all singularities and, thus, creates reality" (ellipses in original).

With regard to Jews, Simmel comments as follows:

the Jews are the best example of the correlation between the central role of money interests and social deprivation. I only want to mention two viewpoints as particularly important for the basic significance of money. Because the wealth of the Jews consisted of money, they became a particularly sought-after and profitable object of exploitation, for no other possessions can be expropriated as easily, simply and without loss. . . . The same specific character of money as lacking in any specific determinacy which made it the most suitable and the least refusable source of income for the Jews in their position as pariahs, also made it the most convenient and direct incentive for exploiting them. . . . The relationship of Jews to money in general is more evident in a sociological constellation that gives expression to that character of money. The role that the stranger plays within the social group directs him, from the outset, towards relations within the group that are mediated by money. . . . The relation between the nature of money and the stranger is already noticeable among some primitive people. . . . The stranger as a person is predominantly interested in money for the same reason that makes money so valuable to the socially deprived: namely, because it provides chances for him that are open to fully entitled persons or to the indigenous people by specific concrete channels and by personal relationships. . . . There is another connection between the sociological importance of the stranger and of money. . . . For good reason, the trader is usually a stranger at the beginning of economic development. . . . The decisiveness of this relationship is demonstrated by its reversibility: not only is the trader a stranger, but the stranger is also disposed to become a trader. This becomes evident as soon as the stranger is not only temporarily present in the society but settles and looks for permanent support within the group. Thus, the citizens in Plato's *Laws* are prohibited from owning gold and silver, and all trade and manufacturing is specifically reserved for strangers. The fact that the Jews became a trading people is due not only to their suppression but also to their dispersal throughout all countries. The Jews became familiar with money business only during the last Babylonian exile, prior to which time it was unknown to them. This is emphasized by the fact that it was particularly the Jews of the Diaspora who followed this profession in large numbers. . . . The fact that the Jew was a stranger who was not organically connected with his economic group directed him to trade and its sublimation in pure monetary transactions. . . . It was of particular importance that the Jew was a stranger not only with regard to the local people, but also with regard to religion. Since the medieval ban on taking interest was therefore not valid for him, he became the recognized person for money lending. The high interest rate charged by Jews was the result of their being excluded from land ownership: mortgages on landed property were never safe for them, and so they always feared that a higher authority would declare their claims null and void. [Simmel here gives several examples of such annulments in the fourteenth century.] The stranger needs a higher risk premium for his enterprises and loans. This connection is not only valid for the Jews, but is deeply rooted in the essence of trade and of money. . . .

The financial importance of some Florentine families during the Medici period was based on the fact that they were banished by the Medici or deprived of their political power. In order to regain strength and importance, they were dependent on financial transactions, since they could not pursue any other business away from home. (223–26)

For a comparative analysis of modernity and money in Simmel, Kracauer, and Benjamin, see David Frisby, *Fragments of Modernity* (Cambridge, Mass.: MIT Press, 1986).

•

3. In *The Origins of Totalitarianism*, Hannah Arendt says that modern anti-Semitism must be understood in the more general frame of the development of the nation-state, and that its source must be sought in certain aspects of Jewish history and specifically in Jewish functions in recent centuries. She says that in Europe, "beginning with the late seventeenth century, an unprecedented need arose for state credit and a new expansion of the state's sphere of economic and business interest. . . . It was only natural that the Jews, with their age-old experience as money-lenders and their connections with European nobility . . . would be called upon for help; it was clearly in the interest of the new state business to grant the Jews certain privileges and to treat them as a separate group" (11). Thus, in the seventeenth and eighteenth centuries, Jews "financed state affairs and handled the financial transactions of their princes" (14). "In contrast to all other groups," Arendt argues, "the Jews were defined and their position determined by the body politic. . . . Their social inequality was quite different from the inequality of the class system; it was again mainly the result of *their relationship to the state*" (14; italics added).

Following the French Revolution, privileges were granted not only to court Jews, but also "to the larger wealthy class, which had managed to settle in the more important urban and financial centers in the eighteenth century," but Arendt explains that

this period came to an end with the rise of imperialism at the end of the nineteenth century when capitalist business in the form of expansion could no longer be carried out without active political help and intervention by the state. Imperialism, on the other hand, undermined the very foundations of the nation-state and introduced into the European comity of nations the competitive spirit of business concerns. In the early decades of this development, Jews lost their exclusive position in state business to imperialistically minded businessmen. . . . As a group, Western Jewry disintegrated together with the nation-state during the decades preceding the outbreak of the first World War. The rapid decline of Europe after the war found them already deprived of their former power, atomized into a herd of wealthy individuals. In an imperialist age, Jewish wealth had become insignificant . . . *the non-national, inter-European Jewish element became an object of universal hatred because of its useless wealth, and of contempt because of its lack of power.* (15; italics added)

Arendt says that early German anti-Semitic parties attacked the Jews as "the secret power behind governments" as a means of openly attacking the state itself (39). But as a political movement, she adds, "nineteenth-century anti-Semitism can be studied best in France, where for almost a decade it dominated the political scene" (42). Arendt attributes the French socialist movement's opposition to anti-Semitism in the Dreyfus Affair principally to strong clerical support of it. "Until then, however, nineteenth-century French leftist movements had been outspoken in their antipathy to the Jews," following the Enlightenment tradition of identifying Jews as capitalists and as financial agents of the aristocracy (47). In a footnote, Arendt places the Utopian socialist Charles Fourier in this tradition (48).

Michel Foucault likewise acknowledges the racism of nineteenth-century socialism, evident in Fourier and the anarchists, and he says that prior to the Dreyfus case, socialists were racists because they had not discussed the mechanisms of biopower (*Genealogía del racismo,* trans. Alfredo Tzveibel [Buenos Aires-Montevideo: Altamira-Nordam Comunidad, 1993]).

Bryan Cheyette, *Constructions of "the Jew" in English Literature and Society: Racial Representations, 1875–1945* (Cambridge: Cambridge University Press, 1993), analyzes constructions of "the Jew" in the English liberal tradition from Matthew Arnold and George Eliot, through George Bernard Shaw, H. G. Wells, and G. K. Chesterton, to James Joyce and T. S. Eliot. In his introductory chapter, he says that the indeterminacy of Semitic representations

meant that "the Jew" can be constructed to represent both sides of a political or social or ideological divide [. . .] Jews are represented as *both* the embodiment of liberal progress *and* as the vestiges of an outdated medievalism; as a bastion of empire *and* one of the main threats to empire; as prefiguring a socialist world state *and* as a key force preventing its development; as the ideal economic man *and* the degenerate plutocrat *par excellence.* [. . .] To some extent, this doubleness points to a received Christological discourse which has constructed Jews as *both* "a deicide nation [*and*] also a nation . . . on whose redemption the fate of mankind hangs." (9; ellipses in original)

Cheyette adds:

While the historicizing of the semitic discourse under consideration avoids the essentialism that may be associated with the eternally "mythic" construction of "the

Jew," it should be stressed that it is as subjects of a "discourse" and not as historical subjects that "Jews" are situated in the literary texts under consideration . . . it is the very slipperiness and indeterminacy of "the Jew"—as constructed within a semitic discourse—that enables an uncertain literary text to explore the limits of its own foundations. . . . "The Jew," like all "doubles," is inherently ambivalent and can represent both the "best" and the "worst" of selves. Unlike marginalized "colonial subjects" who were, for the most part, confined racially to the "colonies" in the late nineteenth century, Jews were, simultaneously, at the center of European metropolitan society and, at the same time, banished from its privileged sphere by a semitic discourse. It is the proximity of Jews within the European imperial orbit that made them *both* a powerful "self" and a powerless "other," a key touchstone for the racial boundaries of European "culture" and the "Englishness" of modern English literature. (11–12)

•

4. In "'I'm Down on Whores': Race and Gender in Victorian London," Sander L. Gilman wrote about Jack the Ripper as a caricature of the Eastern Jew (*Anatomy of Racism,* ed. David Theo Goldberg [Minneapolis: University of Minnesota Press, 1990], 146–70).

The perversion of the Jew . . . lies in his sexualized relationship to capital. This, of course, echoes the oldest and most basic calumny against the Jew, his avarice, an avarice for the possession of "things," of "money," which signals his inability to understand (and produce) anything of transcended aesthetic value. . . . the image of the Jew as prostitute is not merely that of the economic parallel between the sexuality of the Jew and that of the prostitute. For that relationship also reveals the nature of the sexuality of both the Jew and prostitute as diseased, as polluting. . . . For the Jew was also [allegedly] closely related to the spread and incidence of syphilis. . . . The Jews were the carriers of sexually transmitted diseases and transmitted them to the rest of the world. This view is to be found in Hitler's discussion of syphilis in *Mein Kampf.* . . . The hidden source of the disease of the body politic is the Jew and his tool is the whore. (163–64)

"The anthology" would also have notes, for example:

Notes to La Bolsa

Juan José Sebreli ("La cuestión judía") says that "Argentine anti-Semitism had its *historical origin in liberalism,* which is to say, it is present in the very roots of the capitalist and bourgeois organization of the country. All classic Argentine literature is impregnated with a profound racism, the white race is contrasted to the Indians, the blacks, the mestizos and the mulattos" (224). He adds that racism is equally prevalent among nationalist aristocrats and liberals. Sebreli quotes the writer Silvina Bullrich: "Those who, like me, descend from various generations of nation builders, can only look with disdain and pity on those who have neither homeland nor race, who answer to nothing and no one, and end up justifying [the violent anti-Semitic and ultranationalist group] Tacuara" (225).

Sebreli says that *La Bolsa*, in which Jewish financiers are held responsible for the country's economic crisis, is not an isolated occurrence of anti-Semitism in the newspaper *La Nación*. Between 1886 and 1893, the newspaper published a series of articles *opposing Jewish agricultural colonization*, and expressing, undoubtedly, Bartolomé Mitre's opinion on the subject. Other articles expressing contempt for the Jews are found in Sarmiento's newspaper *El Nacional* (Sebreli, 227–28).

In the introduction to *Anti-Semitism in Times of Crisis* (New York: New York University Press, 1991), coeditors Sander L. Gilman and Steven T. Katz write that the image of the Jews, from the Middle Ages on, is not merely a religious one, but also that of a political enemy (14). Throughout the Christian era, Jews have been "Europe's ultimate other," and the secularization of Christian models of the Jew in the eighteenth and nineteenth centuries transposed the "medieval" religious tradition into the "'racial' or 'scientific' anti-Semitism of the late nineteenth century" (1–2). Gilman and Katz conclude by generalizing as follows regarding the studies included in their volume: "The periods examined are all periods of 'stress,' of disequilibrium, where the function of categories of difference seems a necessity in preserving the boundaries of the world in which there is a sense of imminent dissolution. The source of such fears must be located somewhere. In the West, the traditional locus of these fears has been the Jews. . . . The Jews are the 'natural' locus for the origin of all senses of dissolution" (14–15).

In another passage from *Jewish Self-Hatred*, Gilman writes:

> Walter Rathenau stressed the feminine nature of the Jew in his 1897 essay. The relationship between the *feminine physique*, which he ascribed to the Jewish male, and the Jew's discourse, with its feminine attributes, *stands in a long tradition of perceiving the discourse of the woman as different and thus in many ways related to that of the Jew.* . . . Women and Jews misuse language. They both lie. They are both identified by the false, manipulative tone of their discourse.
>
> The linkage of misogyny and anti-Semitism during the latter half of the nineteenth century is not random. For as both Jews and women become more visible on the horizon of European consciousness through their articulated demands for emancipation, both legal and cultural, a natural association takes place. (243–44; italics added)

Gilman says that the question of the language of the Jews is constantly present in the Enlightenment. It takes various forms, but all of them return to the issue of the changing nature (and therefore the unreliability) of the language of the Jews. The idea that *Jews lie,* even under oath before a Christian court, that it is in their nature to deceive, is reflected in the legal practices of that era (106–7). In what Gilman calls the "first German attempt to present the Jews in a positive light," Gotthold Ephraim Lessing's 1749 drama *The Jews,* the author *suppresses* the Yiddish accent and Yiddish itself in the speech of the main character, a "traveler" Jew, in order to present him as an individual possessing "all of the virtues of Western civilization" (82).

The shift from the rhetoric of religion to the rhetoric of race introduces the question of the language of the Jews at the very center of scientific discourse at the end of the nineteenth century. All sciences insist on biological determinism or on the biological model to explain the nature of human difference: language became "a reflex of human biology." Thus, Gilman says, "it makes the special language of the Other a sign of the innate, biological difference inherent in the very concept of race" (213). Science also "discovers" *the racial incapacity of the Jews to belong to the nation* in which they live.

Gilman concludes that "the roots of the image of the Jew as mad, as possessing a damaged discourse, are to be found in the pseudoscience of nineteenth- and early twentieth-century racist biology" (361).

Notes to Los simuladores de talento

The first madmen and simulators in Argentine literature appear after 1880 in the physics exams (in the scene of the truth of science) "like" Jews, metaphorical Jews:

Genaro Piazza, son of a Neapolitan tinker and the first simulator in Argentine literature, is about to steal a numbered ball for his high school physics exam, and he examines the urn with "a Jew's avaricious eye" (Eugenio Cambaceres, *En la sangre,* 1887).

And the "magnet fellow," the madman in Manuel T. Podestá's *Irresponsable: Recuerdos de la universidad* (1889), is compared, also in relation to a physics exam, with "a wandering Jew of the University, a pariah."

Jorge Salessi, *Médicos, maleantes y maricas,* refers to the identification between the Jew and the homosexual in Ramos Mejía's *Los simuladores de talento,* and he adds: "George Mosse, in *Nationalism and Sexuality,* a key book for studies of the relation between notions of state and sexualities, pointed out that in the European cultural imagination of the late nineteenth century, *the conspiracy* of homosexuals ran parallel to the universal Jewish conspiracy; both Jews and homosexuals were considered 'a state within a state'" (244; italics added).

Salessi also indicates that Ramos Mejía's anti-Semitism became state policy when he was employed by the hygienist bureaucracy between 1892 and 1898, and in the educational bureaucracy between 1908 and 1912, at the same moment at which nationalists attacked the Jewish schools of the agricultural colonies in Entre Ríos.

In 1895, when Ramos Mejía was president of the National Council of Hygiene, he undertook persecution of the Jewish colonies then represented as hotbeds of insalubrity. "During Ramos Mejía's presidency in the Department, Jewish immigrants were blamed for the importation of typhus," says Salessi, and "the Jewish immigrants comprised the only cultural group systematically obliged to pass through disinfection." Obligatory disinfections and quarantines were enforced on the island of Martín García (247–48).

Jewish immigration "threatened the interests of the hegemonic groups," Salessi says, and he sketches an economic theory of liberal anti-Semitism, based on the work of Manuel Bejarano published in Los fragmentos de poder, ed. Torcuato Di Tella and Tulio Halperín Donghi (Buenos Aires: Jorge Álvarez, 1969). Salessi suggests that "Argentine anti-Semitism, alternately denied or debated, but always latent and quick to reappear (especially during military dictatorships), has one of its roots in the history of the Argentine latifundio, or landed estate." Agricultural exploitation was subordinated to livestock exploitation, with the exception of a few colonies such as those founded by Baron Hirsch's Jewish Colonization Association. The estate owners feared competition from the Jewish colonies, populated by immigrants who in time could become owners of parcels of land. "Unlike the urban immigrant, the Jewish immigrant colonists represented a foreign invasion in the zone that embodied the economic and symbolic power of the patrician landowning class" (245–46).

So far, Salessi. Let us add that in contrast to Ramos Mejía and his simulator-usurer-Jews in "La fauna de la miseria," his disciple José Ingenieros politicizes the situation: for Ingenieros, both anti-Semitism and nationalism are "political simulations." In the second chapter of the second part of La simulación en la lucha por la vida, Ingenieros identifies as simulation a great deal of propaganda tending to present certain international conflicts over obvious economic interests as racial struggles. Anti-Semitism is another curious instance of simulation in the struggle between races: "as time demonstrated, supposed French anti-Semitism was a mask of clerical-military reaction, which disguised itself in France with the clothing of a war on Judaism in order to enlist the popular masses in this deceit, exploiting the sentiment of hatred toward the rich" (49–50).

He also considers nationalism a simulation: "'Nationalism' is a morbid collective form of patriotism, it is in many cases a simulation by deft and ambitious politi-   .
cians who know how to operate the levers of popularity by exciting the most backward passions of the mob" (51).

For Ingenieros, simulation is *a mass category linked with a certain degree of social evolution.* He refers to professional politicians as simulators *par excellence:* "Only one caste challenges politicians at the apex of simulation: *priests* of all faiths, ancient and modern." Priests are *"consummate pantomime actors"* (55).

Notes to El Kahal *and* Oro

Ramón Alcalde, "De judíos, dineros y Bolsas: Drumont, Bloy, Zola, Martel," *Estudios Críticos de poética y política* (Buenos Aires: Conjetural, 1996), 161–222, says that

> Gustavo Martínez Zuviría (Hugo Wast) had his own theological preoccupations (analogous to those of Gilder and Bloy), which he alleviated by reinserting himself into the anti-Semitic discourse of Martel and Drumont, already expanded by Branfman's *Gniga Kahal* (Book of the Kahal, 1870), August Rohling's *Der Talmudjude* (The Jew of the Talmud, 1871), and *The Protocols of the Elders of Zion* (1902), whose authenticity Wast ingenuously takes for granted. . . . One detail: *Oro* and *El Kahal* are from 1936, Gustavo Martínez Zuviría is Director of the Biblioteca Nacional, a sinecure received from Uriburu; Agustín P. Justo presides over the nation; Mussolini and Hitler have replaced Vittorio Emanuele III and Bismark, and Argentine Jews, who were only a handful in Martel's era, are now several hundred thousand. (163)

Alcalde refers to Jews in the literature of Shakespeare, Walter Scott, Balzac, Maupassant, and the Goncourt brothers, and he analyzes Edouard Drumont's *La France juive* along with Bloy and Zola's responses to it. He points out in Drumont's Jew what he calls "a residue, irreducible for Drumont's anthropology, a Plotinian Emanation of the Judaic One which perturbs all oppositions: the superhumanly beautiful *Jewess*. . . . Beautiful women who seduce and *kill* or inspire others to kill" (187–88).

Alcalde says that "for Zola and Bloy, the important thing is not the Jew as such but the Jew as mythical or real holder of money. *The function and/or the symbolism* of money, which is definitively what makes the Jew what he is, and not the other way around." But he also points out differences in perspective: "Zola seeks first the function and second the symbolism in the *contemporary historical and social world,* described and investigated without prior value judgements," and Alcalde cites Zola's *L'Argent:* "Money, neither attacking nor defending it. Without opposing our so-called century of money to the so-called centuries of honor (those of yesteryear). Showing that money has become for many dignity in life. . . . Then, the irresistible force of money. There is nothing but love and money" (193–94; ellipses in original). Bloy, on the other hand, writes *Salut par les Juifs* ("the only Catholic response to confessional and thus theological anti-Semitism, in which a large part of the French clergy is militantly involved"), taking interest only in the *symbolic statute* of money "within the sacred becoming of the manifestation of God in human temporality" (194). Bloy, Alcalde concludes after analyzing *Salvation,* "inaugurates a social-Catholic thought that, with all its vagaries and contradictions, perhaps contains ingredients for the overcoming of the reductive economicism which has done and continues to do so much damage to socialist political thought and action" (220).

•

Notes for the Final Part of "the Anthology" We Have "Transcribed"

5. In *El antisemitismo en la Argentina,* vol. 1 (Buenos Aires: Centro Editor de América Latina, 1986), Leonardo Senkman refers to the thirty-one-page *El caso Sirota y el problema judío en la Argentina* (Buenos Aires: Movimiento Nacionalista Tacuara, Secretaría de Prensa y Propaganda, 1962).

Senkman says that during the interim presidency of José María Guido (following the fall of Arturo Frondizi), anti-Semitism reached the highest point of a wave unleashed by the Eichmann trial of August 1960 (27). "The wave of anti-Semitic attacks registered since March 1962, reached their culmination with the kidnapping and tattooing (with a swastika) of the student Graciela Sirota" (33).

The reaction of the Jewish community and the official response to denunciations of anti-Semitism and its *impunity* offer material for the study of anti-Semitism. Senkman refers to vacillation on the part of the police in recognizing the racist nature of the attack, and he says:

Nothing is more illustrative than *the pamphlet published by the Movimiento Nacionalista Tacuara* titled *El caso Sirota y el problema judío en la Argentina,* 32 pages, October 1962, which was sold at kiosks. With statistics and quotations of dubious objectivity, it purported to present a historical, political, cultural and economic x-ray of Jews in Argentina. It attempted to show that from their origins, the Jews were *leftists,* first as workers and salaried employees, and later as intellectuals, but at the same time, it adduced that Jewish businessmen consolidated to constitute a solid *capitalist* nucleus. They also accused Jews of *double political citizenship* with the State of Israel and of submitting to a double executive, legislative and judicial power. Economically, the Jews were shown as a *"financial synarchy"* in league with the Frondizi government. The head of this absurd hydra was *two-faced, the Jews managed the country's finances and also its academic culture:* Banks for some and State University for others. It also attempted to show the supposed *responsibility of the Jewish collectivity for the economic crisis.* (28–29)

•

6. *El Plan Andinia o El nuevo estado judío* (Buenos Aires: Nuevo Orden, 1965) was a thirty-four-page pamphlet intended to destabilize the democratically elected government of the Radical President Arturo Illia, and it was printed *a year before the Onganía coup* of 1966. Its author was Walter Beveraggi Allende, according to the previously cited *Brevario de una infamia.*

Evelyne Kenig, "L'antisémitisme en Espagne et en Amérique latine," *Histoire de l'Antisémitisme, 1945–1993,* 165–95, says that in Argentina, where two-thirds of the continent's Jews are concentrated, and where anti-Semitism and Fascist or Nazi movements have a great deal of influence, the most violent moment was in the early 1960s, when Tacuara and other extreme-right groups launched attacks against well-known Jewish citizens and institutions. Nineteen sixty-four was the year in which most anti-Semitic episodes occurred, with 303 attacks. Between 1965 and 1972, the phenomenon disappeared almost entirely. In 1972, anti-Semitic violence took three forms: virulent articles in the right-wing or Arab press and in the Peronist newspaper *Las Bases,* under the signature of López Rega (the *"Astrologer"*), despite the apparent protests of Perón himself. An alleged "Jewish conspiracy" appeared and two bombs exploded in large synagogues at the moment at which a campaign of intimidation was being unleashed. Under the 1976 military regime, the term "Jew" became synonymous with "guerrilla," "extremist," and "communist" (182–84).

Raúl Barón Biza's anti-Semitic novel, *Todo estaba sucio,* appeared in Buenos Aires in 1963, denouncing not only Jews but also "modern women." Some quotations:

When Hitler dreamt of destroying that people which claimed to be descended from Abraham, citizen of Ur—a civilization which flourished between the Tigris and the Euphrates more than five thousand years ago—, he was unaware that following any persecution or massacre, it would reappear powerful and dominant by means of the gold it accumulated, in order to dominate masses of humanity millions of times greater than themselves.

History will vindicate Hitler, despite his military errors, for the sole reason that he attempted to free his homeland from those who bought and sold it in London and New York. (271)

And this:

> The Jew prides himself on the faithfulness of his women in comparison with those of other religions. His secret is circumcision. Obligatory as a sanitary measure in his grimy wandering through the desert, it renders the mucous membranes less sensitive, resulting in a prolongation of coitus. The rapid ejaculation of the un-circumcised leaves the female partner generally unsatisfied and predisposed her to hysteria and divorce. It is one of the wise laws of the Jewish people. The day will come when, as a sanitary measure, all boys will undergo compulsory circum-cision. Baptism in the Jewish manner. (274)

•

7. The magazine *El Caudillo* belonged to José López Rega, the "Astrologer," and one of its directors was Felipe Romeo, later of the RoCa publishing house that published General Ramón Camps, according to Horacio Verbitsky in "Diálogos con la muerte," *Página 12*, 31 August 1997.

Gabriel Ruiz de los Llanos, who "authorized" invasion of "the Barrio of Usury" in 1975, later published *El antisemita* (Buenos Aires: Editorial del Nuevo Amanecer, 1984), a first-person narration in which he repents of his past and tells his story: his father was an alcoholic, his mother supported the family and was in charge at home (and she had pretensions of distinction for her family, founded on certain "good" relations; curiously, this is also the case with Martel, the author of *La Bolsa*). The repentant or psychoanalyzed anti-Semite says that the first Nazi he met was his mother: "she my Nazi, I her Jew" (11). And, "The Jew is, for the anti-Semite, a criminal who, when not committing a crime, is planning something. Condemned without consideration as a being either worthy or unworthy of such condemna-tion, the Jew remains imprisoned in the anti-Semite perspective, no matter what he does" (22).

Coda
1938: Fifteen Minutes for Soiza Reilly

Our Virgil not only wrote about the Moreiras, celebrities, madmen, criminals, anarchists, beggars, and women. He also moved from his chair in history at the Dr. Antonio Bermejo Commercial School for women to the radio: he *inaugurated the radio talk show* in Argentina. He had a fifteen-minute slot in which he discussed problems current in the 1930s and 1940s, and, anticipating Andy Warhol, he was known for the phrase with which he concluded his program: "my fifteen minutes are up." The following are extracts from his chats (which can also figure as "education stories"), published in a seventeen-page booklet by "Columna" ("committed to examining a vital issue of our time") under the title *El judaísmo visto por ojos argentinos* (Judaism seen through Argentine eyes) (Buenos Aires: Columna, 25 January 1938).

I have preferred not to improvise on this theme: I have committed my opinions to paper.

There are many Argentines who have erroneous ideas about Judaism: there are many Creoles who do not yet know how Argentines should think about Jews. What's more, about 80% of the people in the world don't know how to think for themselves. Hence the success of newspaper editorials.

On a certain occasion I happened to hear insults directed at a certain person. I came to his defense because I am from Entre Ríos and in Entre Ríos you don't kick a gaucho when he's down. . . . But I was cut off with this crushing phrase:

"Yes, yes. But he's a Jew!"

I am not going to claim that Jews belong to an exceptional race. My honorable listeners would not permit any such servile flattery. But I will say that Jews are worth of all sympathy for two fundamental reasons:

As a man: I consider Jews my brothers because they belong to the human race.

As an Argentine: I consider them my compatriots, whether because they were born under the same sky or whether because, born in other regions of the earth, they give to my homeland the manly strength of their work, or the light of their science, or the tenacity of their race.

Let us examine some of the objections that are often made to Jews. In the first place, someone might say to me:

"You are talking about something that doesn't exist. In the Argentine Republic the Jewish question doesn't exist; there is no social problem. The Jews live, make money, prosper or suffer misery, under the protection of the common laws. . . ."

Just so. In our generous homeland, open like the magnificent portico of its Constitution, the racial problem of Judaism does not exist. The same laws that protect my existence as an intellectual laborer also protect the Jew and the Mohammedan, and the Buddhist and the English protestant and the Orthodox.

There exists no law of persecution . . . I know! But we cannot deny that there does exist a hidden, surreptitious, constant, secret persecution intended to deny Judaism its right to thrive . . . Why?

What Argentine reason can justify the intent to close the doors of our schools of higher learning to youths bearing Jewish names? If I were authorized to cite proper names, I would give that of an illustrious Argentine psychiatrist—a Creole of many generations—who in a certain Medical School waged a heroic polemic against the councilors when they proposed that, in the written entrance exam, they "flunk" all those with Hebrew surnames or first names reeking of the Old Testament . . .

Jews residing in all countries of the world are accused of a boundless love of money. And what are they to do? They know that if they were to find themselves in need of a bit of bread, their hands would be pushed away by the egoism of their accusers. Why have the Jews devoted themselves with particular preference since the Middle Ages to trading in money? Because ownership of property was denied them. . . . Those were savage times. But in maintaining, well into the twentieth century, the ideas of that period, does one not put himself on the level of those times? They are accused of being usurious lenders. What race is free of them?

A gaucho curse says: May you fall into the power of a Creole lending you money with interest! When a Creole takes up usury! . . .

To advocate that we Argentines persecute the Jews as some countries in Europe do is not only an attitude repugnant to our Argentinism. It is also dangerous and counterproductive. It is understandable that certain countries in the Old World should expel the Jews, as Germany does. Do they expel them because they are Jews? *They expel them in order to expropriate their goods,* in order to take control of the wealth they accumulated through centuries of patience and work . . .

Modern Machiavellianism knows that when a government wants to perpetuate itself in power, outside the law, it has two magical means of throwing sand into the eyes of the people: the Jewish menace or the threat of war with a neighboring country . . .

Let us recall what Mitre said to President Manuel Quintana when the latter wanted to shoot the ringleaders of a failed "revolution": "Doctor Quintana: don't create martyrs. Pardon their lives! Do not create martyrs, Doctor!"

So, this afternoon, I invoke the specters of the authors of the Constitution of '53: with my heart on the edge of my lips, I would say to all those who call for the persecution of Judaism:

Let us not create martyrs, sirs. Let us preserve the greatness of our homeland, sustained until now by the efforts of all the honorable races of the Earth. Only thus will we achieve, as the Preamble states, "the general well-being."

Only thus will hatred be able to cry out from beyond the grave:

"My fifteen minutes are up." . . .

Conclusion

1. This "program" was constructed on the basis of a mass of Argentine stories and novels dating from the beginning of the century through the present. Many have been "told" throughout the manual, but texts from other Latin American countries also form part of the "story of the very much read." What matters are

neither the titles nor the authors but rather the "story" that appears as the virtual set containing and transcending them and allowing reflection on certain cultural formations.

The theoretical fiction of the story is a (literary) apparatus of articulation between political textualities and fables of identity of a line-zone of culture, and it allows for a double reading. On the one hand it appears as a corpus of fictions of exclusion (which is to say, of fictions of elimination of a difference and emptying of a space, with a curtailing of descendants), and could thus be one of the constructions of sexism and racism. On the other hand, and at the same time, it appears as a corpus of dreams of justice, or in other words, as one of the constructions of egalitarian reason. The double reading, or the double politics, seems to be an effect of the encounter between the category of the criminal and the cultural fable of identity.

(The fable of identity is, of course, a fiction of the relation between subjects and communities; it defines—and essentializes—races, nations, regions, genders, classes, cultures; it is articulated in relation to some power, it takes the form of a diptych and it establishes a pact. It is enunciated between two "I's" or voices (it appears as a matrix with two entries); it functions almost always as an apparatus of distribution of differences and determines integrations, exclusions, and subjectivities. In literature, it can be a construction of reading, and it is often related to processes of canonization. The hypothesis that fables of identity are susceptible to a double political reading when constructed on the category of the criminal and when they include representations of the state, is experimental and tentative: it is the "theoretical fiction.")

•

2. Roberto Payró's *El casamiento de Laucha* (1906) was staged by Enrique García Velloso in 1917 in the Teatro San Martín, with a fundamental "correction," as we saw in "Women Who Kill": at the end, Carolina kills Laucha. The story was filmed in 1976 by Enrique Dawi and Emilio Villalba Welsh. The almost inaugural position of *El casamiento de Laucha* (the *pícaro* who deceived the *gringa* with a pseudowedding) lends a particular transparency to the "criminal": we can read the notions of "lesser," second, *pícaro,* or simulator, which characterize him in one of the first moments of the theoretical fiction.

Roberto Payró (1867–1928) is one of the "much read" of the progressive modernizing culture. He was a writer and a professional journalist for *La Nación* from 1891 until his death; he was a friend of Rubén Darío; he participated in the Liberal revolution of 1890; he joined the Partido Socialista in 1894, and he became president of the Sociedad Argentina de Escritores in 1907, the year of its establishment. As director of the Biblioteca de La Nación, he published three classic picaresque novels. He translated Émile Zola's *Fécondité* and *Travail* into Spanish, and in 1902, on the occasion of Zola's death, he gave a talk at the Centro Socialista Obrero. Between 1908 and 1922, he lived in Belgium. He wrote theater (*Marco Severi*, his best-known work, opposes the law of extradition which provided for the deportation of certain peaceful anarchists and socialists residing in Argentina back to their countries of origin), travel chronicles such as *La Australia Argentina*, and various picaresque novels (among them, *Divertidas aventuras del nieto de Juan Moreira*) in which "Creole politics" are represented (the Latin American politics of *caudillismo*, fraud, bribery, and clientism).

"Laucha," a petty thief, second man, and simulator-*pícaro*, could open the history of the representation of the "criminal" in the modern and progressive culture because he reverses the autobiographical "story" of education and marriage of the subjects of the liberal state (his is a false "wedding"); in that reversal and that putting-in-quotation-marks, we read one of the marks of this second culture, *which presupposes an already established "high culture."* Laucha is an ambivalent subject who circulates, in the first person, like money; he is located midway between the interior and the capital, between the old and the new, and also between the different languages and sublanguages: in a "no longer–not yet." And he inserts himself into the tradition of the Spanish picaresque and the gaucho literature with appeals to Estanislao del Campo's "dappled pink," a gaucho named Contreras who draws his knife, and an old gaucho who dies the night of the "wedding"; *the progressive culture presupposes an already established national culture.* Laucha's first person can be inscribed in the history of the simulator and truth, beginning with Cambaceres's *En la sangre* and its scientific and positivist subject (and in the context of Ingenieros and Ramos Mejía: "simulation in the struggle for life"), but with another correlation, because Laucha's oral "first person" is transcribed by a truth-authority different from the scientific subject: the chronicler who heard Laucha's narration-confession in Buenos Aires and who reproduces it in writing. The *subjectivity of the pícaro,* which is what matters, also establishes a crucial difference with respect to the subjects of the liberal state: the criminal's first person, with its voice and rhythm, is found neither in Cambaceres nor in Ingenieros and Ramos Mejía, the authors of the treatises on simulation with their "clinical histories." The *pícaro's* confession opens a fundamental line of literature and a rhetorical change; it opens the novel in first person of the "illegitimate" in name. According to the chronicler who opens the text, Laucha (Mouse), "was his only possible name," an iconic name of the body that is the name-body of an animal: the picaresque genre appears as *Enlightenment speculation* on proper names and the legitimacy of titles.

The autobiographical first person of the *pícaro,* linked with poverty, hunger, illegitimacy, and the crime of truth, would be a *founding character* in literature. And the picaresque genre serves to found the novel; it is related to rights, the law, and the state, both in Spain and in Spanish American literature. According to Roberto González Echevarría, *Myth and Archive: A Theory of Latin American Narrative*, the modern novel originates in the picaresque, *with its questioning of discourses of truth*, and in close relation to the law; the *pícaro* "seeks legitimacy through the codes in which the new authority is hypostatized: *the rhetoric of the new State* . . . he imitates the models furnished by that rhetoric. . . . He is made up by its writing" (56; italics added).

Certain features of Laucha's story were anticipated in *La vuelta de Martín Fierro* in the figure of Picardía: the combination of the first person of the second and illegitimate subject as *pícaro* (framed by another first person, that of "truth," which writes the story "just as I heard it from him," says the writer who opens *El casamiento de Laucha. Chamijo. El falso inca*, 8th ed. [Buenos Aires: Losada, 1971], "and I do not stray many centimeters from the truth" [9]), and the discourse of poverty (the intimacy of poverty: the representation of hunger from within). Laucha says: "always poor, always ragged, going hungry some days, broke everyday" (10); "poorer than the rats" (31); "Misery, like the mean old lady she is, does what she likes with men. . . . She dragged me to the altar, as you'll see . . ." (11; ellipses in original). The denunciation of the state as criminal was also present in the gaucho tradition. But Laucha knows how to read and write, and he has been a "teacher"; with respect to those as miserable as him, he has additional knowledge: *it is this poverty with a cultural difference* that appears to point toward *the birth of a Creole middle class*.

Poverty unleashes in Laucha, as in the traditional *pícaros,* a spatial, social, economic, and linguistic crossing at the moment of the great modernization of the end of the nineteenth century. Laucha decides to go and try his luck in Buenos Aires, and on the way he narrates the economic, monetary, and technological changes: there is a new currency, riverboats are powered by steam engines, refrigeration plants replace salting plants, and the wool that used to be carried to Buenos Aires by herds of oxen now goes by train. He takes the train and misses it, and he gambles and runs out of money near Pago Chico (Payró's Macondo), and he arrives (led by a Spaniard) at the *pulpería* (the place of social circulation) owned by Doña Carolina, an Italian widow (Laucha is a "second man" for her as well). He offers to work for her and stays to live "the culminating adventure of his life": the marriage falsified by the priest.

The center is the crime of truth: falsification and deceit linked with writing, which is Laucha's cultural difference. The falsification of drinks with the "labels written" in the *pulpería* (and his partner is Carolina herself), and the falsification of the marriage certificate (his partner is the priest Papagna, who speaks in a Neapolitan dialect: a language inside another, and the victim is Carolina herself, who speaks in Italian); in both cases, Laucha "translates."

In chapter 6 he falsifies liquor with Carolina as his partner: "Do you know, Ma'am, what occurred to me? Since I know how to make cognac, we could make two jugs of wine out of one, falsify the bitter, the absinthe, the anisette, and everything else, just as we could mix the good yerba maté with the bad, we could do all that here. You'd make a lot more than you're making now, giving your money away to that liquor salesman in Pago Chico, who does the same thing. . . . In Buenos Aires I bought labels with all the names and all the brands of drinks" (24, 28).

In chapter 8, he falsifies the wedding with the priest as his partner, and the priest at first asks, in garbled Neapolitan Spanish, for sixty pesos as a fee for marrying them at the bride's house. Laucha narrates the ensuing exchange.

And the priest didn't say anything for a little while, as if thinking. Then, half laughing, he got up from his chair, walked over to me, and taking me by the lapel of my jacket, he said to me slowly, as if making sure no one else would hear, even though there was no one else in the sacristy . . .

Ah! Since it seems that some of you don't understand Neapolitan, I will make him speak in Spanish.

"But do you want to get married for real? . . . In the parish book?" he asked.

At first I didn't understand what he was trying to say, and I looked at him with confusion.

"Why do you ask me that?" I finally ventured.

"Eh?" the rascal answered. "Because there are those who want to get married, but who don't want the marriage entered into the book. . . . In that case, I prepare a certificate on a separate piece of paper, and I give it to them to keep. So then . . . but you won't say anything about this, will you?"

"Of course not, father!"

"You follow me, then?"

"I reckon I do!"

"So then, if the woman is good, they keep the certificate; but if she isn't good, they tear it up and they make themselves scarce if they feel like it, and the woman can't do a thing, eh? . . . I have permission to perform this sort of marriage, but no one needs to know about it, because it's a Church secret . . . and it's also a lot more expensive than the other marriage . . ."

As if that big rascal priest had permission! It was a story he'd invented to *far l'América* and line his pockets fast even if it meant going straight to hell; that's how eager he was to get back to his country to eat polenta and macaroni.

> But, after a while . . . to be honest . . . I thought that it wouldn't be so bad to get married like that, the way he said, even though it had never, and then less than ever, crossed my mind to deceive the *gringa*, so good and affectionate. . . . That devil of a priest tempted me, and it wasn't my fault, when all is said and done, and since there was no turning back in matters of money, and Carolina had a lot, I fell into the trap, thinking this was a guarantee of security, and I said to the priest:
>
> "And how much would it cost that way, father Papagna?"
>
> "Trechento pesi." (33–34; ellipses in original)

They finally settle on 150.

Laucha associates with the priest in order to falsify his marriage to Carolina. And he is the victim of the police chief Barraba, associated with the gaucho Contreras, who cheated at horse racing. The police chief declares: "The race is legal, Contreras wins." And Laucha: "There's no resistance against force" (46). James D. Fernández, "The Last Word, the First Stone: Lázaro's Legacy," *Journal of Interdisciplinary Literary Studies* 5, no. 1 (1993): 23–37, analyzes the picaresque beginning with the category of *autobiography of resistance*. Fernández sees resistance as a by-product of "the project of breaking up modernity's *grands récits*, of questioning notions of purity, origin and essence, of recognizing—even exalting—hybridities, syncretisms, provisional alliances" (23).

The crucial difference of "Laucha" with respect to the tradition of the subjects of the liberal state (and its connection with the gaucho genre) would reside in the state representations "in" crimes of truth: in the priest Papagna and the police chief Barraba; the "first men" with titles, representatives of the state, are *pícaros* to an even greater extent than Laucha. In a "modern" society totally penetrated by simulation and falsification, the criminal *pícaro* (who is peaceful, who only steals) would be a revealer of the state's crimes of truth.

Laucha ends up robbing Carolina of the little she has left and abandoning her, after confessing to her the false marriage and after the priest, having made his American fortune, returns to Naples "to eat polenta and macaroni." She ends up as a nurse in the Pago Chico Hospital, and Laucha arrives in Buenos Aires, where he dies at age thirty-six, according to the chronicler who opens the novel, before his confession is reproduced: there is no state justice for his crimes. "From his very lips I heard the narration of the culminating adventure of his life, and, in these pages, I have taken pains to reproduce it just as I heard it. Unfortunately, Laucha is no longer here to correct me if I err, but I can state that I do not stray many centimeters from the truth."

☙

Within the "theoretical fiction," Laucha is linked and juxtaposed with the Espila brothers, a pair of losers in Roberto Arlt's *Los locos* and *Los monstruos* (1929 and 1931). The Espilas beg for money in a barrio of Buenos Aires using a false sign and a "scientific" route. They are also second men, illegitimate scientists without credentials. (Laucha knew how to read and write, he was not a gaucho or an ordinary peasant; the Espilas know infinitesimal calculus and the Quixote by heart, but they do not have credentials and they suffer extreme poverty and hunger). This parody of the picaresque (it's "scientific" updating: the false blind man, who is deaf, disguises himself as a "victim of science") is introduced on the last day of the text, the fatal, apocalyptic Friday that closes *Los monstruos,* emptying spaces and curtailing the production of descendants (Barsut kills the Jew, Erdosain kills La Bizca, the Astrologer sets fire to Temperley and flees with the Lame Whore of the Bible). The day begins at ten in the morning with "The Two Rogues" and their sign:

FRIDAY
The Two Rogues
It's ten in the morning.
Seen from a distance of twenty meters, the two men look like fugitives from a hospital. They walk almost shoulder to shoulder. One explores the bases of the houses with his stick, because his eyes are covered by sinister glasses with lenses that look black from the front and violet from the side. A chauffer's hat with a rubber brim exaggerates the elongation of his thin and squalid face, dotted with gray stubble. Moreover, he looks sick, because despite the tepid temperature he wears an impossible overcoat, with brown and reddish checks, whose edges reach almost to his feet. On his chest he wears a cardboard sign that reads:
Blind from the effects of nitric acid fumes. Help a victim of science.
The blind man's guide is dressed up in a pair of gray overalls. Hanging at his side, on a strap that crosses his chest diagonally, he carries a traveler's valise, partially open. Inside, one can make out orange, violet and ochre packages.
"What street is this?" the Deaf Man murmurs.
"Larrazábal . . ."
"Is this on today's itinerary?"
"Oof, what a pain you are . . . Of courze it'z on today'z itinerary. Of courze . . ."
Commentator's Note: Every day the deaf man Eustaquio prepares a route to follow in order to avoid begging in the same streets, arguing that without scientific principles, not even the most productive professions pay off. (477)

Here we see the need for a comment at the foot of the page, the need for a chronicler. Both the Espilas and Laucha and his partners insert themselves into the cultural and literary tradition of the picaresque novel and of the discourse of poverty, a process in which *strategies of survival and rhetorical strategies converge and mingle;* they refer to hunger as the starting point of the crossing, they are "criminals" of truth, and they include "a language inside another" and a chronicler. And they are "second men" who sustain a *symbolic inversion* (in the case of the Espilas they are the only characters who have no contact with the Astrologer, only with Erdosain): they form the polar opposite of the apex of power represented in fictions (as in the Mark Twain's 1882 novel *The Prince and the Pauper*). The *pícaro* is the buffoon who is always aware of the king's position, the restoration of the truth-power equation with a prior excursion through comedy-falsity, says Horacio González, *La ética picaresca* (Buenos Aires-Montevideo: Altamira-Nordan comunidad, 1992).

A quick "excursion." The cultural tradition of poverty and the picaresque opens with the laws of the prohibition of mendicancy in Europe at the very beginning of the modern era, in the fifteenth century. These laws were related to the economic, monetary, and technological changes of the first commercial capitalism and, generally, with "modernizations" (the monetary, technological, state, and economic modernizations that Laucha describes in his voyage from the provinces to the capital), and they show from the fourteenth century onward a hostile attitude toward the begging poor. Incredibly (or ironically) there is a moment at which Christian praise of poverty is replaced by praise of wealth, and that moment coincides with the appearance, and with the codification, of the beggars' crime of truth. And also with the emergence of a new "I" and of the novel as a "modern" literary genre.

From the very beginning of capitalism, from the Renaissance to the Baroque, picaresque literature, literature of manners, and theater do not cease to allude to the deceits, farces, simulations, and falsifications of these marginal vagabonds (and not only literature: legal and penal discourses, religious sermons, canonic doctrines, iconography: see Antonio Serrano González, *Como lobo entre ovejas: Soberanos y marginados en Bodin, Shakespeare, Vives* [Madrid: Centro de Estudios Constitucionales, 1992]). There is a relation between the beggar and the *pícaro* throughout the classical picaresque novel beginning with *El lazarillo de Tormes;* there is a traditional, constant relation between beggars and *pícaros* and crimes of truth. Edmond Cros, *Protée et le Gueux: Recherches sur les origines et la nature du récit picaresque dans Guzmán de Alfarache* (Paris: Didier, 1967), links the *pícaro*'s confession with the universe of mendicancy, conceived as the gravitational field of the dichotomy between the "true" and the "false," which comes to encompass all human behavior. The debate over the poor, Cros says, was soon diluted in a discourse on "criminality." (The relation appears in Baudelaire's "Counterfeit Money," a sort of manifesto of "the fiction" of capitalism, and in a certain "modern" bibliography of simulation.) And, for this reason, there is also a constant, traditional relation between the beggar and the actor, which appears in Alexander Barclay's 1509 *The Ship of Fools,* since the "terminology of the actor" was used in England from the beginning of the sixteenth century to describe the "fraudulent beggars" who "could feign helplessness, disease and mutilation" (William C. Carroll, *Fat King, Lean Beggar: Representations of Poverty in the Age of Shakespeare* [Ithaca: Cornell University Press, 1996], 40, 48). There is also a relation between false beggars and monsters, which is found in the Renaissance encyclopedia of Ambroise Paré, a surgeon who aroused the ire of the medical school, was accused of plagiarism, and submitted to trial. His title: *Des Monstres et Prodiges* (1573), ed. Jean Céard (Geneva: Librairie Droz, 1971). (Ambroise Paré's encyclopedia is still a "popular book," a "best-seller," the most often reprinted book of its kind, says Leslie Fiedler in "From Theology to Teratology," chapter 9 of *Freaks* [233]). There is a relation between the beggar and the prostitute, for the body of the beggar is also merchandise: it is theatricalized, illegalized, naturalized, and animalized. And there is a relation between the beggar and the philosopher, in the tradition of the antitheoretical theory of Diogenes and the cynics, and between them and the state, as is seen in the famous anecdote of Diogenes with Alexander the Great (who said that had he not been Alexander, he would have liked to be Diogenes): when Alexander approached him in the plaza, Diogenes told him to get out of the way because he was blocking the sun (R. Bracht Branham, "Diogenes' Rhetoric and the *Invention* of Cynicism," *Le Cynisme Ancien et ses Prolongements: Actes du Colloque International du CNRS,* ed. Marie-Odile Goulet-Cazé and Richard Goulet [Paris: Presses Universitaires de France, 1993], 445–73). There is also a relation between the beggar and the poet, as is seen in John Gay's 1728 *The Beggar's Opera,* a satire (satire enters English literature through Gay and Fielding) that transpires in the London underworld, with its thieves and prostitutes, in full commercial capitalism: the only thing that matters is money. The *Opera* fuses the figures of the famous English fence and criminal Wild and the conservative prime minister Sir Robert Walpole. A relation is thus established between the beggar (the *pícaro*), the criminal, and the state. *The Beggar's Opera* was performed in London in 1926; later its music was adapted by Benjamin Britten; in 1953 it was directed by Peter Brook; in 1963 the Royal Shakespeare Company mounted yet another production. A film version was made starring Laurence Olivier, and it thereafter returned to theaters and recordings. When Gay was writing, bribery was endemic in court circles and in political life, and corruption was practiced with impunity. E. P. Thompson, *Whigs and Hunters: The Origin of the Black Act* (London: Allen Lane, 1975), says that it was in that period "that *the comparison of statesmanship with criminality* became common coinage" (216–17; italics added) and that political life in England in 1720 bore some resemblance to that of the "Banana Republic." This is a recognized phase of commercial capitalism in which the predators struggle for the crumbs of power and respect neither rules nor rational and bureaucratic forms. Every politician, whether out of nepotism or self-interest, gathered about him a group of loyal dependants.

But what is most notable is the fact that *The Beggar's Opera* (translated into German by Elisabeth Hauptmann in 1927–1928) was the basis of Bertold Brecht's *The Threepenny Opera* (*Die Dreigroschenoper,* 1928), which borrowed the structure, the characters, and also something of the music of the earlier work (Kurt Weill composed the full score). Gay's *Opera* is set at the beginning of the eighteenth century; Brecht's at the end of the nineteenth. In Gay's *Opera,* the beggar appears as the author and poet who opens and closes the performance in dialogue with the actor: "If Poverty be a Title to Poetry, I am sure No-body can dispute mine. I own myself of the Company of Beggars" (John Gay, *The Beggar's Opera, Dramatic Works,* ed. John Fuller, vol. 2 [Oxford: Clarendon Press, 1983]). In Brecht's version, the beggars are the miserable proletarians of the "Friend of the Beggars" Company, a property of the entrepreneur Peachum. G. W. Pabst's film *Drei Groschenoper* (1931), based on Brecht's work, used René Clair's "pan" technique, and added the resources of shadows and angular photography developed by Murnau. Here ends "the excursion."

The *pícaros* and beggars (*who subvert the economy of work, of marriage, and society and who today, in this conclusion, summon us with their crossings*) allow us to glimpse how the crime of truth, when linked with the discourse of poverty (just as it was previously linked with the discourse about Jews) defines certain exclusions and a certain fable of identity: the fable of identity of a secondary culture, which would be founded on the "stories" of marriage (Laucha) and on the "stories" of the "scientists" (the Espilas, but also the criminal Erdosain), and which would include state representations ("first men") in crime, and chroniclers who write.

Beggars also allow us to see how this fable separates itself from others, which form its limits: on the one hand, that of the subjects of the liberal state; and on the other, that of "the unread." With respect to these, we will only mention, in this "terminal station," one other pair of beggars found in a marginal literary discourse, "in crime," and who are not criminals of truth but rather murderers who do not receive state justice. They are, then, two parts or two pairs of poor characters, *pícaros* and murderers, with two different discourses about poverty, which may serve to draw limits between lines or zones of culture, delimited by crime as a critical instrument.

There are many stories of beggars in Argentine literature. "Professional" beggars (like the Italian immigrant Saverio in Armando and Enrique Santos Discépolo's *El organito,* which was first performed on 9 October 1925 at the Teatro Nacional de

Buenos Aires by Pascual Carcavallo's company), anarchists, societies of hobos like those in Juan Filloy's 1937 *Caterva*. (In *Rayuela* [Hopscotch], Julio Cortázar's Parisian *clochard* pays homage to Filloy's novel, recently republished by the Universidad Nacional de Río Cuarto.) But there are not so many "stories of beggars who kill." The beggars who kill are found in two texts, each a contemporary of the *pícaros* Laucha and Espila (contemporary with two modernizing leaps). The first appears in "La vida trágica de una bailarina célebre" (The tragic life of a famous ballerina) by our dear Soiza Reilly, who includes it in his *Cien hombres célebres (Confesiones literarias)* (295–99). The second appears in chapter 4 of Raúl Barón Biza's 1930 novel *El derecho de matar* (The right to kill) (Buenos Aires: M. Alfredo Angulo, 1939). These beggars kill men of means and do not receive state justice: in Soiza Reilly, "the beggar woman of the Paseo de Julio" recounts that she was a famous ballerina who killed the son of a banker in Italy; in Barón Biza the main character tells, in the first person, how he spent all his money on a trip with his lover and how in Brazil he was obliged to beg for money; he met an acquaintance from an earlier period, a "potentate" who refused him money, and killed him: "the right to kill." With them, we have the impression of touching a limit, because the writers of beggars who kill are writers "in crime" in Argentine literature (in *El derecho de matar*, lesbian relations are also represented). "Hard" writers who postulated an aesthetics of hatred, of excess and of revenge. With their beggars who kill, another truth appears, for the common characteristic is the *sudden* social ascent or descent: the beggar woman was born into poverty and arrived at the apex of her art, and that is the moment at which she kills the banker before falling back into poverty; Barón Biza's character sunk socially into mendicancy, killed as a beggar, and later recovered his social status only to end up killing himself when he discovers that his lover and his sister are lovers.

3. To read the Astrologer from Arlt's *Los locos-Los monstruos* as a "first man" is to read from the destinies of truth and from the crimes of truth. And it is also to read that astrological discourse of "truth" in its specific relation to the Latin American state.

Truth and Its Destinies

The Astrologer belongs to a group of "characters" (a series of "monsters" or "madmen") who articulate money or "truth" (always with bodies and numbers in Arlt) with the truth of the Bible, mathematics, and astrology (three different types of "truths" which are believed). Those "characters" have more than one name (or they have a title), and they form a contrast with the "common men," with a single name or without title (another class of monsters), who are the murderers. Let us follow the destinies of the "truths" of the first men "in the mode of winners and losers" and in the trace of the Astrologer.

I

Money with the Bible is the pharmacist Ergueta: "A strange man": a "druggist," a delirious gambler who looks like a "cretin" and a "white slaver," and who knows the Bible by heart. The Bible gives him the numbers with which to play winners and losers at roulette (on the dozens), and it also gives him the Cripple, the prostitute. This pharmacist, Ergueta de Pico, who on the first day of *Los locos* is at the corner of Perú and Avenida de Mayo at ten in the morning, unites the truth of the Bible with numbers and bodies, because he tells Erdosain that Jesus revealed the secret of roulette to him, and that he married the biblical whore (and he also tells him that he will be the king of the world and will rebuild the temple of Solomon). But he gives neither money nor "the truth" to Erdosain, who needs the $600.07 that he stole from the Sugar Company by the next day in order not to be arrested. Ergueta ends up as a "loser"-beggar: he goes crazy, and in "The Revelation" he speaks to God; the biblical Cripple flees with the Astrologer and with the money from the pharmacy, and he is left, in *Los monstruos,* begging on the streets and raving about the end of English imperialism, until they take him away to the hospice.

2

Money with mathematics is called Haffner, a Melancholy Pimp and mathematician who gives Erdosain the check that saves him. When Erdosian arrives at Temperley, he hears the Astrologer's "revolutionary" plan, *and afterward* the Melancholy Pimp (who is armed) gives him the check for $600.07. He "saves" him with the "truth" because he unites money (that of the bodies of the prostitutes) with the numbers of mathematics, and Erdosain begins to believe.

The Melancholy Pimp Haffner makes his money with female bodies and with his numbers. He is a national Al Capone (and perhaps "German" like the captain "Germán," who will appear later the same day in Erdosain's home), and he is "the capitalist" of the Astrologer's revolution. On the other side of the frontier, in Temperley, the bourgeois as gangster or as "mafioso" pimp: *the representation "in crime"* of the capitalism of the 1920s and one of the representations of the mass culture of capitalism, and also the representation of capitalism by German expressionism —for example, that of George Grosz and Bertold Brecht, who adopted the Soviet revolution. "Grosz's war-time drawings were among the best examples of the *gangster* and Wild West mythology," including the figure of the *gold digger,* says Beth Irwin Lewis, *George Grosz: Art and Politics in the Weimar Republic* (Madison: University of Wisconsin Press, 1971). Lewis says that Grosz's drawings form "a visual counterpart" to Brecht's early works (for example, "In the Cities' Jungle," 1921). "Both used as their favorite setting the bar or cheap hotel, which was always peopled by sinister, evil characters. . . . Brecht continued to write within a curious *satirical Anglo-Saxon world until late in the twenties*" (28; italics added).

In "The Ballad de Chicago: Modelo de una sociedad terrorista," Hans Magnus Enzensberger, *Política y delito* (Barcelona: Seix Barral, 1968), says: "The end of the nineteenth century minted a collection of notable mythological figures: the explorer (represented by Livingstone and Nansen), the dandy (Oscar Wilde), the inventor (Edison), the artist as magician (Richard Wagner)." In contrast, says Enzensberger, the twentieth century only erected the myths of the professional revolutionary (personified by Lenin) and the gangster (Al Capone). Enzensberger's enumeration of "modern" myths provides a possible context for the characters of the madmen and monsters. The explorer (Livingstone) appears as the Gold Prospector, as a farce of colonial expansion; the Melancholy Pimp is the dandy (Wilde), but also Al Capone, an industrialist and "capitalism"; the inventor (Edison) appears as Erdosain; the revolutionary (Lenin) appears as Lezin the Astrologer.

Enzensberger says:

Among the extremely scarce mythological figures of the twentieth century, the gangster occupies an outstanding place. The imaginative force of the whole world has appropriated him. . . . But a single name personifies the gangster prototype: the name of Al Capone. Forty years after his "good times," his aura has not disappeared. . . . The only thing that interests us about Al Capone and his world is their mythological function. . . . The myth of the gangster, this figment of collective fantasy, can be located and dated with precision: his era was that of the roaring twenties, or better yet, the fourteen-year period of Prohibition between 1920 and 1933; his place is Chicago, then the second city of the United States. (81–84)

Enzensberger says that Al Capone owes his success not to any attack on the social order of the country, but rather to an unconditional adherence to its premises. "He obeyed the all powerful law of supply and demand. He took the struggle for competition seriously, tragically so. He believed with all his heart in the free play of forces" (107).

The mathematician and Melancholy Pimp Haffner, who gives the "truth" to Erdosain *after* the Astrologer's speech, is the "capitalist" of the Astrologer's "revolution" in the world of the madmen and monsters (Haffner doesn't believe in the "revolution"; he's in it to do business, he says). His capital comes from prostitution, and that is one of the central postulates of the "revolution" just described to Erdosain by the Astrologer, the "revolution" financed and sustained by a chain of brothels. The combination of the mathematician-pimp (the truth of the numbers with the bodies of the prostitutes that give money) is *the same combination* of "truth" of the Astrologer's "revolution," in which Erdosain will come to believe.

(It is the Melancholy Pimp who gives Erdosain the money in Temperley—in the site of the "truth" of Astrology and of the "revolution"—and not the melancholy millionaire [and the relation between money and melancholy is sealed] of whom Erdosain *dreamt before*, that same first day or first chapter, while walking through the Barrio Norte in the afternoon. In the melancholic stroll we can clearly see the relation between "the dream" and "the reality" of fiction, or *the astrological anticipation of the narration* in *Los locos* and *Los monstruos*. For as in divination or mantic [the truth is told through deceit], the terms of the "dream" in Barrio Norte are the same as those of the "reality" of the Astrologer's estate in Temperley, one world within another [like the Barrio Norte] but on the other side of the city, the truth, and the law. Verbal dreams, words, are realized "afterward" in the station and in the train voyage [and it was thus that Erdosain committed suicide in *Los monstruos*], on the site of *the Astrologer's occult sciences*. The dreams are realized later in *Los locos* and *Los monstruos*, first "in simulation" ["fiction" in a second degree] and finally "in crime" in the "reality" of the fiction.)

In the same year of 1929 but in *Los monstruos*, "Haffner Falls" (and very precisely in Barrio Norte), the "revolution" loses its capitalist because the Pimp ends up getting shot by a rival gang of pimps over a problem of bodies and numbers. And in "The Agony of the Melancholy Pimp," as he dreams deliriously about his little blind girl and about his end, he is tortured by Agent Gómez of the police department and dies without confessing. (As we know, this scene belongs to "A Literary History of Torture in Argentina," but we can't stop here to examine it because we are following the "story of the revolution" promoted by the Astrologer or with the winners and losers of "the truth" of the madmen and monsters, in order to try to relate our fiction of the first man with the state and "astrological anticipation" with peripheral formations.)

3

"In" winners and losers, the destinies of "the truths": the devotee of the Bible ends up mad and indigent, the devotee of mathematics ends up murdered and tortured: they are losing truths. We are left with astrology, with its bodies and numbers; with the Astrologer's "revolution," which is the winning plan, because if money (with the bodies and numbers) is the only truth, *the crime of truth in order to keep the money* (the "story" that is believed: the simulation and falsification of language) is the only possible fiction. And the Astrologer's revolutionary plan turns out to be a "story" that allows him to keep the money (the numbers and bodies) of the common or second men when they have lost it all. At that moment he sells them tailor-made "revolutions" and flees with the money.

Let us say that the Astrologer is a political representation because he sells "revolution," "countersociety," and "the colony" (imperial expansion into Chile). He is a political figure (he makes "revolutionary alliances" with anarchists and military officers, he belongs to two sides and acts as a double agent); and he is a *modernista* figure (linked with the occult sciences and the spiritualist sect). But he is also a New Age figure because he adapts the "revolution" to the client's taste: to each his own. He sells "truths" (those of the mass culture of his era): desires for transmutation and justice, "revolutions" and "apocalypse" (and at the end of *Los monstruos*, when he flees with Hipólita, a neighbor confuses him with "a local Methodist pastor"). He offers "the revolution" supplied to the client who believes him, who has or obtains money, and who pays (the Astrologer includes the client personally in his anticipatory "revolutionary" discourse, along with a list of celebrities embodying the dreams of the "common men" in the mass culture of capitalism). At the moment at which the common or second men have lost everything, in the Argentina of 1929, he gives them the "truth" of revolution and keeps the "truth" of money. Erdosain, the future murderer of the "squint-eyed woman," believes him and buys his revolution on the first day of *Los locos*.

The Astrologer's politics is that of "truth" (money, with its numbers and bodies) and that of the beliefs or "truths" of his era; that politics of money and beliefs links his fiction with falsification and racism (as Emma and Gregorio demonstrated in the "Jewish story"). The Astrologer's revolution or story of "truth" is also a fiction of the occult sciences as an underworld that is *on "the other side"* of the frontier of the city and the law, on the side of simulation and crime. (*Las ciencias ocultas en la ciudad de Buenos Aires*, which includes Soiza Reilly's *La ciudad de los locos*, continues, but now in Temperley, in the Province of Buenos Aires.) But the Astrologer is, above all, "a monster" (pure culture: he exists to be read), a hybrid whose body re-sists all attempts to include it in any systematic structure or taxonomy. Jeffrey Jerome Cohen, "Monster Culture (Seven Theses)," in *Monster Theory: Reading Cul-ture*, ed. Jeffrey Jerome Cohen (Minneapolis: University of Minnesota Press, 1996), 3–25, begins with the premise that "we live in a time of monsters" and explores monstrosity as a cultural discourse. The monster demarcates borders and at the same time represents "the Outside, the Beyond": Cohen's seven theses include "The Monster Dwells at the Gates of Difference"; "The Monster Polices the Borders of the Possible"; "The Monster Always Escapes"; "The Monster Is the Harbinger of Category Crisis." The "monster" that is the Astrologer exhibits difference made flesh, the radical difference that paradoxically threatens to erase difference, and that appears as part of a mixed sexual category (castrated) that resists classification. He condenses a simultaneity (he not only joins present, past, and future, socialism and fascism, militarism and anarchism, but also breaks the frontier that encloses them), and he appears in moments of crisis as a third term that problematizes the clash of extremes and questions binary thought. He breaks the either/or bifurca-tion with an "and/or" reasoning: a revolution in the logic of meaning. "The story of the revolution" told by the Astrologer (Lezin/Lenin, or n/z) is the winning plan of the madmen and monsters, the narrative plan of the two novels, and the "Arlt-representation." And it leads us from Locopolis to Apocalypse and from there to the two Peronisms.

For in the plan of the Temperley Astrologer, the plan that announces the coup d'état of 1930 and triumphs with the murder of the Jew, a fire and flight, we could read a formation, at once cultural, political, and "astrological," of peripheral cap-italism in relation to the United States in the crisis of 1929. It would be a "mon-strous" formation (in the sense of the "logic of the monster," Arlt's mode of representation) that opens into the future.

The Astrologer is the "revolutionary leader" (the "first man" or principal mon-ster) of the secret society or revolutionary state of Temperley (*on the other side of the frontier of the capital*), which is a specific type of representation, that of a Latin American counterstate in 1929. The criminal society simulates the structures of the state; the criminals form a state within a state and their structures are the same. That of Temperley is a peripheral counterstate, but it is also "the state" in simula-tion, as is seen in the political reunion which is "The Farce" of *Los locos*, with the Astrologer as leader, the military officer (who spoke the truth when he lied), the communist lawyer, the capitalist Pimp, the Gold Prospector from the south of Chile (who later said that he lied), and the "Minister of Industries," Erdosain. The "state" has a jail with one prisoner, Barsut (kidnapped with his money), watched over by "the Jew": they are the two excluded from the meeting. The Astrologer's secret society could be *the counterstate* (the state of the coup, with its plan for imperial expansion into Chile) and *also* the "real" Argentine state of 1929. The simulation-farce-falsification side or the "astrological" side would represent, at the same time, the state and the counterstate. *This double political representation is an "astrological" feature (or a "monstrous" feature, a feature of Arlt-representation)* because in the Astrologer's political speeches opposites are placed in direct contact. Only through the Astrologer's simulation or crime of truth (and its limits: madness and crime) can we see at once the state and the counterstate.

The "truth" of the Astrologer is evident (as is the "Latin American" cultural formation and the "winning plan" and the "Arlt-representation in monster mode") not only when we see the opposites on the axis of truth and law as themselves *and* the other (as equivalents, as in the tango "Cambalache," the "Argentine classic" of the crisis of 1930: "a burro is the same as a great professor . . ."), but also when we see this fundamental operation with political "representation" on the other side of the frontier. A representation on the side of simulation and crime, wherein simulation (the crime of truth) is itself *and* "truth" and crime is itself *and* "law." Everything exists in *Los locos* and *Los monstruos* from the opposite side: capitalism in the Melancholy Pimp, the working class in the anarchists who manufacture bombs and falsify money. . . . A type of representation without binarisms, in which the opposite terms on the axis of truth and law are put in direct contact, signify each other mutually, and are equivalent from the point of view of value. In this equivalence of terms from both sides of the frontier (of meaning), we can clearly see the type of *"monstrous" representation of the Latin American periphery at the moment of the North American crisis of 1929*. At the moment of apocalypse (the apocalyptic genre as a genre of truth and justice, and also as a genre of resistance and of opposition to the empire) that the Jew Bromberg attempts to interpret, the moment of Ergueta's "Revelation" (with the end of the British Empire), and also the moment of that other apocalypse of "The House of Iniquity Perishes," or the burning of Temperley with the corpse of the murdered Jew.

Because representation "in monster mode" not only identifies opposites and situates itself on the frontier in order to indicate its opposite side. It also implies a multiplication of voices and a proliferation of times and levels of "reality" which make it capable of foreseeing a certain future beginning with the central crisis of 1929 ("The monster stands on the threshold . . . of the future"). For the "dream," the Astrologer's words (the "revolution") are realized always afterward, in another place, space, and with other protagonists who are "legitimate," and on another level of "reality": Erdosain's "revolution" is realized first "in simulation" (the farce of the strangulation of Barsut in "The Wink," which closes *Los locos*). And Barsut's "revolution" is realized afterward, and "in crime," in the final reality of *Los monstruos,* when Barsut murders Bromberg. These are the two sides and the two times (and "realities") of the Astrologer's anticipatory plan, the two "revolutions" he needs in order to win and to disappear with the money in 1929: "The Monster Always Escapes."

The anticipation and the double turn of desire or the "dream" in order to arrive at the "truth," with simulation first and "reality" in crime afterward (and with the narrator-chronicler-commentator-author series with its "realities" and "truths"), the representation of the state and the counterstate and the work with the social and political imagination (of the modern, North American mass culture, which fuses at once technological, scientific, and political elements) make the Astrologer's plan not only a winning one but also one able to predict a certain future: the military coup of 1930 and at the same time the Nazi future, with the squint-eyed woman, the Jew, the gases, and the crematory ovens ("If it's an oven," Erdosain advises in *Los locos,* "you'll need a minimum temperature of five hundred degrees to carbonize the bones as well"). A futurity that each time "comments" on what went before or shows it to have been "a dream" or "fiction" or a farce which precedes "the truth" or "the reality" of the fiction and which can later appear in another "reality."

From Cosmopolis to Locopolis, from Locopolis to Apocalypse, and from there to the two Peronisms. . . . The 1930 road to Perón's "revolution" (and the road of "the reality of fiction" to "reality") passes through the "revolution" of the "first man" monster (the Astrologer), through that cultural formation of the capitalist periphery, a political-astrological-apocalyptic formation of "truth." The cultural continuity between anarchism and Peronism with the winning couple of the "revolution": the "ex-prostitute" and the "Astrologer," who were saved from the justice of the chronicler in 1930 only to reappear in future states alongside the "first man."

According to Michael Hardt and Antonio Negri, *Labor of Dionysus: A Critique of the State-Form* (Minneapolis: University of Minnesota Press, 1994),

> the crisis post–1929 represents a moment of decisive importance in the emergence of the contemporary State. The chief casualty of the crisis was the material basis of the liberal constitutional State. . . . The Wall Street crash of "Black Thursday" 1929 destroyed the political and State mythologies of a century of bourgeois domination. *It marked the historical end of the rights of State,* understood as an apparatus of State power aimed at formally protecting individual rights, through the bourgeois safeguards of "due process," a State power established to guarantee bourgeois social hegemony. It was the final burial of the classic liberal

myth of the separation of State and market, the end of laissez-faire. (26–27; italics added)

•

4. From this perspective we can see how the work of Borges, in which the state does not appear as criminal (and which carries to its imperial culmination the "aristocratic" combination of the encyclopedia and the Creole element), remains outside the second, modern, progressive cultural formations that constitute "the crime story of the very much read."

•

5. The victims or the excluded in *Los locos* and *Los monstruos* (the squint-eyed María and the Jew, or "The Man Who Saw the Midwife") suffer something akin to the "evil eye"; the woman murdered in Ernesto Sábato's *El túnel* is married to a blind man; the deceived Italian woman in *El casamiento de Laucha* speaks in Italian; the victim in *Crónica de una muerte anunciada* (Chronicle of a death foretold) speaks Arabic. There another type of "reality" is touched upon, for these differences are opposed to the "ideology" of the classical subject.

In a chapter titled "The Other Question: Stereotype, Discrimination and the Discourse of Colonialism," in *The Location of Culture* (New York: Routledge, 1994), 66–84, Homi K. Bhabha analyzes the ideological construction of otherness in the discourse of colonialism, an insistent and recurring mode of representation. He explores the stereotype as an ambivalent mode of representation, as well as the *"processes of subjectification"* (subjectivization of subjection) that the stereotype makes possible, both in the colonized and in the colonizer. That "otherness" articulates forms of racial, cultural, and sexual difference in which "the body is always simultaneously (if conflictually) inscribed in both the economy of pleasure and desire and the economy of discourse, domination and power" (67). Bhabha says that *visible and natural differences are the basis of the stereotype: they mark the victim and the object of discrimination* (80). The regime of visibility is fundamental in colonial discourse, which implies a "problematic of seeing/being seen" related to "the *surveillance* of colonial power . . . functioning in relation to the regime of the *scopic drive*" (76). It is linked to fetishism and voyeurism: the stereotype may range, Bhabha says, "from the loyal servant to Satan, from the loved to the hated" (79).

•

6. Laucha could be one of the first texts of the theoretical fiction, or "the crime story of the very much read"; one of the last (and not an Argentine one) is Gabriel García Márquez's "very much read" *Crónica de una muerte anunciada* (1981), which questions the whole "system." There is no truth and no belief in confession, because beliefs are written only in blood on bodies and in names. In it we can read

clearly how the state makes use of beliefs in differences in order to expel someone and empty their space. There are two criminals, the twins Pedro and Pablo Vicario, the town butchers (they kill pigs named after flowers, like the Arabs): the secondariness and the representation that characterize the figure are especially marked. But in reality, as we know, the "guilty party" in the death of Santiago Nasar (who speaks Arabic and has Arab eyes, who is rich and has power) is the whole town, including Angela, of which the Vicarios are the vicarious representatives. The "guilty party" is Angela, for having lost her virginity before marriage, as she told her friends, and for having decided "not to operate." For as we know, everything happens when on the wedding night Bayardo San Román discovers that his wife, Angela Vicario, is not a virgin; Angela "names" Santiago Nasar, and she tells the judge: "he was my author," and she does not lie, because "the Arab," Arab culture, appears to have invented the myth of virginity and female honor. And her twin brothers cleanse their name and their honor by murdering him savagely. (The autopsy performed by the priest in the school is a farce of truth.)

The "guilty parties" are the beliefs in name and honor, and also the beliefs in the crimes of those who are different. The novel revisits the history and the literature of the "holy war": the killing of Moors on the part of the Christians and their chroniclers, and it alludes to Cervantes in the name of the prostitute. The outsider San Román is something like an "inspector of beliefs," and he is directly associated with the state: his father is a colonel and conservative senator, and he arrives for the wedding on the boat of the National Congress. (The bishop, who passed through the town that day, didn't stop.)

The chronicler who narrates, and the judge who arrives in the town to take charge of the case, lack names, and it is they who expose beliefs. The justice of the chronicler (who is positioned between the two clashing families and who is a semioutsider) is that of time, the future, space, the interval, and the change in literary genre (from the chronicle to the epistolary novel and from there to the romantic novel). The judge who cannot bring about justice (a young man full of Spanish and Latin literature, philosophy, Nietzsche, and judicial thought) annotates the brief in red ink: "*Give me a prejudice and I will move the world*," and "*Fatality makes us invisible*." The chronicler says: "The marginal notes, and not just because of the color of the ink, seemed to be written in blood" (*Chronicle of a Death Foretold*, trans. Gregory Rabassa [New York: Alfred A. Knopf, 1983], 99).

•

7. John J. Collins, *The Apocalyptic Imagination: An Introduction to the Jewish Matrix of Christianity* (New York: Crossroad, 1984), refers to the apocalyptic genre found in the Jewish tradition, and he defines it as "a 'scribal phenomenon,' a product of

learned activity" (30), and as a type of esoteric literature. "This genre was characterized by a conventional manner of revelation, through heavenly journeys or visions, mediated by an angel to a pseudonymous seer. It also involved a conceptual framework which assumed that this life was bounded by the heavenly world of angels and by the prospect of eschatological judgment. . . . The conceptual framework is a symbolic structure that can be given expression through different theological traditions" (205). As a "genre that could be utilized by different groups in various situations," Collins says, it has served various functions: "An apocalypse can provide support in the face of persecution . . . ; reassurance in the face of culture shock . . . or social powerlessness . . . ; reorientation in the wake of historical trauma . . . or comfort for the inevitability of death" (205).

Collins affirms the importance of *the relation of the apocalyptic genre to truth*. He explains that "apocalypse" is derived from the Greek word *apokalypsis* (revelation), and he quotes the following definition:

> "a genre of revelatory literature with a narrative framework, in which a revelation is mediated by an otherworldly being to a human recipient, disclosing a transcendent reality which is both temporal, insofar as it envisages eschatological salvation, and spatial insofar that it involves another, supernatural world." . . .
> The main means of revelations are visions and otherworldly journeys, supplemented by discourse or dialogue and occasionally by a heavenly book. The constant element is an angel who interprets the vision or serves as guide on the otherworldly journey. . . . The eschatology of the apocalypses differs from that of the earlier prophetic books by clearly envisaging retribution beyond death. (4–5)

Collins acknowledges at least a "limited overlap between the Jewish apocalyptic literature" and millenarian movements characterized by the following traits: "the promise of heaven on earth soon, the overthrow or reversal of the present social order, a terrific release of emotional energy, a brief life span of the movement, and the central role of a prophetic or charismatic leader. . . . *Hope for the imminent transformation of the social order is generally typical of the historical type of apocalypse*" (206; italics added).

Collins also says that among Christian apocalyptics the book of Revelation was "the first book that was explicitly presented as an *apokalypsis*" and that it bears affinity with the Jewish apocalypses (211). It does not use pseudonyms, and the revelation "is mediated to John by an angel." Its language is poetic rather than descriptive, and its "apocalyptic revelations are symbolic attempts to penetrate the darkness, which provide ways of imagining the unknown" (214–15). Its language tends to persuade, to console, and to provide a vision of the world. "*The apoca-*

lypses often address the issues of political and social liberation, but they conspicuously lack a program for effective action. . . . The apocalyptic revolution is a revolution of the imagination. It entails a challenge to view the world in a way that is radically different from the common perception. The revolutionary potential of such imagination should not be underestimated, as it can foster dissatisfaction with the present" (215; italics added).

Lois Parkinson Zamora, *Writing the Apocalypse: Historical Vision in Contemporary U.S. and Latin American Fiction* (Cambridge: Cambridge University Press, 1989), points out the *critical function of apocalypse,* its promise of justice and salvation, and she says that its narrator *"is radically opposed to existing spiritual and political practices"* but is politically powerless to change them (2; italics added). The narrator's desire is to take vengeance on his oppressors through the justice of God. Parkinson Zamora says that the biblical Book of Revelation is "as much about the capacity of language to conceal as to reveal. John's cryptic imagery and numerology are a response to political necessity," and the text's "ambivalence between concealing and revealing" determines the necessity of interpretation or translation (15–16). She also *differentiates between apocalypse and utopia*: "Whereas apocalypse is impelled by the historical dialectic between evil and good, and confronts the violence of the present, utopia focuses on a future, perfect world. The utopian ideal is envisioned as an external moral and political regime" (17). Apocalypse, in contrast, can be read in reference to historical events and also to the inner events of a subject. "Apocalypse is a historicized myth, a myth about history," says Parkinson Zamora (18), and she analyzes it in contemporary U.S. and Latin American literature.

Jacques Derrida, "On a Newly Arisen Apocalyptic Tone in Philosophy," trans. John Leavy, *Raising the Tone of Philosophy: Late Essays by Immanuel Kant, Transformative Critique by Jacques Derrida,* ed. Peter Fenves Jr. (Baltimore: Johns Hopkins University Press, 1993), 117–71, speculates regarding the apocalyptic structure of truth itself (151): it breaks with time, imposes a "mathematizing mysticism," an "idolatry of figures and numbers," which "goes hand in hand with the phenomena of sect," and imposes a *cryptopolitics* (135). He says that the truth of the apocalypse is the truth of truth.

Derrida lays out a string of meanings for the word "apocalypse": vision-revelation, discovery-concealment (one of the conceptions of truth), prediction, prophecy, vision, contemplation, gaze, inspiration, "mystical illumination," catastrophe, discovery of secrets. And he analyzes the apocalyptic tone that multiplies voices, codes, and tones into a polytonality and a delirium of destination and emission. In Apocalypse, one does not know who is speaking. The general narrator is called the witness and Derrida analyzes the narrative voice and shows its "ruses, traps, trickeries, seductions, machines of war and pleasure." Apocalypse, he says "leaps from one place of emission to the other . . . it goes from one destination, one name, and one tone to the other" (156). "Nothing is less conservative than the apocalyptic genre," and it evades censorship. "We know that apocalyptic writings increased the moment State censorship was very strong in the Roman Empire," says Derrida (159). Signs of mixture of genres, tones, "clandestination," and echoes of quotations are all apocalyptic filiations.

And in "Nietzsche and Saint Paul, Lawrence and John of Patmos," in *Essays Critical and Clinical*, trans. Daniel W. Smith and Michael A. Greco (Minneapolis: University of Minnesota Press, 1997), 36–52, an essay written as a preface to D. H. Lawrence's *Apocalypse* (Paris: Balland, 1978), Gilles Deleuze recalls Lawrence's distinction between the Saint John of the gospel and the other John of the Apocalypse: "the same type of man could not have written the gospel and the Apocalypse. . . . The gospel is aristocratic, individual, soft, amorous, decadent, always rather cultivated. The Apocalypse is *collective, popular, uncultivated, hateful, and savage.* . . . Christ invented a religion of love . . . whereas *the Apocalypse brings a religion of Power*" (36; italics added). Deleuze refers to the currency of Lawrence's text and of the Apocalypse, saying: "It is a book for all those who think of themselves as survivors. It is the book of Zombies" (37).

Deleuze also says that "Lawrence is closely related to Nietzsche," and that he "would not have written his text without Nietzsche's *Antichrist*." He continues: "A certain number of 'visionaries' have opposed Christ as an amorous person to Christianity as a mortuary enterprise. [among them, our Virgil] . . . In Nietzsche there is a great opposition between Christ and Saint Paul . . . Lawrence takes up this opposition once again, but this time he opposes Christ to the red John of Patmos, the author of the Apocalypse" (37). Deleuze says that for Lawrence, John of Patmos "took advantage of the protest of the collective soul" (the expression "collective soul" is Lawrence's, Deleuze says, but we have already come across it in *El alma de los perros,* the best-seller written by our Virgil). Deleuze and Lawrence continue:

> The Apocalypse takes advantage of the claims of *the "poor" or the "weak," for they are not who we think they are: they are not the humble or the unfortunate, but those extremely fearsome men who have nothing but a collective soul.* . . . What the collective soul wants is Power [*Pouvoir*]. . . . The collective soul does not simply want to seize power or to replace the despot. On the one hand, it wants to destroy power, it hates power and strength [*pouissance*], John of Patmos hates Caesar or the Roman Empire with all his heart. On the other hand, however, it also wants to penetrate into every pore of power, to multiply them throughout the universe. It wants a cosmopolitan power . . . in every fold of the collective soul . . . *the power*

of a God without appeal who judges all the others. . . . With the Apocalypse, Christianity invents *a completely new image of power:* the system of Judgment. . . . A counterpower, which is both a power of nooks and crannies and a power of the last men. *Power no longer exists except as the long politics of vengeance, the long enterprise of the collective soul's narcissism. The revenge and self-glorification of the weak,* says Lawrence-Nietzsche. (38–39; italics added)

Deleuze observes that the "system of Judgment" thus appears as the "master faculty of the soul," marking an epochal shift. "The Apocalypse won: we have never left the system of judgment. . . . The Jews had invented something very important in the order of time, which was *postponed destiny*. Having failed in their imperial ambition, the chosen people had been put on hold, they were left waiting. . . . But what is new in the Apocalypse is that this waiting now becomes the object of an unprecedented and maniacal programming. The Apocalypse is undoubtedly *the first great program book, a great spectacle*. . . . A kind of Folies-Bergère with a celestial city and an infernal lake of sulfur" (40–41).

Deleuze marks the opposition in the collective Christian soul between the *apocalyptic vision* and the *prophetic word:* the prophet waits "in time, in life" for something new, "an advent," while Christianity generally can only wait for something *after* death. "Apocalyptic *vision* replaces the prophetic *word*," says Deleuze, and the Apocalypse institutes "an entire theater of phantasms," phantasms which Deleuze characterizes as "the expression of the instinct for vengeance, the weapon of the weak's vengeance" (41). Deleuze also says that the "sedimented and stratified" nature of the book of Revelation fascinated Lawrence and Nietzsche (43). It is the product of a "man of the people," a hard man who represented "the collective and popular soul of Christianity, whereas Saint Paul (and also Lenin, Lawrence adds) was still an aristocrat who went to the people" (43–44). John of Patmos's enemy "is not the pagans but the Roman Empire," Deleuze says, following Lawrence, and "to ensure the fall of the Roman Empire in a vision, the entire Cosmos must be gathered together, convoked, brought back to life—and then it must be destroyed, so that the Roman Empire will itself be brought down and buried under its debris" (44). Now, Deleuze continues, "*it is destruction that is called just*, it is the will to destroy that is called Justice and Holiness. *This is the innovation of the Apocalypse*. . . . *To destroy, to destroy an anonymous and interchangeable enemy, an unspecified enemy, has become the essential act of the new justice*" (45).

Today, Deleuze says, certain thinkers sketch out an apocalyptic future with three features: the germs of an "absolute worldwide State," the destruction of the "habitable" world and the environment, and the persecution of an "unspecified" enemy.

Index